Down the *Susquehanna* to the *Chesapeake*

Down the *Susquehanna* to the *Chesapeake*

JACK BRUBAKER

The Pennsylvania State University Press ~ University Park, Pennsylvania

Library of Congress Cataloging-in-Publication Data

Brubaker, John H.
Down the Susquehanna to the Chesapeake / Jack Brubaker.
        p.   cm.
Includes bibliographical references (p.   ).
ISBN 0-271-0218-5 (cloth : alk. paper)
1. Susquehanna River. I. Title.
GB1227.S87 B78 2002
551.48´3´09748—dc21
2001046359

TO

Christine Conant Brubaker

AND

John Christie Dann

*the North Branch and West Branch
of my life*

Contents

PROLOGUE: *Pine Creek*

If Art Tomack owned this ridgetop grass and wild-flower meadow, he would build an observation tower in it. He would invite visitors to climb his tower and admire the undulant hill-and-vale landscape of Pennsylvania's Northern Tier. And he would tell them something like this: Up here in these old, eroding Appalachians, tall trees flourish on the slopes but settlers have cleared the hilltop plateaus for agri-culture. Up here on these mountain farms in God's country, the fields grow more stones than anything you could eat. Up here, on this beautiful but unbountiful land, hardwoods and hard rocks have conspired to make a hard working life.

And then Tomack would ask his visitors to consider this particular ridge's exceptional watershed—the basis for locat-ing his tower on this hill and not the next one over. Here, he would say, three substantial rivers originate and flow to distant seas. This is the highest ridge, he would explain, and everything that runs to the south is Susquehanna water and everything to the west Allegheny water and to the north Genesee water. This is the Continental Divide in the East.

When he is not dreaming of building a tourist tower, Art Tomack operates a general store in the town of Gold, about a mile north of the watershed meadow and ten miles south of the New York border. Along with frying pans and Hershey bars, he and Betty Tomack sell T-shirts advertising "The Gold General Store: At the Headwaters of Three Rivers." Travelers stop to shop and, more often than you might expect, ask where they can find the beginnings of these rivers.

Art tells headwaters hunters to drive south on Route 449 to Rooks Road, hang a right, and look for the meadow at the peak of the ridge. "The triple divide," as Betty calls it, lies along this plateau, 2,400 feet up in the Appalachian Range. Springs in the meadow on the Slaybaugh farm feed the Genesee River. Meadow springs on the adjacent Torok farm feed the Susquehanna and the Allegheny.

The Genesee, as the Slaybaughs and Toroks and Tomacks and the Tomacks' T-shirts will tell you, empties into Lake Ontario, which feeds the St. Lawrence River and the Gulf of St. Lawrence and, ultimately, the North Atlantic Ocean. The Allegheny joins with the Monongahela to form the Ohio, and the Ohio joins the Mississippi, and the Mississippi runs to the Gulf of Mexico. The third set of springs feeds Pine Creek, the largest tributary of the West Branch of the Susquehanna River. The West Branch meets the Susquehanna's North Branch, forming the Lower Susquehanna, and the Lower Susquehanna washes into the Chesapeake Bay, which runs out to the mid-Atlantic.

The phenomenon that Art Tomack considers worthy of marking with an observation tower—water flowing in three directions from one hill—is unusual on the perimeter of the Susquehanna's drainage area. At most places along the high grounds that divide this river's watershed from its neighbors, rainfall drains in one of two directions: it either trickles into the Susquehanna Basin or runs off toward the Hudson or St. Lawrence by way of a tributary in New York, toward the Allegheny or Delaware by way of a tributary in Pennsylvania, or toward the Potomac or directly into the Chesapeake in Maryland. Before running to rivers, some of this water lingers in groundwater emerging as springs or in aboveground swamps and lakes and ponds, and these are the sources of the Susquehanna.

Pine Creek's headwaters in Potter County's hinterlands and thousands of other Susquehanna sources pepper the periphery of a vast watershed of 27,500 square miles. On the East Coast of the United States, only the St. Lawrence's watershed is larger. The Susquehanna drains nearly half of Pennsylvania, an eighth of New York, and a fragment of Maryland. Its sources are all over the map.

This book concentrates on the river's ultimate beginnings—those swamps and springs farthest by water from the river's mouth—because most travelers searching for sources wind up there. Likewise, most river followers who visit the Tomacks' store are looking not for a secondary source of the Susquehanna but for the primary source of the Genesee.

The ultimate sources of the Susquehanna's branches spring from similarly rural but culturally distinct regions. The origins of the North Branch are associated with the scenic home of the Baseball Hall of Fame at Cooperstown, New York. The West Branch's headsprings and streams flow out of the humble bituminous country of Cambria County, Pennsylvania. Hard ball and soft coal.

This narrative follows the flow from these dissimilar sources to the Chesapeake. Chapters focus on particular places along the course. Some chapters discuss an aspect of the Susquehanna that applies not only to that place but to others along the river. Most chapters examine how the river has changed over the years.

Before we begin this journey, it might be helpful to clarify the geography of the Susquehanna Basin by dividing the long and convoluted river into sections.

Most people cut the Susquehanna into three parts. The 316-mile-long North Branch and 228-mile West Branch join at Northumberland-Sunbury to initiate the 128-mile Lower Susquehanna, also known as the Main Stem. The wide, shallow, island-jammed Lower Susquehanna, sweeping by and, in flood, through Pennsylvania's capital at Harrisburg, is what most people think of when they think of this old river.

The Susquehanna's North and West branches are long enough and far enough apart and flow through sufficiently disparate terrain to have characteristics very different from those of the lower river and each other. Some confusion could have been avoided if these branches had retained individual names, but their complex aboriginal designations have all but disappeared.

Most Pennsylvanians consider the North Branch the Susquehanna's primary course. The West Branch is shorter and somewhat narrower and provides less volume to the

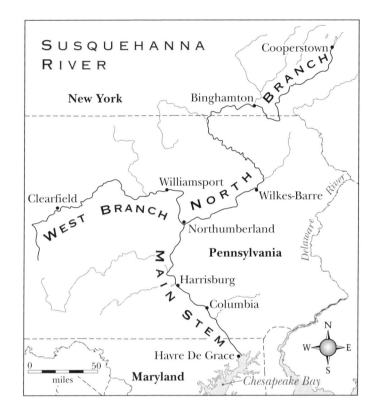

flow at the confluence, so the Commonwealth of Pennsylvania calls it one of the Susquehanna's "major tributaries." Dedicated West Branchers appreciate this demeaning designation as much as they enjoy watching Penn State lose a football game.

More than 31,000 miles of streams with 31,193 names—thousands of rivulets and hundreds of significant rivers and creeks—feed the tripartite Susquehanna. Unlike most big rivers, the Susquehanna has several tributaries that are

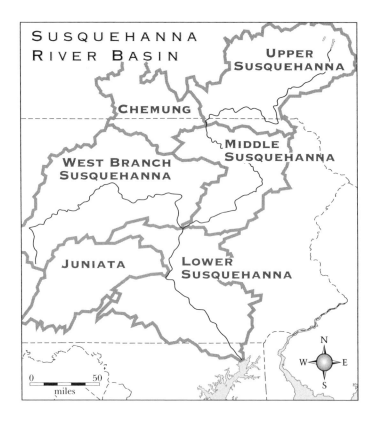

SUSQUEHANNA
RIVER BASIN

UPPER
SUSQUEHANNA

CHEMUNG

MIDDLE
SUSQUEHANNA

WEST BRANCH
SUSQUEHANNA

JUNIATA

LOWER
SUSQUEHANNA

N
W—E
S

0   50
miles

only that tributary's drainage, also mainly in New York; and the Middle Susquehanna, which extends to the confluence with the West Branch. The West Branch and Juniata River watersheds form two more subbasins and the Lower Susquehanna the sixth.

These subbasins make sense from a water-management perspective; and setting apart the Chemung, West Branch, and Juniata systems helps emphasize the watershed's remarkably lopsided reach to the west. However, these designations do little to identify the dramatically changing characteristics of the Susquehanna as it flows from cedar swamps in New York toward cypress swamps in Maryland.

This book uses variant translations of the Algonquian word "Susquehanna" as descriptive designations for sections of the river. No one knows with certainty what the word means, but dozens of etymologists and historians have proposed at least sixteen translations. Six of them seem to define general segments of the Susquehanna and the river's changing nature as it moves south. Chapters are clustered beneath these designations.

Chapters under "Spring-Water River" cover the North Branch's sources. The rest of the North Branch, winding into Pennsylvania and back into New York and back into Pennsylvania, is the "Long Crooked River." The arcing West Branch is the "Long Reach River." "Broad, Shallow River" flows from the confluence at Northumberland-Sunbury to Columbia. "Rock River" runs through the Susquehanna Gorge, from south of Columbia to Tidewater. "Great Bay River" washes into the Chesapeake.

These divisions not only differentiate and define sections

nearly as substantial as the main stream where they enter it. These include the 100-mile-long Juniata, the 74-mile Chenango, and the 38-mile Chemung.

To organize this river's vast and varied watershed, the Susquehanna River Basin Commission, which coordinates the basin's water resources, divides it into six subbasins. North Branch drainage comprises three parts: the Upper Susquehanna, which includes much of New York's Susquehanna drainage; the Chemung River, which includes

of the Susquehanna but help emphasize the river's significant reach through three states. In recent years,
Chesapeake enthusiasts have focused on the Susquehanna
principally as it relates to an endangered bay in Maryland.
In this view, Pennsylvania's Susquehanna has all but lost
its own identity and the river in New York has become an
afterthought. As the Chesapeake Bay Foundation, the
Alliance for the Chesapeake Bay, and other groups promote bay-related environmental issues, reinforced by the
Chesapeake 2000 Agreement, the river sometimes seems
an appendage of the bay.

It is the other way around, of course: the Chesapeake is
the appendage of the flooded Susquehanna. The river's
ancient mouth opened into the Atlantic Ocean off the
coast of present-day Virginia. During the great ice meltdown, the rising ocean seeped inland to form the estuary
around that lowest stretch of river. But the Susquehanna's
earlier course has not disappeared: its deep trench runs
through the bay, forming its primary shipping channel.

Today the Susquehanna is the bay's only indispensable
tributary. The East Coast's largest river contributes an
extraordinary 19 million gallons of water a minute—
90 percent of the upper bay's fresh water and 50 percent
overall. Without that steady influx to hold back the briny
Atlantic, the Chesapeake could not support its rich mix of
estuarine life. Given the river's pervasive influence,
"Susquehanna Bay" would be the Chesapeake's more accurate designation.

At an average speed of 20 miles a day, the nation's sixteenth longest river rambles from Potter County springs

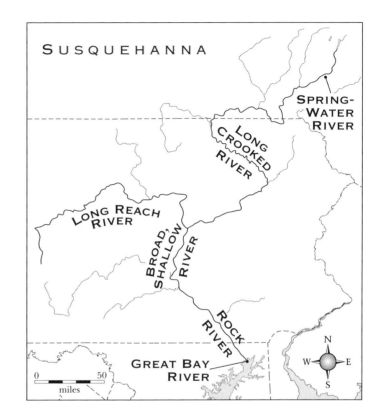

and other sources deep in the outlands of Pennsylvania
and New York to and through the nation's largest bay.
As it changes shape, it shapes the land along the way.
Its journey is the story.

SPRING-WATER
RIVER

Jordanville

Ocquionis
Creek

Richfield Springs

Shadow
Brook

Lake
Canadarago

Lake
Otsego

Oaks Creek

Cooperstown

Phoenix Mills

Milford

Portlandville

Goodyear Lake

Oneonta

Unadilla River

N
W · E
S

North Branch Susquehanna River

Otego

Unadilla

Bainbridge

Sidney

New York

0   5   10

miles

Spring-Water River

Ocquionis Creek

I stood in that meadow with sun reflecting back from the isolated drops of water and realized that for a river like the Susquehanna there could be no beginning. It was simply there, the indefinable river, now broad, now narrow, in this age turbulent, in that asleep, becoming a formidable stream and then a spacious bay and then the ocean itself, an unbroken chain with all parts so interrelated that it will exist forever, even during the next age of ice.

—THOMAS APPLEGARTH upon reaching a source of the Susquehanna in James Michener's *Chesapeake*

RAIN FALLING ON A BARN ROOF near that source of the Susquehanna River farthest from the Chesapeake Bay rolled off the south eaves toward the Susquehanna and the north eaves toward the Mohawk. So it is said. The claim cannot be verified because the barn was destroyed decades ago. In its place is the largest monastery of the Russian Orthodox Church outside Russia. Now rain falling on the monastery property drains either into soggy regions to the north that feed the Hudson by way of the Mohawk or into a swamp

☙ *Ocquionis Creek, the ultimate source stream of the Susquehanna, flows from this swamp near Jordanville, New York, into Lake Canadarago. In the background is Holy Trinity Monastery of the Russian Orthodox Church. (Photo by Christine Brubaker.)*

This mucky puddle is as unremarkable as the monastery that soars nearby is unforgettable. One of the nation's great rivers rises beside a cathedral with brilliantly gilded onion-shaped domes, where bearded, black-habited monks go about their monastic duties just as their brethren do thousands of miles away.

In 1930, two young Russian immigrant monks purchased the Starkweather farm, including its old water-dividing barn. The monks planted crops and began work on a complex of buildings that would attract other Russians and sightseers from around the world. They constructed a chapel and, in 1950, the cathedral. An expanding brotherhood then built the main monastery and opened a five-year college-level seminary. Today the monks of Holy Trinity Monastery operate a large printing plant and continue to farm.

To the monks, the cedar swamp is wasteland and a nuisance when it overfills. To Bruce Harter, who until recently lived on land adjoining the monastery property, this swamp is the birth water of the Ocquionis (an Iroquoian word, supposedly and inexplicably meaning "he is a bear").

Harter and his father and grandfather before him watched Ocquionis Creek trickle out of the swamp and across their land toward the village of Jordanville. Harter has always thought that the Ocquionis (also known as Fish Creek) is the ultimate source of the river. His father and grandfather believed the same.[1]

Ocquionis is a tranquil source. "There has never been a flooding, except once," Harter says. He is standing in the side yard of his former Jordanville home, looking toward the narrow course the Ocquionis takes down through the

on the south side of the watershed ridge. The overflow from the swamp forms the beginning of the Susquehanna's North Branch.

These wetlands stand about 1,500 feet above the sea, considerably lower than some other elevations along the Susquehanna's northernmost reaches, which can rise over 2,000 feet. Lakelike after snowmelt or spring rain, the swamp shrinks to ankle depth in drought, with green and brown bottles sticking out of the gunk. Northern white cedars and swamp grass rim the tannin-dark water. Relatively warm and probably spring-fed, the swamp rarely freezes in winter.

fields from the monastery, half a mile away. "The monks got the Department of Environmental Conservation to blow a beaver dam at the edge of the swamp in the spring of '49 and that caused the flood."

Beavers occasionally dam the creek south of Jordanville as well, and that may explain how the tiny Ocquionis provided sufficient water to baptize some of the original settlers. In the decade after the War of Independence, a wave of revivalism swept through the United States. When that wave reached the Ocquionis, those dunked in the deepened creek named the town for the biblical baptismal river.

The Ocquionis is barely three feet wide where Route 167 crosses it in Jordanville, a village of fifty-some houses in Herkimer County. The creek winds west and then southeast to the hamlet of Cullen, where it is joined by a tiny branch and becomes unjumpable. Nester Shypski, one of many Russian Americans who live in this area and take pride in the monastery up on the ridge, shows where the creek runs underground for half a mile or so on his 175-acre farm. He also points out "chyle holes"—deep caves into which rainwater disappears before joining the Ocquionis.

When the creek reaches the village of Richfield Springs, it is running about twelve feet across. Shallow and filled with rocks, it spills its sometime swamp and baptismal and underground water into Lake Canadarago. It also carries in sulfur from dozens of springs immediately north of the lake. The Oneidas appropriately called this area Ganowanges ("stinking waters").

Richfield Springs adds to the stink, conveying effluent from its wastewater treatment facility into the creek less than a mile above the lake. In the late 1800s, the village built one of the first sewage treatment plants in upstate New York. That relatively primitive plant failed in the 1950s and '60s. Raw human sewage mixed with the sulfur and wastes from dairy operations and a pea-processing plant to degrade the lake severely and create a rare aromatic experience.

In the early 1970s, Richfield Springs, with state and federal support, constructed one of the nation's first three tertiary treatment plants, designed to remove nitrogen and phosphorus. This operation eliminated most of the nutrients flowing from the village into the Ocquionis and Canadarago. The quality and clarity of water in the lake improved dramatically.

Glaciers scoured out Canadarago and Otsego, its sister lake to the east. The glaciers pushed moraines (boulders, gravel, sand, and other geologic clutter) to the southern ends of these largest natural lakes in the Susquehanna watershed. Meltwater, rapidly filling the two basins, soon breached the lakes' moraine dams, and they drained down to their approximate present elevations. They continue to drain southward, unlike the better-known Finger Lakes farther west, which drain northward because their southern moraines remain unbreached.

Fed by the Ocquionis and three other tributaries, Canadarago is considerably smaller and shallower than Otsego—about four miles long, one and a quarter miles wide, and, at its greatest depth, 44 feet. Yellow perch, walleye, pike, tiger muskies, pickerel, and large- and smallmouth bass thrive in the comparatively warm water. Searching for the best fishing spots, hundreds of boaters cross wakes on the modest lake each summer.

Except where farmers plow right up to the shoreline, the

lake is surrounded by cottages of mixed quality, trailer parks, and motels catering to a seasonal trade that doubles Richfield Springs' population in July and August. The dense summer population around the lake succeeds an earlier, grander seasonal settlement that centered on the sulfur springs and was confined, for the most part, to the village proper.

At the southern end of Canadarago, water spills over a dam designed to elevate the lake by several feet. The outlet stream is called Oaks Creek. It is a fine fishing stream, filled with brook trout.

Some ten miles south of the lake, Oaks Creek joins the Susquehanna's North Branch. Just beyond this commingling of waters, this forerunner of all the long, shallow stretches of the Susquehanna can be waded during low flows without wetting the knees.

Lake Otsego

An exclamation of surprise broke from the lips of Deerslayer . . . when on reaching the margin of the lake he beheld the view that unexpectedly met his gaze. . . . On a level with the point lay a broad sheet of water, so placid and limpid, that it resembled a bed of the pure mountain atmosphere compressed into a setting of hills and woods.

—JAMES FENIMORE COOPER, describing his hero's first sighting of Lake Otsego in *The Deerslayer*

WILLARD HARMAN UNFOLDS a multicolored map of Lake Otsego's watershed. The watershed, covering seventy-five square miles, is shaped roughly like an inverted triangle, with the bottom point at the Village of Cooperstown. The triangle's sides angle narrowly from the lake, then spread and run far north of it, deep into the Town of Springfield. All of the water that falls into this area, within northern Otsego County and a small section of eastern Herkimer County, feeds Otsego Lake and, eventually, the Susquehanna.

"We have created two Otsego Lake protection districts," explains Dr. Harman, a professor with the State University of New York College at Oneonta and director of its Biological Field Station on this lake. "One of them is in the proximity of Otsego Lake and has a bunch of restrictions related directly to the lake itself. The other one, more than twice the size of the first, protects the aquifer throughout the Town of Springfield."

A burly biologist with a habit of talking himself nearly out of breath, Bill Harman is the driving force behind regulations on the lake and in its watershed. As a scientist and a member of Springfield's planning board, he worries as much about pollution entering the springs and ponds and streams north of the lake as he does about more direct degradation.

"Our interest is primarily in the lake," he says. "However, when you have a facility like this, you don't just stop at the lake. The lake, like the Susquehanna, is not just a hole in the ground with water in it. What comes off the land around it greatly impacts on its character and what lives and doesn't live there. And so we find ourselves more and more interested in what's going on in the lake's watershed, which really is more the headwaters of the Susquehanna than the lake itself is."

Like Lake Canadarago, Otsego is watered by a number of creeks and brooks, most of them growing from swampy sources near the Mohawk-Susquehanna watershed divide.[2] One of these swamps, Maumee, lies in Herkimer County, just south of the Jordanville swamp that drains into Canadarago.

Otsego's primary tributaries are Cripple and Hayden creeks and Shadow Brook, all flowing into the northern end of the lake. The easternmost, Shadow Brook, extends about six miles and has the largest watershed. It flows almost entirely through farmland, picking up significant amounts of nitrogen and phosphorus from manure runoff and transporting them into Otsego. These nutrients undermine the lake's ecology but have no adverse effect on the enormous carp that spawn each spring at Shadow Brook's mouth in picturesque Glimmerglass State Park.

In portaging from the Mohawk River to Lake Otsego, the Iroquois followed paths near Shadow Brook. Three Dutch traders probably came this way in 1614, six years before the Pilgrims landed at Plymouth. These traders began at Albany, canoed up the Mohawk, portaged across to Otsego, and continued down the Susquehanna to Tioga Point. After Native Americans captured and released them, the traders descended the Susquehanna as far as the Wyoming Valley before crossing to the Delaware River and returning to New York.

In 1737, Cadwallader Colden, New York's surveyor general, noted that goods could be portaged from the Mohawk to Otsego—a distance of fourteen miles—and then transported down the Susquehanna in flat-bottomed boats. George Washington, passing this way in 1783 on a postwar exploring expedition, observed Lake Otsego and the portage path to the Mohawk.

In the 1820s, Governor DeWitt Clinton and others proposed that a canal be constructed to extend from the recently completed Erie Canal (which parallels the Mohawk) along Shadow Brook to Otsego and down the Susquehanna. The plan never attracted widespread support. In the next decade, construction of a superior alternative—the Chenango Canal, connecting the Erie Canal at Utica with Binghamton on the Susquehanna—killed the idea.

Because Shadow Brook is Otsego's largest feeder stream and because of this long history of travel and anticipated travel along it to the lake, some local residents say it should be considered the Susquehanna's primary source. Every source has supporters.

Neither Shadow Brook nor any other tributary or landscape feature of this region prepares a visitor for Lake Otsego. In an agricultural area where mediocre soil insufficiently rewards all but the most determined farmers, Lake Otsego is a 50-carat diamond in a 14-carat setting. The Iroquois called it O-te-sa-ga. The word may mean "a place of greeting," and Native Americans certainly met and gathered here. In several of his nineteenth-century novels, James Fenimore Cooper called it the Glimmerglass. Subdued by a haze that often accompanies sunrise at Otsego on calm mornings, the lake can indeed seem to glimmer. Cooper described the lake in *The Chronicles of Cooperstown* as

≈ *The pleasure boat* Adelaide *on Lake Otsego, 1901. (New York State Historical Association, Cooperstown, New York.)*

"a sheet of limpid water, extending . . . about nine miles, and varying in width from about three-quarters of a mile to a mile and a half. It has many bays and points, and as the first are graceful and sweeping, and the last low and wooded, they contribute largely to its beauty. The water is cool and deep, and the fish are consequently firm and sweet. The two ends of the lake . . . deepen their water gradually, but there are places, on its eastern side in particular, where a large ship might float with her yards in the forest."

Like most glacial, deepened valleys, Otsego's basin is bathtub-shaped and steep-banked. It gathers most of its water from the north and west because its eastern sides are steepest, rising 400 to 600 feet above the water surface. Otsego's average depth is 74 feet, maximum 166 feet, making it one of the deeper lakes in New York.[3] Sited so close to the Susquehanna-Mohawk watershed divide, it is also one of the state's higher bodies of water—1,195 feet above sea level.

Nearly half of Otsego's shoreline, unlike Canadarago's, is forested and protected from development. Most of the lake's east side remains natural, thanks to ownership of vast acreage by Cooperstown's philanthropic and paternalistic Clark family. Crucial sections of the western slope, however, are wide open to erosion. Rain washes silt into the lake and landslides occur periodically at several locations. Increasingly powerful motorboats and increasingly numerous personal watercraft add to the problem if they raise wakes close to shore.

The north end of the lake and much of its northern watershed lie on limestone, which buffers acid rain as well as runoff from the acid sandstones and shales that underlie the southern section. Glacial scouring exposed the limestone, which is dissolved by water rushing in from Shadow Brook and other streams and then settles to the bottom of the lake as a white marl. That marl, along with blue sky and the lake's green plankton, contributes to the lake's distinctive turquoise color on its best days.

Unlike Canadarago, Otsego is a cold-water fishery—one of the best in the world, according to its devotees. Its cooler lower levels shelter native lake trout and landlocked salmon. Fishing boats occasionally haul in a trout weighing more than twenty pounds. Landlocked salmon can grow to half that weight. Anglers also prize the Otsego bass, a native whitefish called a grayback by locals. It is closely related to another popular lake whitefish, the cisco or greenback, a species introduced to the lake in the 1930s.

All of the cold-water species (with the exception of lake trout and landlocked salmon, whose numbers are increased by annual stocking) have been declining in recent years, largely because they must compete for food with introduced warm-water species. Six species of new fish, including alewives, have been dumped into the lake illegally since the 1980s. Alewives look much like small shad, but there is nothing small about their effect on Otsego. Alewives eat huge meals of crustacean zooplankton, thereby starving Otsego bass, ciscos, and other fish that formerly dined on that food. Before it began disappearing inside alewives, zooplankton ate algae, cutting the souplike growth in Otsego to near zero. Now algae bloom on the lake each summer, reducing the water's clarity and threatening to turn its turquoise to pea green. When algae die, they sink, decompose, and deplete the lake's deep-water oxygen, further jeopardizing the cold-water fishery. Thus have alewives, an unwanted species, destabilized the entire lake culture.

Since 1988, more than thirty species of fish have been captured in the streams that feed Otsego, and most of these warm-water species also thrive in the lake. They include large- and smallmouth bass, perch, sunfish, suckers, and catfish. The bass especially are popular among Otsego's anglers.

Young freshwater eels still occasionally enter Otsego after swimming all the way from the Sargasso Sea, in the North Atlantic Ocean. They come to Otsego by way of the Chesapeake and the Susquehanna, somehow getting past huge hydroelectric dams on the Lower Susquehanna and low-head dams farther north. The arduous trip, one way, takes about a year. As adults, these eels make the return trip to the Sargasso.

Eels are scarce in the lake now, but years ago they filled Otsego and the river. Art Andrews, a retired New York State Department of Environmental Conservation (DEC) officer, recalls that during the Depression his father worked the Cooperstown water pump on the Susquehanna, just below the river's outlet from the lake. When eels migrated back to the Sargasso in autumn, Andrews's father would shut down the pump wheel, place a big bag over the outlet, and harvest *Anguilla rostrata*. He sold them downriver in Oneonta for 25 cents each.

Otsego once was rich with shad and herring as well. Before dams, the river and lake teemed with the spawning migrations of these anadromous fish. Wrote Fenimore Cooper in *The Pioneers,* "Enormous shoals of herrings were discovered to have wandered five hundred miles through the windings of the impetuous Susquehanna, and the lake was alive with their numbers."

Now, on perfect summer afternoons (and Cooperstown does have them, despite enduring 200 overcast days during an average year), Otsego Lake is filled with fishing boats searching for trout and bass, sailboats searching for wind, tour boats searching for Deerslayer's haunts, and motorboats cruising the scenic waters with water skiers in tow. An increasing number of boats, combined with escalating development around the lake, more pollution entering the water, and the ubiquitous alewives, have prompted calls for greater controls on lake and watershed to preserve an outstanding fishery and Otsego's other recreational assets.

Not to mention saving Cooperstown's drinking water. Until recently, the village's residents drank lake water with only chlorine added. State and federal regulations mandated a new filtration plant and additional chlorine treatment in the mid-1990s, but many residents would have been satisfied to continue drinking unfiltered, unchlorinated water. At the Biological Field Station on the west bank of the lake, SUNY-Oneonta faculty members still drink their lake water straight as they work to provide straight answers on how area residents can protect Otsego.

Bill Harman came to Cooperstown in 1968 to establish a research location for Oneonta students. The university constructed the field station three years later just north of the well-known Farmers' Museum and Fenimore House. It holds offices and labs and launches research vessels exploring Otsego's flora, fauna, and water quality. Harman runs the field station as an educational center for researchers, students, and the community. He is a true believer in keeping a "relatively pristine" lake from deteriorating.

"It's pretty apparent that this is one of those unique situations where the system is just the right size and shape so that with the human population we have, what we do becomes very evident," says the professor. He is preparing to take another class of students out in a boat to show them what nutrients washing into the lake are doing to plant life. "In most places you're either fighting a losing cause or you don't have much to worry about. Here we just happen to be in a situation which is very close to the edge."

In an effort to monitor lake quality and increase public awareness of Otsego's challenges, Harman and other faculty and student researchers systematically test the lake, its tributaries, and the Upper Susquehanna and compare those tests with historical data. Harman and others have published *The State of Otsego Lake: 1936–1996*, a 300-page description of changes in the lake's ecology.

That report and earlier studies found that the lake's water quality improved in the early 1980s, thanks to a statewide ban on high-phosphate detergents and installation of an upgraded sanitary waste disposal system at Glimmerglass State Park. Quality began to decline again in the mid-1980s and has continued to deteriorate, largely because of development on the lake's west shore. The number of lakeside homes increased from 147 in 1937 to 407 in 1994, with construction accelerating at the end of the period. Total phosphorus levels in the lake doubled in the 1990s, increasing algal growth at the same time that alewives diminished the populations of algae-eating zooplankton.

Bill Harman directs the SUNY-Oneonta Biological Field Station on Lake Otsego at Cooperstown. The station monitors water quality in the lake, its tributaries, and its outflow—the Susquehanna. (Photo by Christine Brubaker.)

Phosphorus is Harman's primary concern. It flows into the lake from malfunctioning septic systems and in manure runoff from dairy farms, which occupy about 95 percent of the watershed's cleared land. A Biological Field Station report in 1996 concluded that Otsego retains over 80 percent of the phosphorus that reaches it. Unless that percentage is reduced, the report said, the lake will suffer severely.

To Harman, implementation of remedies for the lake's high nutrient levels and other ills is as important as data collection. He is an activist scientist; beyond research and teaching, he wants to transform the thinking of the more than 2,300 people who reside in the lake's watershed year round and its thousand or more summer residents. He wants them to take better care of their septic systems, keep their cattle out of streams, and monitor the bait they dump into the lake.

The field station has strong allies. Conservative landowners who want to protect their own interests as well as Lake Otsego compose the Otsego County Conservation Association. Otsego 2000, a more activist group, would like to protect the lake while also promoting new business in Cooperstown. Motorless Otsego, a third conservation group and the most radical, would remove all gasoline engines from the lake.

Not everyone agrees with the conservationists. Another point of view exerted itself forcefully during a lengthy argument in the mid-1990s over whether or not the DEC should build a public boat launch at Glimmerglass State Park. The DEC and some residents believed more boaters should be encouraged to use Otsego, accessible to the public now only by way of a launch in the Village of Cooperstown. Harman, Otsego 2000, and others claimed the launch is adequate and that more boats, particularly if launched from the state park, would further destabilize the lake. Governor George Pataki eventually scotched the project.

Mike Empey, a licensed fishing guide and president of the Otsego County Sportfishing Association at the time, thought the boat launch should be built. He believes Harman has not proved beyond doubt that the quality of the lake water is declining. He says Harman and the Biological Field Station have engaged in "eco-science

practiced as religion," at the expense of people who want to use the lake.

Empey's brother, Ken, agrees: "If there had been a referendum, popular opinion would have been overwhelmingly in favor of a public boat launch." Ken Empey serves on the planning board for the Town of Warren in Herkimer County, at the extreme northern edge of Otsego's watershed. Cooperstown and other Otsego County towns want Herkimer residents to participate in watershed improvement efforts, but Empey and many of his neighbors want nothing to do with that. "It doesn't look like a good deal to us. They would like to control the whole watershed because of the lake, but we don't have easy access to the lake."

In 1992, watershed municipalities formed the Otsego Lake Watershed Council to reconcile varying viewpoints while developing a master plan to protect Cooperstown's drinking water, preserve the lake and the land around it, and provide for recreational use. Council members called for the *State of Lake Otsego* report so they would have a scientific basis for action. They quizzed groups of lake users to discover their priorities. They held public hearings, issued a management plan, and hired a watershed manager.

Harman believes independent elements of this voluntary plan will be implemented as consensus develops on lake-protection priorities. He hopes the consensus will support better farm management practices and wastewater treatment and stricter navigational rules and fishery management. "It's kind of a mix between what a lot of people think of as a legislative hammer to hold over somebody's head," he explains, "and a peer-pressure kind of thing where you think, gee, if I don't clean my act up, all my neighbors are going to think I'm a turkey. That latter means of getting at things seems to work a lot better in many situations."

Here at the headwaters of the Susquehanna, as at so many places along the river's length, competing interests want to maintain the quality of drinking water in the lake while also fishing and boating in it and living and farming in its watershed. That goal may be attainable; but given the vagaries of nutrients and alewives, alongside some watershed residents' concerns that the environmental case has been overdrawn, ultimate resolution remains as clouded as Otsego's glimmer.

The Outlet

I dream of a blue lake sleeping . . .

And I see a village gleaming . . .

And out from the lake's broad bosom

A river is gliding slow.

—Mrs. E. J. Bugbee of Fayette, Iowa, in a letter to the editor of the *Cooperstown Republican and Democrat,* 1858

When James Fenimore Cooper published *The Pioneers* in 1823, he pluralized his subtitle addendum: *or, The Sources of the Susquehanna.* In his introduction to a later edition, however, the author noted that "New York having but one county of Otsego, and the Susquehanna but one proper source, there can be no mistake as to the site of the tale."

That site is Lake Otsego and the channel draining it.

Ocquionis Creek and Shadow Brook are ultimate sources of the Susquehanna. The outlet from Lake Otsego is the river's traditional source. This is where most people searching for *the* source stop.

"The site is gravelly, stiff clay," wrote the river explorer Richard Smith after visiting the place in 1769, "covered with towering white pines, just where the river Susquehanna, no more than ten or twelve feet wide, runs downward out of the lake, with a strong current." Majestic pines still ascend Lake Otsego's eastern cliff, but the outlet has changed. Since its damming in 1905, this section of the Susquehanna runs three times wider, but without force. The concrete dam several hundred yards downstream from the outlet significantly deepens and slows water in lake and river.

Fenimore Cooper described the predammed outlet in *The Deerslayer:* "[Beyond] the fringe of bushes immediately on the shore of the lake . . . [was] a narrow stream, of sufficient depth of limpid water, with a strong current, and a canopy of leaves, upheld by arches composed of the limbs of hoary trees. Bushes lined the shores, as usual, but they left sufficient space between them to admit the passage of any thing that did not exceed twenty feet in width, and to allow of a perspective ahead of eight or ten times that distance."[4]

In the mid-1840s, several years after Cooper wrote *The Deerslayer,* the noted journalist Nathaniel Parker Willis visited Cooperstown and asked the novelist to show him the source of the Susquehanna. Cooper, then in his fifties and widely recognized for his literary accomplishments, led the

☞ *Patriotic canoeists at Clark's Bridge, an elaborate foot crossing just downstream from the Susquehanna's outlet from Lake Otsego, 1888. (New York State Historical Association, Cooperstown, New York.)*

younger Willis to the outlet. "It was something to see two such sources together," Willis reported, "the pourings-out from both fountains, from visible head and visible head-waters, sure to last famous till doomsday." Willis admitted that upon entering Cooperstown he had ridden over Main Street Bridge "with neither tributary look nor thought" toward what flowed beneath—the Susquehanna's outlet from Otsego. He really needed Cooper to guide him there.

In 1899, six years before Cooperstown residents dammed the river, Charles Weathers Bump, on assignment from the *Baltimore Sun,* stood on the bridge Willis had crossed and looked back toward the Susquehanna's start. "We gazed down upon as pretty a brook vista as can be seen any-where," he wrote. "Leafy trees and bushes overhung the water in profusion, and some grew quite in midstream, with their roots clinging to mossy rocks. The water was so calm and clear as to reveal, with the aid of a friendly sun, the charms of the river bottom, and the stream seemed to us to have a mood akin to ours, unwilling to leave the 'Glimmerglass' for an onward hurry to the Chesapeake."

Carl Carmer visited the outlet in the early 1950s, as he was preparing to write *The Susquehanna* for his Rivers of America series. The dam had changed the scene. "A few yards from the lake it is not quite four feet deep," he observed, "and there children swim, shadowed sometimes by the high bank across from Riverbrink [the first home on Cooperstown's River Street, which parallels the stream]. Canoes drift here and fishermen, hardly expecting a catch, idle with short lines dangling in water so clear that the fish can see them."

🦢 *The Susquehanna, in foreground, runs out from Lake Otsego. The view is from Cooperstown's Main Street Bridge. (Photo by Christine Brubaker.)*

Generations of village residents have gathered for recreation and sometimes celebration at the lake's outlet, where the water remains relatively clear. Many of Cooperstown's visitors, however, are as oblivious of the North Branch's start as N. P. Willis was initially in the 1840s. No one has made it easy to recognize that a river begins here. The Susquehanna River Basin Commission erected the first plaque marking the source in 1996; it stands at a less-than-obvious site in a grove of maple trees fifty yards from the water.

The low-key nature of all things unrelated to baseball contributes to the Susquehanna's relative obscurity in Cooperstown. Besides, the tiny park at the river's start was privately owned and quietly guarded until 1957. Then Fenimore Cooper's great-grandson donated an acre and a quarter to the Village of Cooperstown with the condition that it remain forever undeveloped. From the juncture of River and Lake streets the village constructed a flight of stone steps leading to the lake, river, and floodplain. The terraced Cooper tract is called Council Rock Park.

Old state markers at the top of the steps commemorate two singular features of the lake. One is Council Rock. The other, a metal plaque bolted to a boulder on the outlet's eastern shore, marks General Clinton's dam, a temporary military device that helped the Continental Army win the War of Independence.

Mohawks gathered at Council Rock, which rests in the lake a few yards from the outlet. Arrow points and chips have been found in large numbers on the shore, often called Indian Point. Council Rock is (and apparently was, even before Cooperstown's dam raised the level of the lake) the only rock rising above lake water, so Native Americans as well as early white settlers considered it a landmark.

Deerslayer and Chingachgook meet at Council Rock in *The Deerslayer*. Cooper describes the feature at the opening of the novel, as Deerslayer and Hurry Harry canoe from Otsego into the Susquehanna's outlet: "The rock was not large, being merely some five or six feet high, only half of which elevation rose above the lake. The incessant washing of the water, for centuries, had so rounded its summit, that

it resembled a large beehive in shape, its form being more than usually regular and even."

Louis Jones, a Cooperstown folklorist, reported an "old Mohawk Indian" story connected with Council Rock. A black-robed missionary disparaged the Mohawks' religion. In contrast, he told them, *his* God could perform great miracles. He could move mountains, for example. Then a Mohawk chief asked the missionary a question. If he had such complete faith, the chief wondered, did the missionary believe that his God could move Council Rock? The missionary said his God could do that. "Well, then," said the chief, "we will test your faith. We will roll the rock on top of you and your faith being what it is, your God will move it off your back." The Mohawks rolled the rock on top of the missionary. They say his skeleton is still beneath the boulder.

While the Native Americans may have gotten the best of one missionary, they did not survive white settlement. The Revolution ruined the Iroquois. By the late 1780s, tribes had abandoned settlements at Cooperstown and at the huge village at Onoquaga (along both sides of the North Branch well downstream at what are now Afton and Windsor). For several decades, small groups of Iroquois returned to the Cooperstown area in the summer months to hunt, fish, sell goods to whites, and beg for food. By 1850, as Fenimore Cooper's daughter, Susan, noted, white settlement had obliterated everything related to Native American occupation except Council Rock.

A poignant memorial to the Iroquois—a large mound of earth with a medium-sized oak tree growing at its center—

lies off Main Street just east of the outlet. Workers uncovered a number of Native American skeletons while grading this property in 1874. The property owner, Mrs. Alfred Corning Clark, gathered the bones and buried them at the foot of the mound. She marked the mound with a granite slab and an epitaph composed by the Reverend William Wilberforce Lord, village rector and a poet. It reads:

White Man, Greeting!
We, near whose bones you stand,
Were Iroquois. The wide land
Which now is yours was ours.
Friendly hands have given back
To us enough for a tomb.

The inscription on the boulder plaque at the Susquehanna's outlet is not similarly poetic and is only partially informative: "Here was built a dam the summer of 1779 by the Soldiers under Gen. Clinton to enable them to join the forces of Gen. Sullivan at Tioga." An uninformed visitor may well wonder: How could a dam help this army?

General James Clinton led half of the crucial Sullivan-Clinton expedition against the Iroquois and their British sponsors. He was second in command to General John Sullivan. George Washington directed Sullivan to cross into central Pennsylvania from Easton and ascend the Susquehanna to Tioga. He ordered Clinton to move from Albany along the Mohawk to Canajoharie, cross to Otsego Lake, and travel down the Susquehanna to meet Sullivan.

Clinton arrived at the foot of Otsego in early July 1779. He held his army of 1,800 men and 220 bateaux there until early August, waiting for the lake waters to rise behind a dam his engineers had constructed at the outlet. Some accounts say the water level rose a foot. Some say two or three feet. One says four feet, which is about the additional amount of water held in the lake by the 1905 dam. The reason for the damming was simple: Clinton's boats were too heavily weighted with supplies to descend a summer-shallow Susquehanna. Without additional water, those boats would have run aground on fallen trees or rocks, or they would have banged against the river's clay banks and stopped dead in a slow flow. Clinton's engineers planned to create an artificial flood similar to the "splashes" used by raftmen and loggers in the next century to raise the level of water on Susquehanna tributaries to a useful rafting stage. At the outlet, soldiers placed logs collected from the adjacent woodland atop a boulder foundation and waited for Lake Otsego to rise.

On August 8, after pressure had built for five weeks behind the rock-and-log jam, Clinton's soldier-sailors moved the bateaux into the river. At six o'clock that night, they broke the dam. The river, which had been nearly dry, filled quickly. The boats, manned by three soldiers each, took off at the peak of the flood the next morning and ran thirty miles down the swollen river. Clinton's soldiers marching alongside the Susquehanna traveled just over half that distance.

The flood swelled the North Branch for more than 100 miles and forced major tributaries, including the Chenango

☞ *Canoeists in the General Clinton Canoe Regatta's two-person pro race begin a seventy-mile paddle out of Lake Otsego and down the Susquehanna on Memorial Day 2000. The race from Cooperstown to Bainbridge, New York, is the longest single-day flat-water race in the world. (Tri-Town News, Sidney, New York. Photo by Anna Ritchey.)*

River at Binghamton, to reverse course at their mouths. The *Gazetteer of the State of New York* reported that the sudden change in water level at midsummer terrified the Iroquois, who thought the Great Spirit had intervened on the side of the soldiers. When Clinton finally joined forces with Sullivan at Tioga on August 22, the Iroquois found more to dread: the combined force of 5,000 men marched into their country and laid waste to village after village, field after field.

While waiting for the lake to rise, Clinton's troops had celebrated the revolutionaries' third Independence Day with considerable firing of artillery and drinking of rum. In commemoration, Cooperstown residents traditionally have made their own racket at the outlet each July. An artillery piece dubbed the Cricket exploded here a half century after Clinton's flood. On the Fourth of July, about 1870, some residents, annoyed by the boat-snagging boulders remaining from the dam, dynamited the impediments as the climactic event of the day's celebration.

The Susquehanna's outlet also has hosted more mundane activities. James Fenimore Cooper, grandson and namesake of the novelist, described some of the nineteenth-century pleasures Cooperstown residents enjoyed at the junction of lake and river in his *Reminiscences of Mid-Victorian Cooperstown:* "In dry times the residents would draw water in barrels and hogsheads from the river here. Here the bold and lawless youth of the town would enjoy the forbidden pleasure of swimming in the nude, going under water when an infrequent boat passed; and here on rare Sundays the more modest Baptists were dipped."

The Course

This part of the Susquehanna is about as wide as a living room and it meanders like the course of a parcheesi game. Trees broken by spring floods had toppled into or across the river. We hacked our way through or lifted our craft over.

—RALPH GRAY on canoeing the first miles of the Susquehanna, *National Geographic Magazine,* July 1950

WHEN DAME'S ROCKET LIGHTS UP THE Susquehanna riverbank with vibrant lavender and pale pink flowers in late May, scores of canoeists paddle furiously out of Lake Otsego and down the narrow river course. Professional and would-be Olympic racers from the eastern United States and Canada are competing in one- and two-person races in the longest single-day flat-water race in the world—seventy miles from Cooperstown to Bainbridge.

Begun in 1963, the General Clinton Canoe Regatta commemorates the commander who sent his boats speeding downriver during the Revolution. ("I suppose regatta participants wouldn't think it was such a gala affair if they realized that Clinton was really going down through here just to destroy the Indians' food and hope they starved to death for the winter," says Joe Homburger. Homburger watches the race each year from his front yard on the river at Phoenix Mills.)

The event is called a regatta rather than a race because it includes a wild variety of additional events that lure mostly local amateur paddlers of all ages. Participants stage preliminary sprint and relay and fun races at various points between Cooperstown and Bainbridge throughout Memorial Day weekend. The seventy-mile events, also known as the world championship flat-water endurance races, are held on Memorial Day itself. They begin early in the morning, usually before fog has lifted from Lake Otsego. How long they last depends on the level of the river water as well as on the quality of the paddling.

The first several miles of the Susquehanna, before it joins Oaks Creek, provide the most challenging stage of the race. Canoeists can take an hour or more to reach Phoenix Mills. Wood often fills the narrow Susquehanna, which local residents refer to as "the crick." River sponsors chainsaw a path downstream before the race begins, but sufficient obstacles remain. If water is low, canoes bump into rocks and tires on the river bottom. If it is really low, they scrape over islands of gravel.[5]

After that stretch, and especially below Milford, the river deepens and widens and, for the remainder of the journey, provides one of the most scenic racing waterways in the country. The Susquehanna's beauty (along with a desire to attract tourists) inspired a Bainbridge insurance agent, Charles Hickley, to begin these races and the Bainbridge Chamber of Commerce to continue them.

Thousands of spectators stand on Susquehanna bridges and sit on lawn chairs along the banks to watch the pro paddlers glide powerfully along the course. One of the racers leading the two-man professional division more often than not has been Serge Corbin of St. Boniface, Quebec.

Corbin has entered more than half of the races and has won every time. Thanks to better-trained athletes and lighter equipment, winning times dropped from 11 hours and 45 minutes in 1963 to a record 6 hours, 34 minutes in 1990.

The professional racers never pause in their precision paddling, except to portage small dams at Cooperstown, Goodyear Lake, and Oneonta, before skimming across the finish line at General Clinton Park at Bainbridge. Here they join amateur paddlers from earlier races in a carnival atmosphere that draws crowds from the rural region. While kids enjoy rides and games, their parents may tour the regatta's tiny museum to admire the clunky seventy-two-pound canoe in which Al Camp and Jim Root won the 1969 race. By comparison, Serge Corbin's latest graphite canoe weighs twenty pounds.

Aside from regatta participants, Joe Homburger sees about twenty people paddling and dragging their canoes along his stretch of river each summer. Some enjoy a day's adventure and some hope to canoe the entire Susquehanna. Lake Otsego's outlet has been the starting point for some extraordinary recreations.

The most celebrated expedition ever to travel the length of the river passed Phoenix Mills long before Homburger began monitoring traffic. Ralph Gray and five other paddlers used three heavy wood-and-canvas canoes to descend the Susquehanna from Cooperstown at a comparatively leisurely pace in the summer of 1949. Newspapers covered the tour as it progressed and tens of thousands of people turned out to cheer the paddlers all the way to the Chesapeake. With unusually low July water and without an advance crew to cut away trees, the group faltered below the Cooperstown dam. The men walked their canoes over the worst driftwood piles and stony shoals. Even so, the rough riverbed shredded the bottom of one canoe. "As *Susque* or *Hanna* [two of the canoes] scraped on gravel bars and rocks," Gray reported later in the *National Geographic,* "dairy cows grazing in adjacent pastures looked up in wonderment. Or was it quiet scorn? We began to feel a little foolish before our constant gallery of well-bred herds."

An Alliance for the Chesapeake Bay group tugged its canoes through the debris out of Cooperstown and paddled on to Binghamton in June 1996. Each spring since 1990, canoeists participating in the Alliance's Susquehanna Sojourn have taken a week's vacation to cover a substantial stretch of water. At night they hear local experts discuss the river's ecology and history. Sojourner groups have paddled the entire Susquehanna and its major tributaries without encountering a stretch as ragged as those first few miles below Cooperstown.

Not everyone uses a paddle to propel himself down the Susquehanna. Russ Chaffee, a thirty-nine-year-old teacher from Sayre, Pennsylvania, swam all 444 miles in twenty-eight days during the summer of 1966. The only person ever to swim the length of the Susquehanna (as well as the length of all the Finger Lakes), Chaffee said he wanted to emphasize swimming's recreational values. Upon arriving at the Chesapeake Bay, he reported, "I was struck with the wideness of the Susquehanna. Of all the rivers I have seen in the world, few can match it in this area."

The wide river caused no problem more dangerous than the juvenile Susquehanna. Just downstream from Otsego's outlet, the current swept Chaffee beneath an undercut bank. He held his breath for what seemed like several minutes until he could break away. Then he continued swimming and occasionally climbing over accumulated debris in the narrow channel, on his way to the broader river and the bay.

Cooperstown

Cooperstown's location as the first community at the headwaters of the Susquehanna River gives it a special downstream responsibility to those towns who drink from the river, and ultimately to the fishermen who make their living from the Chesapeake Bay that it feeds, 400 miles south of Main Street.

—Michael Whaling, environmental activist, in a letter to *The Freeman's Journal,* Cooperstown, April 1999

William Cooper, father of the novelist, founded Cooperstown in 1787. Because he thought of the Susquehanna as the area's primary conduit to downstream markets, he laid out his village on a north–south axis on the west side of the river. He built his house near the river but facing the lake, and first settlers called the town Foot of the Lake as well as Cooperstown.

Perhaps inspired by General Clinton's Revolutionary example, Cooper proposed to build a dam across the Susquehanna's outlet to build up a head of water to help float boats downstream during low flows. He collected the money needed to construct these works, but the New York legislature refused to pass an enabling law, fearing that Pennsylvania communities would benefit at the expense of New York cities. Since then, Cooperstown has focused more on the lake than on the river, and many of its most substantial buildings face the former.

More than a century after the founder's river plan foundered, the Cooperstown Water Company built its concrete dam across the Susquehanna just downriver from the outlet. This blockage raised Lake Otsego and helped provide a steady supply of drinking water for the village's 3,000 residents. The company employed water wheels and gravity to move this higher water along an aqueduct running through town. About 1960, Cooperstown abandoned water power and began to pump drinking water through the town with electricity. The town chlorinates lake water, runs it through a rapid sand filter to remove solids and chemicals, and chlorinates it again before pumping it to drinkers.

If Cooperstown's water distribution system has not required the dam to help distribute drinking water for more than four decades, why not remove the impediment instead of forcing everyone canoeing out of the lake to portage almost immediately?

"The purpose of the dam," maintains a state water quality management plan drawn up in 1976, "is to regulate the level of Otsego Lake within certain limits in order to main-

tain the recreational potential of the lake." If the lake fell to its natural level, Sunken Island, at Otsego's northern end, would no longer be entirely underwater, and boating in that area could be hazardous. Moreover, the lake's shoreline would change, in some places radically, disturbing property owners and boaters.

The artificial water level causes unnecessary erosion to unstable shorelines and damage to the lake's ecology, says Bill Harman at the Biological Field Station. "If the lake was back to its original level, we'd be in a lot better shape," he claims. "However, if you lower it, you've got all of the silt which has washed out and has built up a new wave-washed terrace three feet higher than the original. That's all going to be re-eroded again. I wish it wasn't up, but now we've got a situation where we effectively can't drop it."

The town will not remove the dam for another essential reason: it regulates the flow of the first miles of the Susquehanna. River flow must be steady to flush Cooperstown's treated sewage fast enough to keep the nutrient-enriched water from wiping out aquatic life. The village's sewage treatment plant sits about a mile downriver from the dam, just behind Cooperstown High School. The system provides primary and secondary treatment of solid and liquid waste. In the late 1980s, at the insistence of the Department of Environmental Conservation, Cooperstown added $1 million worth of rotating biological contractors to squeeze out remaining toxins, primarily ammonia. After chlorination, a pipe carries the waste water another quarter of a mile downstream before dumping it into the river that runs out of Cooperstown's basin of drinking water.

As a member of Cooperstown's water and sewer boards, Dr. Ted Peters has monitored the water coming and going for several decades. A retired research scientist at Cooperstown's Mary Imogene Bassett Hospital, Peters says that "new" water from the lake is better than Perrier (because it does not have benzene in it). He says Cooperstown's "used" water is no better or worse than any other community's waste.

"This is where the water is best on the Susquehanna," agrees David Sanford, chairman of the village water board.

"It's all downhill from here," adds John Mitchell, chairman of the Otsego Lake Watershed Council.

Dam operators have some control over what happens to the village's downstream discharge. They take off heavy boards at the top of the concrete structure during low flows, permitting more lake water to spill into the riverbed and dilute the effluent. "When I took over as chairman of the sewer board," recalls Peters, "the state was trying to tell us that the Susquehanna was an intermittent stream because we could close it down completely by putting those boards on and slowing it down to a trickle." The DEC now requires the village to keep at least 11 cubic feet of water per second moving over the dam in order to discharge sewage into it safely. That's not a lot of water—the river sometimes is little more than ankle deep below the dam—but it's enough for the state to classify the Susquehanna as a "regulated" stream.

Thanks to a steady river flow and comprehensive sewage treatment, water quality in the first few miles of the Susquehanna has improved, says Leonard Sohacki, a biologi-cal limnologist who works with Bill Harman. Sohacki began sampling the river between Cooperstown and Otego, just beyond Oneonta, in the early 1970s. Cooperstown today releases fewer nutrients to the river and far fewer than Otsego's tributaries contribute to the lake. The river assimilates the village's effluent without major stress on fish.

At Phoenix Mills, three miles downstream from Cooperstown, the biologist Joe Homburger agrees that water quality has improved since the 1970s. But he has fished through some bad times in between. Homburger handles DEC permits and chairs the Cooperstown Water Board's Watershed Supervisory Committee. He shares Harman's intensity on environmental issues. When it comes to fishing, he may be even more focused. "The fishery shifted drastically about 1982–83," says Homburger, "because the chlorinator at the sewage treatment plant was not operable, so they guessed at the dosage of chlorine. The chlorine was astronomical: it killed the fish. The river quality was terrible. As a matter of fact, there weren't any fish to speak of in this river."

The Susquehanna's first few miles had been a fertile fishery for centuries. William Cooper said he returned to his fledgling village with provisions in the spring of 1789 and found the colonists starving. They quickly ate everything he had brought and turned to picking the roots of wild leeks, which were not particularly satisfying as sustenance but contributed considerably to communitywide halitosis.

"A singular event seemed sent by a good Providence to our relief," Cooper wrote in *A Guide in the Wilderness*, his colorful account of Cooperstown's settlement. "It was reported to me that unusual shoals of fish were seen

Joe Homburger fishes in the Susquehanna at his home in Phoenix Mills. The *Department of Conservation biologist encourages improved water quality for better fishing. (Photo by Andrew Baugnet.)*

moving in the clear waters of the Susquehanna. I went, and was surprised to find that they were herrings. We made something like a small net, by the interweaving of twigs, and by this rude and simple contrivance we were able to take them in thousands. In less than ten days each family had an ample supply with plenty of salt."

After canal dams on the Lower Susquehanna blocked the herring and shad migration in the early nineteenth century, plenty of other fish continued to thrive in the upper river. Until the early 1980s, Joe Homburger regularly caught an unusual assortment of fish. Because the Susquehanna running by his property is in transition from cold-water lake to warm-water river, it contains several species that slip over the dam from the lake, as well as fish that are born and die in the riverine system. Homburger began needling DEC officials in 1984 and kept it up until the agency required Cooperstown to monitor its sewage discharge with more care. Operators cut back on chlorine and the contractors reduced ammonia. The river began to rebound in the late 1980s and Homburger has been fishing more successfully at Phoenix Mills.

"Ted Peters thought the state was being overzealous in what they wanted them to do for treatment levels and the amount it would cost," Homburger says, "but the fact of the matter is there were no fish in this river and I think a river of this magnitude and renown and distinction ought to have fish in it."

Pete Farmer, who grew up in Cooperstown and regularly returns, has a slightly different perspective on the chlorine. Before secondary treatment of sewage began in 1968, he recalls, "toilet paper, slime, and algae" filled the North Branch. "That river really used to stink. But the chlorinator took away the smell and it took away the slime, because nothing grows with that chlorine in there. The river doesn't stink as bad now and they strain out the turds, so it's great for swimming—but the fishing's lousy."

How one assesses water quality often depends on where one stands along the stream. A DEC water engineer suggests all municipalities discharge their sewage effluent upstream from their water supply. "He's of the opinion that they would be inclined to monitor things a great deal more carefully," Homburger notes. The biologist laughs and strokes his dark beard. "I kind of like that, but I don't think I could ever get the village to relocate their outfall from the river to the lake."

Goodyear Lake

Whenever you build a dam, you alter the whole characteristic of a river. It stops being a river and it becomes a lake. It becomes a siltation point. The fish are changed; the algae, the food cycle, the energy source are completely changed. It's not a healthy situation.

—GEORGE SCHUMACHER, professor emeritus of biology,
State University of New York at Binghamton

FROM COOPERSTOWN THE NORTH BRANCH meanders south through a wide, flat-floored valley deepened, as were its source lakes, by the glacier that scarred this watershed. The fledgling Susquehanna Valley accommodates the river, state Route 28, and the Cooperstown and Charlotte Valley Railroad, along with small villages and large dairy farms. Each Fourth of July, it also carries reverberations from Cooperstown's fireworks explosions.

At Portlandville, about eighteen miles south of Cooperstown, the little river suspends its winding course. It suddenly widens and deepens and slows. Here the Susquehanna's northernmost hydroelectric dam has robbed the water of almost all riverine characteristics, and so the North Branch for several miles above the dam is called Goodyear Lake.

Girard Goodyear owned much of the land in this vicinity in the late nineteenth century. With the aid of a small dam, he operated grist- and sawmills. Between 1905 and 1907, the Goodyears and their in-laws, the Colliers, built the current hollow-core concrete dam to increase water power and generate electricity to run a trolley from Oneonta through Cooperstown and on into the Mohawk Valley.

After the trolley went out of business in the late 1930s, Associated Gas & Electric (now New York State Electric & Gas (NYSEG) purchased the dam. When the utility began concentrating on nuclear power in the late 1960s, it decided to tear it down. Owners of surrounding cottages did not like the idea of living beside a mud flat instead of a lake. They sued and stopped demolition, then raised $25,000 to help a Canadian entrepreneur purchase the facility. Subsequent owners have improved the dam and continue to sell power to NYSEG.

Thus was preserved Collier's Dam on Goodyear Lake— a feature that renders the Susquehanna at this point so alien to its nature that some summer visitors never realize they are playing not in a self-contained lake but in retarded river water.

A major reason for their faulty perception is the irregular shape of the 370-acre lake. Goodyear widens, then narrows,

☞ *The Susquehanna's first large dam holds back Goodyear Lake at Portlandville. The dam's raceway (in foreground) washes through generators to create power for New York State Electric & Gas. (Photo by Christine Brubaker.)*

the recreational and commercial attractions far outweigh ecological disturbances to the waterway. Beginning in the 1920s, families built summer "camps" on Goodyear and began boating, fishing for bass and walleyes, swimming, and holding dances in a pavilion constructed at the southern end. Many owners turned these camps into permanent homes. Today more than 400 year-round houses ring the lake and scores of weekend visitors bring cartop craft to a new public boat launch.

In 1955 Fred Knott Sr. bought the area around the dam. He demolished the dance pavilion and built a motel in its place. Knott's Motel on the Lake is the major commercial enterprise on Goodyear Lake and Knott and his son have been community leaders. A former president of the Goodyear Lake Association and former overseer of the hydroelectric operation, Knott Sr. watched Goodyear change before retiring in Florida. "The quality of the water is better than it used to be," he says. "We had a little swimming area thirty or more years ago, which the state tested for bacteria and phosphates and found safe for bathing. That doesn't mean it wasn't polluted or was safe to drink. The lake was acting as a big sump for phosphates. The dam was stopping all the phosphates right here."

Water quality improved after Cooperstown and other upstream communities upgraded sewage treatment. When the residents of Milford, a small village midway between Cooperstown and Portlandville, installed individual septic tanks in the early 1980s, the water changed dramatically. Previously, about half of Milford's residents had piped their raw sewage into a central conduit that ran out East Main

hosts good-sized coves here and there, and extends a lame leg for a quarter of a mile east of the dam. This scalloped form is nothing at all like the straight-banked, run-of-the-river "lakes" behind the big dams on the Lower Susquehanna. Canoeists unfamiliar with Goodyear Lake's geography have paddled up the east leg and then had to backtrack to portage the dam.

For most people who live around the two-mile-long lake,

Street and dumped its contents into a small stream feeding the Susquehanna. Sewage odors could be intense on warm summer evenings and algae blooms in the vicinity turned the North Branch green from bank to bank.

Len Sohacki, the SUNY-Oneonta biological limnologist, takes samples from the river and its tributaries, wading into the water under low-flow conditions. His sampling locations include Cherry Valley Creek at his home, near where the little stream runs into the Susquehanna at Milford. Sohacki says Cooperstown's effluent and barnyard runoff from cattle farms lining the river offset Milford's improvements. "Even in low-flow conditions, the phosphorus load entering the lake is great," notes Sohacki. "Planktonic organisms make use of this phosphorus. They convert it into an organic form and develop situations where lake waters become pea-soup green."

While phosphorus degrades the lake, Sohacki says, water downstream is biologically superior because most of the phosphorus remains behind the dam. As long as nothing disturbs this nutrient receptacle, it improves the quality of the free-flowing river.

Just south of Goodyear Lake, the released Susquehanna turns southwest and flows toward Oneonta, home of another athletic hall of fame—soccer this time. Oneonta has an elaborate sewage treatment system, similar to Cooperstown's. At Otego, a few miles farther downstream and the end point of Sohacki's study area, the river has almost recovered from Oneonta's waste stream.

At Oneonta, for the first time in its long journey, the Susquehanna seems more river- than creeklike. It stops winding and can be contained, happily for modern road engineers, between Route 28 and Interstate 88. An embankment running along I-88 protects the city from high water. This dike and the highways also effectively isolate the river from the residents of Oneonta.

Parts of the North Branch have been rechanneled to accommodate I-88, but those alterations are minor compared with changes wrought by severe flooding many years ago. According to a local historian, an 1816 flood dumped a massive load of stone and mud into the river, forcing the channel to shift outward from the center of the city. Today the wider, deeper Susquehanna, skirting the City of Oneonta on the south and dividing it from the Town of Oneonta, seems "just stream enough for a flow of thought," as Thoreau said of the Concord near his home. This river is ready to roll.

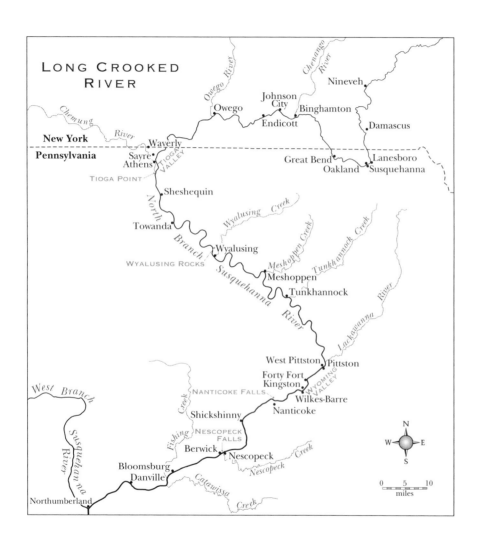

LONG CROOKED RIVER

Long Crooked River

Great Bend

The physiographic history of the Susquehanna river is a tragic story. The old river has experienced many vicissitudes. It has suffered the fateful effects of rock control and of robbery by rival streams. It was beheaded, dissected and diverted by pirate streams, and in Tertiary time was partly reversed in its direction of flow. In later time it was blocked, reversed and finally entirely extinguished in New York by the resistless continental Quebec glacier. The final withdrawal of the ice sheet has permitted the renewal of the river, but with altered and subdued character.

—HERMAN FAIRCHILD, *The Susquehanna River in New York and Evolution of Western New York Drainage*

THE SUSQUEHANNA HAS BEEN WEARING away at the rocks along its present path for 100 million years or more, creating distinctive valleys running the lengths of its branches and main stem. Standing on Mount Vision, which rises 500 feet above Lake Otsego at Cooperstown, a sightseer looks down the beginning of the broad, flat-floored North Branch Valley. Standing on Route 553, running along the Eastern Continental Divide south of Bakerton, Pennsylvania, an observer looks up the beginning of the narrower, rolling West Branch Valley. The river's source streams are small and shallow now, but they have cut deep, wide paths through these hills. The ongoing battle between water and rocks, with floods and ice floes lending heavy support to the river, has created a contorted path along much of the course. The river sidesteps the most resistant rocks, washes straight through the soft stuff, and again winds around rigid ridges.

The distance from Cooperstown to the Chesapeake is 444 miles by river, but only about 300 by the most direct roads. A log traveling along the full length of the West Branch in Clearfield County, Pennsylvania, would float 100 miles, while a crow passing through that county would fly half that far. Especially in its upper reaches, the river meanders between eroded riverbanks, making hundreds of small horseshoe curves that account for much of the extended water mileage.

This is the way it usually happens. Occasionally geologic upheavals push a river even farther off course. Such extraordinary events may have created two of the larger convolutions of the Susquehanna. Route 15 south of Williamsport cuts through a wind gap on Bald Eagle Mountain and heads southeast toward the present course of the West Branch at Milton. According to one geologic theory, this is an old valley of the Loyalsock Creek, abandoned when the present

course of the West Branch captured the Loyalsock's flow. Another theory suggests that the West Branch itself ran through this gap before a glacial ice dam blocked the course. As ice behind the dam melted, it formed glacial Lake Lesley, which backed up water all the way to Lock Haven. The ice dam eventually forced this huge glacial melt to flow east. This water carved through rock to form the present extended channel of the river, which curves around Muncy before flowing south toward Milton.

Part of the river's North Branch channel has changed even more radically, according to Herman Fairchild's study of the evolution of Susquehanna drainage. The New York State Museum published Fairchild's 99-page analysis in 1925, before the evolution of some contemporary theories about geology in general and the Susquehanna specifically. His detailed study remains a standard reference.

Fairchild believed the Susquehanna's glacial drainage began much farther north, perhaps as far north as Canada, but at least from the Adirondack area, the southern edge of which rises some thirty miles north of Cooperstown. The geologist also thought the upper Delaware River was an early Susquehanna tributary. (Contrarily, some modern geologists believe the North Branch at one time flowed southeast into the Delaware.) Many millions of years ago, Fairchild said, the westward-flowing Mohawk River began wearing away its valley between the Adirondacks and the current sources of the Susquehanna. The Mohawk eventually beheaded the Susquehanna's original sources. Fairchild thought that a study of the stream valleys north of the

Mohawk might find correlations between those valleys and the Susquehanna's present headwaters. This "accident to the Susquehanna," as Fairchild termed the beheading, left the remaining river flowing from its present headwaters into Pennsylvania and then, in a path approximating that of the present Tunkhannock Creek, almost directly south from the vicinity of Lanesboro through Nicholson to the present North Branch course at Tunkhannock.

Fairchild examined an area five miles south of Lanesboro and found what he believed to be part of the Susquehanna's old channel marked by a wind gap. The geologist theorized that another developing stream flowing west along New York's border captured the south-flowing Susquehanna's water and turned it into its course, which became the present North Branch running west toward Binghamton. The old Susquehanna course, beheaded by the present course, became Tunkhannock Creek. Fairchild believed that the dry channel he had found near Lanesboro had connected the two waterways.

So the current Susquehanna course, narrowed by a forested tableland that rims both banks, flows south to Lanesboro, where it turns abruptly west. The river flows westerly for about ten miles and then turns north again just past the town of Great Bend. It reenters New York and loops through Binghamton before eventually turning south again at Waverly and running southeast through Pennsylvania and back to Tunkhannock to join the older river valley. This is how Herman Fairchild explained creation of the Great Bend, the Susquehanna River's most conspicuous physical anomaly.

The Great Bend, dipping from Broome County, New York, into Susquehanna County, Pennsylvania, and back into Broome, drains a hardscrabble farming area sprinkled with small river towns. Some of these towns have biblical names—Nineveh, Damascus—that seem out of place in a region intimately associated with the birth of Mormonism.

In the 1820s, some four decades after Jordanville's first settlers received baptism in the Susquehanna's source waters at Ocquionis Creek, Joseph Smith turned the Susquehanna proper into "the Jordan of Mormonism." Smith, founder of the Church of Jesus Christ of Latter-day Saints, or Mormons, said he took instructions from John the Baptist before he and his first convert, Oliver Cowdery, baptized each other in the Susquehanna at Harmony (now Oakland Township) in Susquehanna County. The founder and Emma Hale Smith, the first of his dozens of wives, resided for several years in a three-room house a hundred yards or so from the river in Harmony. At that place Smith translated the golden tablets he said he had found on a hill near Lake Ontario. His translation is the Book of Mormon. The Mormons have commemorated these events in a shrine along Route 171 on the Oakland side of the river just downstream from Susquehanna and Oakland. A series of six repetitive markers and monuments tell these stories in a modest but impressive park rimmed by evergreens and separated from the river by railroad tracks.

Given to flamboyant religious visions and prophesies, Smith took advantage of the red-hot religious temperament

The central monument of a Mormon shrine in Susquehanna County, Pennsylvania, depicts John the Baptist providing instructions to Joseph Smith, founder of the Church of Jesus Christ of Latter-day Saints, and his first convert, Oliver Cowdery, before they baptized each other in the Susquehanna. (Photo by Christine Brubaker.)

of the New York frontier to speed his rise as Mormon prophet. Meanwhile, he engaged in less lofty pursuits, several associated with the Susquehanna, that disturbed many of his neighbors in the Great Bend. The Mormon historian

Rodger I. Anderson thoroughly examined Smith's neighbors' accounts and found no reason to dispute their authenticity.

W. R. Hine, a Susquehanna raftman, reported that Smith looked into a clear, egg-shaped "seer stone" and saw Captain Kidd sailing on the Susquehanna during a freshet. Smith then translated a message telling where Kidd had buried two pots of gold and silver along the river. He dug for the treasure without success. Smith also told Samuel T. Lawrence that he had discovered a rich mine of silver on the bank of the Susquehanna in Pennsylvania. He invited Lawrence to help him dig for this silver and share the profits. Lawrence paid the two men's travel expenses to Pennsylvania, where they discovered no silver.

In addition to these and other documentations, a bitter folklore lingered along the Great Bend well after Smith left the area. Charles Bump reported the tale of a "miracle" Smith supposedly tried to perform on the Susquehanna:

On a certain Sunday Smith announced that he would walk on the waters of the Susquehanna near Nineveh. A large crowd assembled and to the amazement of the unbelievers the feat was accomplished. Smith announced a second performance for the following Sunday, started out boldly upon the water, but suddenly went down, to his great chagrin. A mischievous boy had removed one of a lot of planks which had been laid about six inches below the surface.

If a proposal by the U.S. Army Corps of Engineers had progressed from paper to river, there would be considerably more water to try to walk on at Nineveh. In 1976 the corps announced plans for five dams in the Binghamton area. The largest would have loomed 125 feet above the river between the towns of Great Bend and Susquehanna. Water held behind this monster dam would have inundated thirteen Susquehanna towns from Oakland, Susquehanna, and Lanesboro in Pennsylvania through New York's villages with ancient names and all the way up to Unadilla, well beyond the Great Bend. The dam would have created a sixty-mile-long reservoir flooding thousands of acres. Corps planners estimated it would have provided recreation for 3 to 6 million visitors a year. It also could have been used to control floods on the Susquehanna, and the corps planned to study the possibility of tapping it for hydroelectric power and as a water supply. Residents almost universally opposed the idea. Farmers, anglers, environmentalists, government officials, and a Cub Scout pack, complaining that the dam would destroy its camping area, gathered at a public meeting to tell the corps to shelve its plan. The corps took the advice, and so a significant chunk of the North Branch of the Susquehanna did not become a giant lake.

The Pennsylvania Electric Company does use Susquehanna water to generate electricity at the Oakland Substation, just downstream from Oakland and Susquehanna. The utility's comparatively modest 10-foot dam is the first major obstruction on the river south of Goodyear Lake. It is also one of the few modern industrial manifestations along this rugged and secluded reach where the Susquehanna turns so dramatically before flowing on toward its first sizable city.

Binghamton

For an elusive, even mutable, and happily indestructible beauty always attends on the Susquehanna. The history of man along its course borrows from, rather than lends to, its quality. The river itself is the power.

—Hubertis M. Cummings, "Song of a River," 1952

A burgeoning, industrial Binghamton rises grandly alongside the confluence of the Susquehanna and Chenango in an 1870s painting by Henry Wolcott Boss. Water and farmland dominate the foreground. The Susquehanna Valley's picturesque hills ascend into the smoke-hazed, cloud-bedecked background. In between sprawls the town. Nature and the human structure imposed on nature are fully integrated in this nostalgic view of Greater Binghamton.

The Boss work and other Susquehanna paintings prompted a sweeping thesis by Roger Stein, curator of a 1981 exhibition at Binghamton and author of its comprehensive catalog, *Susquehanna: Images of the Settled Landscape*. Stein, an art history professor at SUNY-Binghamton, maintained that artists have treated the Susquehanna differently from most American rivers. Whereas more glamorous waterways have been celebrated for their lush visual elements, he said, the Susquehanna generally has been painted, as by Boss, as a quiet, inhabited landscape.

Stein's exhibit formed part of the Confluence series of

programs presented by the Roberson Center for the Arts and Sciences on Binghamton's Front Street. In a prefatory note to the exhibig catalog, Diane Truex, the Roberson Center's director, related the siting of the museum to the exhibit and to Stein's thesis of the settled landscape:

The Susquehanna River has played an important role in defining our sense of this region. The city of Binghamton was founded at the confluence of the Susquehanna and Chenango, and the plan of its streets was shaped by the direction of movement along and across the rivers. The museum's main entrance faces the confluence itself, and both rivers are visible from several places within the building. Roberson's own collections include historical works depicting the area and works by regional artists. Thus the Susquehanna River, as fact and as image, continues to influence the daily life and aesthetic experience of the residents of our region.

The Susquehanna's influence on Binghamton might have been greater. Unfortunate decisions, some made more than a century and a half ago, have relegated the football-field-wide river to something less than a starring role in the community's growth.

Binghamton lies, notes the city's centennial booklet of 1967, "at the juncture of two major highways, Routes 17 and 81, as well as at the meeting place of the Chenango and Susquehanna Rivers." The author of that booklet did not arbitrarily name the highways before the rivers; the area's roads have been more important than its rivers for more than a century. Neither did he list the Chenango before the

Susquehanna by chance. "People think of Binghamton as a Chenango River town," says the Broome County historian Gerald Smith. "If you talk to somebody in the Endicott or Johnson City areas, or elsewhere in the Susquehanna Valley, they'll say they live along the Susquehanna. But if you talk to somebody in Binghamton, they'll say they live along the Chenango."

The Chenango is the Susquehanna's third longest tributary (after the West Branch and the Juniata). The Chenango's sources, extending from deep in the counties of Oneida and Onondaga, drain rich central New York land lying within forty-odd miles of Lake Ontario.[1]

Early settlement favored the Chenango. Otsiningo, the area's primary eighteenth-century Iroquois settlement, sprawled along the Chenango from its confluence with the Tioughnioga River to the present site of Binghamton. Binghamton's first white settlers lived at Chenango Point, on the west bank of the Chenango, considerably above its confluence with the Susquehanna. Binghamton's population extended slowly along both rivers in the early nineteenth century, and for a brief period shippers considered the Susquehanna as important as the Chenango for transporting lumber and other goods. Both rivers are shallow, however, so rafts and other conveyances could be held up for weeks until sufficient water enabled passage.

The Chenango Valley served as the primary water conduit after 1837, when workers opened the Chenango Canal to the Erie Canal at Utica. While the Chenango Canal never made money (no canal did except the Erie), it effectively bypassed the North Branch above Binghamton, thus reducing the economic effectiveness of the Susquehanna in

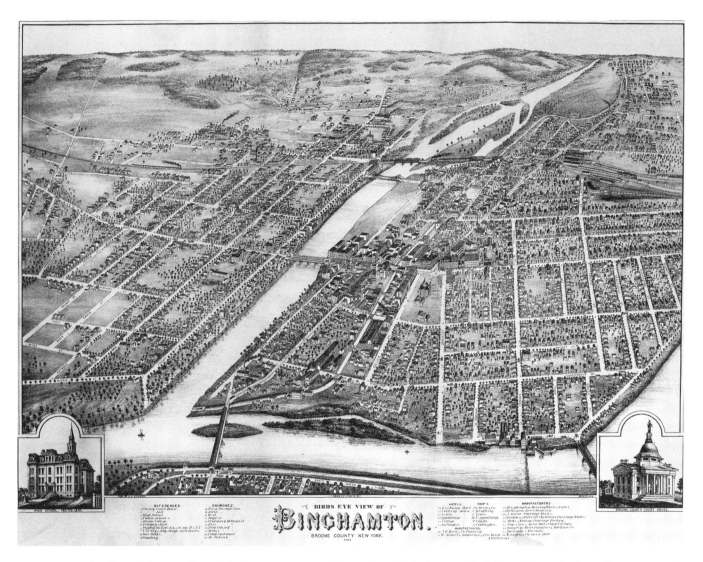

H. H. Brosius drew Birds Eye View of Binghamton, Broome County, New York, *in 1873. The lithograph's emphasis on rivers suggests the prominent roles the Susquehanna (at bottom) and Chenango played in the community at that time. (Broome County Historical Society, Binghamton, New York.)*

☙ *The confluence of the Susquehanna and Chenango rivers at Binghamton. The Chenango enters the Susquehanna at left. A concrete-covered gas pipeline crossing the Susquehanna inhibits boating. (Photo by Christine Brubaker.)*

New York. The canal also spurred growth, largely along the Chenango.

The canal closed in 1875, its work by then superseded by railroad commerce; but the Chenango River remained the residential and industrial focal point of the area. Today development fans out around the Chenango. More industries, producing more pollution, lie along that river. Development lines highways that follow the Susquehanna through Binghamton but does not spread far from the river's banks. The Susquehanna's big industries are downstream, at Johnson City and Endicott.

In the 1960s, Broome County developed Otsiningo Park along the west bank of the Chenango, just outside

Binghamton's northern boundary. The park quickly became the area's recreational focal point and strengthened the Chenango's claim as Binghamton's primary river. Binghamton Symphony concerts and other events draw thousands of visitors each summer.

Binghamton's segment of the Susquehanna also has provided recreational possibilities, but they are all in the past and almost no one is talking about future prospects on a river now lined with roads and levees. From the late nineteenth century through the mid-twentieth, beaches and bathhouses spotted the Susquehanna's shore. Endicott and other towns west of Binghamton also had beaches, but residents had abandoned all of them by the 1960s. They died as Otsiningo and other new Broome County parks replaced them and as river pollution made bathing impossible and sightseeing unsavory. Even when the Susquehanna's beaches flourished, however, long stretches of waterfront in between were poorly maintained—a condition that a nationally recognized city planner had deplored in 1911.

Charles Mulford Robinson, a planner from Harrisburg, Pennsylvania, prepared a report called "Better Binghamton" for the city's Mercantile-Press Club. He cited two "curious facts" related to the possible improvement of the Susquehanna and Chenango riverbanks: "The first is that every one with whom I talked in Binghamton, or who sent communications to me, spoke of the riverbanks as the city's great aesthetic opportunity. The second fact is that among the municipal ordinances the only reference that I find to this great asset of the city is that garbage and the bodies of dead animals shall not be thrown upon the banks of the rivers."

Residents tossed much more than dead animals along the

rivers, Robinson observed, not disguising his disgust for the manner in which Binghamtonians treated their waterways. He recommended well-lighted footpaths and parks all the way along the rivers, except on the south side of the Susquehanna, where hills limited recreational development. Robinson suggested that municipal legislation soon would catch up to popular opinion about the value of these two rivers. In the Susquehanna's case, especially, he was wrong. Long after Robinson's report, in a letter to *The Conservationist* magazine in 1964, an area resident called the Susquehanna "the Garbage Disposal of New York State." Wrote Chester Majka, of Johnson City: "The river from Sidney, N.Y., to the Pennsylvania border is nothing but a garbage disposal for cottage owners, permanent residents and farmers all along the way. These people are using the river for their trash, garbage, sewage, and anything they feel they want to dispose of, even animal carcasses."

Broome County initiated the only serious effort to improve North Branch frontage in the 1970s. The county began negotiating for property easements along the river to link existing public lands. New county officials, unsympathetic to the cause, claimed that easements invariably reduced a property's value and undermined personal property rights. That program died and nothing has been suggested to follow. City officials are reluctant to encourage a comprehensive greenway program because they believe the Susquehanna's course through Binghamton is too long.

Something else happened over time that C. M. Robinson never could have imagined. Popular opinion about the value of waterways changed. Earthen dike and concrete flood-wall projects built after the disastrous flood of 1936 isolated the

Susquehanna and the Chenango from the public. Residents no longer saw the water except from the window of a car as they passed over a bridge. Binghamtonians began looking elsewhere for recreation.

The tendency to use rivers as open sewers in the 1940s, '50s, and '60s exacerbated the poor general perception of them—a perception that persists among many residents today. "When we first moved here in the fifties," recalls George Schumacher, who taught biology at the SUNY-Binghamton campus and has retired in the area, "the joke was that if you went swimming in the Susquehanna, you would use only the breast stroke, so you could push the large materials to the side as you swam upstream, just skim that stuff off the surface." Schumacher never went swimming in the river, but he did collect algae downstream from the Binghamton–Johnson City sewage treatment plant in Vestal, just across the river from the university. Toilet paper, napkins, and disposable diapers clogged his nets. "You couldn't make a draw through the water without getting this white fabric-like coating all over the nets," he says. "We have taken major steps to reduce all that."

No city along the Susquehanna has done more to improve water quality than Binghamton. The Binghamton–Johnson City system is the Susquehanna's biggest sewage plant, after Harrisburg's. Before releasing sewage to the Susquehanna, operators treat more than 20 million gallons of effluent a day from 75 percent of the homes and businesses in Broome County. An upgraded plant, to be completed in several years, will reduce nitrogen in the outflow. Binghamton also is developing a sophisticated process to deal with sewage overflow that occurs after heavy rains add water from storm sewers to the mix.

State studies show that the Susquehanna at Binghamton is only slightly affected by upstream pollution. Binghamton's sewage moderately degrades the water quality. The river is classed as "clean" ten miles below the city's sewage plant and "excellent" at Owego.

Schumacher regularly fishes in the river, often using a Susquehanna Tube Spinner. Manufactured in Binghamton, the spinner rotates at a precise angle on a tube to attract the attention of hungry walleyes. Both the Tube Spinner and better water quality have improved Schumacher's fishing. In the 1950s, when toilet paper and worse filled the river, the professor considered carp and suckers a lucky catch. Now he reels in walleyes and tiger muskies and chain pickerel and smallmouth bass.

Schumacher often finds himself on the river without company. The Susquehanna in the Binghamton area, as farther north, is underutilized. SUNY-Binghamton students never use the river, he says, because they have been "inundated" by antipollution ideals. "They want the water to be pure and clean and of drinking quality—today. If they find a worm floating downstream or a beer can occasionally, well, that's unforgivable. My answer to that is they should have seen it in the fifties or the forties."

Although they may not know it, SUNY students drink the Susquehanna, after it has run through the treatment plant. Some 100,000 water customers in Binghamton and parts of the towns of Chenango, Dickinson, Kirkwood, and Vestal also drink Susquehanna water. Area industries draw enormous amounts of water from both the Susquehanna and the Chenango.

Most people don't think much about the water they drink or use in any other way until the river floods. "A good part of the publicity the river gets is bad press," notes John Titus, a biology professor at SUNY-Binghamton. "There are certain sections that are prone to flooding, so that's a major concern most springs. People think about the river when it's raining a lot. Other than that, I don't see a lot of attention paid to the river."

Taking the long view, the historian Gerald Smith sees some positive change. "We're coming back to the idea that you not only put bridges over rivers but take a look at the rivers, too," he says. "They're not only beautiful, but they had a special significance in our development. Unfortunately, we haven't done a very good job of keeping connections. Binghamton has sort of pulled away from the rivers and now we're trying to pull people back."

Rockbottom Dam

If an engineer designed an efficient, unattended, self-operated drowning machine, it would be hard to come up with anything more effective than a low-head dam.

—Virgil Chambers, chief of the Bureau of Boating, Pennsylvania Fish and Boat Commission

On a pleasantly warm afternoon in September 1975, two men capsized their raft as they shot over the Rockbottom Dam. Turbulent rotary currents sucked the men back into white water roiling at the bottom of the low-head dam on the Susquehanna River at Binghamton. They struggled to keep their heads above water until three Binghamton firefighters in an aluminum boat got close enough to free them. But then the dam's backwash tipped the rescuers' boat and captured one of the firefighters. Caught in the circulating water, John Russell rolled around and around until he drowned.

The next day, two colleagues tried to recover Russell's body from the swirling river. Fire Chief John Cox and Captain Donald McGeever launched the aluminum rescue boat below the dam and edged it toward the white water. Before they could reach the body, the powerful backwash snagged and capsized their boat and they also drowned in the Rockbottom's unforgiving undertow. Examining the water at the dam a few days later, under normal river conditions, a U.S. Coast Guard officer said he had never seen a current as strong as that at Rockbottom Dam.

Others have drowned at the dam, just upstream from where the Chenango joins the Susquehanna, but the deaths of the three firefighters provided the most dramatic example of what a low-head dam can do even to people who are most aware of its danger. A local television crew had gone there to tape Cox and McGeever's rescue effort. Binghamton rescue workers now use the film of their drownings to train new personnel. The film is called *The Killing Machine.*

For a proven death trap, the Rockbottom appears relatively innocuous. Depending on the level of the Susquehanna, water drops only three or four feet after passing the crest. An unsuspecting boater can shoot over the top before realizing the dam is there. Binghamtonians wade into

the shallow water below the Rockbottom to catch walleyes and other fish that cannot pass upstream. If the anglers get too close, the churning white water can grab them, too.

What makes the Rockbottom and hundreds of dams like it on the Susquehanna and its tributaries so dangerous is the hydraulic action immediately downstream.[2] On such low-head dams, as opposed to higher dams, the momentum of the plunge over the obstruction carries water straight to the river bottom. This water then curls upward and backward to create a backwash. When the curling water surfaces to meet new water coming over the dam, the mixture plunges down again and the cycle repeats. In each cycle, some water escapes and flows downstream, but new water is always entering the mix. The system works like a huge washing machine.

This continuous circular motion or "boil" captures most solid objects that enter it. A person theoretically could escape by diving to the bottom of the river and crawling downstream beyond the boil line and then surfacing. Such escapes are rare. Objects can get caught in boils for weeks at a time, or for years. A metal barrel circulated in the Rockbottom boil all through the 1980s.

Despite its deadliness, the Rockbottom Dam is permanent. If it were removed, Binghamton would lose the five-and-a-half-foot pool behind it that provides a steady water supply to the city. The dam also slows the water, making it easier to treat at the city's filtration plant and providing some control over floodwaters. For better and for worse, Binghamton is stuck with the Rockbottom Dam.

Two Broome County industrialists, General Joshua Whitney and Colonel Hazard Lewis, built a timber dam at this location in 1828. They and others constructed gristmills and used the manufactured pool to power them. Later owners raised the dam a few feet and added a concrete cap. The City of Binghamton purchased the Rockbottom in 1931 and began piping upriver water to homes and businesses.

After the 1975 accident, city workers built up the river bottom at the dam's base, reducing the depth of water and so diminishing the backwash effect, at least when the river is not in flood. Rescue crews also changed their methods, practicing rescues without getting into the river and using a large steel boat instead of the aluminum boat whenever they had to enter the water. But nothing could eliminate all risk at the Rockbottom.

This is the first of four water hazards a Susquehanna traveler encounters in the Binghamton area. Two concrete-covered gas pipelines cross the river at the Chenango's entry and farther downstream, creating small backwashes of their own. The Goudey Dam, another low-head, poses danger at Johnson City. Because canoeists must portage four times within several miles, few use this section. Powerboating is impossible.

Like the Rockbottom, Goudey Dam performs a crucial function. Goudey Station uses water from the dam's pool as coolant for a New York State Electric & Gas coal-fired plant, one of the largest consumptive users of Susquehanna water in New York. Without that water, thousands of NYSEG customers would not be able to turn on their porch lights or order lingerie from Victoria's Secret over the Internet.

More important to anglers, the used water returned to the river by the power plant attracts walleyes. When walleyes move upstream to spawn in the spring, they congregate in the warmed, turbulent river below the dam. Generations of area residents have been casting their lines for walleyes and other fish at Goudey since the utility built the dam in the 1920s.

Thirty-year-old Natbai Mircea drove down from Johnson City to fish below the Goudey Dam on a Sunday in July 1989. His knee-high rubber boots slipped on algae-covered rocks. The unforgiving backwash of the low-head snared and drowned Mircea, as it has other anglers and boaters. Goudey is another case of a low-head dam that is useful, even necessary—and potentially deadly.

Warnings for Goudey and Rockbottom are posted upstream, but many people ignore the signs and they are not useful to anglers approaching from below. Binghamton's second assistant fire chief, Martin Tillapaugh, told the *Binghamton Press & Sun Bulletin* after Mircea's drowning, "If you get caught in that boil, your chances are slim to none. If I were going in the river, I'd be damn sure I knew where all the dams are and not rely on warning signs."

Owego

The small streams emptying into the Susquehanna are innumerable; and eight or ten miles back from the river the arks are built, and the materials of the rafts collected, ready to launch with the first thaw.

—N. P. WILLIS

NATHANIEL PARKER WILLIS, journalist, poet, astute observer of nineteenth-century American life, lived for a time in an attractive country home along the Owego River. His house, now a bed and breakfast, stands a quarter of a mile upstream from the village of Owego at the river's conjunction with the Susquehanna. Willis learned to love Owego—the town and its people and its natural surroundings. He enjoyed a prime view of river craft and their crews as they passed his little estate on the way to Owego and on down the Susquehanna. In 1840, he wrote about what he saw in considerable detail in *Letters from Under a Bridge*. "As [the Owego] swells in March," he said,

the noise of voices and hammering coming out from the woods above, warn us of the approach of an ark; and at the rate of eight or ten miles an hour, the rude structure shoots by, floating high on the water, without its lading (which it takes in at the village below), and manned with a singing and saucy crew, who dodge the branches of the trees, and work their steering paddles with an adroitness and nonchalance which sufficiently show the character of the class. . . .

At the village they take wheat and pork into the arks, load their rafts with plank and shingles, and wait for the return of the freshets. It is a fact you may not know, that when a river is rising, the middle is the highest, and *vice versa* when falling—sufficiently proved by the experience of the raftsmen, who, if they start before the flow is at its top, cannot keep their crafts from the shore.

Willis further observed that as long as rivermen were willing to pilot their rafts and arks to Susquehanna ports in southern Pennsylvania and to Maryland towns at the head of the Chesapeake, "those who are contented to stay at home and cultivate the rich river lands of the country, are sure of high prices, and a ready reward for their labour."

Smaller boats began transporting people and freight on the Susquehanna's North Branch more than a century before Willis described ark travel. Native Americans, traders, and travelers used the waterway as the most natural pathway through the mountainous wilderness of southern New York and northern Pennsylvania, where travel over land was difficult. In the 1720s, for example, German settlers in New York's Schoharie Valley, east of Cooperstown, built canoes, floated down the Susquehanna, and settled in Berks County, Pennsylvania.[3]

In 1737, Cadwallader Colden, New York's surveyor general, recognized the significance of the Susquehanna to his province's commerce: "Goods may be carried from this lake [Otsego] in battoes or flat-bottom vessels through Pennsylvania to Maryland and Virginia, the current of the river running everywhere easy without any cataracts in all that long space."

Colden overstated the navigational ease of the Susquehanna. Because the river is so shallow, merchants and farmers floated most boats downstream only with high water. Moreover, when they reached the Main Stem in southern Pennsylvania, the boats faced numerous obstructions. River traffic restricted to New York and northern Pennsylvania—from Binghamton to Wilkes-Barre, for example—moved more easily in less rocky water.

〜 *A Susquehanna River ark. Arks plied the North Branch from the 1790s until the mid-nineteenth century, carrying lumber, grain, and other goods downriver. Pointed on both ends, arks ran about ninety feet long. (Drawing by Chris Emlet.)*

Commerce faced more uncertainty on the Susquehanna than on any other major river in North America. Maryland and Pennsylvania, in competition for the Susquehanna trade in the first decades of the nineteenth century, blasted away channel impediments, but Pennsylvania eventually gave up and built adjoining canals.

Although business flourished on the Susquehanna only seasonally before canals, shippers in New York and northern Pennsylvania received a substantial payoff. In 1827, *Nile's Weekly Register* reported that "the trade which quietly passes down the Susquehanna and which chiefly settles at Baltimore, is, of itself equal to about one half of the whole value of domestic articles exported from Baltimore to foreign places." For years after the Erie Canal opened in 1825,

many farmers in New York counties bordering the Susquehanna continued to send their produce to the Chesapeake and points in between.

Northern Pennsylvanians did the same. Charles Fisher Welles, the great-grandfather of the Athens historian Elsie Murray, "ran the river" from his home near the New York border to Baltimore early in the nineteenth century. He took lumber, wheat, pork, and whiskey with him and brought back china, calico, and blankets in exchange. He poled his boat all the way back up the river.

One-way rafts and arks, the craft that N. P. Willis watched pass his house at Owego, traveled the Susquehanna from the end of the eighteenth century through the nineteenth. They replaced the earlier and heavier flatboats and keelboats, as well as the forty-foot-long Durham boats poled up and down the Susquehanna by five-man crews (and, more famously, across the Delaware by George Washington's soldiers). At the peak of traffic in the 1820s, thousands of rafts and arks descended the river each spring.

A raft was a simple construction of logs or boards floated to market, while arks carried cargo other than the material of which they were made. Rafts were squared off on the ends; arks were pointed on both ends. The size of a raft depended on the size of the lumber it carried. Arks ran up to ninety feet long and twenty feet wide. Rivermen steered both arks and rafts with oars and poles.

Lumbering and timber rafting flourished on both branches of the Susquehanna until lumbermen depleted the supply of white pine and hemlock on the North Branch in the 1840s. Major North Branch timbering and raft-building centers included Oneonta and Binghamton in New York and Athens and Towanda in Pennsylvania. Foresters spent all year cutting trees, awaiting spring freshets to ship them. On a perfect day for lumber launching, crews crowded the river, maneuvering their rafts down tributaries and then along the Susquehanna toward lumber markets in southern Pennsylvania or Maryland.

Substantial North Branch ark traffic began about 1807 and slowed considerably after 1840 with the opening of the Susquehanna and Tidewater Canal on the lower river. Each spring, farmers and merchants crowded the loading dock of every New York river town. In Unadilla, the firm of Noble & Hayes loaded arks at a cut in the riverbank opposite its store. That cut is still there.

Historians discovered firsthand how difficult ark travel must have been when they floated a one-third-scale ark as part of Steuben County's bicentennial celebration in 1996. Agents of the entrepreneur Charles Williamson had built and launched Steuben County's first ark on the rising Cohocton River in March 1800. During a typical spring freshet two centuries ago, arks made the trip from southern New York to Baltimore in eight days. The relatively inexperienced crew of the "bicentennial ark" hoped to guide the boat down the Cohocton and Chemung to the Susquehanna and on to the Chesapeake in ten days. Tied to a launching date in early June, they could not wait for a freshet and started off in low, slow water. The little ark got hung up on rocks in the Chemung and on sand bars and rocks in the North Branch. Dubbing themselves "Riders of the Lost Ark," the frustrated Steubenites trucked the boat all the way to Wrightsville, Pennsylvania. After floating through hydroelectric plant reservoirs on the Lower Susquehanna and being portaged around their dams, the craft and its weary crew finally arrived at the Chesapeake nearly two weeks after leaving home.

It always has been difficult to plan transportation on the Susquehanna; early shippers occasionally found their goods rotting along the shore when water remained low in spring. Predominantly one-way navigation also frustrated northern Pennsylvania communities that wanted to ship coal and other goods upstream. To do that, they had to wait for the canals, finally completed on the North Branch in the 1850s—just in time for burgeoning railroads to put them out of business.

Tioga

If one carefully looks at a map, and notes the drainage pattern, the significance is striking. All the tributaries converging into the Susquehanna, give the effect of a long arrowhead aimed south, the point of which is the meeting place of all their waters, Tioga.

—Richmond E. Myers, *The Long Crooked River*

The arks that Charles Williamson loaded with grain and lumber in the spring of 1800 and shipped downriver into Pennsylvania represented an essential element of a grandiose plan to develop a million acres in central New York. Acting for Maryland investors eager to tap into the New York trade, Williamson founded the town of Bath on the Cohocton River and began clearing creeks and land and building roads for commerce. With unswerving optimism, this "Baron of the Backwoods" planned to gather goods from the Genesee River country and transport them over to the Cohocton and Chemung and then south, by way of the Susquehanna, to the Chesapeake Bay and Baltimore. Charles Williamson expected to make a fortune.

This scheme seemed reasonable at the time because of the major channeling of North Branch waters at the place now known as Athens, a small but storied town in Bradford County, just south of the point at which the Susquehanna crosses into Pennsylvania for the second time. Williamson did not understand that the shallowness of all these water-

ways would severely limit commercial traffic. He overbuilt and overpromoted the Bath area and then could not deliver the goods.

The formidable Chemung River joins the Susquehanna at Athens. Only half as long as the Chenango, the Chemung benefits from a watershed nearly twice as large. Thanks to the contributions of substantial tributaries, the Chemung runs nearly as wide as the Susquehanna at the confluence. The Cohocton and Canisteo rivers flow into the Chemung from the northwest, the Cowanesque from the west, and the Tioga from the south. When rivers flood at Athens, the Chemung generally makes more of a mess than the Susquehanna.

Athens actually lies at the center of an even vaster web of water. As early New York settlers in Broome, Chenango, and Otsego counties to the north and northeast discovered, upper tributaries of the Susquehanna interweave with sources of the eastern Finger Lakes and, by short portages, link with tributaries of the Mohawk and Delaware. Likewise, the Chemung's uppermost tributaries connect, by portages, with tributaries of the western Finger Lakes and the Genesee and Allegheny rivers, and by them with the Great Lakes and the Ohio River. Just below Athens, the North Branch tributaries of Sugar and Towanda creeks nearly connect with tributaries of the Chemung's Tioga River and the West Branch's Pine Creek. Via these shortcuts and carrying their canoes only briefly, the Iroquois regularly passed back and forth between the North and West branches.

Canoe traffic could move in any direction on this network, but rafts and arks floated only downstream and only at high water. When Williamson realized he was limited to one-way, one-season shipping, he abandoned his dream development.

Early surveyor maps label the peninsula below Athens, where the Susquehanna and the Chemung close in on one another, the "Indian Arrow." This arrow points straight into the heart of Pennsylvania. When Williamson wanted to impress potential Bath settlers and investors, he pointed to the arrow and all of his claims made sense.

N. P. Willis described the confluence of the waters at this arrow: "'A!' Imagine this capital letter laid on its back and pointed south by east, and you have a pretty fair diagram of the junction of the Susquehannah and the Chemung. The note of admiration (exclamation point) describes a superb line of mountains at the back of the Chemung valley, and the quotation marks express the fine bluffs that overlook the meeting of the waters at Athens."

The best bluffs from which to examine this meeting of waters rise south of the confluence at Turn of Rocks, a 150-foot hill between the east bank of the Susquehanna and Route 199. From here, where the augmented North Branch runs nearly 300 yards across, one has a clear view of the confluence and the fertile fields of potato farms and the southernmost homes of Athens contained within the green arrow. Partway down the peninsula, the converging rivers compress the arrowhead, then spread out briefly before narrowing toward their juncture. Louise Murray, a historian of the Athens area, explained the geography this way: "Now the streams flow almost together, then suddenly spread out again, forming the peculiar peninsula just above their confluence, long ago called Tioga Point."

Tioga (Teaoga to the Iroquois) was the original name not only of the peninsula but of the town. Tioga may mean "meeting of the waters" or "forks of a river." Or it may mean "a gate," as in the passageway to another territory. Whatever it means, early settlers decided to abandon "Tioga" in favor of "Athens." They thought the place should be known for its hills rather than its waterways. Doubtless they also preferred the classical to the aboriginal designation. "Tioga" survives nearby in multiple testimony to the powerful historical influence of the Susquehanna-Chemung confluence. The county directly west of Bradford is named Tioga and the Tioga River runs through it to the Chemung. The towns of Tioga and Tioga Junction stand along that waterway. And immediately north of Bradford County is Tioga County, New York, the oldest county (established 1791) in that section of the state.

More than twenty distinct tribes of Native Americans lived on the Tioga peninsula at one time or another, enjoying access to both rivers. Ted Keir, a retired earth sciences teacher at Athens High School and an accomplished archaeologist, has participated in many digs at Tioga Point. His excavations of pottery, projectile points, and other materials date from the early Archaic period to white settlement. Keir stores some of these objects in a basement museum at his house on Athens's North Main Street. The Tioga Point Museum on South Main displays area artifacts for public viewing.[4]

Native Americans would have gravitated to Tioga because of its natural attributes in any case, but the compression of the peninsula's midsection made life simpler for early canoeists. A plaque on the Route 199 bridge crossing the Chemung onto the peninsula commemorates the "carrying

☙ *The Chemung River (left) joins the Susquehanna at Tioga Point, here viewed from Turn of Rocks, a downriver overlook. (Tioga Point Museum, Athens, Pennsylvania.)*

path" at Tioga's narrowest point. Native Americans canoeing down the Chemung docked here, crossed 190 yards to the Susquehanna, and paddled north, thereby avoiding a longer trip down around widening land to the rivers' confluence and then back up the Susquehanna.

Mary Patterson lives on South Main Street, just downriver from the bridge and not far from the old carrying path. The Chemung is in her backyard. The Susquehanna is in the backyard of her neighbor across South Main. In 1972, Tropical Storm Agnes flooded both rivers and the waters met in the street. Floodwater rose about a foot around Mrs. Patterson's house. Her Susquehanna neighbor had two feet of water swirling around hers.

At this narrow neck in August 1789, General Sullivan constructed a diamond-shaped fort. The fort commanded approaches from both rivers while Sullivan waited for General Clinton's force to float down the North Branch on the artificial flood from Lake Otsego. After marching up the Susquehanna from the Wyoming Valley, Sullivan's troops had crossed the swollen river from the east bank below Tioga Point. The soldiers held hands to avoid being swept away by the current. Then they marched up the west bank of the faster-running Chemung and forded it onto the peninsula.

The formidable stockade, with a two-story blockhouse and mounted cannon guarding each angle, served as a supply base as Sullivan's force, augmented by Clinton's, marched into the heart of New York's Iroquois country. When the triumphant army returned to Tioga after laying waste to Iroquois lands, Sullivan instructed his soldiers to

dismantle the fort. They threw its twelve-foot palisade logs into the Susquehanna and burned the blockhouse. The Sullivan expedition then marched south, while its wounded and sick and supplies floated in boats down the river.

Four contiguous villages, Athens, Sayre, and South Waverly in Pennsylvania and Waverly in New York, today form a thin line of human habitation in this region of wide waters and narrow hills. In this peaceful place, Ted Keir and his wife, Evelyn, make their homes—their primary residence in Athens and the place where they go to relax, a rustic cottage on the Susquehanna's east bank.

Keir grew up in the Athens area and has spent much of his life on the Susquehanna, boating and fishing and searching for Native American artifacts along its banks. He has served with several citizen groups working to improve life in Bradford County and water quality in its streams, and recently completed a term as president of the Pennsylvania Fish and Boat Commission. A tall, athletic, intense man, Keir speaks about the Susquehanna to anyone who will listen.

"I've given talks in places where I find people who have lived along the river all their life and have never been in a boat on the river, never swam in it—it's just there," he says. "To me that's a shame because I love the river. I love water, period, but I particularly love the river."

There is probably less river to love these days than before loggers cut down the water-retaining forests and before the water-draining human population increased. "I think the water table has dropped and that the river was much more navigable years ago," says Keir. "These native building sites that we find along these tributaries suggest the Indians

≈   *Ted Keir, past president of the Pennsylvania Fish and Boat Commission, points to the Susquehanna from his property on the river's east shore in the Tioga Valley. (Photo by Christine Brubaker.)*

probably used canoes on our larger creeks, and we know that eel and shad moved up and down the tributaries. Some of them get almost dry now in the summer."[5]

The course of the river also has shifted. Downriver at Sheshequin, where he has done much archaeological work, Keir has found fishing net stones at a Native American village site dating from about 5,000 to 3,000 B.C. "That's probably close to half a mile from the river now," he explains, "and certainly they wouldn't have had their village site way back there—not being on a creek—that far from the river. Their net stones would not be back that far from the water." Keir believes the river may have changed course three times within the archaeological time period.

A more recent river change is considerably more evident. The Susquehanna here is much cleaner. Keir remembers communities in New York and Pennsylvania piping raw "white" sewage, filled with toilet paper, into the water. Except for the Tioga River, running north out of coal country and tainted by acid mine drainage, water quality in the area today consistently rates high.

"When I was a kid," Keir says, "we would go out on the bridge and look down and the North Branch would be so clear we could watch the fish, and then in the fifties and sixties you never got the river clean enough hardly to see the fish, but we can now; it's cleaning up now and the fish are coming back. We're getting species of fish that we didn't have before and there's natural propagation and plant life. The river's coming back."

Wyalusing Rocks

It is along the North Branch of the Susquehanna, from Tioga Point near Athens to above Pittston, that Susquehanna beauty most fully flames. Even as glimpsed from the highway, it is clearly the central scenic feature of the Endless Mountains. . . . [This section] should be high on the national list of protected scenic rivers. Indeed, it could be a national park.

—John M. Kauffman,
Flow East: A Look at Our North Atlantic Rivers

At Wyalusing Rocks, several ledges, their jagged edges seeming to overhang the water, cap a sandstone-and-shale hill that rises a sheer 500 feet to provide one of the most spectacular overlooks in north-central Pennsylvania. The expansive view from Wyalusing Rocks inspired the western Pennsylvanian Charles Wakefield Cadman to compose the 1909 hit song "From the Land of the Sky-Blue Water."

Cadman's Native American theme was appropriate: this place must have served as an observation point for successive generations who inhabited villages at the present site of the town of Wyalusing, two miles downstream. Known locally as "Indian Lookout," Wyalusing Rocks, on the bulge of a horseshoe bend in the river, afforded observers clear sightings of canoe traffic straight downriver and curving westward upriver.

Thousands of Native Americans passed Wyalusing Rocks on the Great Warriors Path running from the present New York State to the Carolinas. General Sullivan's soldiers took this path. The river these early travelers saw has not changed significantly, but the scene on the other side has. Today's view includes extensive farm fields rising gradually on North Branch terraces toward the Kittatinny Range, popularly called the Endless Mountains. According to Wyalusing's first white settlers, fields of thick bluegrass originally filled these flats.

Travelers on today's Route 6 (the Sullivan Trail) may choose to look over the river from Wyalusing Rocks or from the Marie Antoinette Scenic Lookout, three miles north. Also situated on a long river bend, Marie Antoinette affords similar views of the water and farmed flats on the other side.

Just upstream on these flats stood Azilum, or Asylum, a village founded by Royalist refugees from the French Revolution. Responding to an invitation from American friends in 1793, the refugees built a village and, on a nearby Susquehanna island, a dance pavilion, where they held flamboyant formal parties in an effort to forget the fall of the monarchy. According to legend, the French constructed La Grande Maison with the expectation that Marie Antoinette would join them.[6]

The Sullivan Trail overlooks stand at the center of the longest section of wild river on the North Branch, in a region as pristine as any in Pennsylvania. From Tioga Point to the Lackawanna River's entry at Pittston, the Susquehanna winds some ninety ruggedly scenic miles through Bradford and Wyoming counties and a small slice of Luzerne.

The river takes its time getting to Pittston, forming large, symmetrical bends while gathering additional water from numerous creeks. Steep cliffs rising on one side of the river do not always offset farmed terraces on the other. From just south of Wyalusing to Tunkhannock, the river valley becomes a canyonlike, relatively inaccessible wilderness.

Many have championed this long, winding section. An English traveler, Isaac Weld Jr., who canoed down the North Branch in the mid-1790s, wrote:

> I think there is no river in America that abounds with such a variety and number of picturesque views. At every bend the prospect varies, and there is scarcely a spot between Lochartzburgh [an early name for Athens] and Wilkesbarre where the painter would not find a subject

well worthy of his pencil. The mountains, covered with bold rocks and woods, afford the finest foreground imaginable; the plains, adorned with cultivated fields and patches of wood, and watered by the novel river, of which you catch a glimpse here and there, fill up the middle of the landscape; and the blue hills, peeping up at a distance, terminate the view in the most pleasing manner.

Federal officials began to think about designating this section a national "wild river" in 1962. "From Laceyville, Pennsylvania [just below Wyalusing], all the way into New York, it is possible to travel that river in its natural state and not see a single community," said Richard Gross, a biologist who headed a Department of the Interior task force studying streams in the Northeast. "You might as well be on the Alagash in Maine. I was on a completely wild river. This is what we want to preserve."

The Interior Department made grand plans to protect the river, clean up spots that needed renewal, and provide recreational opportunities along the way. River advocates enthusiastically supported these proposals; other observers objected that federal wild river status would restrict future uses for the waterway. Speaking to and perhaps for them in a 1966 critique of the wild river plan, U.S. Representative Daniel J. Flood, an influential Luzerne County Democrat, said the North Branch was indeed a superior waterway, worthy of conservation—but "we must not forget that the Susquehanna River is to serve man, and, if the people of the Susquehanna Basin are to prosper, the river must be used to best meet the needs of these people."

As it turned out, the federal government never made a choice between preserving the river's natural resources and using those resources "to serve man." The government suspended comprehensive plans for the Susquehanna after the Nixon administration abandoned the Model Rivers Program in favor of cleaning up America's lakes.[7]

Pennsylvania established its own scenic rivers program in 1972. In its first inventory of streams three years later, the Wild and Scenic Task Force gave prime consideration to the North Branch from Athens to Pittston and the tributary Meshoppen Creek. But the state has had no more success than the federal government in turning prospect into project.

In the early 1990s, the state and the Susquehanna North Branch Advisory Committee, a Wilkes-Barre-based organization monitoring the river and its tributaries, concentrated on the Meshoppen. The short and narrow creek, with its two impressive waterfalls and excellent seasonal white water running through isolated terrain, seemed perfect for wild-and-scenic designation. But representatives of the Pennsylvania Landowners Association (PLA) turned out for a late public hearing on the project and raised questions about what scenic river status might mean for creekside landowners. Within three weeks they killed the proposal.

"PLA came in and made up outlandish stories. They ruined the project," says Maryann Hrubovcak, assistant director of the Pennsylvania Scenic Rivers Program at that time. "You get up to a rural area and people's contact with government is minimal. Any contact with the Department of Environmental Regulation may not have been positive. PLA convinced the landowners not to trust us."

Adjacent landowners have expressed reservations about proposed scenic river status elsewhere in the Susquehanna Basin, including an eight-mile stretch of the West Branch between Montoursville and Muncy, a segment also nominated as a national wild and scenic river. Rick and Sue Sprout, retired science teachers who live at nearby Picture Rocks, on Muncy Creek, support both designations. The Sprouts have canoed the entire Susquehanna and regularly kayak the placid water and easy rapids from Montoursville to the Muncy's mouth. "We have gone down this stretch in the summer and never seen a single soul," says Rick Sprout. "You only see two cabins along the way. Except for occasional tractor noises, and trains and planes, there's no hint of civilization."

But here, too, landowners fear that publicity accompanying national or state protection would encourage hordes of tourists to boat past their farms. Don Wilson, a Muncy resident and waterfowler who supports scenic river status for that section, says some of the landowners have another reason to oppose the designation. "That's nothing but farmland along there; it's prime farmland," he explains. "When you make this stretch a scenic river, these people are cut off from developing it."

Scenic river initiatives are not always a losing cause, although sometimes enactment seems to take forever. Federal officials processed a nomination for Pine Creek as a national wild and scenic river in 1968. Pennsylvania also nominated the West Branch tributary as a state scenic river four years later. Many landowners opposed both designations. All plans languished until 1989, when the Pine Creek

〰 *This undated photograph shows a man on a ledge of the Wyalusing Rocks. Farm fields stretch toward the foothills of the Endless Mountains on the other side of the North Branch. The camera points downriver. (Pennsylvania State Archives, Harrisburg, Pennsylvania.)*

Headwaters Protection Group, a grass-roots effort to protect water quality and halt attempts to locate a landfill in the watershed, recommended that a segment of the northern Pine Creek Gorge be reconsidered. Pennsylvania finally granted scenic river status in 1991.

Other designated scenic rivers flowing into the Susquehanna include all or parts of Lick Run in Clinton County; Stony Creek in Dauphin County; the Yellow

Breeches Creek and LeTort Spring Run, a tributary of the Yellow Breeches, in Cumberland County; and Octoraro and Tucquan creeks in Lancaster County.

Efforts to designate any other section of the river or its tributaries must originate locally. The Pennsylvania Department of Environmental Protection (successor to DER) has learned a lesson: If citizens who live along the river do not support protective status, no amount of planning by state government or regional environmental associations will produce more than a paper plan.

Wyoming Valley

Just above the mouth of the Lackawanna the Susquehanna breaks through the mountain . . . that forms the northwestern boundary of Wyoming Valley. At Nanticoke Falls it breaks out through the same mountain, and about eight miles lower down again overcomes it. It is difficult to account for this singular and apparently useless freak of the otherwise dignified and onward Susquehanna. It looks like the mere wantonness of conscious strength—a sort of Sam Patch ambition to show that some things may be done as well as others.

—Oscar J. Harvey and Ernest G. Smith, *History of Wilkes-Barre, Luzerne County, Pennsylvania*

Dr. Gerald Reisinger speaks with characteristic bluntness about who controlled the Susquehanna in the Wyoming Valley until white settlers practically stole the place: "The Iroquois named the Susquehanna. It's our river. The Wyoming Valley was once treated as sacred ground—a meeting place for many tribes. It was totally sacred. This river valley was a Vatican." The stocky Kingston naturopathic physician, descended from a Seneca grandmother, feels as protective of the Iroquois heritage in this valley as he does of the river. "It was pure water, a vital part of the estuary when the Iroquois were here. Then settlers moved into the valley and polluted the river."

Reisinger crunches gravel and shells as he walks along the Susquehanna's west shore at Kingston. He toes a freshwater clamshell into summer-low water where Native Americans once fished for shad with stone-weighted seines made of bushes and vines. "The Iroquois came here to do their fertility rituals and their councils and hunting and fishing and it was a sacred burial area," he says. "It was just so lush and fertile, and utopian, you might say."

The green valley of Wyoming begins where the Lackawanna joins the North Branch across from West Pittston. Near that point rises a massive outcropping, now Campbell's Ledge State Park. Here the river sharply shifts direction and runs seventeen miles down the valley to Nanticoke Falls, where adjacent hills squeeze in to end Wyoming. On both sides of the river all through this valley lie fertile bottomlands, which the Iroquois called Wassawomeke.[8] These alluvial floodplains are narrow at some points but spread for miles at others, notably midway in the valley, where Wilkes-Barre and Kingston face each other across the river. Sharp inclines, like Campbell's Ledge and Prospect Hill, rise from the floodplains and define the entire length of the valley.

The Iroquois considered this extraordinary valley crucial to the defense of their confederation. Wyoming controlled critical pathways, on land and water, between the northernmost reach of the Iroquois Confederacy at Onondaga and the confluence of the North and West branches of the Susquehanna at what the Native Americans called Shamokin. To help protect their claim to Wyoming, the Iroquois invited displaced tribes to move here. The Shawnees settled at Plymouth, the Nanticokes at Nanticoke, the Mahicans on Shawnee Flats, the Mohegans at Kingston, the Tuscaroras near the mouth of the Lackawanna River. These tribes fished in the North Branch and farmed the adjacent flats, hunted in the nearby hills, and, as European settlers increasingly made their way into the area, defended their territory.

From at least the 1670s and for a century thereafter, the Iroquois controlled Wyoming. Pennamite settlers from Pennsylvania and Yankee settlers from Connecticut invaded in the 1760s and fought to determine who owned the valley. Then they united to fight the British during the Revolution. The Iroquois, still believing the valley was theirs, aligned themselves with the British and American Loyalists. In 1778, these allies defeated Continental forces in the Battle of Wyoming, then slaughtered scores of soldiers and settlers in what has become known as the Wyoming Massacre. General Sullivan's massive reprisal the next year effectively wiped out the Iroquois presence in the valley.

Today the Native Americans are coming back and the river's water quality is coming along. Paul Waterman, chief of the Onondaga Nation and leader of all Iroquois, has visited Wyoming several times to spur its modern residents to take responsibility for the water and the valley. "Our people traveled up and down this river," Waterman said at Pittston in 1997. "We let you use her and are here now to reclaim her. Look what you have done with her."

Before white settlers completely polluted the water, early travelers lavishly praised this river valley. They viewed Wyoming and the Susquehanna as essential elements in the American paradise. As late as the early 1870s, as he prepared notes for William Cullen Bryant's *Picturesque America,* R. E. Garczynski found his spirit soaring at the sight of the valley from Prospect Rock, high above Wilkes-Barre. "Through the points of brilliant light with which the sun lights up the white houses," he wrote, "the Susquehanna glides like a gracious lady-mother, making soft sweeps here and noble curves there, but ever bordered by fringes of deep, emerald green. The whole valley is green, save where the towns toss up to heaven their towers and spires from numberless churches, and where behind, as if in hiding, black mounds and grimy structures mark the collieries."

Probably unknown to Garczynski and most other Wyoming sightseers, beneath this green and coal-pocked valley lies another, buried valley that once held an older Susquehanna flowing deeper in the earth. The erosive force of the latest glaciers filled this earlier depression in the

The Valley of Wyoming *by Jasper Francis Cropsey, 1865. Cropsey specialized in painting pleasant pastoral landscapes, often along the Susquehanna. This view looks upstream toward Wilkes-Barre from a hill on the southern side of the valley. (The Metropolitan Museum of Art, New York, Gift of Mrs. John Newington, 1966.)*

bedrock with porous clay, sand, and gravel—quicksand-like sediments now saturated with water.[9]

The Iroquois and the first white settlers appreciated the Wyoming Valley's beauty and the rich deposits on its floodplain, but later residents pushed this topsoil aside, digging far beneath the good earth in search of black rocks that would catch fire. Early mining companies took chances tunneling beneath the buried valley because veins of coal here are unusually rich and free of impurities. To avoid disaster, most companies tried to keep a rock cover of at least thirty-five to fifty feet between the mines and the riverbed. Despite precautions, miners pierced this "roof" several times. The deadliest incident occurred at Nanticoke in 1885: water broke into a shaft and killed twenty-six miners.

By the middle of the twentieth century, everyone who mined coal understood the danger. S. H. Ash, a safety official in the Department of the Interior's Bureau of Mines, wrote in 1950: "If an opening should be driven from mine workings beneath the buried valley into the water-bearing deposits or if, because of subsidence, a cave should occur and water from the Susquehanna River flow suddenly into the mine workings, a major catastrophe could result. It is probable that a stream the size of the Susquehanna would resist all efforts to contain it in time to avert a large loss of life and could result in the loss of a major portion of the Northern field."

Within less than a decade, the ultimate error that Ash warned against occurred. On January 22, 1959, a mine roof under the Susquehanna collapsed and the river poured through an enlarging hole into dozens of connected mines directly beneath and adjacent to the river. The accident occurred primarily because greedy and corrupt mining company officials had authorized cuts into coal veins within a few feet of the bed of the river itself. The Susquehanna determined the precise timing of the disaster. An unseasonable thaw beginning in mid-January broke the ice cover and raised the river level from two feet on January 19 to fifteen and a half feet on the morning of the collapse and nearly twenty-two feet the next day.

At the River Slope Mine, a mile and a half downstream from Pittston at Port Griffith, the Knox Coal Company had leased from the Pennsylvania Coal Company the right to dig beneath the east side of the river. The high-quality anthracite in the area encouraged Knox officials to ignore Pennsylvania Coal rules establishing a "stop line" above which mining was not permitted. That line was fifty feet beneath the bed of the river. For several months before the accident, Knox had been mining illegally above the line, clearly marked in red on maps. Water in the sediments of the buried valley had begun to leak into the mines. Miners wore helmets, raincoats, and boots as "droppers" fell steadily from the roof.

Late in the morning of January 22, two men cleaning up an area in a vein of the River Slope Mine heard a ceiling support crack in a large chamber closest to the riverbed. As they and the assistant foreman, John Williams, investigated, the roof of this chamber suddenly collapsed. "I no more than put my foot in the place and looked up, than the roof gave way," Williams reported. "It sounded like thunder. Water poured down like Niagara Falls." The three men sprinted up a slope to safety. Three other members of their crew drowned as water, ice, and debris from the river poured into the mines with enormous force. At the surface, Williams telephoned the mine superintendent, who relayed a message to all points to evacuate the mines.

To someone in a helicopter hovering over the area, the river would have looked like a giant bathtub whose drain had just been pulled. A massive whirlpool filled with huge chunks of ice formed over the hole and 100,000 gallons of water a minute swirled downward through the buried valley into the mines. The men who remained below heard a continuous, deafening roar. All passageways quickly filled with ice water. Most of the thirty-nine miners who escaped in the first minutes of the accident walked through ice-filled water up to their armpits and rising. Some swam.

Older miners helped younger ones find exits through a labyrinth of quickly filling passageways. One workman scaled a sixty-foot-deep air shaft and reached the surface three hours after the collapse. Thirty-two more men came out the same way four hours later. At that point, mine officials and federal mine inspectors decided the risk was too great to continue probing for survivors. Eighty-one men had been working in the mine at the time of the collapse. Sixty-nine survived. The bodies of the others disappeared.[10]

Tunnels connected many of the underground workings throughout the Wyoming anthracite field, so the potential existed for the invading river to wipe out practically all mining activity. In an effort to avoid disaster, federal and state mine officials mounted a massive effort to stem the flow. Pennsylvania Department of Mines workers helped miners divert tracks of the Lehigh Valley Railroad toward the cavity. They pushed 30 railroad gondola cars and 400 mine cars along the tracks and into the hole. They dumped in 12,000 cubic yards of dirt, 900 bales of fine wood shavings, truckloads of boulders, tons of coal waste, hundreds of hay bales.

The next day workers began constructing two earthen cofferdams 200 feet upstream and downstream from the break. Each dam stretched 500 feet from the river's eastern bank to Wintermoot Island. These dams further reduced the flow down the drain. Workers then installed twenty-two deep well pumps throughout mine shafts near the break site and began pumping out water as it poured in. These pumps could not keep up with the inflow. As late as March 23, some 20,000 gallons of water a minute continued to penetrate the tunnels. Workers drilled holes into the mines from the dry riverbed inside the cofferdams and pumped in 1,230 cubic yards of concrete and 26,000 cubic yards of sand. This seal, completed on May 27—more than four months after the break—cut the flow of water to 400 gallons per minute, an amount the pumps could handle.

Mines throughout the Wyoming Valley had been ruined by more than 10 billion gallons of river water. State inspectors immediately shut down operations in ten mines. Dozens more closed within days. Thousands of miners lost their jobs. During the year before the incident, the Wyoming Valley's anthracite field had produced more than 148,000 tons of marketable anthracite per week. That production dropped to about 54,000 tons a week within days after the catastrophe and eventually fell toward zero.

~ *Coal mining ended in the Wyoming Valley on January 22, 1959, when the floor of the Susquehanna collapsed, allowing the river to flow into mines beneath. Here a massive whirlpool of water and ice disappears into the hole in the river. (Luzerne County Historical Society, Wilkes-Barre, Pennsylvania.)*

Anthracite production had been declining dramatically even before the Knox Mine Disaster. Competition from natural gas and oil, the high cost of pumping mine drainage, and other factors had reduced the profitability of coal. Still, before the accident, the Wyoming field produced about half of all anthracite mined in Pennsylvania. The Susquehanna's inundation ended deep mining of coal in the Wyoming Valley forever.

Wilkes-Barre: Coal

Any unbiased observer who tours the hard and soft coal

sections of Pennsylvania may easily be pardoned for swal-

lowing the Russian line [that in the long run capitalistic

countries will destroy themselves]. What does he see?

Mountains of gob, miles of muck and culm fires a century

old. Everywhere the thoughtless greed of man spills over

into red rivers flowing through green valleys.

—Basse A. Beck in the *Sunbury Daily Item,* 1963

As a boy in the early 1930s, Ray Lybolt twice canoed the Susquehanna from Owego nearly to Harrisburg. Those trips began a lifelong love affair with the river. A retired construction worker and active archaeologist who lives near the river at Tunkhannock, Lybolt remembers two specific things about the Susquehanna's quality during his early journeys. Although raw sewage floated in the river, he scooped up

what looked like pure water surrounding the feces and drank it. The other thing he remembers is the color: after he paddled past the mouth of the polluted Lackawanna and into the Wyoming Valley, the water turned black and stayed black the rest of the way. "The river was like a huge black stain," he says. "You put your hand six inches under water and you couldn't see your hand." Washing out of abandoned mines or eroding from enormous riverside piles of anthracite waste, Wyoming Valley coal turned the river dark. Swimmers emerged with a thin coating of coal dust. The coal discolored the water and everything in it.

The stain was not the worst of it. Worse was acid mine drainage—what happens when oxygen and water react with pyrite, a mineral impurity of iron and sulfur common in coal, to form sulfuric acid and ferrous sulfate. Acid mine drainage lowers water's pH. Other chemical changes occur as the mixture washes into a stream, including the creation of iron hydroxide, which stains rocks bright orange (called "yellow boy") or even brighter ("red mo"). Mine drainage can kill everything in the river, either through its own acidity or by stealing oxygen from the water to form its chemical products. Ray Lybolt could not see his hand, but if the water had been clear he would have seen that his hand was the only living thing in the river.

Through the Wyoming Valley and southward the Susquehanna turned sickly in the early twentieth century. By the 1940s, the water quality worsened when a lack of mining regulations and enforcement allowed acid mine drainage to undermine the ecology of much of the river and many of its tributaries. No one had worried about coal killing the river when the industry got rolling in the early nineteenth century. Then mining promoters had touted the rich anthracite fields, thought to be the largest in the world, as an economic boon to the region. They were right about that. Wilkes-Barre on the Susquehanna and Scranton on the Lackawanna owed their early population growth and prosperity to the black rock that polluted both rivers.

Formed millions of years ago when pressure from overlying layers of sand and mud squeezed the water out of decaying vegetation, the carboniferous treasure ran in veins throughout the region. Native Americans probably burned coal before Europeans arrived, just as they dug for Pennsylvania oil centuries before Edwin Drake "discovered" it. Moravian missionaries spotted coal as they passed through the Wyoming Valley in 1750.

Abijah Smith opened the first coal mine in the valley in 1807. He loaded an ark with his product and poled it down to Columbia to sell to Lancaster County blacksmiths. There the anthracite sat, unused, on the riverbank. Blacksmiths preferred charcoal—being softer, it was far easier to ignite—and they had plenty of that near home.

The following year, a Wilkes-Barre judge and tavernkeeper, Jesse Fell, held a very public demonstration, burning anthracite in an open grate without the aid of bellows. This experiment convinced several observers that coal could be used for domestic heating, and the idea spread rapidly from hearth to hearth. Abijah Smith dispatched two more arkloads to Columbia. This time he took along grates and lit coal fires inside homes. The demonstrations worked: he sold all of his coal. Anthracite production swelled. A group of

Baltimore investors purchased land at Wilkes-Barre in 1831 and started mining on a large scale. By 1840, homeowners and even blacksmiths were using hard coal throughout the mid-Atlantic states.

Initially, miners cleaned coal underground by hand, using wrought-iron rakes to separate large pieces from smaller and leaving the smaller pieces inside the mines. After 1830, workers began sizing and cleaning coal outside mines. They dumped the anthracite on a perforated cast-iron plate and used sledgehammers to break the large pieces into lumps of sizes suitable for sale. Smaller pieces passed through perforations in the plate. Miners dumped these discards (called culm or spoil) onto huge piles.

Mechanical coal breakers, introduced in 1844, revolutionized the industry: they could process and screen a ton of coal in a minute, as opposed to standard manual output of three tons per day. In the rush toward mechanization, miners ignored waste. The breakers lost 15 percent of the coal they processed, as opposed to 6 percent lost by hand breaking. Adding to the problem, mechanical breaking required large quantities of water, which the breakers returned directly to waterways.

Until the 1870s, miners discarded all anthracite smaller than a chestnut on culm dumps, wasting millions of tons of fine coal, much of which eventually eroded into the Susquehanna or tributaries. Occasionally, while clearing land to expand their facilities, mining operations simply pushed these waste piles into waterways. At one point a mountain of culm reported to be nearly a quarter of a mile high blocked much of the Susquehanna's course above Wilkes-Barre.

This attitude toward Wyoming Valley mining operations predominated in the nineteenth century: while culm piles might be unsightly, mining for "beautiful gems" that "sparkle in the sun" was noble work. A correspondent for *Harper's New Monthly Magazine* wrote in 1853 that he "learned to look upon the mines as very comfortable nooks, and upon the miners, despite their terrible visages, as very clever and Christian people."

Those who examined the waste more closely had a different opinion. An observer in 1857 said that Roaring Brook, a tributary of the Lackawanna, had "blackened sides." An 1878 travel guide reported that "many streamlets, orange-tinted with mine sulfurs, run down the hills, seeking the Susquehanna."

In a 1904 study of water quality in the Susquehanna drainage basin, M. O. Leighton estimated that one-fifth of the water flowing through the Wyoming Valley was acid mine drainage pumped from mines directly into the river.[11] He further described the damage to waterways: "The appearance of a small stream into which coal-mine wastes are discharged is peculiar. The bottom of the channel is colored a light yellow, and there appear no signs of vegetation of any kind. All fish life in a stream is immediately destroyed at the first appearance of coal mine waste. Where culm as well as acid mine waste is dumped into the channel the appearance is well-nigh beyond description. Many of the small brooks emptying into the Susquehanna River in the Wyoming Valley have no permanent channel. The old channel has been filled by deposits of culm, and the stream takes a new course whenever freshets arise, often covering fertile fields with culm and doing great damage."

While acid mine drainage poisoned aquatic life, coal sediment gradually transformed the course of the Susquehanna. Changes occurred all the way to the Chesapeake. Floating coal formed new islands and expanded others. Coal sediment reduced the river's depth. The change in composition of eroding sediment to predominantly coal waste destroyed natural habitats and further reduced life in the channel.

Searching for ways to reduce waste, Pennsylvania commissioned a series of studies. Mining engineers and geologists advocated improved mining and processing techniques. Neither of these initiatives prompted change, but the market did. The price of anthracite increased about the year 1900, so mining companies began selling smaller lumps of coal, thus reducing the amount of anthracite that reached the water.

Hard coal production in Pennsylvania peaked in 1917, when miners drew out over 100 million tons. After World War I, homeowners began switching to less costly and more convenient home heating fuels, including oil and bituminous coal from western Pennsylvania. Anthracite production stabilized during World War II but dropped precipitously thereafter, with an increasing amount of hard coal coming from strip rather than deep mines. By the time of the Knox Mine Disaster in 1959, miners throughout the state were extracting only 18 million tons of anthracite each year.

Decades of wasteful mining and acid mine drainage have left black and orange markings on this valley and downstream sections that decades of damage control have not entirely removed. Dredges have recovered much of the coal large enough to be useful for industry and home heating from the water, but piles of culm remain along the river's banks. Since the early 1980s, electricity-generating companies have been removing and burning culm. To reduce continuing erosion from remaining piles, the state has added alkaline sludge to offset acid, then seeded the mixture with rye grass to hold it in place.

Controlling acid mine drainage has been much more difficult—both because acid is considerably harder to remove from water than is coal itself and because the coal industry fought all efforts at reform for so many years. Pennsylvania's basic antipollution law, the Clean Streams Act of 1937, excluded coal mine drainage from all enforcement. Acid mine drainage, along with raw sewage, swept down the Susquehanna without regulation into the 1960s.

The effects of acid on North Branch waters are not so noticeable as on the West Branch, where heavy drainage from bituminous mines has created entirely sterile water in some sections. In North Branch water, the most adaptable fish can live tenuously despite the steady inflow of acid, thanks largely to the buffering capacity of lime feeding heavily from the Chemung River. The Chemung flows through extensive limestone formations in New York.[12]

Unusually high flows of acid can overwhelm lime's ameliorating influence. In the autumn of 1961, large pumps began expelling 25 million gallons of water a day from Wyoming Valley mines flooded by the Knox Mine incident. The result: all fish died along more than fifty miles of the Susquehanna south of Wilkes-Barre—the worst fish kill in Pennsylvania history. Admitting that the state led the nation in miles of water polluted by acid mine drainage, an embarrassed Pennsylvania General Assembly ended pollution exemptions for the coal industry in 1965. Two years later, state voters approved a $500 million expenditure (Operation Scarlift) to clean up waterways damaged by acid mine drainage.

Controlling drainage is a laborious, expensive, never-ending task. Most acid flows from deep abandoned mines that can be difficult to reach. Alternatives are few. The openings of mines must be sealed or water diverted from them. Lime can be fed into mines to neutralize acid. Wetlands filled with phragmites, cattails, or sphagnum moss can help filter acid leaking out of mines. The state's Reclaim Pennsylvania program permits the remining of abandoned mines on condition that the sites be cleaned up. Mining companies have remediated an estimated 98 percent of all acid discharges on remined lands.

Despite remediation efforts, the latest water quality assessment by the Department of Environmental Protection (DEP) lists acid mine drainage and agricultural pollution as by far the largest sources of water degradation in the state. Mine seals do not last forever, lime treatment is costly, and the success of wetland treatment varies according to conditions. Therefore, the DEP is not optimistic about making major improvements in the most polluted areas without a large infusion of funds. Pennsylvania currently receives about $22 million a year from the federal Office of Surface Mining—a fragment of the estimated $5 billion needed to clean up all problems in the state.

Moreover, acid mine drainage is not the only poison oozing from the Wyoming Valley's abandoned mines. Periodically, toxic wastes have been dumped illegally into some of the thousands of bore holes feeding into the labyrinth of mines beneath Wilkes-Barre. One of the worst cases of chemical poisoning began in the summer of 1979 and continued well into 1980. Trucks from two New Jersey firms illegally dumped millions of gallons of oil and toxic chemicals, including cyanide, into a bore hole leading to abandoned mine shafts in the Butler Mine tunnel at Pittston. The waste flowed through the tunnel and on into the Susquehanna for months, polluting the river all the way to Harrisburg. The oil, cyanide, and other toxins threatened fish stocks and Danville's water supply and cost millions of dollars to clean up.

The Environmental Protection Agency (EPA) thought it had completely cleaned the site, but Hurricane Gloria proved otherwise in 1985. Thousands of gallons of toxins, including cancer-causing chemicals, flooded out of the mine and into the Susquehanna. Now the EPA does not say it has cleaned up the mine, but says rather that it is "monitoring" it, prepared to minimize toxic releases.

Wilkes-Barre: Flood

We slipped and slid down the street. The mud was incredible, four inches thick and treacherously slippery. The smell that rose from it lay heavy on the air, the smell of dead fish, rotting food, and polluted river water. Everything was strangely quiet. The city sat silently after its defeat to the river.

—ANTHONY J. MUSSARI, *Appointment with Disaster*, quoting
Maria Csala on her return home after the Susquehanna
flooded Wilkes-Barre in 1972

ON JULY 26, 1972, MORE THAN A MONTH after the bloated Susquehanna River washed over coal mines and everything else in the Wyoming Valley, Elwood Disque wrote in his diary: "Went to Wyoming Valley Mall to make Red Cross purchases: shirts, underwear, dinette set, cooking utensils, towels, etc. A disturbed person in the bus (there are now many) claimed it was the end of the world. Every one thinks he is the only one who was in the flood and wants a lot of sympathy. But we are all in the same boat."

Tropical Storm Agnes swamped Wyoming Valley's boat with thousands of flood refugees. After a wet early June, during which some fifteen inches of rain fell upstream of Wilkes-Barre, Agnes dropped another twelve inches over much of central New York and Pennsylvania. An unprecedented amount of water falling directly into the river and rushing in from tributaries swelled the North Branch to record levels, overrunning levees and inundating nineteen square miles of the valley with water twelve to thirty feet deep.

Agnes (also known in Wyoming as "Agony") disrupted life along the entire Susquehanna River. Milton Shapp, Pennsylvania's governor, called the storm "unquestionably the greatest disaster in the history of the state." President Richard Nixon took a broader view, calling Agnes "the greatest natural disaster in the history of the United States." Wilkes-Barre suffered at the center of the catastrophe.

In the late spring of 1972, as Elwood Disque walked along streets paralleling the river to his teaching duties at Wilkes College, he studied the city's thirty-seven-foot earthen dike. The longtime German professor, then in his mid-sixties, knew that if a flooded Susquehanna overran that barrier, water might fill the basement of his home on Birch Street, two blocks from the river in South Wilkes-Barre. But when he decided not to evacuate that June, Disque did not know that Agnes, a flood of an entirely different order, would fill the whole valley. He did not know that the water would rise through his house, trapping him for four days, and that he would spend more than a year cleaning up the mess left behind after the flood receded.

Early on the morning of Friday, June 23, telephone calls from two neighbors woke Disque, a bachelor who lived alone. Afraid that the dikes would not hold, the neighbors said they were evacuating immediately. As they and others left Birch Street that morning, Disque ate breakfast, cleaned the upstairs of his house, and called several friends. "Since I was one of the oldest residents of the area I knew it would be difficult to return to our homes because of martial law," he wrote in his diary. "Therefore I decided to stay. Why not? (I had been a refugee once and that was enough.) We had never had water in the house before. Why should this time be any different?"

Nevertheless, Disque moved as many possessions as he could from the basement and the first floor to the second floor. Late that morning, he stepped onto his front porch to take a break. Moments earlier, the North Branch had breached the levee at Riverside Drive and Ross Street, between his house and the Wilkes campus. "I saw this huge wave of water rushing down the street," Disque said. "By the time I got to the dining room I was up to my knees in water. I took a loaf of bread, peanut butter, a knife, a can opener (I don't know why), a package of meat loaf and

went to the second floor. The water continued to rise."

Disque filled his bathtub with water for drinking and took food, a pail of water, and his mattress to the attic, where he slept. "I woke up about 8:00 A.M. [June 24]," he wrote,

hearing the furniture banging against the ceiling of the first floor. I did feel rested. Then I looked out the window. The ranch style homes were well covered by the water. I turned on the [battery-operated] radio. The Susquehanna River now extended 5 miles on both sides of its banks—a large lake of mud filled with acid and oil and a roof top jutting out here and there. I suddenly realized I would be living in the attic longer than one day. . . . When I went to the bathroom on the second floor I stepped into water. It had reached 3 steps of the attic stairs. . . . The water was quite cold. I dried my feet at the foot of the stairs and went back to bed to keep warm.

Over the next two days, Disque watched the fast-moving water from his attic windows. He saw wide-eyed cats and wild animals riding lumber through the flood. He flagged down an emergency helicopter. Trees and high voltage wires kept the craft from drawing near his home. Waves created by the propeller washed over two-story houses across the street.

Then the floodwaters began to recede. Disque watched porch roofs reappear. He saw that the flood had tilted or overturned some garages. When he awoke at 5 A.M. on June 26, Disque saw ground.

A house burns as a Coast Guard boat patrols South Franklin Street at the height of the flood caused by Tropical Storm Agnes in June 1972. The view is south from the Sullivan Street intersection. (Luzerne County Historical Society, Wilkes-Barre, Pennsylvania.)

"This morning I waded through the mud on the first floor," he wrote. "Every thing is a total ruin. . . . The buffet, china closet and book cases had turned over. My large freezer had been turned on its side. . . . Much to my dismay I could open no doors or windows downstairs. They were swollen shut. I hope someone turns up soon and leans the ladder, which drifted into the yard, against a second story window so that I can get out. I'm not going to jump yet."

On Tuesday, June 27, half a week after his ordeal began, Disque spotted two men checking on a neighbor's house and asked them to hoist his ladder. He climbed down into the mud and debris on the floodplain.

After a brief exploration, he returned and almost immediately began cleaning house. Over the next several weeks, he washed everything, often more than once. After Wilkes reopened, Disque walked over the drying mud to teach summer school classes, but he spent most of the rest of his waking hours scrubbing away mud and grit and trying to rid his home of the stench of what the flood had left behind. Nearly every day brought a new and usually negative revelation. He found his garden ruined. Electricity, gas, and telephone remained dead for weeks. Walking around the city, he "was reminded of the bombed out cities in Europe during the Second World War." He and others accepted food and clothing provided by the Red Cross. Disque fared better than many. He wrote: "I never thought I'd see American women poking around with umbrellas through rubble in front of stores for sheets, girdles, stockings, panties, etc."

The summer sun dried the mud to dust. Bulldozers knocking over broken homes and construction trucks rumbling through town carting away debris raised the dust into enormous clouds that actually blocked the sun. Meanwhile, Disque continued the tedious task of cleaning his house, object by object and room by room. Even with considerable help from friends, the work proved more difficult than he had imagined. He spent one entire day scrubbing his refrigerator.

"The endless grinding, grinding, grinding of the pushers, bull dozers and trucks is getting to me," he wrote on August 8. "Will it ever stop? Came home, rested, went to bed. The endless monotony of life is getting to me—cleaning, scrubbing, getting tired and going to bed." Disque vacillated that summer between determination to clean up the house and go on living in it and frustration and a desire to leave it all behind.

He spent a full year washing walls and replacing flooring and painting the exterior of his house; but on the first anniversary of the flood, while his neighbors held a celebratory block party, Elwood Disque stayed home to examine slides of Florida real estate. On August 2, 1973, he made this final entry in his Agnes diary: "The frustrations and disillusions continue—no wonder I finally decided to move to Florida and to start life over again. I now enjoy the beautiful sunshine and warm weather and no longer am annoyed by the dust, dirt, and unhappiness caused by living in a depressed area."

Thousands of Wyoming Valley residents went through what Disque did, but most eventually decided to stay. Hundreds of millions of dollars in federal and state flood aid cushioned the catastrophe, but no amount of money could wipe away all the devastation of water and mud. Twenty-five thousand people, many of them in Wilkes-Barre, lost all or part of their houses. All but 20 of Kingston's 6,000 homes suffered some flood damage. Water and mud infiltrated more than 2,700 commercial buildings and scores of industries and schools throughout the Wyoming Valley. The Agnes cleanup eventually cost the region $2.2 billion—half of the total Agnes loss in seven states.

The 1972 flood was the worst but far from the first to devastate Wyoming. The narrows at Nanticoke slows water flowing through the valley, making it especially susceptible to flooding. Between 1784 and 1972, the North Branch overflowed its Wyoming banks nearly seventy times.[13] Many of these floods have been recorded in detail. The Pumpkin Flood of October 1786, for example, propelled two-ton stones several miles downstream and picked ripe pumpkins by the thousands from fields and washed them all the way to the Chesapeake.

As Wyoming's population increased, so did flood damages and citizens' requests for relief. Early in the twentieth century, the U.S. Army Corps of Engineers surveyed the North Branch, especially the flood-prone Wilkes-Barre area, and recommended construction of tall levees to protect the most developed areas; but Congress never appropriated funds for the project and local communities decided not to foot the bill.

In March 1936, Susquehanna floodwaters rose more than thirty-three feet at Wilkes-Barre, inundating much of the valley and causing $7 million in damage in Wilkes-Barre and Kingston alone. In response to that devastation, Pennsylvania's congressional delegation successfully lobbied for passage of the National Flood Control Act. That legislation appropriated $27 million for projects along the Susquehanna in Pennsylvania and New York, including a $9.1 million system of earthen levees in the Wyoming Valley. The Corps of Engineers designed the system to hold water cresting at thirty-seven feet. Four feet higher than the river's crest in 1936 would be more than high enough, practically everyone agreed, to avoid another calamitous flood.

By the summer of 1972, coal-mining operations had undermined the levees and they had subsided several feet in places. Nevertheless, Wilkes-Barre and Luzerne County officials believed they could contain any amount of water coursing down the North Branch. Flood stage is twenty-two feet at Wilkes-Barre. By the evening of June 22, the river had risen above that level. By late that night, well before Elwood Disque's neighbors urged him to leave his house, the river was rising at more than a foot an hour. Luzerne County Civil Defense personnel began talking about the possibility of a forty-foot crest—three feet above the levees. At 2 A.M. the Civil Defense director, Frank Townsend, called for 10,000 volunteers to help stack sandbags on top of the levees to elevate them to forty feet. Thousands of valley residents responded and worked frantically all morning, shoveling sand into any kind of bag they could find (including pillowcases from a city hotel) and piling the bags atop the levees.

By 4 A.M., Townsend knew the effort would fail. The

river was still rising from thirty-six feet. He ordered an evacuation of low-lying areas in Wilkes-Barre and Kingston. Thousands of residents left the valley, but many sandbaggers refused to quit as water began seeping through and splashing over the top of the porous levees. The workers still hoped to avoid what already had occurred downriver at Plymouth. Sewer construction had opened a large cut in the dike earlier that spring, and Agnes-driven water poured through there first. Plymouth had been evacuated at 11 P.M. on June 22, and by the early morning of June 23 the whole town was under water.

The North Branch breached the Wilkes-Barre levee about 10:30 that morning and washed into Elwood Disque's dining room minutes later. In a book about the Agnes flood, Anthony J. Mussari, a history professor at King's College and at that time an editorialist for WNEP-TV in Wilkes-Barre, recalled the scene as the levee broke:

> Hundreds of young people [were] running away from the levee. Water was pouring over the green steel pilings which were designed to prevent just that. The smell of natural gas filled the air and people were yelling about the possibility of an explosion. . . . Gas pipes were rattling; manhole covers were popping. In the midst of these alarming sounds, people were glaring in anger and frustration at the dike. . . . There was a sense of imminent death and destruction in the air. Heavy clouds hovered over the valley. Central city Wilkes-Barre was almost deserted, and yet some still clung to the belief that the Wyoming Valley was not vulnerable to a major natural disaster.

William Shock was helping to pile sandbags on top of the levee at Riverside and Ross when the dike broke. He did not run fast enough. Several days later, after floodwater had receded, someone found Shock's body in the mud. (Five other Wyoming Valley residents died as a result of the flood, most from heart attacks.)

Shortly after the Ross Street break, the Susquehanna breached the levee a few blocks south at Irving Street, tearing apart most of the homes on Irving and Charles. Rushing water created a whirlpool that scoured Charles Street itself, creating a gorge in its place. Elsewhere, the flood knocked houses from their foundations and washed them into other houses. Several bridges and hundreds of cars washed downstream. The flood rose over watertight homes and filled them by pouring down the chimneys.

The levee broke on the Kingston side shortly after the river ran into Wilkes-Barre and water quickly covered everything in town. Within hours, early on the afternoon of the 23rd, the levee broke at Forty-Fort, upstream of Kingston. Surging floodwaters washed into a riverside cemetery, ripping caskets from the ground and sweeping them down the river.

The water rose Friday night and into Saturday, June 24. The Susquehanna did not crest—at 40.6 feet—until Saturday at 7 P.M. It did not begin to fall substantially until the next day, dropping below the top of the levees at noon. All along the valley, along the entire Susquehanna, water that remained above flood level for several days altered the landscape and the lives of thousands.

Everyone who lived in the Wyoming Valley in June 1972 has an Agnes story. When Civil Defense finally blew the emergency evacuation siren at 11:14 A.M. on June 23, Francis Michelini, president of Wilkes College, was helping his library staff move rare books from a basement vault. Michelini returned to his riverside home and waited for the water to rise so he could launch his boat on South Franklin Street. He spent the rest of that day and night motoring around the streets with two firefighters, ferrying those who had been stranded to higher ground. "I heard the bottom of the boat scrape something," recalled Michelini. "It was the roof of a car. We learned to look for antennas."

Peg Hoffman was living with her eighty-four-year-old mother near Wyoming Avenue in Kingston. Wyoming Avenue, the town's main drag, is a mile from the river. As the flood rose, "we put the cat in a pillowcase and took mother out of the house in a boat. We went right over the electric wires. Oh, she thought this was a lark." After the family returned, "the whole place stunk. We had mud between the outside wall and the plaster and it just stunk. The carpet and the matting underneath it stunk. After the water went down, the good furniture still stood there. The bad furniture came unglued and fell apart on the floor."

Maria Csala was seventeen years old that summer. She offered Anthony Mussari detailed impressions of the disaster that greeted her family when they returned home four days after the flood. Then she explained the clean-up process:

It was all too different, too amazing, too horrible for us to really comprehend. But day by day, week by week, we found that summer what it was like to put back together a world that we thought was lost for good. It all went painstakingly slow. Little by little the mud was shoveled out and carried away in buckets; the junk that was ruined was heaped in huge piles in the street; all the pipes in the cellar and Dad's tools had to be oiled against rust; the walls were hosed and scrubbed down, then all that water had to be swept out of the house, the floorboards had to be pulled up, the paint had to be scraped off the walls; the many dishes and pots and pans and utensils had to be washed and rewashed, then sterilized in bathtubs full of Clorox, and so on and so forth until I thought I'd go mad.

In a way, Agnes washed and sterilized the valley's entire human-made landscape. Thanks to enormous amounts of federal funding channeled into the region by its aptly named congressman, Dan Flood, Wyoming remade itself. The valley adopted an unofficial slogan: "Newest old community in the nation." Ruined historic homes and commercial buildings yielded to newer structures. Redevelopment replaced all four corners of Wilkes-Barre's square—a particularly positive change in a downtown that had been sliding for years. Outside industries moved into a revived city and valley. Developers planned new housing projects.[14]

Immediately after the flood, concerned citizens formed the Susquehanna River Basin Association (now the Tri-State Association) to help develop flood- and drought-control plans. The Susquehanna River Basin Commission updated its flood forecast and warning system. The National

Weather Service measurably improved its forecasts with the help of computers and satellites. "I think it was probably the flood that started a lot of the positive changes," says Damon Young, an early director of the Tri-State Association. "It was like the war in Europe. It gave the community a chance to start over fresh and correct some of the problems they had in the past."

The threat of high water never ends. A flood in 1996, precipitated by ice jams, came within inches of running over the levees. In the spring of 1997, the Corps of Engineers began a five-year $147 million project to raise the Wilkes-Barre and Kingston levees by another three to five feet and make other modifications to the flood-control system throughout the valley.

The higher levees remain below the crest of Agnes flooding in some places where major settling has occurred. Levees settle all along the line because the Wyoming Valley—with its buried valley, springs, swamps, and abandoned coal mines—is constantly caving in. (An entire South Wilkes-Barre neighborhood sank into the ground a few years ago.) However, engineers claim flood-control reservoirs on Susquehanna tributaries upstream of the Wyoming Valley reduce the chances for another Agnes-type disaster to near zero.

Perhaps. In an article written for the Susquehanna River Basin Commission on the twentieth anniversary of Agnes, John D. Graham, a civil engineer, worried about the future:

Unfortunately, the facts show that we are not prepared for the "Flood Next Time." We haven't learned our lesson.

Telltale signs of our apathy are all around us. We continue to remodel and construct homes in the flood plain; we are aware of the need to improve our flood warning system, but refuse to pay the monetary price for its installation and operation; we resist purchasing flood insurance coverage and drop the coverage we had; we ignore flood-damage reduction programs; and we forget about the dangers of flooding in order to build next to the water.

Compared with its mile-and-more width downriver, the Susquehanna at Wilkes-Barre is a modest 700 or so feet across. In dry weather, it runs at an average of four feet deep or less—dozens of feet below the tops of the levees. Given normal conditions, it is easy to believe the river can be kept in its course by increasing the height of levees and manipulating dams at flood-control reservoirs.

Given normal conditions, Wilkes-Barre is considering using an inflatable dam to raise the Susquehanna to boating level during summer months. The structure, which would cost an estimated $7 million, officially is part of the area's flood-mitigation plan, although its primary function would be recreational: another $7 million would be spent to construct parks and marinas around this seasonal river pool.

Creating an attractive recreational pool would not be that simple. An engineering consultant says a dam would be worthwhile only if Wilkes-Barre fully cleans up its antiquated sewer and storm water systems, which regularly spill excess sewage into the river. The estimated cost of that project ranges up from $40 million.

The inflatable dam plan has divided area residents and

☙ *Canoeists paddle down the North Branch at West Pittston. They are Kim Cappellini, women's crew coach for Wilkes University and the Wyoming Valley Racing Club; her son, Sean Cappellini-Boyle; and Gere Reisinger, men's coach and water chairman for Susquehanna River Watch. Campbell's Ledge rises in the background. (Photo by Christine Brubaker.)*

legislators. U.S. Representative Paul Kanjorski contends that a recreational "lake" on the river would draw thousands of boaters and anglers and millions of dollars. State Senator Ralph Musto says the proposal would waste millions of dollars to pool polluted water.

The Kingston naturopath Gere Reisinger believes a recreational pool would draw more people to the Susquehanna and therefore encourage cleaner water, which he uses regularly as coach of Wilkes University's crew. He also thinks cleaner water would provide an impetus to improve parks along the shore. Reisinger joined Charles Urban, founder of Susquehanna River Watch, and others to help restore Wilkes-Barre's Nesbitt Park, on the Kingston side of the river. They had hoped to clean up the adjacent natural area of Kirby Park as well, but that effort has stalled because the city government and the park's owner have not supported it.

The landscape architect Frederick Law Olmsted Jr. designed Kirby Park with bridle paths and an arboretum, a greenhouse and a zoo. Residents virtually abandoned the area after the Kingston levee separated the river and parks from the town in the late 1930s and it went to seed. Rampant undergrowth catches debris, behind which water stacks up during floods. Adding assault to neglect, the Corps of Engineers ripped up part of the area while it expanded the base of the levee to support additional earth on top.

Reisinger says the flood-control project presents a more significant problem: the expanded levee further constricts the flood channel just above the spot where the North Branch broke through to flood Elwood Disque's house in 1972. "The river begins to curve at the Market Street Bridge [just upstream of Kirby Park]," he explains. "All New York and Pennsylvania water is rushing down to that curve. Now the levee extends sixty more feet into the flood channel on either side of the river. So it creates more constriction and velocity. They hauled in more riprap to hold the sides of the levee. With riprap you've lost more flood channel—so you have this crazy equation going. . . . It would have been better never to have built the levee."

To rim the river with levees, the engineers dug thousands of tons of dirt from the mountains. To line the levees with riprap, they blasted thousands of tons of rock. In Wilkes-Barre and Kingston, most people go about their daily business as if living in walled cities in the twenty-first century is standard procedure.

Nescopeck Falls

I paddled into these rapids, and within seconds I was being drawn toward what looked like a drop-off. I paddled hard toward the left bank, and narrowly missed being sucked over a few ledges and into a raging bottleneck. . . . The whole river was effectively funneled into an area under the bridge only fifty yards wide. Extremely dangerous!

—Keto Gyekis on traveling through Nescopeck Falls
in a sea kayak in the summer of 1998

Not quite halfway along the Susquehanna's seventy-mile course between Wilkes-Barre and Northumberland,

Berwick and Nescopeck face each other across the water. A sizable industrial town, Berwick stands on a terrace 80 feet above the river's west bank. The little village of Nescopeck lies on the flat bottomland on the east side.

Nescopeck Creek enters the North Branch just below the village. Nescopeck meant something like "deep, dark water" to the Native Americans. Some residents today call the waterway Black Creek because it is even darker: it is the color of coal.

Nescopeck once was clear and full of fish, but miners ruined it a century ago. They flushed massive amounts of coal waste, collected through a water drainage tunnel called Jeddo, into the tributary Little Nescopeck Creek. The drainage from the tunnel blackened the Little Nescopeck and the Nescopeck and killed all the fish. Acid mine drainage continues to flow out of the Jeddo Tunnel and the Nescopeck remains a dead stream.

Polluted as it is, Nescopeck Creek is one of the Susquehanna's better white-water canoeing tributaries. It rams its way through several mountains by way of deep gorges before spilling into the Susquehanna. Where it enters the main stream, the Nescopeck has dropped an enormous amount of stone and gravel. This deposition extends well out into the North Branch, compressing the current toward the west bank and creating a white-water chute known as Nescopeck Falls. These falls drop over a ledge of Blue Ridge granite extending across the riverbed.

Early canoeists respected Nescopeck Falls, shooting them with care or portaging in high water. Moravian missionaries bound for Ohio in June 1772 found the river flowing rapidly at Nescopeck. Bishop John Ettwein said the group carefully worked the well-packed canoes across the falls by hand and ropes "and not without much anxiety."

Early rivermen also used ropes to haul boats upstream over the falls. William Hollins, a Baltimore businessman, reported in 1825 that crews extended a line from their boat to the upper rocks at Nescopeck, "whilst others pole and guide the boat among the rocks, and the rest are hauling on a rope, either in the water or on shore."

Larger boats experienced even more difficulty passing through Nescopeck Falls, which became a central player in ending the short-lived dream of long-distance steamboat travel on the Susquehanna.

In 1825, workmen constructed three steamboats—the *Susquehanna,* the *Codorus,* and the *Pioneer*—according to designs specially tailored to conquer the difficulties of navigating a shallow river by using steam power. Wood heated two huge boilers that propelled the eighty-two-foot *Susquehanna*'s stern wheels. The other two boats were side-wheelers. The boats spent the winter of 1825–26 at York Haven and each voyaged upriver in the spring. The *Susquehanna* ran up to Northumberland and back. The *Codorus* headed up the North Branch as far as Binghamton. The *Pioneer* traveled the West Branch to Williamsport and Jersey Shore. Large crowds greeted them wherever they went. Bands played stirring music. Cannons blasted charges over the water.

The Susquehanna River commissioners for Maryland, on behalf of eager Baltimore merchants, persuaded the *Susquehanna*'s crew to make a second trip in late April. Captain Cornwell and his engineer, Quincy Maynard, experienced little difficulty until they reached Nescopeck Falls on the afternoon of May 5, 1826. Although the *Codorus* had passed through the falls successfully several weeks earlier,

the *Susquehanna*'s captain acknowledged a risk. A number of passengers left the boat and joined a large cluster of spectators on shore.

The crew of the *Susquehanna* added wood to the fires beneath its boilers and headed for a central channel through the falls. About two-thirds of the way up the channel, the boat lost momentum. It drifted back to the foot of the rapids and toward the west bank of the river, where it struck a large rock. One of the boilers exploded at both ends. The burst of boiling water killed John Turk and Ceber Whitemarsh of Green, New York. William Camp of Owego, New York, died a few hours later. Quincy Maynard died the next day. Exploding water scalded the fireman and several passengers. The accident burned or hurt in some other way practically everyone on board.

Colonel Joseph Paxton of Catawissa, a small community downstream at the Catawissa Creek's junction with the North Branch, rode on the *Susquehanna* that afternoon. He described his experience: "I stood on the forward-deck with a long ash pole in my hand, and was in the act of placing it in the water hoping to steady her, when the explosion took place. Two young men standing near me were blown high into the air, and I was hurled several yards from the boat into the water. I thought a cannon had been fired, and shot my head off. When in the water I thought I must certainly drown, but, making a desperate effort, succeeded in reaching the shore. I was badly scalded, and lost my hair and a portion of my scalp."

Battered but reparable, the *Susquehanna* returned to York Haven to join the *Pioneer* long before the *Codorus* came home. Stranded in New York by low water, the *Codorus*

≈ *Captain Joel Walp of Wilkes-Barre piloted the steamboat* Greyhound *until 1902. Here the boat steams upriver from Plymouth to Wilkes-Barre about four years earlier. Notice the canoe in the water in front of the boat. (Paul W. Roberts, Plymouth, Pennsylvania.)*

finally ran down the river when rain fell in mid-July. After this experience, John Elgar, the York mechanic who had constructed the boat and accompanied it on its tour, decided the Susquehanna was too shallow for commercial steamboat navigation. None of these boats ever steamed again. Canal dams, which Pennsylvania began constructing in the late 1820s, ended long-distance steamboat navigation on the river.

However, Pennsylvania did not complete the North Branch Extension Canal from Pittston to the New York border until 1856, so several new steamboats fitfully provided strictly regional travel between Wilkes-Barre and points north. In 1835 the Susquehanna Steamboat and Navigation Company began running another boat named *Susquehanna* between Owego, New York, and Wilkes-Barre. It carried passengers and freight, including, on one occasion, coal tugged along on barges. The boat made few trips: parts kept breaking and low water in summer and ice in winter reduced opportunities for travel.

In the spring of 1838 the second *Susquehanna* completed its final voyage—from Owego to Wilkes-Barre—on a freshet. The boat ran the 150 miles, across some twenty dams, in twelve hours. As the *Susquehanna* steamed down the waterway, the journalist N. P. Willis observed established and prospective modes of transportation. "It was sometimes ticklish steering among the rafts and arks with which the river was thronged," he wrote, while "the gangs of laborers at the foot of every steep cliff, doing the first rough work of the canal, gave promise of a speedy change in the aspect of this almost unknown river."

Subsequent efforts to run steamboats north of Wilkes-Barre also failed, as the Wilkes-Barre attorney and historian F. Charles Petrillo explains in *Steamboats on the Susquehanna*. For example, the citizens of Bainbridge, New York, launched the *Enterprise* in the spring of 1851. As long as the river remained high, commerce with Wilkes-Barre continued. But when the water fell after the spring of 1853, the boat ran aground along the North Branch, fatally injuring its hull. The *Enterprise*'s failure ended regional commercial navigation on the North Branch.

The successful launching of the *Hendrick B. Wright* at Wilkes-Barre in 1874 began a new age of strictly local steamboat transport. Numerous steamers (including a third *Susquehanna,* whose boiler also exploded, landing in the river along with several crew members in 1883) carried passengers for short distances in the Wyoming Valley and in other communities from Tunkhannock to Owego.

These fancy new steamboats (the cabin of the *Mayflower* featured oak and walnut paneling and carpet on the floor) provoked a culture clash in Victorian Pennsylvania. Laborers and their children had been accustomed to swimming nude in the river for many years. Steamboat travelers took offense. The *Luzerne Union* sided strongly with the steamboaters in an editorial:

For several days past, large numbers of men and boys have been so indecent as to expose themselves, in and out the water, while passenger boats, carriages, and pedestrians, are passing near them, and it is the duty of all moral citizens to teach these shameless offenders a valuable lesson. Whenever these parties are caught on the shore or in the water in a naked condition, those who wish to reform them should seize their clothing and retain them until the names of the offenders can be secured. . . . The steamboat companies must see that this public bathing is stopped, or decent passengers will avoid going upon the river.

Steam navigation struggled into the 1890s, but by then trolleys had forced many boats out of business. Competing for a declining number of passengers, some frustrated steamboat captains began ramming other boats. This wildness further discouraged ridership.

In the autumn of 1902, Captain Joel Walp abandoned the *Greyhound* and the *Wilkes-Barre,* the last steamboats to operate in the Wyoming Valley, in Nanticoke Creek. They became regionally famous wrecks, eventually washed away by floodwaters.

Bloomsburg

Large floods from severe storms have been experienced in the past on the Susquehanna River at Bloomsburg. Greater storms have occurred on other watersheds in the general geographical region. Such storms could occur over the Susquehanna Watershed causing floods larger than any that have occurred in the past.

—Report of the U.S. Army Corps of Engineers after the flood of 1972

FROM THE NORTH BRANCH'S SOURCE WATERS in New York to the confluence of branches at Northumberland, many more tributaries enter the Susquehanna from the west than from the east. These western tributaries are generally larger and have more feeder streams, so the whole drainage network on that side is substantially more complex.

Two creeks that enter the North Branch just below Bloomsburg exemplify this watery imbalance. Fishing Creek flows in from the west immediately below the town. Catawissa Creek cuts through the eastern riverbank about two miles downstream. Fishing Creek is considerably larger than Catawissa because it is fed by a dozen fair-sized creeks that have scores of tributaries of their own. Catawissa is nearly as long as Fishing Creek, but its waters are increased by just two tributary creeks and a dozen or so short runs.

Fishing Creek is not only the more abundantly watered but the more storied stream. The creek's west and east branches rise well up on North Mountain in Sullivan County and combine as they exit the highlands. Then Fishing Creek runs some 30 miles before entering the Susquehanna. The Native Americans called the creek Namescesepong, which may mean either "stream of fish" or "smells fishy." Today it is a good, clear fishing stream and smells a lot better than it did when residents pumped raw sewage into it.

James McClure and other early immigrants settled in the triangle of land between creek and river. Shortly before the end of the Revolution, Lieutenant Moses Van Campen, who married one of the McClure daughters, constructed

SEPT. 27, 1975

MAR. 18, 1936

1902

MAY 30, 1946

MAR. 13, 1936

APR. 2, 1960

⁀ *Dan Bauman, coordinator of Bloomsburg's flood protection project, discusses the town's high-water adventures at the flood marker between the Susquehanna River and Bloomsburg Airport. (Photo by Christine Brubaker.)*

McClure's Fort around the family's riverside property. The fortifications saw little action but provided a refuge for frightened settlers during tense times.

This area also figured in an abortive military maneuver during the Civil War. Rumors reached Union ears that Confederate sympathizers had built a major fort above the headwaters of Fishing Creek to command the approaches to North Mountain and control all the land between the Susquehanna's branches. To combat this so-called Fishing Creek Confederacy, a thousand soldiers moved into Bloomsburg in August 1864. They established a camp and parked two cannons on the Bloomsburg Fairgrounds, set just back from Fishing Creek's entry to the Susquehanna. One morning in early September, Major General George Cadwallader divided his little army into three columns and sent them scrambling up North Mountain to oust the insurgents. At the top, the columns met each other—and no one else. Cadwallader returned to Bloomsburg and proclaimed the Copperhead Rebellion a farce.

Since that summer of 1864, activities in the Susquehanna–Fishing Creek floodplain have been considerably less militant. The fairgrounds host one of Pennsylvania's largest and oldest agricultural expositions. The Town Park, forty-three acres along the Susquehanna, features one of the older and more pleasant riverside greens in the basin.

Several industries now operate in the floodplain. Magee Rieter Automotive Systems (generally known as Magee Carpet) is the largest, employing about 700 people to make carpet for cars. Bloomsburg's high school is here. So is its sewer plant. Several hundred homes line streets set back from the river.

Dan Bauman lives in one of these homes, on Third Street. His was the last house flooded in 1972 because Third Street runs uphill from here. The land continues to rise until it hits the heights, where Bloomsburg University students have the best view in town.

Flooding is a recurrent reality to the park, fairgrounds, carpet plant, Dan Bauman's house, and other low-lying areas of Bloomsburg. A flood in lower Bloomsburg, known as Scottown, actually constitutes two floods. The first high water washes down Fishing Creek, overflowing into Scottown on one side and Fernville, just outside Bloomsburg, on the other. Then a few hours or even days later the Susquehanna itself overflows, pushing Fishing Creek's waters upstream, and the river and creek flood Fernville and Scottown again. All this flooding is predictable. It has happened so often that Bloomsburg has created a map showing precisely which homes will get wet when the river reaches a certain flood stage.

Tropical Storm Agnes sent waters raging through much of Scottown and Fernville, causing damages of nearly $18 million. Hurricane Eloise provoked the Susquehanna and Fishing Creek to flood all the same places a little less deeply three years later. Concerned citizens then created the Fernville-Scottown Survival Committee.

Bauman, a foreman with a Bloomsburg construction company, had served as chairman of an area cleanup committee after Agnes. He took charge of the Survival Committee. The group coordinated removal of a sizable island that had been channeling Fishing Creek floodwaters into Scottown homes. The committee's further plan—to build a dike along Fishing Creek, and maybe extend it the whole way around the horseshoe and up along the Susquehanna—did not materialize. This project has been Bauman's obsession ever since.

For three decades he has promoted a levee to protect lower Bloomsburg. He boosted the levee as Bloomsburg's mayor and now he coordinates the town's flood protection project from his basement office. Decades of material related to floods and Bloomsburg and Bloomsburg in flood fill his large, often-flooded recreation room. "I'm getting burned out now and this is my last hurrah—getting this dike built," says the portly project director. "The corps finally concluded that we've got a flood problem, which I've been telling them for twenty-seven years, and we're doing a feasibility study. Everything is moving in the right direction."

Bloomsburg is the only large town on the Susquehanna between Wilkes-Barre and Sunbury without a flood protection wall. The Corps of Engineers first examined the possibility of building a levee at Bloomsburg after the 1936 flood and found that the project would not be cost effective. That is, the value of property to be protected from flooding did not equal the expense of providing that protection. Subsequent studies reached the same conclusion.

Several years ago, Magee Carpet added several hundred employees. Given those new workers, added to scores already working at Ore-Ira Foods and more than a thousand residents of Scottown, the corps's cost-ratio examination after the flood of 1996 finally worked in Bloomsburg's favor. The engineers recommended a $2.1 million feasibility study of a U-shaped flood-protection system, including an earthen levee along the Susquehanna and a concrete flood wall along Fishing Creek. If results of the study are positive and if Congress and the Bloomsburg Town Council agree, the project will go forward, with an estimated completion date of 2006. "The corps are perfectionists," says Bauman, explaining why this process will take so long. "They drive me up a wall, but they are good. Good and expensive, too." The projected cost of the levee is at least $15 million. Bauman suspects the project actually will cost several million dollars more than that. The town would pay 35 percent.

Like any flood mitigation project, the Bloomsburg proposal has complex implications. If floodwaters cannot expand into Scottown from Fishing Creek, they will wash with greater force into Fernville. So should the Fernville side of Fishing Creek also be walled, or should homes over there be raised on their foundations, or should they be razed and residents sent packing under a government buyout program? Some Fernville residents dislike all options. One of them wrote to the *Bloomsburg Press Enterprise* after Bloomsburg approved the feasibility study: "You know you're from Fernville, Pa., if your options in the current proposed Flood Plan are SINK or SWIM!"

Bauman and other levee promoters see more urgency to the situation since Wilkes-Barre raised its levee. "Once you've raised that levee, downstream has a problem because the flooding impact is much greater now," says George Turner, a member of the Bloomsburg Town Council and president of the Columbia County Historical Society. "It's not spreading upstream, it's spreading downstream."

No one has to convince residents of Scottown and Fernville of the problem. The frequency of flooding has increased over the years. Bauman's and Turner's figures show that thirteen floods occurred from 1936 to 1972—about one flood every two years and ten months. Between 1972 and 2000, high water covered the triangle between the Susquehanna and Fishing Creek eleven times—about one flood every two years and two months. Flooding has been exacerbated not only by upstream levees but by increased development in the floodplain, fewer wooded areas to soak up rain and snowmelt, and inadequate storm water management.

"Storm water management is the answer to flooding," says Bauman. "You'll never see it. The lobbying groups are too strong. It's the Realtors and the developers. They don't give a damn where they build. So we keep building in the floodplain and we keep building without holding water back."

While Bauman believes his pro-levee arguments outweigh any opposition, he and the town government are taking no chances. They hired a public relations firm to help sell the project, and they developed an answer to what may be the most pressing question of all: Why should residents who live on Bloomsburg's heights help pay the town's share of the levee bill when their homes do not require protection from rising water?

"The argument is this," says an activated Bauman. "The president of Magee Carpet says if we have another Agnes flood, the plant's gone: we'll never recuperate. So we lose seven hundred jobs. We lose that tax base. And the other thing is how many people down here don't have flood insurance. If they all get wiped out and if the government says we're not helping you out this time, who's going to pay for this? All Bloomsburg residents will pay. So everyone would benefit from a levee." Bauman pauses to consider the naysayers. "I would say there's probably twenty people that are the noisemakers and the rest of the people realize that it's for the good."

What is "for the good" of Bloomsburg generally has been acted on over the years. "Bloom" fancies itself a progressive town, with one of the better schools in the state university system, a renowned theater group, and a first-rate fair and riverside park. The town thrived in the nineteenth century because the Pennsylvania Canal and then the railroad followed the river, transporting metal products forged of iron drawn from nearby mountain deposits. Manufacture of textiles, including car carpets, kept the town going in the twentieth century, with most shipments moving by truck on Route 11.

Without the river and the transportation routes alongside it, Bloomsburg might be just another hick hamlet in the triangle of forests, farms, and crossroad villages between the North and West branches. Except for river communities, notably Bloomsburg, Danville, and Northumberland on the North Branch and Lewisburg on the West Branch, this region has few population centers.

Ascending in a hot-air balloon from Danville in the summer of 1842, the pioneering aeronaut John Wise viewed a wild landscape as he headed south. Someone taking that tour today would see much of what Wise saw, with the exception of development along the waterways. "The atmosphere was very hazy, which limited my prospect to an area of about 35 miles in diameter," Wise wrote in a letter to the *Berwick Sentinel*. "The confluence of the two branches of the Susquehanna, with the two bridges and the towns of Northumberland and Sunbury made a beautiful view. . . . The river was soon lost to my view by the intervention of the clouds, and the country beneath presented one vast wilderness as far as the eye could reach."

There is another way to approach the confluence—by way of the Long Reach of the West Branch, which begins gathering its waters along the Eastern Continental Divide in the coal regions of Cambria County.

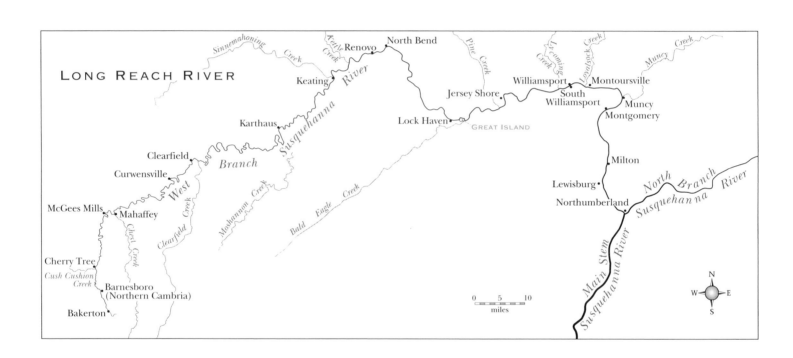

LONG REACH RIVER

North Bend

Renovo

Keating

Sinnemahoning *Creek*

Kettle *Creek*

Susquehanna *River*

Karthaus

Clearfield

Curwensville

West

Branch

Clearfield *Creek*

Moshannon *Creek*

McGees Mills

Mahaffey

Ghost *Creek*

Cherry Tree

Cush Cushion *Creek*

Barnesboro
(Northern Cambria)

Bakerton

Bald *Eagle* *Creek*

Lock Haven

Jersey Shore

GREAT ISLAND

Pine *Creek*

Lycoming *Creek*

Loyalsock *Creek*

Muncy *Creek*

Williamsport

South
Williamsport

Montoursville

Muncy

Montgomery

Milton

Lewisburg

Northumberland

North *Branch*

Susquehanna *River*

Main *Stem*

Susquehanna *River*

0 5 10
miles

N
W E
S

Long Reach River

The Headspring

In nature and in fact [the Susquehanna] is a vast flattened tree-form of water always in motion. It is forever being born from ten thousand springs at ten thousand points of birth in upland springs and initial mountain rills.

—H. M. Cummings, *Scots Breed and Susquehanna*

Water trickling from the West Branch's sources in Cambria County takes about four days to reach the confluence at Northumberland. Dick Davis explains where this journey begins: "When you're driving along Route 553, you can see it as plain as anything. You look to the north: that's Chesapeake water. You look to the south: that's Gulf of Mexico water."

On maps, you can tell where the watershed division known as the Eastern Continental Divide runs because no blue lines cross it. On land, you can tell where the divide runs because Route 553 (Ridge Road) follows it. Water headed for the West Branch and the Chesapeake trickles down the 2,100-foot-high ridge and moves north. Water headed for Blacklick Creek drains down that ridge to the south. The Blacklick feeds the Allegheny, which runs to the Ohio, the Mississippi, and the Gulf.

"All of the water on this side enters the West Branch, one way or another," says Davis, an affable Ebensburg educator turned businessman and active member of the Cambria County Historical Society. "You could pick any one of these springs or streams and say, well, this is the real one, this is the source. But the traditional headwaters of the Susquehanna are on land that used to belong to a farmer named Strittmatter. I've never heard anyone seriously dispute that."[1]

Faber Farabaugh never disputed it. In 1917, Farabaugh's father bought Andrew Strittmatter's farm. Along with the property came the story of the historical headspring of the West Branch. That spring currently lies smothered by road cinders in a grassy wetland where Faber Farabaugh used to plant oats.

"This was the beginning of the West Branch. This would be the furthest away from the Chesapeake. This was the headspring of the Susquehanna River," Farabaugh would say as he pointed out the traditional headspring to irregular visitors. Farabaugh died several years ago. His widow maintains their modest home along Route 219 just north of its juncture with Route 553, about a mile south of Carrolltown.

Before the spring began drying up in the early 1960s, the Farabaughs drank straight from it. In wet springs and summers, a small stream from the spring still runs from the depressed wetland through a culvert under Route 219. Channeled within a deep gully, it passes the faded-red Farabaugh barn and washes down the hill toward its rendezvous with the North Branch, 240 miles away. No water from any West Branch tributary travels more miles to Northumberland.

The spring waters are augmented by intermittent surface drainage from farther up the ridge, from the peak of the Continental Divide. During rainstorms, that water washes around the house of the Farabaughs' son, Fred, and past some volunteer apple trees into the grassy spring area.

Except with heaviest rains, the headspring of the West Branch is no more than a damp place in the grass. Fred and Debbie Farabaugh's children barely wet their shoes running through it. Several years ago, the family vacationed on the Chesapeake Bay at Annapolis, Maryland. "They thought it was amazing," Debbie Farabaugh says, laughing as she remembers the look on her kids' faces as they compared their puddle at home with the big bay. "That it starts here and ends up there—they thought that was amazing."

It is easy to locate this traditional headspring of the West Branch. It lies on the east side of Route 219, equidistant between the Brick Road intersection and a Pennsylvania Historical and Museum Commission marker dedicated to Dr. Lawrence F. Flick, an antituberculosis pioneer. A semipaved pulloff leads into the site. The spring lies in the tall grass about fifty feet back from the road.

After cinders fouled that spring, Faber Farabaugh used another that originates on the barn side of Route 219. The flow from the second spring strengthened as the headspring weakened. Farabaugh installed a small concrete reservoir to hold enough water for his family. They drink it straight out of the ground and so do the cows. The cows stand downstream a bit, in a ditch washed out by water from the second spring when it floods.

A few hundred yards southwest on the Farabaugh property lies a third source of West Branch water. Until the Pennsylvania Railroad punched a tunnel underneath Route 219 early in the twentieth century, the third source did not exist. Now that stream, unleashed by tunnel excavation, flows with more volume than either the headspring or second spring.

In the mid-1980s, the *Pittsburgh Press* published an article called "The River That Has Its Head in the Mouth of a Tunnel." The *National Geographic*'s March 1985 story on the Susquehanna also spread the notion that the West Branch issues from a manufactured hole in the ground.

"That tickles me," Farabaugh said of the tunnel claim. "That's not natural: it's manmade water. And the tunnel's not as far from the Chesapeake as the headspring. We never considered that the source." Still, he conceded, nobody expected water to flow out of that railroad tunnel, so the novelty opening has attracted more interest than the cindered headspring. "Water's a funny thing," Farabaugh concluded. "You can never quite tell where it's going. It's unpredictable."

West Branch Susquehanna Rescue decided not to select a single source when it erected a sign to mark the "Home of the Headwaters" several years ago. The environmental group placed an impressive redwood marker next to Soup 'r Sundaes, just south of the Farabaugh property on Route 219. Diplomatically, rather than definitively, the marker reads: "This site is near several springs that mark the beginning of the West Branch of the Susquehanna River."

🐟   *The Susquehanna's West Branch rises from a wet place in the grass, once an active spring, on the property of Fred and Debbie Farabaugh in Cambria County. Debbie stands with her children, Dana and Luke, at the edge of the wetland. The camera looks west toward the West Branch Valley. (Photo by Christine Brubaker.)*

Bakerton Reservoir

A huge reservoir was constructed for the Bakerton Water Company in the summer of 1920 at a cost of approximately $100,000. A pipe line from the reservoir to the town was laid and a dozen or more fire plugs were placed throughout the town, thus giving citizens of Bakerton ample fire protection such as they never had before.

—Mary Frances Inzana in Bakerton's centennial history, 1989

WESTERN PENNSYLVANIANS CALL ALL LONG STREAMS that issue from springs "cricks." They call shorter streams "runs," although runs may be wider and deeper than cricks. Most Cambria County residents call the early miles of the Susquehanna's West Branch, which is fed by several good-sized runs, "the crick."[2]

Asked where the crick begins, many Cambrians, if they have any idea at all, will say "near Carrolltown." Some will say "near Bakerton"—a village that, unlike Carrolltown, actually lies along the crick a couple of miles north of its source springs. Some will say "near Elmora." Elmora is the name—no one knows why—of the post office in Bakerton.

And then a few locals will say that the West Branch of the Susquehanna River flows out of the Bakerton Reservoir. The Bakerton Reservoir collects all water that drains north from the Continental Divide into the West Branch valley, pipes out a supply for Bakerton-area fire plugs and kitchen spigots, and releases the rest as the West Branch. It could be said that the Bakerton Reservoir is the most obvious source of the West Branch, just as Lake Otsego, on a considerably larger scale, is the most obvious source of the North Branch.

Approximately 400 by 800 feet, the reservoir originally held up to 12 million gallons of water behind a 28-foot-high concrete dam. Two streams drain some fifty-eight acres to fill the reservoir. One of these streams is the West Branch, flowing from the headwaters on the Faber Farabaugh farm. The other is a smaller, nameless stream issuing from a spring just north and east of the headspring. This water runs through a pipe from the reservoir to an adjacent filtra-tion plant and on to Bakerton and nearby communities in West Carroll and Barr townships. While many area residents have their own wells, more than four hundred families use water from the reservoir. The filtration system, a simple affair but state of the art when it was completed in 1986, adds chlorine to kill bacteria and coagulant to separate dirt particles from the stream. As the water warms in summer, plant operators use potassium permanganate to scrub out excessive amounts of iron and manganese.

"Generally, the water quality's pretty good," says Bob Frazier, West Carroll Township's primary handyman and water guru. "If we get a heavy rain, I have to do some fooling around to get the turbidity out. The iron and manganese are coming from the old mines, but that's not a major problem anymore. We get a lot of agricultural runoff. It's all fields up through there and you can see channels from runoff. We get dirt and manure in the reservoir and then I add more coagulant."

Would Frazier drink water straight from the reservoir, without treating it?

"At certain times, it wouldn't be so bad. There's a lot of people go down to these springs that aren't any good and they'll take that water because they don't like the chlorine we put in the water. DEP says those springs are filled with bacteria, so they're no good, but a lot of people have adjusted to that bacteria." Frazier looks off toward the source streams. "We drink water right out of the crick when we're out hunting, but we can't let that water go downtown."

Sometimes nature does not let the water go downtown. During periodic droughts in the 1990s, says Bill Jones, a former West Carroll Township supervisor and Water Authority member, the main problem was not the quality of the water coming out of the springs but its quantity. Jones worked closely with Frazier when the drought of 1993 nearly dried up all sources. Ordinarily two feet wide where it enters the reservoir, the West Branch dwindled to six inches that summer. The reservoir level dropped below the pipe that feeds the treatment plant, so the township paid the U.S. Army to haul in water and piped in more from Carrolltown's wells.

Unlike New York, which regulates the amount of water issuing from Otsego into the North Branch, Pennsylvania does not require a minimum flow from the Bakerton Reservoir. "We're supposed to keep as much water coming down as possible," says Jones, "but if it's not there, it's not there. The Chesapeake Bay didn't get any water from us in September of '93."

In 1997 the state Department of Environmental Protection declared the old dam unsafe and told West Carroll Township to abandon it or rebuild its cracking breast. The township did not have the resources to do either. With DEP's reluctant approval, the township lowered most of the breast by five feet. That measure reduced the threat of dam failure. It also reduced the amount of water the reservoir can hold. In addition to the five feet taken off the top, accumulated silt has removed about ten to twelve feet of storage space at the bottom. The fill has cut the reservoir's effective capacity to about 3 to 4 million gallons—a third or less of the original capacity. The township had to ration water during the drought of 1998. "When

we're not in a drought, the supply is adequate," comments Joan Shrenkle, secretary of the township's water authority. "We're on a metering program now. When people are aware they have to pay for it, they watch the amount of water they use."

The water authority plans to rebuild the dam to DEP specifications with federal and state grants and to dredge out the silt. That project would increase capacity and reduce the likelihood that Bakerton residents would have to drink brown water or take "mud showers." It would ensure use of the crick as the area's primary water supply for decades to come.

Barnesboro

You should be here. This place is all coal.

—A Barnesboro man writing to his brother, 1907

FED BY FOX RUN FROM THE EAST and Browns Run from the other side, the West Branch widens substantially before it cuts through Spangler and Barnesboro, adjacent mining villages recently combined as Northern Cambria. Here inflow from Walnut, Porter, and Gardner runs further expands the river's straight shot through town. The channel was considerably more crooked before the flood of 1936 abruptly straightened it out.

Nearly twenty-five miles of tributary streams feed the first ten miles of the West Branch. Many of them are naturally alkaline and so partially offset acid from abandoned coal mines. Walnut Run, in fact, hosts a thriving trout fishery.

But fish generally do not live in the West Branch itself—all the way through Cambria County. "A few suckers can live in that water, but there's no fisheries population here," says Chris McDevitt, Cambria's waterways conservation officer. "I don't recall anyone fishing in the West Branch in Cambria County."

Barnesboro was named for its first major coal miner and fish killer. Beginning in the early 1890s, Thomas Barnes and Alfred Tucker, an investor, extracted millions of tons of "black diamonds" from beneath this land. They laid tracks along the river and sent their treasure to heat steel mill furnaces in Johnstown and to fire the boilers of steam locomotives chugging out from Pittsburgh. Barnes and Tucker opened many of their two dozen productive mines immediately on the banks of the Susquehanna or its tributaries.

Bituminous coal underlies nearly half of the West Branch's total drainage area, including much of Cambria, Clearfield, and Clinton counties, so Barnes and Tucker and subsequent mining companies had plenty to haul to the surface until well into the twentieth century. Miners dug many of these mines on an upslope so that water from them naturally drained directly into the river and its tributaries. The entire West Branch began paying for the fast development of the coal industry as slugs of acid, propelled by heavy rainstorms, washed down the river. Sometimes the overwhelming influx of acid killed fish all the way to Northumberland.

Major periodic acid spills continued to pollute the entire West Branch well past the middle of the twentieth century. Rick Sprout, the canoeist who lives downstream near Muncy, remembers swimming in an acidic West Branch in the 1960s: "After a big rain up at Clearfield, we would get a two- or three-day-long aqua-green slug of mine acid. You knew it was coming because you could actually look down and see the river change color. It would last for a day, two days, three days, and then the river would get cloudy again."

Although the acid irritated their eyes and skin, Sprout and his friends went snorkeling during slugs. They rowed a boat until they spotted something interesting on the river bottom. Then they dived in and snorkeled around. "The water was transparent during a slug," says Sprout. "You could see twenty feet to the bottom of the river. It was perfect for snorkeling. You still get that clarity upstream from Lock Haven, but down at Muncy, it's not as bad as it used to be."

Deep mining contributed much of the acid to these slugs; later strip mining, often right up to the edge of streams, added more. "During the Second World War, they stripped in this area because the guys said that anything that was black you could sell," says James J. McDermott, a Clearfield resident and past president of the Clearfield Historical Society. "Unlike today, there was very little restriction on getting the coal out of the ground. What you did with the water and everything from the mines was not controlled. We had a lot of mine drainage. We had no fish in the river."

The state did not seriously enforce laws prohibiting coal pollution in waterways until 1970, when it targeted Lancashire 15, a large mine stretching out from the west bank of the West Branch in North Bakerton. The Barnes and Tucker Coal Company had sealed that mine in the spring of 1969, but water seeped in nonetheless, and the company said it could not afford to pump out and neutralize it. As the mine reached the overflow point over the next year, environmentalists and editorial writers railed. The state threatened. Maintaining that its mining permit predated state pollution regulations, Barnes and Tucker ignored the warnings. In June 1970, acidic water broke out of the mine. A million gallons a day washed down the West Branch, killing fish for 200 miles. Environmentalists railed some more and the state threatened again. Barnes and Tucker sat tight, and when the state began to neutralize the overflow with lime, the coal company refused to repay the costs.

Pennsylvania sued. After lengthy legalities, the Pennsylvania Supreme Court upheld the state in 1977, supposedly settling for all time who is primarily responsible for cleaning up coal pollution.

Until recently, Barnes and Tucker treated 7 to 9 million gallons of water a day from this vast mine, part of which extends well over into the neighboring Allegheny watershed. Because the company has not mined coal for years and has earned only modest amounts from leasing coal reserves to other operators, it ran out of money and went bankrupt in 2001. So the state has inherited the water-treatment problem after all. State mine acid mitigators pump water from Lancashire 15, seven miles through mine tunnels, neutralize it with lime, and run it into a tributary of the Allegheny River. Thus West Branch water winds up in the Gulf of Mexico, where, according to Barnes and Tucker's last president, Al Wenturine, it improves the water quality.

🖎 Enormous "bony dumps" of waste coal are the most prominent reminder that bituminous coal was once Cambria County's lifeblood. Here the West Branch winds past the million-ton Barnes-Watkins refuse pile in North Bakerton. Acid mine drainage turns the water a bright orange-brown, while "red dog," or burned coal, streaks the bony dump. (Photo by Christine Brubaker.)

"Right now, I believe that the water, even untreated with lime, would be of benefit to the Susquehanna River," Wenturine says. He is sitting in his spare office in Ebensburg, where he managed the last fourteen employees of a company that had 1,600 workers as late as 1982. "That water is alkaline, not acidic. Its pH level is high. Needless to say, the environmental people of Pennsylvania don't necessarily agree with me."

Getting down on his knees on the office floor, Wenturine unrolls a large map of all the old mines in the Bakerton-Barnesboro area. Diagonal lines on this map indicate mining areas. The whole map is covered with diagonal lines. All of these mines are connected, so water runs in from other mines that no longer have caretakers. "This is all flooded," Wenturine says, sweeping his hand across the map. "It's one big, massive lake underground. That's a tremendous reservoir of water. If I pulled another map out, you'd see more down here—and more out this way." Some of the water in this subterranean pool may be alkaline, but much will turn acidic. If it reached the West Branch, it would kill anything left to kill.

As Barnes and Tucker exhausted its revenues treating an old problem, Pennsylvania also spent millions trying to mitigate the effects of acid mine drainage in other sections of the abandoned lake of mines in Cambria and other bituminous areas. As with clean-up efforts in the anthracite fields, results have been mixed.

The state terms the West Branch intermittently degraded from its sources all the way to the mouth of Chest Creek in Clearfield County. Periodic sections of good-quality water shelter surprising fish populations outside Cambria. Smallmouth bass thrive around Cherry Tree, and Chest Creek adds alkalinity that greatly improves the quality of water running the whole way from there to Clearfield. Stocked trout thrive upstream of Clearfield, but from there on, for more than a hundred miles, toxic mine drainage kills most fish and nearly everything else. Clearfield Creek is

the first major tributary that provides a daily rush of acid from abandoned deep mines. Other prime acid conveyers include the Sinnemahoning Creek and its Bennett's Branch. The worst of all is twenty-six-mile-long Moshannon Creek, nicknamed Red Mo, after the color of its stained streambed.

All these streams, clear as chlorinated pool water, run over bright-orange rock. Natives who travel outside the region are surprised to find flowing water with color and submerged rocks without. Contrarily, nonnative canoeists are amazed to see the bottoms of their paddles and the bottom of the river—but not one minnow or a spot of algae.

The quality of West Branch water changes fast after Bald Eagle Creek's entry. That creek and its tributaries, flowing northeast through limestone beds, contribute sufficient alkalinity to neutralize most of the acid running down the West Branch from Bakerton and Barnesboro and Clearfield. Life returns to the river: it turns green (or brown with runoff), fish begin to thrive, and by the time it reaches Jersey Shore, just downstream from the entry of limestone-rich Antes Creek, the West Branch has recovered completely and supports a healthy bass population.

Shortly after Ted Clista began monitoring water quality for the state in 1967, he received a letter from a man who had just canoed the West Branch from its upper reaches to Northumberland. The paddler complained because the river looked "clear" enough above Lock Haven but appeared "dirty" below that point. He wondered why DER could not "clean up" the lower section of the West Branch so it would be as appealing as the upper part of the course.

"He had it precisely backwards," says Clista. "He was admiring the damage from acid mine drainage."

Canoe Place

To see the phenomena of the water and see the earth from the *water side,* to stand outside of it on another element, and so to get a pry on it in thought at least, that is no small advantage. . . . I vastly increase my sphere and experience by a boat.

—Henry David Thoreau, *Journal,* March 25, 1860

Along a bank of Cush Cushion Creek, within a few yards of its juncture with the West Branch at Cherry Tree, Indiana County, stands what may be the most unusual monument along the Susquehanna. Topped by a weather vane, a simple granite obelisk marks Canoe Place and the site of the landmark wild black cherry tree. After the French surrendered sovereignty over their land east of Pittsburgh to the English in 1758, the heirs of William Penn purchased millions of acres in western Pennsylvania from the Iroquois. On the West Branch, the limits of this purchase ran from the mouth of Tiadaughton (now Pine) Creek to the black cherry tree.

R. Dudley Tonkin, a Cherry Tree native, summarizes the conditions of this purchase in *My Partner, the River:* "The Penns were to have the territory on the north and west side of the West Branch to a point where a canoe would strike bottom at a canoeing stage of water. The waters of Cush Cushion Creek entering from the west had widened the river and had thrown up a gravel bar across it. The canoes paddled upriver struck bottom on this gravel bar."

At this Canoe Place, Native Americans portaged over to Diamondville on Two Lick Creek, some ten miles to the west. Then they paddled down Two Lick to its junction with Blacklick Creek. The Blacklick leads to the Conemaugh River, which joins the Kiskiminetas River, which runs into the Allegheny at Freeport. So the cherry tree at Canoe Place marked the location at which water transportation on the West Branch ended and the most direct land transportation to the Allegheny watershed began.

When officials surveyed the future counties of Cambria, Clearfield, and Indiana in 1803–4, the cherry tree assumed further significance as a corner boundary marker for all three—until, about 1837, a flood washed away the landmark. Continuing erosion and Pennsylvania Railroad construction severely altered the course of the West Branch, moving it east and letting the mouth of Cush Cushion Creek take over the old river channel. The builders of the memorial obelisk in 1894 placed it on the cherry tree's original site, now along the Cush Cushion, not the West Branch.

After several ferocious Cush Cushion floods that damaged homes in the vicinity, the state constructed a massive levee along the creek in the mid-1990s. The earthen levee keeps the memorial obelisk dry, but residents must climb on top of the ten-foot-high barrier to see the Cush Cushion at all.

Raftmen assemble for a photograph in 1896 on the last six commercial rafts to leave Cherry Tree. The recently erected obelisk commemorated the site of the black cherry tree that had marked the place upstream of which canoes or rafts could not pass except in highest water. Notice the enormous raft paddles. (Lycoming County Historical Society and Thomas T. Taber Museum, Williamsport, Pennsylvania.)

The West Branch here runs perhaps thirty feet wide and not much deeper than its tributary. Massive levees also line the river. As upstream development drives floodwaters ever higher, the state has raised the levees. High water through Cherry Tree now runs out of sight but many feet above the little town. In seasons of average precipitation, however, this section of the West Branch barely carries enough water to float a boat, so most modern canoe journeys begin well downstream of Cherry Tree, at Clearfield.

The Wild West Branch is so designated largely because of

the isolated, relatively unpopulated hundred-mile stretch from just east of Clearfield to just west of Lock Haven. Since the decline of the lumber and coal industries, the population of this area has dwindled. You can drive for half an hour along back roads through these woods and not pass another car or see more than a handful of houses.

This isolation is one of the West Branch's attractions. Another is the nature of the river itself: it generally rolls along at a more rapid clip than the North Branch and boasts significantly more white water; but few places on the river test a paddler during normal flows. A spring canoe trip down the West Branch can be exciting enough to maintain a paddler's interest but sufficiently uncomplicated to be relaxing.

"This is the reach that makes the West Branch such a treasure," writes Edward Gertler of canoeing from Clearfield to Lock Haven in *Keystone Canoeing*. "As big rivers go, this ranks as a wild one. Recognizing this quality, many paddlers take along their gear and camp out along the way. Numerous grassy benches and, at the mouths of side canyons, hemlock groves make fine campsites."

Canoeists beginning a trip at Clearfield encounter several water hazards. Treated Clearfield sewage mingles with yellow acid water flowing down Clearfield Creek to create a killer blend. Moreover, below the dam of the coal-fired Shawville Station, the discharged water can reach 120°F on summer days and will burn the feet of canoeists walking through the shallows.

After Shawville, the scenery turns wilder. Between Karthaus, where Mosquito Creek spills in from its picturesque gorge, and the Sinnemahoning Creek at Keating lies the most scenic reach on the Susquehanna. Along the twenty-five miles between these tiny villages, once major coal and timber centers, no highway follows the river. The only way most people can see this part of the West Branch is by water.

Pennsylvania's premier river writer, Tim Palmer, writes in *Rivers of Pennsylvania:* "Karthaus is at the head of the West Branch Canyon, a section of the river with vast complexes of ridge lines, ravines and shadows. Forming a rugged gorge, layers of forested mountains are seemingly set one upon another as winding waters unfold view after towering view." Elsewhere, Palmer has said this West Branch "canyon" provides Pennsylvania's only competition for the wildest section of his favorite river, the Youghiogheny.

The Karthaus-Keating run might have been lost forever if a Corps of Engineers flood-control project had been constructed at Keating. The engineers began studying a Keating Dam in 1934 and by 1976 projected that a structure 400 feet high, creating a fifty-mile-long reservoir, would cost $700 million. Too much, concluded the corps, thereby preserving the West Branch Valley for canoes and kayaks.

Clearfield Boy Scouts created the most detailed guide to canoeing the West Branch in 1967. The six-day tour specifies prime overnight camping spots along the eighty-mile course between Clearfield and North Bend. O. Lynn Frank, Scout leader and state timber management official, wrote a forty-page booklet describing this tour, followed by many groups and individuals besides Scouts. Lynn called his tour the Chinklacamoose Wilderness Canoe Trip, after an aboriginal village sited where the old rafting and lumbering town of Clearfield now stands.

Clearfield

ALL PEOPLE THAT ON EARTH DO DWELL

SPEAK SOFTLY—TREAD LIGHTLY

TO HONOR THE RAFTMEN—THE LOGGERS

THEIR MOTHERS AND WIVES

OF PENN'S WOODS

CARRY ON

—Inscription on a granite marker erected by
R. Dudley Tonkin at Cherry Tree in 1955

WHEN CLEARFIELD REBUILT ITS OLD TIMBER dam, the town consulted R. Dudley Tonkin for specifications. Tonkin had made his first West Branch tour with his log-rafting father, Vincent, in 1888. He had then spent his life selling and planting trees and chronicling the history of logging and timber rafting on the Susquehanna. Tonkin probably knew more about rafting and how to build a timber dam than anyone else living in the middle of the twentieth century.

The original Clearfield dam held water high for rafting; the replacement, called the R. Dudley Tonkin Memorial Timber Dam, holds back the carp and suckers and sunfish that have adjusted to the West Branch's acidified water until they can be hooked by Clearfield anglers.

"It's built so that rafts will go down over it without taking anything out," explains James McDermott at the Clearfield Historical Society, a mid-Victorian building that overlooks one of the Witmer parks, just upstream from the dam. "It's sort of a gentle slope over the top and down the other side so that the logs could go over smoothly even without high water."

McDermott's grandfather, a contemporary of Vincent Tonkin, rafted out of Clearfield. He cut wood from autumn to March and took it downstream with the spring's high water. Many families in Cherry Tree and Clearfield have ancestors who worked as woodsmen and raftmen. Some of them worked in the coal mines instead of the forest in winter, but a large number of them rode rafts or drove logs downstream with the flood.

"Few of those loggers lived to be very old, you know," says McDermott. "Life was hard. They lived to thirty-five or forty years old—that was about as much of this work as you could take." Some people say there are no photographs of smiling loggers because loggers had nothing to smile about.

Early settlers cut timber (a term soon corrupted into "lumber," which originally designated an excessive amount of timber) in the seemingly endless Appalachian forests of the West and North Branch basins. They cut wood to clear the land and so that they and their neighbors could build and burn. The first sawmills supplied wood for frontier homes and barns. But entrepreneurs soon discovered a rich market for wood, especially white pine, downstream, where the forests were not so prolific.

During most of the nineteenth century, and especially during its middle decades, millions of rough logs and millions of board feet of finished lumber moved southward by

⚬ *Workmen sort logs, preparing to drive them down Pine Creek to the West Branch in the spring of 1908. Notice the raft with a large shed, probably sleeping quarters for loggers. (Lycoming County Historical Society and Thomas T. Taber Museum, Williamsport, Pennsylvania.)*

way of the cheapest and most efficient transportation available: the river and its tributaries. Thousands of lumber rafts and innumerable individual logs floated to river ports in southern Pennsylvania or Maryland each spring. Many of them traveled to Marietta, where wagons and later railroads conveyed their wood to Lancaster and Philadelphia. Others continued to Port Deposit. Some floated all the way to the Chesapeake, where steamboats tugged them to Baltimore and other bay ports.

White pine became the masts of sailing ships, the beams of Victorian homes, and the foundations from which many East Coast cities and towns arose. To say that early America was built of white pine is barely an exaggeration, as anyone who has examined the construction of extant eighteenth-

and nineteenth-century homes knows. Not only was pine wood plentiful, especially in the vast, thick forests of western and northern Pennsylvania, but it is one of the most versatile of all building materials. White pine is straight and strong enough to weather sea winds or support the weight of many people, but light enough to be cut easily and to float readily. It is durable, whether hot or cold, wet or dry: it rarely warps or rots. The supply of white pine seemed as limitless as the demand, and so the largest lumber industry the world had yet seen developed in and near the West Branch Valley.

Some of these virgin trees had been standing for 200, even 300 years. They had grown up to 150 and more feet tall and measured up to 40 and more inches wide at the base. Builders favored the tallest trees, whether or not they used the entire length. So when timbermen felled the trees, they examined each specimen, marked the straightest length, and abandoned the rest. The waste, at first, was enormous.

The operation was loud. "When the work was fairly started," wrote A. T. Brewer of tree cutting, "the noise was something like a Gettysburg battle. The tall pine came down with a resounding crash producing a cloud of snow and debris, leaving the smaller trees in its wake (not swept to the ground) swaying and swishing like the sound of shells and solid shot. These crashes following each other at short intervals during the day made a terrific roar and seemed to shake the earth."

Using axes and crosscut saws, timbermen cut trees closest to the river and its tributaries to minimize hauling distances. They peeled the bark from most logs so they could be hauled more easily on land and would glide over obstructions in water. Teams of horses "skidded" these logs to the water on slides made of hardwood logs or on sleds over snow. Workers assembled the logs in enormous piles on the banks of streams at places called rafting grounds. There they made rafts (a labor called "rafting in") in expectation of the spring thaw and high water.

Timbermen assembled all rafts essentially in the same way, whether they were "spar rafts" constructed of the longest, straightest logs designed for ship masts; or "timber rafts," made of smaller, squared logs cut for more general building use, or "lumber rafts," collections of logs that already had been milled.

The West Branch historian Lewis E. Theiss, who frequently visited lumber camps and made four trips down the river on log rafts, explained the process: "Imagine fifteen lead pencils laid side by side and held together by two wires, one crosswise near each end of the section, stapled to each log. Then imagine several such sections laid end to end, and the whole fastened together. In effect, such was a log raft. As log rafts had to go through several chutes in the canal dams, their width was thereby limited. They were commonly twenty-eight feet wide, to fit the width of the chutes they must run—and 150 to 200 feet long."

First, the raftmen had to get their construction into the water and floating downstream. This task ordinarily was no problem on the river itself, which carried abundant water in spring, but it could be difficult on the small tributary creeks where most of the timbering was done. Here timbermen constructed "splash dams" to control water flow. They formed these dams of logs and earth, much like General Clinton's temporary dam on the North Branch at Cooperstown. Raftmen placed their crafts in the stream below these dams, opened crudely fashioned gates, and rode the flood from tributary to river and downstream. Remnants of these dams remain in several creeks.

Single rafts or "fleets" of two joined rafts had an oar mounted in a block of wood at either end. The oar stems were customarily fifty feet long and the blades sixteen feet long. To dip one of these giant poles required a man to hold its stem well overhead. Turning a raft by pushing a heavy oar across the deck caused enormous pressure on the small of the back. A quick turn in a narrow section of water often required three men on each oar, and so rafts generally carried crews of six to ten.

Unless held back by a headwind, rafts moved faster than the current because of their weight. Raftmen could make a trip from Clearfield to Marietta in three to four days under the best conditions and traveling through the night, but this journey required an expert pilot and a crew willing to run a few risks to get past rapids and over dams in short order.

Rafting pilots memorized the water and manned the front oar. They often specialized in sections of river. Rather than one pilot taking a raft all the way to the Chesapeake, several might divide the job. Challenges on the Lower Susquehanna included rapids, rocks, sharp turns, and channels that, courtesy of flooding and erosion, changed nearly every season. If a raft ran up on a rock or hit a bridge pier, raftmen said it was "stoved"—a condition that occasionally plagued even the most expert pilot. Such an accident often

did more harm to rafters' bodies than to the pliable raft.

Raftmen lived colorful lives and wore colorful clothes, including red and blue shirts. They cut a hole in the seat of their checked trousers so a patch of bright shirt would show through. Most sported mustaches. Some wore bearskin caps. Many drank copious amounts of alcohol. They were quick to take up a fight or help a friend. They were an exceptional group of men, especially in view of their abysmal pay.

Several of Pennsylvania's governors had been raftmen. William Bigler, who served as the state's chief executive in the 1850s, earlier had ridden rafts from Clearfield to Harrisburg and was known throughout the region as the "Clearfield Raftman."

The most significant entrepreneur of the West Branch lumber industry was John Patchin of Curwensville, a town just upstream from Clearfield. Beginning in the 1830s, Patchin, "the Spar King," purchased some 40,000 acres of trees along the West Branch. Dudley Tonkin said Patchin had the ability to "smell" good pine. He dispatched hundreds of timber rafts and employed hundreds of raftmen.

Some unexceptional men plagued the industry, including "Bumble Bee" Askey, so named because he hummed tunes instead of singing them. During the rafting season, Askey and his gang would plant a block and tackle in the river at Moshannon Falls, below Karthaus, and wait for the trap to snag a passing raft and lodge it in the rocks. Then the scammers would amble down to the river, uncover the block and tackle and pull the raft free—for a price.

The most famous West Branch river man was Cherry Tree Joe McCreery, who was born just after the nineteenth century began and nearly finished it out. McCreery started running the river in the 1820s, when the first timber rafts floated out of the headwaters towns of Cherry Tree and Burnside and McGees Mills. Standing 6 feet 5 inches tall, McCreery was known for his prodigious strength and dexterity. He has been called Pennsylvania's Paul Bunyan, and some Cherry Tree Joe stories are patently Bunyanesque.

Though it has been said that McCreery's raft ran over and ruined the wild cherry tree in his hometown and that he once single-handedly lifted a timber raft clear of an obstruction, set it down in safe water, and jumped aboard, rafting was not his primary occupation. He spent more time driving free-floating logs. "Rafters are sissies. They will not get their feet wet," Cherry Tree Joe told John S. Fisher, another rafter who would become a governor. "I have been up to my waist in coldest water day and night every spring and fall for forty years."

McCreery not only preferred driving logs, a practice that came into its own later than rafting and grew into a far bigger business, but he was the most proficient "jam cracker." He broke a seven-mile jam of loose logs at the mouth of Chest Creek about 1875, when he was some seventy years old, by locating the key log and, in effect, pulling the plug.

McCreery and other early drivers guided logs along streams too small for rafts to a sawmill or a place where they could be lashed together. On the river itself, rafts ruled until the middle of the nineteenth century because rafting was safer and less likely to lose drifting logs, and it required fewer workers.

But in the late 1840s John Leighton, a woodsman from Maine, persuaded a fellow New Englander and Williamsport transplant, James Perkins, to finance the Susquehanna Boom Company. The company built the first boom to snare floating logs at Williamsport in 1851. Lock Haven and other large lumber centers soon built their own booms. Booms reduced risk and payroll costs by ensuring that loose river logs would not float out of reach of their owners. So logging replaced rafting as the predominant form of timber transportation on the West Branch.

Hundreds of 20-by-40-foot timber cribs, each 22 feet high, anchored the Susquehanna Boom. Boom builders sank these cribs, filled with rocks and linked by iron chains, at fifty-foot intervals along a nine-mile diagonal line across the current.[3] They tied huge floating logs to each other and to the cribs to form a wall in the water. This log wall stopped all wood moving down the river.

The Susquehanna Boom stretched upriver from the river's southern shore, against Bald Eagle Mountain, through a level stretch of water known as the Long Reach, to Quenshukeny Creek at Linden. At the head of the boom at Linden, the last crib stood about 100 feet from the north shore. A "shear boom" log, reaching from this crib nearly to the riverbank, channeled logs into the Long Reach holding pond. A "fly boom," extending the few remaining feet from the sheer boom to the northern shore, served as a gate to allow timber rafts to pass through the boom.

Each spring, as the last ice melted and loggers prepared to launch their winter's cut of pine toward the river, workers chained boom logs together on the diagonal. "Boom's hung, let the logs come," cried the boom operators, and timbermen began floating their logs from upstream.

A full boom held hundreds of thousands of densely packed logs. A logger could walk for miles on floating wood. Until logs could be moved to sawmills or on downstream to another boom or to markets on the Lower Susquehanna, owners identified them by stamping or branding each end. "Boom rats" sorted the logs by brand. The boom operators charged timber companies to haul their logs out of the river for milling or to store them for later use.

The transition from rafting to log driving radically changed the timber industry and the West Branch landscape. R. Dudley Tonkin explained: "The two systems can be shown by a present-day agricultural comparison. The raftsman in the woods, to cut his product, can be likened to a man in a corn field selecting the finest stalks without cutting or destroying the lesser stalks. The logger enters the forest and cuts clean, as an eight-foot binder in a wheat field. In other words, clear cutting."

Lumber driving and the booms helped propel Pennsylvania to the forefront of lumber-producing states in 1860 and 1870 and maintained the state's position as one of the primary lumber producers until the end of the century. The new methods also speeded deforestation, provoking increased erosion and flooding.

If rafting was dangerous, log driving could be close to suicidal. As soon as ice began to break from the streams in spring, drivers started moving their merchandise to the river. Their boot heels held inch-long spikes, called calks or corks, so they could ride icy logs and jump from one log to another in swift currents. They carried iron canthooks for hooking and moving the ends of logs, and pikes to propel them through the water. One slip could be fatal in a waterway crowded with heavy logs.

Gibson Antes watched log drivers on the Susquehanna at Williamsport between 1884 and 1894. Echoing Joe McCreery, he said in a 1962 interview: "They were real *men*, because those men would go into the water, ice cold water possibly in March, as soon as the floods came, and would be in ice cold water possibly up to their waists, maybe a whole day. And they claim that those men slept in the clothes that they wore. They wore heavy woolen underclothes, and they lay down and slept in them."

Log drivers were showmen, as James Mitchell reported in his *Lumbering and Rafting in Clearfield County:* "Along the towns on the river the drive caused great excitement among the children, and their elders gathered on the river bank to see the sights. Many of the loggers would perform on the logs for the onlookers and many of them would ride a single log down stream."

Solving a log jam was one of the riskiest jobs. The year before McCreery loosed the logs on Chest Creek, the most famous jam ever stopped all river traffic dead at Lock Haven. A large raft got wedged in the town dam's chute. Before long, two canal boats, more than two hundred other rafts, and tens of thousands of loose logs blocked the channel upstream and jammed the river from bank to bank. Running beneath and overtop each other, an estimated 30 million board feet of logs eventually piled up to a sixteen-foot height. The jam held back the current, which then exerted terrific pressure on the logs. By carefully manipulating logs and rafts, Joe Colbert and a crew of sixty men eventually broke the mass of lumber, which then floated down to the boom at Williamsport.

Log driving also was dangerous initially because raftmen opposed it. Loggers not only took work from raftmen by transporting timber more cheaply but, when they could get away with it, delayed river traffic and then charged raftmen for passing through their booms. Raftmen rebelled, especially on Clearfield Creek, one of the primary rafting tributaries. In the spring of 1857, raftmen attacked loggers at Salmon Hole. They shot several men, destroyed the loggers' camp, and drove iron spikes into their logs, which could wreck saws at the mills. That convinced loggers to abandon Clearfield Creek, but the law favored log drivers and they succeeded elsewhere.

In 1883, the Susquehanna Boom held 1,874,655 logs, its peak performance. One-quarter of these trees were not white pines. Lumbermen were logging out the pine forests by the late 1870s, so they began clear-cutting hemlock. Inferior to pine as a building material, hemlock until that time had been tapped primarily for its bark, which contained acid used in the tanning process. Now it would be used as a substitute for pine.

Stands of hemlock always exceeded pine in the West Branch Valley, so the lumber industry received a boost until the end of the century. While loggers cut more trees, however, the number of logs in the boom gradually declined as logging railroads took over transport. With remaining pine

and hemlock trees standing farther and farther from water, running rails into the logging camps made more and more sense.

By early in the twentieth century, even railroads could not reach big old coniferous trees because they did not exist. What Joseph Dudley Tonkin, R. Dudley Tonkin's son, called the "Great Take Away" was complete. The greed of the timber industry and an insatiable demand for its products had combined to cut down an estimated 200 billion board feet of Penn's Woods. By 1908, the state's forest cover had been reduced to 30 percent. The Susquehanna Basin's percentage was probably less than that. Whole mountains had been stripped of trees.

Early travelers along the West Branch had found dense, dark forests covering virtually all of the land. Several referred to the valley as the Dismal Vale. Conrad Weiser reported in 1737 that "the wood was so thick, that for a mile at a time we could not find a place the size of a hand, where the sunshine could penetrate, even in the clearest day." Eight years later, the Moravian bishop Spangenberg wrote: "The forest is so dense that for a day the sun could not be seen, and so thick you could not see twenty feet before." All of this was gone.

In the mid-1980s, a Lycoming College professor asked students to find the stand of virgin timber closest to Williamsport. The students searched for a long time before spotting an isolated group of 200-year-old white pines 20 miles north of the city in the watershed of Lycoming Creek.

In the early years of the twentieth century, Gifford

Pinchot and other pioneers in the forest conservation move-ment prompted Pennsylvania to turn hundreds of thousands of acres of deforested land, much of it along the Susquehanna's West Branch, into state forests. New stands of trees soon covered the region, but these were mostly hard-woods (oak, maple, black cherry) rather than pine or hem-lock. Pinchot, chief of the U.S. Forest Service and later governor of Pennsylvania, described forestry as "the art of using the forest without destroying it." Much modern lum-bering on public and private land has reflected that thinking.

Today's timber company operations are comparatively dull. Felling and finishing relatively small second-growth timbers at portable sawmills and hauling them out of the renewed forest by truck does not require a rugged raft or a splash dam, a jam breaker or a boom rat.

Anticipating a day when the idea of lumber floating on the Susquehanna would seem a romantic novelty, Henry Wilson, a one-time resident of Cherry Tree, wrote a region-ally famous ballad called "Cherry Tree Joe McCreery." Lumbermen sang the ditty during the declining years of their enterprise. Its last verse:

In years to come, when no rafts run
On our dear little river,
And the cheery cry of "Land, tie-up,"
Shall be heard no more—forever;
Down Rocky Bend and through Chest Falls,
On winter nights so eerie,
The phantom raftsmen chase the ghost
Of Cherry Tree Joe McCreery.

Kettle Creek

What we have on the river today is managed floods. This river, before they put flood-control dams in, never fluctuat-ed so fast. Years ago, when we had high water, you could see the river gradually coming up. But today you're looking at the river and the next thing you know you've got a three-foot raise. Where did it come from? We didn't have that much rain. Well, those guys up there at the control dams get jittery and crank open the gates and let her out.

—DON WILSON, downstream at Muncy

THE MAJOR FEEDER CREEKS OF THE WEST BRANCH splay from the center of Howard William Higbee's famously detailed map of Pennsylvania's streams. Five of these creeks, as wide at their junctures with the West Branch as the river itself, drain from the north. Anywhere else but north-central Pennsylvania, these would be rivers. Here they are Sinnemahoning, Kettle, Pine, Lycoming, and Loyalsock creeks.

Kettle captures all water between Sinnemahoning and Pine. It runs in a trench eroded thousands of years ago through the wilds of southern Potter County into Clinton County. Near its end it turns white as it rushes over rocks toward a level entry into the West Branch at Westport. Filled with trout, the creek has been popular with anglers since well before President Grant made this his favorite fishing spot in the 1870s.

Kettle Creek's long, lovely course has one large, jarring element. Something over eight miles back from the creek's confluence with the Susquehanna, an earthen and rock-fill dam rises 165 feet above the streambed. For two miles behind that dam, Kettle Creek is not a rocky mountain stream but a gorge-filling, lakelike 160-acre reservoir. The Army Corps of Engineers moved 89 inhabitants and 478 coffins out of the area before completing the dam and flooding Kettle Creek in 1959. The new reservoir in relatively lakeless Pennsylvania immediately attracted swimmers and anglers and campers.

The 1,350-foot-long dam contains a spillway in the right abutment to allow a revised edition of Kettle Creek to flow downstream. A separate gate-controlled outlet tunnel can be closed off entirely during high flows so that all water can be held until the flood has receded. Designed to control a drainage area of 226 square miles, the dam essentially has turned Kettle Creek into a regulated stream with a pool in the middle.

The corps dedicated the Alvin R. Bush Dam at Kettle Creek in the summer of 1962. At the ceremony, Colonel Warren R. Johnson, the corps's Baltimore District engineer, warned that such dams alone would not guarantee protection from flooding. "By moving into the floodplain where earlier commercial or residential developments were unsafe," he said, "these communities find themselves with a second undesirable and dangerous situation to replace the one they just erased." Floodplain management, he concluded, remained essential.

That is not to say that concerns about continued floodplain development have ever restrained the corps from building dams. Since Congress passed the National Flood Control Act of 1936, the corps has dammed fourteen of the Susquehanna's tributaries to control the flow of about 12 percent of the headwaters. The dam on Kettle Creek is one of four flood-control structures in the West Branch Basin. During a flood, the corps operates these dams as a system to reduce the flow of the river at Lock Haven and Williamsport. The others are the Curwensville Dam on the West Branch itself, the George B. Stevenson Dam on the First Fork of the Sinnemahoning, and the Foster H. Sayers Dam on Bald Eagle Creek. Eight dams, half of them in New York, regulate tributaries on the North Branch. Two of the Pennsylvania dams control the Lackawanna River. The other two, Tioga-Hammond and Cowanesque, control water in northern Pennsylvania. By manipulating floodgates, operators of these two enormous dams can influence the North Branch flow as far south as the Wyoming Valley. The last two flood-control dams are on contributors to the Susquehanna's Main Stem—Raystown, on the Raystown Branch of the Juniata River, and Indian Rock, on Codorus Creek, which flows through York on its way to the Susquehanna.

To emphasize the recreational aspect of these facilities, the corps refers to the water impoundments as lakes rather than reservoirs. The larger of the reservoirs, such as Cowanesque and Raystown, place no restrictions on horsepower and draw thousands of boaters and other vacationers. But the federal government would not have spent more than $7 million to create a big swimming hole at Kettle

Creek or more than $100 million to manufacture a motor-boat paradise at Cowanesque; not until the 1960s did the corps, at the prompting of Congress, even consider using the reservoir behind any dam for recreation.

These "lakes" have been successful as recreational facilities, impressing even some people who originally opposed damming several of the most scenic free-flowing streams in the Northeast. Whether they have been as successful in achieving their primary goal of flood control is debatable. The dams were of limited value in June 1972. The unprecedented amount of water Tropical Storm Agnes dropped on the area might have overwhelmed all controls in any case, but the reservoirs failed because water filled them before the flood. Instead of being drawn down, as in the spring, in anticipation of high stream flows they could hold back, they stood full to the brim for the benefit of summer swimmers and boaters.

When these reservoirs have been drawn down, they have reduced flood damage. The Susquehanna River Basin Commission (SRBC) reported after Hurricane Eloise flooded the midstate in September 1975 that the flood-control dams had served as "an important mitigating factor." After the extraordinary flood of January 1996—the worst in the Susquehanna Basin since Agnes—the SRBC estimated that North Branch flood-control dams had reduced damages by $1.4 billion.

If Congress had given the green light, the corps might have regulated the entire Susquehanna by damming each tributary and placing strategically located tourniquets on the river itself. Many more dams have been proposed than constructed, including the big plans at Keating on the West

Branch and Great Bend on the North Branch. Smaller proposed dams have not been built on dozens of tributaries. Chances are slim that the corps will build more flood-control dams in the Susquehanna watershed, but not because the engineers would not like to build them. The corps's business is building things; if its engineers can force the lower Mississippi not to leave its present channel by employing enormous control structures, they surely could dam the Susquehanna into impotent sections. The engineers will not be doing that because Congress will not provide the money.

Robert Lindner, chief of the planning division in the corps's Baltimore District, defends flood-control dams. "If you look at the drainage areas that are controlled by these various reservoirs versus the size of the entire Susquehanna River Basin," he says, "we control a relatively small percentage of the total drainage area." Lindner reflects on those dams and the ones that got away: "If my only interest was flood control and I was a god, there would be dams all over the place—but there are other concerns besides flood control, so certainly we don't want to do that."

Some of those concerns—the negative things that dams do, beyond simply blocking the free flow of water—include burying riffles, killing normal riverine vegetation, stopping migrating fish, warming water by ponding it, collecting sediment, and, as Colonel Johnson warned at the dedication of the dam on Kettle Creek, encouraging more development in the floodplain.

On the plus side, besides providing for flood control and recreation, two of these reservoirs—Cowanesque and Curwensville—store water to supply the river during low flows. Under the direction of the SRBC, the corps releases stored water during droughts to offset consumptive use. Consumptive users evaporate water, incorporate it into a product, or otherwise do not return it to the river system. These users, primarily electric utilities, pay the SRBC an annual fee. The SRBC passes the money to the federal government.

Lindner hopes to involve the corps with other federal and state agencies in planning for the region's long-range water supply needs. He believes more reservoirs will be built on the Susquehanna in the distant future to ensure adequate water supplies for a growing population, "but not until water becomes a life issue and not an economic issue."

Lock Haven

Probably if we went back in history, we'd find evidences of flooding in the Susquehanna much greater than since the white man has been in this country. The reason we built levees and other flood-control structures is because it is nature's way to have flooding. So you have a choice: either you get the floods or you do something about it.

—Robert W. Lindner, U.S. Army Corps of Engineers

In 1911, the year Charles M. Robinson developed the Better Binghamton plan, the city planner John Nolen prepared a similar proposal for the Civic Club of Lock Haven.

Unlike Binghamton, which essentially ignored Robinson's recommendation to improve the North Branch riverfront, Lock Haven implemented elements of Nolen's plan along the West Branch. Residents cleared away scrub and planted trees and shrubbery at the entrance to the old covered bridge leading to the Susquehanna's north shore. They seeded lawns and placed benches to create a park along the river's previously neglected south bank along Water Street. The town looked again to the river, which was its reason for being.

In the mid-1830s the Church brothers, Jeremiah and Willard, understood that the West Branch Canal would be opening locks on both sides of the river here. To get in on the action, they bought a 200-acre farm in the delta between the West Branch and Bald Eagle Creek, which runs into the river at a severely acute angle from the southwest, and plotted the "City of Lock Haven for Rafts." The "Lock" derived from the West Branch Canal locks, the "Haven" from the flat and relatively still water that provided a safe harbor for lumber rafts.

During the middle decades of the nineteenth century, Lock Haven developed largely around the river and canal trade. Canal boats carried goods up the West Branch and downriver to the Chesapeake and points between. Rafting crews running the West Branch traditionally paused at Lock Haven. Free-floating logs fed the town's sawmills or rested in the Lock Haven Boom before passing down to ports on the Lower Susquehanna.

Lumber barons built many of the homes on Water Street. They actually overbuilt most of these houses with enormous

logs that have kept them standing through multiple West
Branch floods. One resident constructed his home of lumber,
then encased it in brick. After he died, his wife covered the
brick with wood. The walls of the house are four feet thick.

The earliest homes at Lock Haven faced the river. The
later, more elaborate Victorian homes faced away, with
expansive backyards running to the water. Whether these
later occupants wanted more privacy in their backyards as
commerce moved from the river to the street, or whether
they wanted to use those yards and the river as a dump, the
effect in Lock Haven was the same as in most Susquehanna
towns: the river and riverbank became the place to do and
put things no one wanted to see out front.[4]

The waterfront cleanup of 1911 changed the town's focus
once again. Lock Haven's residents took great pride in their
park and their views down and particularly up the river.
Other large towns along the Susquehanna and its branches
erected earthen levees or concrete walls to protect them
from flooding after the 1936 disaster, but Lock Haven maintained its greensward and coped with periodic inundations
of the first stories of its riverfront homes. Even when the
West Branch ran sick with acid mine drainage and nothing
could live in the water, the people did not turn away. They
wanted their view of the river. But the water rose high again
in 1972 and the levee builders, like ambulance chasers, followed that flood to the bank.

Because of its location just upstream from the confluence
of the West Branch and Bald Eagle Creek, Lock Haven
stands wide open to floods. When the river runs high, it
blocks and backs up creek water, which then covers the

≈ *Residents of the Lock Haven area watch Independence Day festivities on the West
Branch in July 2001. They are sitting on concrete bleachers built into a 15-foot-high levee that
rims the town. The viewer looks across the river to Lock Haven from the north shore. (Photo
by Philip Huber.)*

town. The 1936 flood is the high water of record; the river
rose to thirty-three feet—more than eleven feet above flood
stage. Agnes drove the water to only thirty-one feet in 1972
but worked significantly more mischief. The flood covered
55 percent of the city and ruined planes at Piper Aircraft's
plant along Bald Eagle Creek. That disaster helped prompt
Piper's decision to abandon the city a dozen years later.
Two years after Agnes, the Army Corps of Engineers began
serious preliminary designs for Lock Haven's flood protec-

tion. From the beginning, this plan was unique. The Lock Haven levee would be U-shaped, stretching down the West Branch to a point just inside its confluence with Bald Eagle and then curving sharply back along the creek. It would be the only levee in the United States that would nearly surround a city. (The subsequent proposal to build a smaller U-shaped levee along the North Branch and Fishing Creek at Bloomsburg features a considerably less severe U and would not create the same sense of community encirclement.)

Lock Haven's dirt-and-rock levee would run a total of seven miles and stand fifteen feet high. During a flood, metal doors would close off all city entrances that breached the levee, including the concrete Veterans Bridge, which replaced the covered bridge at Jay Street. The levee in essence would isolate the river and creek from Lock Haven.

This plan attracted controversy the way a flood makes mud. Residents argued the levee's pros and cons until Lock Haven City Council agreed in 1990 to provide $4.4 million as the local share for the project, signaling the corps and Congress to authorize federal funds and fire up the bulldozers. The corps regularly updated total anticipated expenditures from an initial $11.6 million to an actual $72 million.

The plan's local supporters, including Mayor Diann Stuempfle, maintained that the levee project not only would protect the city against future floods but would provide hundreds of jobs during its five-year construction period and encourage new industries to bring more jobs to a city insulated against disaster.

Members of the West Branch Valley Flood Protection

Association opposed the levee and higher taxes to support it. Among at least a dozen specific arguments, they said water would seep beneath the levee to flood the town. They also said levee construction would ruin the riverside park, and Water Street's lovely Victorian homes would lose much of their backyards and all of their river view.

Many of the leaders of the Flood Protection Association lived in those substantial Water Street homes and in an upscale development on an upriver bluff rising nearly 800 feet above any flood. Mayor Stuempfle and other pro-levee leaders, mostly middle-class business people whose modest homes and stores lie in the center of the delta and generally bear the brunt of flooding, did not buy the antilevee arguments of residents whom Robert Yowell, director of the city's Flood Protection Agency, called "those privileged few."

Privileged perhaps, but not few. After two years of turbulent debate, during which the corps cut down the park's trees and began moving earth in preparation for the project, levee opponents ran a slate of candidates for mayor and council in 1992 and won 70 percent of the votes. The new mayor, Bob Edmonston, initiated a suit to halt the project, saying, "What could be more absurd, in a time of [national] fiscal crisis and economic recession, than to force a costly project down the throat of a small town that doesn't want it?"

He was too late. Congress had authorized funds on the basis of the previous council's decision and the corps determinedly pressed ahead. The courts rebuffed the city's challenge and construction proceeded on schedule. The corps completed the levee in 1994, in plenty of time to hold back a major flood two years later. The governor declared

Clinton County a disaster area, but that flood did not touch Lock Haven. Someone placed a wreath of thanks on a monument commemorating the levee's construction near the Jay Street bridge.

The flood of 1996 persuaded some former levee opponents to change their minds. Others remain skeptical. As walkers and joggers pound along the four-mile asphalt path on top of the levee's Susquehanna section, Dr. Larry Lytle sits high and dry in his spacious home on the upriver bluff and discusses flooding and the levee. Lytle was one of the antilevee councilmen elected in 1992. "I'm glad the levee was in place in 1996," he says. "It saved a flood for the lower part of Lock Haven. But there's great doubt in my mind whether it was really tested. If we have a scenario like Agnes in 1972 and the water table is high and we have a lot of rain, we could have a lot of water inside the levee. Lock Haven could still become Lake Haven. The levee gives a false sense of security."

Lytle concedes that the corps has gone out of its way to make the project palatable, constructing the levee walkway and a beach. The engineers even incorporated concrete bleachers in the levee at the Jay Street bridge. The bleachers face the river so that viewers can watch boat races and floating rock concerts. Lytle says none of that makes up for the loss of a lovely riverfront, nor has projected industrial development materialized in a town with unusually high unemployment.

And there's always the flood next time. "We've found that our emergency system is good—but we've also found that we've changed what the river does, and we've always known that the river can be an unpredictable beast," noted an editorial in the *Lock Haven Express* after the 1996 flood.

The levee monument includes an inscription recording major West Branch floods that "have left the people of Lock Haven robbed of their homes, possessions and means of life." All of those floods—eighteen of them—have risen higher than twenty-five feet, the figure local officials selected in 1994 as the base line for major flooding.

When the unpredictable beast tested the levee for the first time two years later, the water surged to precisely twenty-five feet and stopped rising.

Great Island

An island is small enough to call one place. You can see the whole thing; walk around it. Stopping at an island is like singling a person out of a crowd. You can know a person and you can know an island.

—Tim Palmer, *Youghiogheny: Appalachian River*

An island so big that it seems to have fallen out of thin air into the wrong river divides the West Branch flow just downstream from Lock Haven. Great Island's 367 acres make the Susquehanna bulge like a snake that has ingested a large live meal. As a geographic reference point, the island upstages substantial Bald Eagle Creek, which runs into the sliver of river on the island's south side.

Nearly a dozen owners divide Great Island. Most operate

Aerial view of Great Island looking down the West Branch from Lock Haven. The 367-acre island, unusually large for this section of river, is one of thousands in the relatively shallow Susquehanna. (Photo by Philip Huber.)

farms modest in size but fertile in production of corn and other vegetables and fruit. The island-dwelling Ramm family sells produce at a small roadside market on the mainland just across the bridge to Lock Haven. Between that bridge and the other bridge, across the northern ribbon of water, the island measures just under a mile.

No flood wall protects this place. After the Lock Haven levee directs high water past the town, the released river sweeps directly toward the island. Farmers were surprised in January 1996 when floodwater channeled by the levee did not wash higher on Great Island. "My impression, totally unscientific," the island farmer Tom Svec told the *Lock Haven Express,* "was that there was a surge that dissipated very quickly, which was very strange." The Svec home and others on the island remained dry.

The Iroquois and Delaware and many peoples before them made Great Island their principal home. Their traces remain in the form of graves and campfire pits and pottery periodically exposed by floods or archaeologists. Some authorities say the Senecas called the West Branch Great Island River (Gawanowananeh Gehunda) because of this island's importance to them.

Camped on both ends of the island, Native Americans hunted game here and on the mainland and snared shad, sturgeon, suckers, and smallmouth bass with gill nets. The eastern camp stood opposite the mouth of Bald Eagle, near the downstream end of the island. High waters have eroded away the location of the village on the upstream end.

From Great Island, generations of Native Americans launched dugout canoes and forty-foot-long pirogues to carry themselves and goods up and down the river. To Great Island, legions of visitors trekked across half a dozen major trails. One was the Great Island Path running from Sunbury through the wind gap in Bald Eagle Mountain that long ago carried West Branch water.

Newhaleeka, the chief who controlled the island when white settlers arrived, lived in the village at the western end. According to legend, Newhaleeka admired a rifle and a keg of whiskey owned by William Dunn, who came here from York in 1768. Dunn traded the gun and whiskey for the island, a deal Newhaleeka regretted after he had polished off the whiskey.

Dunn built a cabin and lived on the island. While creating Dunnstown on the mainland, near the present site of Lock Haven, he bought the island again—this time from the commonwealth, which had invalidated the whiskey purchase and labeled Dunn a squatter. The island Dunn purchased from Pennsylvania in 1785 for £30 per 100 acres differed substantially from the island that splits the West Branch today.

Thomas Tucker, a deputy state attorney general, surveyed Dunn's island in October 1785. He figured its size at 267 1/2 acres (approximately 100 acres smaller, or £30 cheaper, than now) and drew its shape differently. Chronicling the history of Great Island in 1894, the West Branch historian John F. Meginness noted that the island's shape had changed somewhat from a drawing made just twenty years earlier. He credited both long- and short-term changes to "great floods."

As an altered piece of land in the middle of the river, Great Island has plenty of company. Islands are the Susquehanna's most changeable features. Various surveyors who examined islands in the Susquehanna and Schuylkill rivers for the Commonwealth of Pennsylvania between 1759 and 1761 made pen-and-ink drawings and reported islands' acreages and names. Two and a half centuries later, most of the names are the same but almost all of the shapes and sizes have changed markedly. Some of those islands no longer exist and new islands have appeared.

When Stephen F. Lintner, a physical geographer, compared a survey of the Lower Susquehanna River channel made by Benjamin Henry Latrobe in 1801 with conditions on the river in 1976, he found that bedrock islands had remained relatively stable but alluvial islands had changed and, for the most part, expanded drastically. Most remained in the same places but had been highly modified through erosion by flood and ice, as well as by deposition from floods, high flows, and coal washing down from the Wyoming Valley. Some islands had expanded and joined others. Contrarily, floods and ice jams had cut channels through islands.

Sometimes an island simply moves with the flow of the river. Canfield Island, downstream from Great Island, between Williamsport and the mouth of Loyalsock Creek, steadily "walks" downriver toward the Loyalsock. As the island's upper end erodes, the lower end collects silt. James Bressler, a Williamsport archaeologist, says this explains why the record of habitation, beginning about 5000 B.C, shows occupation moving down the island.

Sometimes the flow moves with the island. The head of an island can turn the river's current at an angle. Depending on the configuration of two islands close togeth-

er, they actually can reverse the flow. More often, water is merely becalmed upstream of an island.

A major flood may eliminate small islands in one location and create new ones elsewhere. Tropical Storm Agnes wiped out little St. Catherine's Island, about a mile above Garrett Island at Havre de Grace, Maryland. At the same time, it deposited 500 acres of virgin islands several miles below in the Chesapeake's Susquehanna Flats. Despite efforts by the Maryland Department of Natural Resources to save the new islands by planting them in swamp grass, much of that acreage has since eroded.

Ice changes islands faster than anything else. Donald Oyler, who lives where Conodoguinet Creek runs into the Susquehanna across from Harrisburg, has watched ice obliterate islands. "Floodwaters don't damage islands that much," he says. "Once the water gets high, the current is more toward the top than it is toward the bottom, where it would cut an island out. It's the ice that does it. The ice just cuts out these little grass patches before they can become good-sized islands." Contrarily, after several winters without major ice movement, an island's size can increase dramatically.

Human activity in and near the river also has created and destroyed islands. Dammed water covers islands, coal sediment distorts their shape, and erosion from developed and deforested shores contributes substantially to island extension. Alluvial deposits collect around bridge abutments and train trestles, sometimes attaining considerable size. The Corps of Engineers' periodic "channelization" of various sections of the river and its tributaries to widen and flatten stream beds and reduce potential for flooding has eliminated innumerable small islands. A large portion of the Wyoming Valley's Wintermoot Island washed away in 1959 when the bottom fell out of the Susquehanna above the Knox Mine.

According to early Pennsylvania law, anyone with a land bridge to an island owned the island. So some riverside landowners expanded their property by depositing fill in narrow channels and wiping out islands. The state did not care about islands and began selling all it owned in 1793. Shad fisheries purchased many of them. The state more or less supported private ownership for the next two centuries.

Pennsylvania reasserted its interest in the river's smaller islands in 1990, proposing to take active ownership of any that still belonged to it. No one had any idea how many that might be. Islands are difficult to count in the Susquehanna, not only because they come and go but because there are so many of them. In all of the Chesapeake Bay, rising tides have left fewer than fifty islands. Between Easton and the Delaware Bay, the Delaware River contains sixty-two islands. The shallow, rocky Susquehanna hosts thousands of islands.

More than two hundred of them force the river to braid the twenty-four-mile stretch of the Susquehanna between Halifax and Harrisburg's City Island alone.[5] They are part of the Susquehanna River Trail, opened in the summer of 1998 as Pennsylvania's first water trail. The Central Susquehanna River Trail Association, in conjunction with the Alliance for the Chesapeake Bay and several state agencies, created this unmarked water route to encourage river traffic and low-impact primitive camping on islands. Camping is permitted on ten of the more sizable islands, not including Wade and Sheets, where yellow-crowned and black-crowned night herons and great egrets have a lodging priority. This water trail eventually will extend up- and downstream.

Susquehanna islands today support two state parks, a nuclear plant, a minor-league baseball park, a catfish farm, and numerous livestock operations. More natural islands host wildlife sanctuaries and state game lands. A conglomeration of housing, both substantial and seasonal, dots many large islands, and here and there on a Susquehanna beach, a weathered net awaits warm weather and a volleyball.

Williamsport

One cannot see much live pine at Williamsport; but down by the river-side, and at the boom, one can see nothing but logs of every size and length. The children of the street play upon them, fearlessly jumping from one to the other, as if there were no cold, black water underneath.

—R. E. Garczynski, *Picturesque America*, 1872–74

"The river and the Susquehanna Boom were the center of all the wealth, so it was the lumbering industry which usurped the riverfront." James Bressler, Susquehanna enthusiast, archaeologist, and authority on the Native Americans of Lycoming County, explains why Williamsport's riverside landscape looks as it does. Working in the basement library of the Lycoming County Historical Society on Fourth Street, he is separated from the West Branch by four blocks of industrial and commercial development, Interstate Route 80, and a massive levee. The lumber industry once sprawled over all this space.

"Thirty sawmills, one after another, occupied this whole riverfront." Bressler punctuates the air to show where the mills stood. "The boom in the river was packed with logs and an endless belt took these logs up over the bank of the river and dumped them into the millrace. The millrace connected with all the millponds and mills along the waterfront. There was no place to build millionaires' homes there, so in back of the mills is where the lumber barons built their homes."

In the latter decades of the nineteenth century, lumber magnates constructed Millionaires' Row, an ostentatious string of Victorian and neoclassical mansions along eight blocks of West Fourth Street. The men with the money wanted everyone to see it. Their wealth came largely from the success of the Susquehanna Boom, one of whose later owners, Maylon Fisher, built the "Million-Dollar Mansion," a pretentious Greek Revival home that cost that much to build and furnish. From 1850 on, the boom that spanned the West Branch, holding all logs from upstream, transformed Williamsport into "the lumber capital of the world," home to a few dozen very rich people and thousands of workaday lumbermen.

Williamsport's nine-mile-long boom outperformed similar but smaller structures at Lock Haven and elsewhere because of its size and especially its location along the Long Reach, a straight stretch of quiet water running between the

mouths of Pine and Lycoming creeks. A dam enhanced this level area by backing up the water. Also, Williamsport lies at the widest part of the narrow West Branch Valley, thus allowing ample space for construction of the sawmills and planing mills and ponds needed to process all those logs. And—by river and canal and later by railroad—Williamsport stood closer than Lock Haven to downstream markets. Because of the busy boom, which processed 1,850,951 logs in its peak year, Williamsport boomed; but it never could grow big. In this town, geography is destiny.

In *Man, Land and Time,* the archaeologist William A. Turnbaugh separates the West Branch Valley between Lock Haven and Muncy from all other features in the Appalachians. He calls this "narrow ribbon" the Susquehanna Section. Most of this land and water ribbon spreads one and a half to two miles wide, broadening to a maximum of six miles at Williamsport and South Williamsport. Steep mountains running east to west frame the valley. Before highways, the mountains rendered the area inaccessible except by water.

Even today, relatively few people live inside the valley and far fewer just outside. Lycoming is Pennsylvania's largest county, but much of it remains undeveloped. Ninety percent of Lycoming's 115,000 people, including Williamsport's 30,000-plus, live on 3 percent of the county's land—in that strip along the river where all the water runs when it rains. Numerous and intense storms, sometimes combined with fast snowmelt in spring, overfill tributaries rushing down from the mountains. Heavy tributary runoff rapidly fills and overflows the West Branch channel. During highest water, much of the valley floor can become a mile-wide river, flooding thousands of homes.

The first five recorded floods—in 1744, 1758, 1772, 1786, and 1800—supported a Native American tradition of a great flood every fourteen years and encouraged early settlers to count forward to the next one. Nineteenth-century floods altered the time pattern while increasing destruction. The worst flood of the mid-century occurred on St. Patrick's Day, 1865: it swept away or severely damaged all bridges between Farrandsville, just upstream of Lock Haven, and Northumberland.

High water frequently fractured the Susquehanna Boom, sending logs by the hundreds of thousands swirling toward the Chesapeake. The boom broke in 1860, 1861, and 1865. And it broke on May 18, 1868, just days after a huge log drive from Sinnemahoning Creek had deposited more than 44 million feet of timber in it. Between 12 million and 15 million feet of logs that hundreds of men had spent weeks ushering down the Sinnemahoning and West Branch tore loose for the bay.

The boom broke again, catastrophically, in 1889. The deluge in the spring of that year is best known for causing the flood that wrecked the South Fork Dam on the Conemaugh River, north of Johnstown, sending a twenty-foot wall of water rushing into the city to drown 2,200 residents. The same stalled storm system that ruined Johnstown dumped eight inches of rain on the West Branch and the Juniata River in less than thirty-six hours.

Washing from the headwaters of the West Branch and tributary streams to the north, the 1889 flood overwhelmed all towns along the way. Fifty people drowned, including a dozen whose house was destroyed by logs rushing along

Antes Creek near Jersey Shore. Bridges that had been rebuilt after the 1865 flood were washed away again as floodwaters rose more than five feet higher. Seven feet of water covered much of Williamsport. The West Branch Canal washed out. Then the boom broke. They called it "the big break."

"Rushing down the river the flood reached Williamsport in the early hours of the morning of June 1st," wrote the historian John Bach McMaster.

The 75 million feet of lumber from Lock Haven, set free by the breaking of the Lock Haven boom, began to run into the boom of Williamsport. . . . At nine it went out and 150,000,000 feet of sawlogs began a journey to Chesapeake Bay. Then followed every kind of manufactured lumber, sashes and door frames, pickets and shingles, from the yards along the river bank, mills, bridges, houses and trees. The railroad station was swept of everything movable. The track was washed out and littered with broken cars, boards, trees and sand; and communication of every sort was destroyed. Three-fourths of the city was under water and more than one-half of the people were sufferers from the flood.

The flood caught James R. Skinner of Brooklyn and a friend several blocks from their Williamsport hotel. "By wading we reached the place of a man who owned a horse and buggy," Skinner recalled.

These we hired and started to drive to the hotel, which is on the highest ground in the city. The water was all the time rising, and the flood kept coming in waves. These waves came with such frequency and volume that we were forced to abandon the horse and buggy and try wading. With the water up to our armpits we got to a [floating] outhouse, and climbing to the top of it made our way along to a building. This I entered through a window, and found the family in the upper stories.

Floating outside were two canoes, one of which I hired for two dollars and fifty cents. I at once embarked in this and tried to paddle for my hotel. I hadn't gone a hundred feet when I capsized. . . . After a struggle in the water, which was running like a mill-race, I got afloat again and managed to lodge myself against a train of nearly submerged freight cars. Then, by drawing myself against the stream, I got opposite the hotel and paddled over.

Skinner's friend did not get that far. His canoe leaked and he spent the night on a house roof.

Williamsport's misfortune flowed downstream. The Susquehanna Boom crashed into the Loyalsock Boom, which led to the suing of the owners of the former by the owners of the latter and, in an unexpected turn of events, merger of the companies. The combined logs from these booms crashed through the wooden sides of the covered bridge at Lewisburg just before rising floodwater destroyed all five spans of that structure.

The 1889 disaster and another severe flood five years later (which again took out the Williamsport boom) damaged boom cribs and mills and other equipment beyond repair, and washed hundreds of thousands of logs and millions of finished boards downstream. Many mills went bankrupt.

The West Branch lumber industry would have declined even without these floods. Extensive clear-cutting had nearly exhausted timber resources. By the turn of the century, the forests of Michigan and Wisconsin had replaced Penn's Woods as the nation's primary lumber region. The repaired Williamsport boom closed forever in 1909. A decade later, the last Williamsport mill sawed its last log and that part of the lumbering business also disappeared.

The flood of 1889 set into slow motion the control mechanisms that would transform Pennsylvania's response to floods. Primarily because of the tragedy at Johnstown, the state established the first permanent water-level gauging station on the Susquehanna at Harrisburg. The Corps of Engineers conducted the first survey of the West Branch in 1890. The river never could be made navigable, the corps reported, and was not worth improving. More ominously, the study noted, "there is no practicable method of confining its water, in times of great flood, to the general course of the channel."

Subsequent destructive floods persuaded the corps to build expensive levees at Williamsport. They run on both sides of the river, unlike the single-bank levee at Lock Haven. Williamsport and South Williamsport remained dry behind their levees in 1972, except for some furious but localized flooding along West Branch tributaries. But because the levees had been built *in* the river, narrowing the channel, the flood burst out downstream and caused greater destruction there than otherwise would have occurred. Williamsporters, however, were pleased: The vicious cycles

Williamsport Boom employees and loggers pose during the boom's last years in the late 1880s. Notice the fellow sitting on top of one of the cribs that linked large floating logs to form the boom. (Lycoming County Historical Society and Thomas T. Taber Museum, Williamsport, Pennsylvania.)

of ruin and reconstruction had ended and their city could plan for a future that would not include periodic inundations by water and muck.

Nevertheless, the downside of diking—isolation of the city from the river—is as severe here as at any other place on the Susquehanna. Motorists can see the water from Route 80, which runs on top of the north levee for some distance; or they might notice it as they pass across a bridge to attend the Little League World Series in South Williamsport. Joggers can see the river from a path that follows another section of the north levee. Otherwise, for most residents, the West Branch does not exist.

"The dike dramatically changed the way people here relate to the river," says John F. Piper Jr., a professor of history at Lycoming College. "Historically, people essentially lived on the river. The Reading Railroad was right down on the riverfront. You got off the railroad and could personally spit into the river. People could walk to the end of their street and fish. In the winter, they'd use it for ice skating. In South Williamsport a canoe club was very popular. There were steps down to the water. You just walked right down to the river." The corps completed the levees in 1955. "The next year the city fathers discovered that they needed to build ice skating rinks," says Piper, "and then they had to build public pools—partly because of pollution but partly because you can't get to the river easily to swim in it."

Piper grew up fishing and swimming in the river, but his children have had nothing to do with it. As a young teenager, Piper's son wondered where he could go to fish.

The Pipers live four blocks from the river. Piper had to direct his son there; he would not have thought of that resource on his own.

"People just can't relate to the river," Piper says. "It's not like growing up—you know, people grow up on a farm, they grow up on a mountain, they grow up on a river. Here you sort of grow up behind the dike, and that's not any of those things."

In memory of the Susquehanna Boom, which helped Williamsport prosper so many years ago, the city holds a Boom Festival each June. A parade includes floats with a logging-era theme. Boats race on the river, but much of the festival's entertainment occurs well back from the waterfront. The festival does not focus on the water. Williamsport's river, like its boom, is history.

Muncy

I saw people thrown, fly in the air, and a woman floating in

the water, the sea scouts saving people and the shed fly to

pieces. You can see that all your life, the people in the water.

—Kenn Reagle, *Headwaters and Hardwoods,* quoting Lorma Ferrell,
who watched the Last Raft hit the middle pier of the
Reading Railroad bridge at Muncy in 1938

Some fifteen miles east of Williamsport, the West Branch turns at a right angle along its glacial channel and rolls directly toward its meeting with the North Branch at

Northumberland. The town of Muncy (named for the Munsee tribe and the creek that enters the West Branch just upriver) lies along this elbow in the course.

Because of the Munsee Valley's strategic location, paths led in all directions to destinations on the North Branch and the Allegheny. Many tribes visited here to hunt and fish. Before traveling west to settle in the area of what would become Muncie, Indiana, the Munsees themselves built an enormous fortification and a burial mound north of the river.

Samuel Wallis established the first white settlement in Lycoming County at this place in the 1760s. A few years later, William Penn's son, John, claimed this land for one of the Penns' expansive manors, displacing Wallis. Muncy soon became the most important travel destination on the West Branch as settlers built their houses along narrow streets set well back from the crooking river.

Muncy's golden era began with the arrival of the West Branch Canal in 1834. From the 1830s through the 1870s, a large class of merchants turned Muncy into one of the richest towns in Pennsylvania. These merchants built grand homes and established a considerable educational and cultural community before Williamsport's enormous lumber trade overshadowed the commerce of its downriver neighbor. During the latter decades of the lumbering era, Muncy established its first real industries, including sawmills and planing mills, and began its transformation into a working-class town.

Logs and log rafts floated past half a dozen significant rafting "points" in the Muncy area. Raftmen used points to determine location and anticipate hazards. One of those points was the site, just downriver, where the Reading Railroad built a succession of bridges, concluding with an iron structure on concrete piers in 1929. Nearly a decade later, as a thousand people watched from atop that bridge, the West Branch's "Last Raft," making a nostalgic journey from McGees Mills to Harrisburg, crashed into one of the bridge piers. As spectators shouted in horror, seven men drowned.

The rafting and writing Tonkin family and like-minded rivermen did not consider failure when they conceived the idea of running the Last Raft. Vincent Tonkin began planning to take one last trip down the river as early as 1905. He died before he could make the excursion, but in 1912 his sons, R. Dudley and V. Ord, coordinated construction of a raft from pine logs Vincent had reserved for that purpose. That March, they and the pilot Harry Conner and others floated the raft from Cherry Tree to Williamsport, where they sold the wood to a lumber company. They planned to make another rafting trip each decade of their lives, but twenty-six years passed before they actually tried it again.

In the winter of 1937–38, the Tonkins began searching for pines to make what would become their last Last Raft.[6] Aging lumbermen cut trees from three separate tracts to make a half raft running 112 feet long and about 27 feet wide. They fastened the timbers together, as they had always done, with supple white oak saplings and pins made of ash. They fashioned fore and aft oars fifty feet long, with sixteen-foot blades. Said an observer, "They were some paddles."

The builders placed the customary shanty in the center of

The crew and passengers on the Last Raft prepare to enter the raft chute through the Williamsport Boom on their way to Muncy. Harry Conner, the pilot, stands foremost. (Lycoming County Historical Society and Thomas T. Taber Museum, Williamsport, Pennsylvania.)

the raft and an uncustomary outhouse on the raft's stern. Then they waited for a tin cup in R. Dudley's backyard to gather an inch of rainwater so they would know the river held sufficient water to float their raft.

Some newspaper editors and not a few experienced rivermen had cautioned about the risks of this venture. Too many changes had been made along the river since 1912, they said: Lock Haven had built a dam without a chute for rafts; the Williamsport chute had been damaged in the flood of 1936; the Reading Railroad had doubled the number of piers holding up its bridge at Muncy, forcing a tighter fit. The *Montgomery Mirror,* in what now seems a shocking foreshadowing of tragedy, captioned a photo taken of the raft early on its tour: "Ghost of Dead Industry Floats Down Its Styx."

On the misty morning of March 14, 1938, more than 5,000 people crowded the banks of the river at McGees Landing to watch the takeoff. Tonkin "tied loose" the Last Raft, and the craft, riding low in the river, with water slopping over its edges, moved downstream. Pilot Conner, seventy-five years old, manned the front oar. Ed Sunderlin took the rear. Other crew members included Levi Connor, who had supervised construction; John Byers, another steersman; Clyde Folton, a cook; and John Cooper and Harry Tozer.

Crew members braced themselves for passage by Rocky Bend and Chest Falls, widely considered the most dangerous rafting points on the West Branch. They guided the craft through the current, around rocks, and away from the shore, until it headed straight for a boulder near the end of the run. "For one breathless moment, the raft seemed to hang poised above this rock," reported Joseph Dudley Tonkin, son of R. Dudley, in *The Last Raft.* "Then surely, as the lead of the water bore off to the right, the cumbersome timber changed its course to pass unharmed with all of twelve inches to spare."

By the evening of that first day, the Last Raft had passed all the way to Clearfield, where bells and whistles, cheering crowds, and a mayoral speech greeted the rafters. The crew left town the next morning in high spirits, buoyed by enthusiasts along the riverbank. A woman waved a large American flag while her husband played "The Star-Spangled Banner" on his cornet. When the raft moved into deeper water, fleets of powerboats, rowboats, and canoes traveled alongside.

This type of reception greeted the excursionary raft all along the way. Tens of thousands of people, some of whom traveled hundreds of miles, came to watch. Old-time lumbermen, who took their families to see a representation of the industry they had spent their lives serving, stirred much of the enthusiasm. Scores of local dignitaries and others rode the raft for a few miles just to say they had participated in the momentous event. Reporters wrote daily stories for all the newspapers along the West Branch and many other papers across the United States. Thomas Proffitt, a Universal Newsreel cameraman, filmed highlights of the raft's construction and trip to show in movie theaters.

The trip had its quiet moments. As Harry Conner prepared to direct the raft through Moshannon Falls on March 16, one H. D. Tozer (apparently no relation to the crew member Harry Tozer) approached him. "Sixty years ago today," he explained, "my father, Gilbert Tozer, drowned when the raft on which he was working struck Wood Rock, just on the other side of these falls. I've brought a little wreath with me and I wonder if Mr. Tonkin will have the Last Raft pull over close enough to the rock so I can place it there." Soon the raft swung close to Wood Rock. Several crew members held Tozer's hand while he leaned out and placed his memorial wreath on the boulder.

There were merry moments as well. Before tying up at Renovo the next evening, members of the crew "arrested" Conner for exceeding the river speed limit. The prosecution proved that Conner had been averaging better than five miles an hour. The jury returned a verdict of guilty and sentenced him, despite his fifty years as a pilot, to spend ten minutes at the rear oar.

The raft passed over the Lock Haven dam on March 18. Joseph Dudley Tonkin described this uneventful but dramatic passage: "For a moment the front platform of the raft seemed to hang suspended in space as the weight of the timber held it see-saw fashion on the brink. The flexible sections seemed to creak complainingly as they poised for the plunge—then—SPLASH—the front section nosed under with Harry holding his position that was by this time waist deep in racing water. As the headblock popped immediately to the surface, the rear platform made the six foot drop and sank several feet in turn."

The next day the raft arrived in Williamsport, and on the morning of March 20 shot safely through the flumelike and photogenic Williamsport dam chute. Harry Conner headed

for Muncy.

Forty-seven crew members and visitors rode with Conner as the raft approached the town. That was enough over optimum capacity to press the logs low in the water and diminish the steersmen's ability to change the craft's direction on short notice. In addition, centrifugal force created by the river's radical change of course at the Muncy elbow forced the raft toward the east bank.

At the first of the little town's bridges—which carries Route 405 from Muncy to Montgomery—the current swept the raft toward a pier. Hard work at the oars moved the nose of the raft past the bridge support, but its side grazed it, jostling the passengers.

"What happened at the second bridge was vastly different," reported the West Branch historian Lewis Edwin Theiss, who at that time owned a farm just below the Reading Railroad bridge and helped care for some of the Last Raft survivors. "There the current sets diagonally toward the shore at certain passages between piers. To avoid hitting a pier in this current, it is necessary to steer directly toward it and allow the current to sweep the craft to one side sufficiently to enable it to pass through the bridge span."

Following this wisdom, Conner guided the raft straight for the fifth of the bridge's nine piers. Reports conflict on precisely what happened, but clearly neither the current nor the two men at the oars modified the raft's course. It hit that pier head on, shattering the shanty and possibly killing immediately Thomas Proffitt, who had his back against it to steady his newsreel camera. Then the river swept the raft to the right and its rear end hit the sixth pier. The log assembly tipped on its side, dumping all but one of the passengers into icy water.

"Things happened so quickly thereafter, that my recollections are all too hazy," wrote Leo A. Luttringer Jr., editor of *Pennsylvania Game News* and a passenger when the raft crashed. "I remember going over, coming up, and swimming a short distance to a piece of driftwood. I also remember someone making futile grabs for my shoulder, catching once or twice and almost pulling me down."

The front oar hit John Bain, breaking several of his ribs. "Somebody yelled to me, look out for the oar!" Bain testified at a coroner's inquest in Muncy. "I jumped and the handle of the oar caught me and I fell on my back and in an instant it swung back from the other direction and washed me overboard."

Encumbered with heavy boots and clothes, the men in the water searched for any possible way to keep afloat. Oliver Helmrich, a sixteen-year-old journalism student at Williamsport High School, fought his way back aboard the raft, which incredibly had not broken up but had righted itself and continued floating downstream. Michael Abiuso, of Sunbury, had been watching the raft's approach from a motorboat downstream of the bridge. He began hauling swimmers from the water and transporting them to shore. A number of trained Sea Scouts did the same.

The bodies of Conner, Proffitt, and five other drowned men drifted several miles with the current. Dr. Charles F. Taylor, Montgomery's mayor and a dentist, had been scheduled to get off the raft at his hometown, five miles downstream. Instead, the river washed his body there. After extensive dragging and careful dynamiting of the river, searchers found the last of the bodies a month later.

R. Dudley Tonkin had left the raft and gone downstream to study the route ahead when the accident occurred. After the inquest, he and other surviving crewmen returned to the Last Raft, which had tied up just below Muncy. They finished the journey to Fishing Creek, north of Harrisburg, where they sold the last timber two days later.

Asked why he planned to complete the doomed journey after his old friend Harry Conner had drowned, Levi Connor said, "I want to finish this trip just for old times' sake. That's the way Harry would want it."

The crash ruined much of the photographic record, but someone retrieved Proffitt's waterproof film from the bottom of the river. Wide-eyed audiences in movie houses across the nation viewed the silent footage. The film shows the raft making its way along the West Branch, running the dams and being greeted by huge crowds at Lock Haven and Williamsport. As it nears Muncy, the raft seems to travel faster, plowing through the high March water. The final frames show the raft headed for the railroad bridge. A man in the front reacts with alarm as he realizes the raft will hit the pier. He backpedals frantically. The screen turns black.

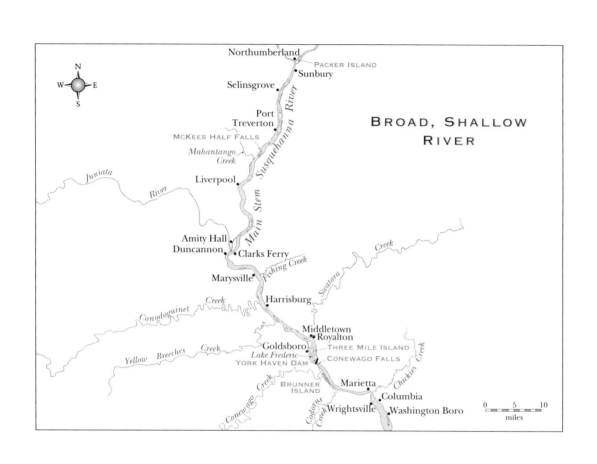

Northumberland

PACKER ISLAND

Sunbury

Selinsgrove

BROAD, SHALLOW
RIVER

Port
Treverton

MCKEES HALF FALLS

Mahantango
Creek

Susquehanna River

Juniata

River

Liverpool

Main Stem

Amity Hall
Duncannon

Clarks Ferry

Creek

Marysville

Fishing Creek

Swatara

Harrisburg

Creek

Conodoguinet

Middletown
Royalton

Goldsboro

THREE MILE ISLAND

Lake Frederic
YORK HAVEN DAM

CONEWAGO FALLS

Chickies Creek

Yellow Breeches Creek

Conewago Creek

BRUNNER
ISLAND

Marietta

Columbia

Codorus Creek

Wrightsville

Washington Boro

0   5   10
miles

Broad, Shallow River

The Confluence

The view from [Blue Hill's] summit is one of unsurpassed beauty and loveliness. In the foreground lies the ancient borough of Northumberland on a sloping mesa, with Montour Ridge in the rear. From the east roll the waters of the North Branch like a silver ribbon to unite with the West Branch and form the Susquehanna, which at this point majestically starts on its voyage to the sea amid green islands and rugged hills.

—JOHN F. MEGINNESS, *Otzinachson: A History of the West Branch Valley of the Susquehanna,* 1856

IN THE SUMMER OF 1743, John Bartram, a Philadelphia botanist, engaged the interpreter Conrad Weiser to guide him up the Susquehanna River and on to the Iroquois council at Onondaga, New York. A traveling companion, Lewis Evans, took notes from which he produced the first reliable map of the northern Pennsylvania wilderness. Shikellamy, an Iroquois chief, accompanied the trio.

On their return, somewhere just north of Shamokin (by which name the Iroquois designated a large area now occupied by Northumberland and Sunbury), the party stopped for the night alongside a good-sized creek at the foot of a large hill covered with tall trees. "This is like a bridge between the N.E. and N.W. branches of the Susquehanah," Bartram wrote in his journal. "Here is also a spring from whence the water runs to both branches."

Their camping spot must have been somewhere on Montour Ridge, which determines which branch will receive the rain that falls in this region. Tributaries of Chillisquaque Creek, which joins the West Branch some six miles upstream from the confluence, draw water from the west side of the ridge. Tributaries of Mohoning Creek, which runs into the North Branch at Danville, draw from the east. From atop Montour Ridge, about a thousand feet above the North and West branch valleys, John Bartram could see spring water flow either way.

From the summit of Blue Hill, a vantage point several miles south of Montour Ridge and just across the West Branch from Northumberland, an observer today may look down on these branches and find it hard to believe any water in them issued from a common source. The West Branch ordinarily washes into the confluence with a greenish hue. This water is relatively clear because acid mine drainage has depressed life. The North Branch comes in orange-brown and murky because of its own acid mine drainage and overall greater pollution; but it is filled with life.[1]

"Everybody wants to boat up the West Branch because it's a lot clearer. You don't have the algae buildup," says Stan Rohrbach, who directed Shikellamy State Park for fifteen years and keeps his hand in the park system in retirement. "But take water quality samples and you will find the North Branch is cleaner. Roll over twenty stones on the West Branch and count the life that's underneath and then roll over twenty stones on the North Branch. You'll find that you have a hell of a lot more life going on on the North Branch than you do on the West Branch."[2]

Unless the West Branch is in flood, the slightly larger North Branch pushes it to the side as the two stream together. The branches meet but do not commingle: a definite diagonal dividing line stretches from Pineknotter Park, at the tip of the Northumberland peninsula, southwest toward Blue Hill. Especially on still days when sunlight glints off the water, that line looks as if it has been drawn along a surveyer's chain.

A biologist would discover this division even if it were not so visually pronounced. Beneath the water, all along that line, fish dart about in constant turmoil. The big fish that thrive here—smallmouth bass, walleye, catfish, black bass, carp—feed on minnows. Minnows like to hide in the darker, more fertile waters on the North Branch side of the line. The bass and walleye chase minnows into the lighter water of the West Branch so they can see them and eat them. To save themselves, the faster minnows scoot back to the shelter of North Branch water. "The fish go back and forth here; it's a favorite place," says Rohrbach. "Smart fishermen fish on the break line."

Whether they scout the dividing line or not, plenty of central Pennsylvanians and a steadily increasing number of tourists fish and boat here. Deepened by a seasonal dam about three miles downstream from the confluence, this part of the Susquehanna in summer becomes Lake Augusta. The 3,060-acre water playground extends some three and a

☞ *The English artist William Henry Bartlett included seven Susquehanna drawings in* American Scenery, *his 1840 collaboration with the American journalist, N. P. Willis.* View of Northumberland (on the Susquehanna) *illustrates the scene from Blue Hill, with a canal boat and river arks in the fore-ground. The view upriver shows, from left to right, the edge of Blue Hill, the bridge over the West Branch, houses at Northumberland, the bridge over the North Branch to Packer Island, and the bridge from the island toward Sunbury.* (American Scenery.)

half miles up both branches. Excellent daily fishing and thirty smallmouth bass tournaments a season draw thousands of anglers. Boating without horsepower limits attracts hundreds more, who churn the water into a froth. The state marina on Packer Island holds 110 boats, but a sunny summer weekend will encourage five or six times that many Sunday sailors to run up and down the branches.

Two-mile-long Packer Island splits the North Branch in half as it reaches the confluence, giving boaters an extra channel to navigate. From water level, it seems as if three rivers—the West Branch and the divided North Branch—join here to become one mile-wide waterway that soon takes on the character—expansive, shallow, rocky—of the Lower Susquehanna.

In addition to hosting part of Shikellamy State Park at its southern tip, Packer Island supports a residential area, a campground, and an airport, from which an amphibious plane periodically takes off to land in Lake Augusta. Examining the layout from the park end of the island, a visitor can begin to imagine how ideal this location—two picturesque river valleys melding into one—must have seemed before modern roads and bridges connected all of its elements, fostering dense development and heavy traffic.

"It may truly be said that this site was not chosen by man, but was decreed as a center of human activity by the Great Architect of the Universe." wrote the authors of Sunbury's bicentennial history in 1972. To anyone who seriously studies this region's geography, that bit of local hyperbole does not seem far off the mark.

This confluence duplicates the situation at Tioga Point, where the North Branch and Chemung join, but on a far grander scale. With major water routes running in three directions and a dozen land trails radiating in four, Shamokin became the most important native settlement in Pennsylvania before the French and Indian War. At least twelve distinct tribes representing Iroquoian, Algonquian, and Siouan linguistic stocks lived together here in the early eighteenth century. That tribal diversity and the strategic location guaranteed that practically everyone traveling through central Pennsylvania would visit Shamokin.

Native Americans gathered in this early American melting pot not only because of its strategic geographic position but because the fishing was fantastic and the river's oft-flooded banks provided rich alluvial soil for farming. Some say Shamokin means "the place of the eels." Before dams intervened, eels streamed up the river to live their adult lives and streamed back down to the sea to spawn and die. Those that made it this far north in their life journey had to choose one of the branches. They provided a tempting target for spear or net.

As Native Americans inevitably congregated at this place, so did arriving Europeans. The Reverend Philip Vicars Fithian considered the changing of the guard as he canoed across the waters at the confluence in the summer of 1775: "I could not help thinking with myself how the savage tribes, while they were in possession of these enchanting wilds, have floated over this very spot. My heart feels for the wandering natives. I make no doubt but multitudes of them, when they were forced away, left these long-possessed and delightsome banks with swimming eyes."

Sloping gently from the foothills of Montour Ridge toward the water, Northumberland fills the crotch of the Y formed by the Susquehanna's branches. The founders laid out this town three years before Fithian visited and it contained nearly a hundred homes by the end of the eighteenth century. Congress briefly considered Northumberland as a site for the nation's capital, and it lost a bid to become Pennsylvania's capital by one vote.

Joseph Priestley settled at Northumberland in 1794 after his English political and religious enemies drove him across the Atlantic. He built a large white clapboard home and laboratory on the east side of town, looking across the North Branch to Packer Island. The man who had discovered "dephlogisticated air" (oxygen) in London continued his experiments in Northumberland, passing steam over heated charcoal to create the first carbon monoxide. He adjusted rapidly to his new situation. "The town is beautifully situated between two branches of the Susquehannah," he wrote his sister, "each as large as the Thames at London, bounded by rocks and hanging woods."

New residents and travelers often described this region with superlatives. Priestley's son, Joseph Priestley Jr., and son-in-law, Thomas Cooper, traveled here the year before the old chemist arrived. In *Some Information Respecting America,* Cooper wrote of his journey upriver to Northumberland: "The noble masses of wood and mountain, the Susquehanna sometimes rolling through rich val-

This view downriver at the confluence of the North and West branches at Northumberland shows the North Branch marina at Shikellamy State Park on Packer Island. The West Branch enters from the right past the tip of Blue Hill. Sunbury buildings are visible in the distance. (Photo by Christine Brubaker.)

leys, and sometimes washing the base of stupendous rocks, almost everywhere taking the form of a lake, and interspersed with numerous islands, well wooded, of all forms, and stretching out in a variety of directions; these combined with the brightness of the atmosphere . . . made this journey one of the pleasantest I had ever experienced."[3]

Travelers who crossed the North Branch from Northumberland found the site of modern Sunbury an equally pleasant place to settle and with considerably more room to expand. British soldiers constructed Fort Augusta here in 1756, complete with an underground tunnel to the Susquehanna so that canoe parties could enter the structure without exposing themselves on land. Augusta quickly became the most important British fort on the river—the parallel of Fort Pitt, at the confluence of the Allegheny and Monongahela.

The Penn family laid out Sunbury in 1772 and in the next century it served as an important lumber-processing area, with its own small log boom. With fortunes made from sawmills and planing mills, the town's wealthiest citizens built substantial homes along the Susquehanna. In the early twentieth century, residents of these homes, separated from the river by a row of cherry trees in River Front Park, enjoyed some of the most scenic views along the Susquehanna. Because Sunbury received the worst of every flood, however, floodplain residents eventually demanded a protective wall and the riverfront homes lost their view.

Without a wall or levee, floodwater rushing down the North Branch naturally expands into low-lying Sunbury. Blue Hill forces the approaching West Branch water over in that direction, too. The combined force of the two branches has been eroding the riverbank here for centuries. In his history of the West Branch Valley, John Meginness noted that Fort Augusta had been built forty yards from the river, but the encroaching water had moved to within a few feet of the fort's site a century later.

Sunbury's riverfront took its last major pounding from the flood of 1946. The Corps of Engineers began constructing a flood-control system the next year and completed it in 1951. Because the riverbank had been eroded so severely and

Route 147 crowded the water, the engineers had no room to build expansive earthen levees. Sunbury's starkly vertical flood wall is the longest concrete structure anywhere along the Susquehanna. In conjunction with pumps, storm drains, and other controls, the wall kept Sunbury relatively dry when Tropical Storm Agnes ruined Wilkes-Barre in 1972. On the concrete that summer, someone scrawled, "We Love You Wall!"

Not everyone loved the wall. Riverside homeowners complained that they no longer could see the river from ground level. Someone said the concrete divider gave Sunbury "the feel of an empty swimming pool." Critics suggested that if the levee had not broken at Wilkes-Barre in 1972, higher water rushing downstream would have topped the wall. Therefore, they claimed, it not only was aesthetically displeasing but would not necessarily save the city from another flood.

John Skotedis, whose family operates Tedd's Landing Restaurant across the Susquehanna from Sunbury, detests the solid gray barrier. Skotedis grew up in Sunbury, after the wall's construction. He says he may as well have lived fifty miles from the Susquehanna: the river is not part of anyone's life in the town. "The flood wall saved the town but totally alienated the community from the river," he says. "It killed the town as far as I'm concerned. Sunbury's housing values are lower than the rest of the area—no one wants to live there. Now all those beautiful houses on Front Street are either apartments or doctors' or dental offices. You would think today we could avoid something as drastic as totally detaching a community from its environment, its resource."

Shamokin Riffles

The world contains many impressive dams. The Aswan
Dam in Egypt, the Hoover Dam in the western United
States. But where in the world can you find the longest
inflatable dam? It's right here in the Susquehanna Valley.

—Brochure distributed to tourists by the Central Susquehanna
Valley Chamber of Commerce in Sunbury

THE WORLD'S LONGEST INFLATABLE DAM spans Shamokin
Riffles, a rock ledge extending across the Susquehanna just
below Sunbury. Since the late 1960s, the eight-foot-tall rubber dam has raised the water level and created Lake Augusta
in season. Initially, the dam also created a headache for its
operators.

Pennsylvania's Bureau of State Parks installed seven
huge rubber bags filled with both air and water. These
bags spanned the 2,100-foot width of the river from late
spring until early fall. A state work crew then deflated the
bags in place to allow a normal run of the river until the
next spring.

Problems occurred almost immediately when water
remaining in the bags after their first deflation sloshed
around, abrading rubber against piers that anchored the
bags on the ends and against a concrete foundation slab
running along the river bottom. After reinflation, the torn
bags quickly lost air, leaving gaps in the dam. Lake
Augusta's level fell. Boaters went elsewhere.

After the flood of 1972 destroyed all but one of the bags,
the state purchased heavier rubber. The nine bags now in
place are twelve mils thick and contain only air, substantially reducing the possibilities for abrasion and tearing. During
its months of operation, the dam maintains a pool depth
averaging six feet in an area of the Susquehanna that otherwise could be forded.

This pond has become one of central Pennsylvania's
prime recreational assets, drawing ever-larger powerboats
from a wide region. Popularity has a downside: the big
boats make waves that chew into Packer Island. To end
annual erosion of about a foot, Shikellamy State Park has
lined the southern end of the island with riprap. Otherwise,
because it is seasonal, the dam's ecological damage is limited: the deflated dam does not catch silt floating downriver
with high flows in the early spring.

Boats with limited horsepower scoot about in the shallow
water downstream of the dam, where anglers catch impressive numbers of fish. Pennsylvania operates a boat access
here, although many anglers simply wade into the shallows
and cast their lines.

The state did not choose this dam site arbitrarily. An earlier dam at Shamokin Riffles, completed in 1829, created
something like Lake Augusta, not as a recreational resource
but to help launch a brisk but unprofitable and relatively
brief trade on the Pennsylvania Canal.

Pennsylvania's canal commissioners designed a statewide
system connecting Philadelphia with regions west of the
Allegheny Mountains. Governor John Andrew Shulze broke
ground for the Eastern Division of the Main Line of the

Pennsylvania Canal in 1826. This section ultimately ran from Columbia to the Juniata River. A year later, work crews began to construct a canal segment along the Susquehanna's west bank from the Juniata to Northumberland. This thirty-nine-mile stretch, called the Susquehanna Division, connected the Main Line with the soon-to-be-built North Branch and West Branch divisions. Those divisions began at Northumberland and eventually extended to Athens and Lock Haven, making Northumberland the hub of a network of canals extending throughout central Pennsylvania and connecting with canals reaching into the Delaware and Allegheny watersheds.

In 1831 the state built a six-span covered bridge from the end of the Susquehanna Division at Blue Hill across the West Branch to Northumberland. Teams of mules walking on this bridge towed canal boats into Northumberland's pool, from which they could proceed along the North or West Branch divisions.

Without the original Shamokin Dam, the system would not have worked. One of several dams built at various locations to support the Pennsylvania Canal system, Shamokin Dam diverted water into the canal and facilitated operation of the locks. The wooden dam stood 9 1/2 feet high and 2,783 feet long—nearly 700 feet longer than its inflatable successor.

Shamokin Dam did more than create the canal pool: it encouraged steamboats and other craft to use the entire slack water area. In the late 1800s, the Sunbury entrepreneur Ira T. Clement built a fleet of steamboats to tow canal boats from branch to branch, haul sand dredged from bars in the West Branch, and transport coal and iron to and from points on the North Branch.

Sailboats and rowing clubs also used the pool until an ice flood washed out Shamokin Dam in 1904. Members of two Sunbury rowing clubs persuaded sponsors to hold the annual regatta of the National Association of Amateur Oarsmen on the river at Sunbury in July 1888. Crews of collegians from all over the country raced on a measured course. Participants told the *Sunbury Item* they had never rowed in better water.

John Skotedis revived the sport in this region when he returned to work in his father's restaurant after rowing on the Schuylkill River as a Temple University student. Students at Bucknell University, having difficulty rowing in shallow West Branch water at Lewisburg, asked Skotedis to coach them. He formed a first-rate crew, using the deeper west side of the river when the dam was down and any section when the dam was inflated.

He retired as Bucknell's crew coach in 1992 but has remained an active rower. He has noticed more people using the area's primary natural resource in recent years, although he believes many people do not relate to the river at all. "The average person underestimates the value of the river," he says. "A lot of them are caught up in the clichés, that it's useless and polluted. We've had major floods in '36 and '72 and they might know someone who's drowned in the river. The constant reminders of parents to their young children to stay away from the river make a lifelong impression. Because of that, the Susquehanna has been underutilized."

Port Treverton

They used to say that coal travels downstream about 12 miles a year when there wasn't no flood, just ordinary high water, so it should all be down by this time; there shouldn't be any in the water, but there is.

— FLANDERS KELLER, Susquehanna coal dredger

ALL ALONG THE SUSQUEHANNA'S SHORE, visitors find things they might find along any river: driftwood, animal tracks, rusting metal cans, fish skeletons, pokeweed growing up an eroded bank. On beaches and islands south of the Wyoming Valley and especially downriver of Sunbury, they also find something they will see nowhere else but on the Susquehanna—"river coal." It paints dark streaks in light river sand and can darken the water itself; if you walk in it and then wash your sandals in a bathtub, it comes off black and gritty.

Fine particles of this coal corrupt beaches, ruin rich island farmland, and taint the water; but pollution from old anthracite mines and culm piles would be considerably more serious if scavengers such as Flanders Keller had not spent their lives extracting coal from the river. A little old man who wears a billed cap almost constantly and a smile as faithfully, Keller dredged coal from the Susquehanna for more than six decades before retiring in 1996. Known throughout the region as "a real Susquehanna character," he water-skied until he was eighty and after that worried local residents by flying a seaplane beneath low river bridges. His house, like most in Port Treverton, sits on a bluff overlooking the river and Route 11/15. What's left of his coal-dredging operation rests about a mile downriver, among trees and scrub bushes lining the water.

Here small, lightweight pieces of suspended coal drift toward shore, pass over a riffle. and then float through a rough area that was a small island before Keller "pushed it off" with a front-end loader several years ago to preserve his primary dredging area. It seems impossible that coal fragments could float in tiny channels through this broken sediment to coat the beach, but thousands of tons have found a way. Generally, coal stops where the current is sluggish. Asked why coal winds up at this particular spot, Keller says briskly, "Coal just stops wherever it wants to."[4]

Keller did not run a pretty operation. His abandoned heavy machinery wears a crust of rust, as you might expect of equipment that has been in and out of the river and always in the rain for more than half a century. This looks like a riverside junk yard.

This is how it worked. From the dredge, a flexible suction pipe extended into the water. On the end of the pipe, a T-shaped "bonnet" sucked up river muck, including mud, coal, coallike slate particles, and anything else that happened to be in there. A pump drew this conglomeration back through the pipe to the dredge. Meanwhile, a winch wound the dredge against an anchor, slowly sweeping the contraption along the riverbed. "Just like mowing grass," explains Keller.

The dredger ran this muck through a "riffle line" on the

dredge to wash out sand and dirt, then conveyed it to a barge floating in water right next to the shore. A "scraper line," pulled by a cable, moved the material from the barge onto a truck on shore. Keller drove the truck up onto a hopper. There the coal washed over a shaker, the smaller and lighter pieces floating along and heavier pieces of coal and slate falling through a screen. Finally, the coal washed through three fine screens, separating it by size. "Barley" coal is the finest, with particles the size of sand. "Pea" coal is about half an inch or larger. "Buckwheat" is in between.

Keller sold barley coal to Pennsylvania Power & Light Company (now PPL Utilities), which used it to power its Sunbury Steam Plant, just south of Shamokin Riffles. Residents of Port Treverton and nearby areas bought Keller's buckwheat and pea coal to use in their hand-fired home stoves.

In one especially good year during the mid-1990s, Keller took a thousand tons of coal from this spot. Upstream mining had ended and all of the waste coal should have moved down the river years before, so where did a thousand tons come from?

"I can answer a lot of questions about the river, but that I can't answer, because after they passed that new clean streams law, they weren't going to put anything in the river no more," says Keller, smiling slyly. "After they passed that law, for about two or three weeks we didn't get no coal. But then we didn't take the processing plant down right away. We thought we'd wait till after deer season—and by that time the coal started to come again and it's been slow but steady ever since."

Whether this new coal is coming from abandoned culm piles or riverbanks that are washing out or illegal mining operations, Keller cannot say. He does say the amount coming downriver now represents a tiny fraction of the coal tonnage that floated past Port Treverton during the days of active mining.

Dip-netting scavengers began hauling coal out of the river about 1880. They ferried a net or a screen with a handle out to a bed of coal, climbed out into the shallow water, and sifted the larger pieces from dirt and sand. Later, dip-netters developed screen handles ten or more feet long, allowing them to work from a larger flatboat in deeper water.

Commercial-scale coal dredging began in the 1890s, when entrepreneurs realized the market for fine coal extended beyond the home furnace to businesses that could buy truckloads. Clarence and Walter Liddick of Clarks Ferry remembered when the Susquehanna, running black with coal at the turn of the century, prompted rival dredging outfits to compete with fists and clubs for choice digging sites.

Early dredges were of two types. The most common resembled Keller's. The other type, which dredgers eventually phased out, employed buckets on an endless chain. The buckets dipped into the water to pick up coal, sand, and dirt and dumped their loads onto screens on the dredge. The sand and dirt escaped through the screens and workers loaded the remaining coal on barges.

Up to a point, the river itself sorted coal. Larger, heavier pieces generally sank in upstream areas. (Keller keeps a hunk of coal as big as his head in his basement.) South of

Harrisburg, dredgers always had a hard time finding coal larger than marble size. The finer coal swept down and sometimes over the dams on the Lower Susquehanna and into the Chesapeake. Finest coal has reached the mouth of the Patapsco River at Baltimore.

Dredging for coal turned into a big business in the early decades of the twentieth century. One expert estimated that 900 million tons of coal had accumulated in the river by 1904. In 1942, the U.S. Bureau of Mines listed twenty-one independent dredging fleets on the Susquehanna and another nine on tributaries. The bureau said these operations had salvaged 943,944 tons of coal in 1940 alone. So many dredges operated in the vicinity of Harrisburg that writers began referring to them as the "Pennsylvania Navy."

These "little water parasites," as James Boyd called coal-dredging operations in his 1935 novel, *Roll River,* could operate successfully only as long as a generous supply of coal kept washing down the river. When miners began to appreciate the value of smaller sizes of coal and reduced the waste they allowed to enter the water, the river removal business suffered. By 1951, only ten dredgers operated on the river and four on tributaries.

One of them was Flanders Keller, who bought his first dredging "outfit" from a bankrupt gravel company in Williamsport and floated it down the river. He ran his dredge into the same bridge pier at Muncy that the Last Raft had hit—"only I was just about standing still, you know, so I didn't do any damage"—and cruised on to Port Treverton. Keller committed himself to coal dredging and decided to buy other outfits as their owners quit. Eventually

A dredger operates a paddle-wheel boat with coal-retrieving apparatus along the Susquehanna's West Shore in 1902. Part of City Island and bridges leading to Harrisburg are visible in the background. (Pennsylvania State Archives, Harrisburg.)

he owned the largest dredging operation. From 1945 to 1950, he sold at least 60,000 tons of coal each year to PPL's Sunbury plant.

Other large users of river coal included the American Car and Foundry Company at Berwick, the Bloomsburg Steam Heating Company, the Steelton plant of Bethlehem Steel, and PPL's power generator at Holtwood.

Holtwood Dam stopped the lightest and farthest-traveling coal immediately after its construction in 1910. By the mid-1920s, the amount of coal particles building up in the pond behind the dam concerned Holtwood's operators. They built a steam-generating plant next to the hydroelectric facility and began dredging what they called "fines" (fine coal pieces) to fuel it. Holtwood became the only power plant in the world producing both hydro and steam power.

From 1925 to 1953, huge dredges moved slowly back and forth through the Holtwood pond, drawing out the anthracite and loading it on barges. Workers sorted and dried the coal, blew it into furnaces, and ignited it. Coal-produced heat condensed water into steam to operate turbines that generated electricity for hundreds of thousands of PPL customers.

After 1931, the new Safe Harbor Dam stopped most of the coal that previously had floated 8 miles downriver to Holtwood. After 1953, with the Holtwood reservoir's coal load exhausted, dredgers moved to the pond behind Safe Harbor. Working from early March through mid-December, the crew salvaged about 500,000 tons of coal a year. Bad weather rarely stopped operations.[5]

Marion "Gus" Towner of Millersville worked as a shift foreman of dredging operations in both dam ponds. "The fellows did work through some very unusual weather conditions," he recalls. "They were always most concerned with the high flow on the river. That was very hard to handle. In 1972, when that big flood came, we brought everything downriver and tied it up securely."

Towner's crew saved the dredges and barges, but Agnes ended PPL's coal operations on the Susquehanna. The flood swept an enormous amount of debris, including coal, from the Safe Harbor pond downriver and eventually into the Chesapeake. Dredging no longer could compete with other methods of obtaining coal and Holtwood began trucking in anthracite from Schuylkill County. After passage of the Clean Air Act of 1990, Holtwood's operators burned less polluting bituminous coal. The plant closed, a victim of high coal costs, in 1999.

Today only Keller and Bernie Sudol of Danville still keep dredging equipment on the river. Sudol purchased his outfit from Keller before Keller junked much of the rest of his fleet. He quit operating about the same time Keller did, and that was the end of coal dredging.

An inscription on a plaque at the sunken garden in Harrisburg's Riverfront Park reads: "Sunken Garden is the excavated foundation area of dwellings once occupied by migrant river coal dredgers working the Susquehanna River bottom during the 19th and early 20th Centuries." An uninformed visitor observing the relatively coal-free Susquehanna today might comment, "Why in the world would dredgers look for coal in the water?"

Millersburg

The wild geese are flying north and the Millersburg Ferry is in operation. Spring has indeed sprung.

—Annual postcard message to Pennsylvania newspaper editors from
Jack Dillman, former Millersburg Ferry captain

Old joke: A fellow is standing on the bank of a river. He spots another fellow standing on the other side of the water. "How do I get to the other side?" he shouts across. And the other fellow yells, "You're already there!"

If voices could carry across the mile-wide Susquehanna at Millersburg, that might be a common dialogue. When the town's ferryboats are not running—that is, most of the year—only such a humorous perspective would carry travelers to the other side. The closest bridges cross the Susquehanna at Sunbury–Shamokin Dam, twenty-eight miles north, and Duncannon–Clarks Ferry, fourteen miles south.

The Susquehanna's last ferryboats cruise between Millersburg, population 3,000, and the Perry County shore, population one campground. They operate on most days from May to October, provided one of three captains is working and running water is sufficient to float a boat. Don't figure on a scheduled departure time; the ferries leave when they have passengers.

Finding passengers, especially on summer weekends, is rarely a problem. As the oldest remaining transportation company in Pennsylvania, employing the last existing wooden stern-wheel paddleboats in the United States, the Millersburg Ferry draws international interest. During any summer week, passengers from several continents, along with the locals, board one of these colorful ferryboats to ride across the water and back into time.

They cross obliquely from Kramer's Landing at Millersburg past Halfway Island to Crow's Landing at Ferryboat Campsites. The view from a boat in midstream can be spectacular on a clear day. Mahantango Mountain, cut by the northernmost of the Susquehanna water gaps, looms upstream. Downstream, the wide river stretches away toward Harrisburg. This 20-minute scenic ride is as close to really seeing the Susquehanna as some people get.

The *Falcon*, built in 1975 and modeled on an earlier boat by that name, makes the crossing with a gas-powered 1948 Farmall combine engine that periodically requires rare and costly spare parts. The *Roaring Bull*, reconstructed in 1998 by the Millersburg Ferry Boat Association, employs a modern Duetz air-cooled diesel engine that cost a small fortune but is easier and cheaper to maintain. The engines of both turn wooden paddles that churn the water as the boats move methodically from shore to shore.

Each boat tows a barge attached to its starboard side. A barge can carry four cars at a time or as many as seven Amish or Mennonite buggies, with horses unhitched. The ferries themselves carry up to fifty-two passengers. A car and driver can make the trip for $4. Walk-on passengers pay $1. Most days it is possible to save a buck by crossing the shallow river on foot. Knowledgeable river folk recommend using a stick to poke for deep holes along the way.

The Susquehanna must have at least eighteen inches of water in it or the *Falcon* and *Roaring Bull* will get stuck on sand and gravel bars or the rock bottom of the river. Nearly every spring, ferry operators rebuilt a downstream wall of river rocks and mud that stretched across the Susquehanna and held back enough water to allow the ferry pilots to use their three channels. The river fell so low during the drought of '99 that the Ferry Boat Association spent $15,000 to build a more permanent boulder wall.

Don Lebo, Cliff Tschopp, and Bill Sheaffer are the Ferry Boat Association's current U.S. Coast Guard–certified captains. All grew up along the river and understand its changeable nature. Sheaffer, a science teacher at Millersburg

High School, has fished in and boated on the Susquehanna for two decades. He has been working on a history of Millersburg and the ferry, and he tells stories about both as he pilots travelers to the other side.

Sheaffer explains his fascination with the ferry: "Of the boats on the river—the *Hiawatha* [a Williamsport riverboat], the Millersburg ferry, and the *Pride of the Susquehanna* [a Harrisburg riverboat]—the ferry is the most difficult to run. But it's the most historic—it's closest to the river." He pauses, considering his decade of work on the ferry. "It's relaxing to be on the water, but it's a tough job. I'm tired at the end of the day."

Jack Dillman, now a captain of the *Pride of the Susquehanna,* spent several decades as a ferry captain, coal dredger, and self-described "river rat" at Millersburg. He enjoyed everything about the job except the weather. If wicked weather loomed, Dillman refused to cross. But one afternoon in 1982, after he had carried six Mennonite buggies and wagons from Millersburg to Perry County and was taking five more, a thunderstorm caught him in the middle of the Susquehanna.

"It was thundering with lightning and the works, and the wind blew us right up against the dam," Dillman told the *National Geographic* in 1985. "So there I was with three buggies, two wagons, seven horses, and a bunch of Mennonite boys waiting for it all to go away. Fortunately the boys and the horses all took this in stride. All except for one horse, that is. You can still see his teeth marks on the rail."

Sheaffer rarely waits for the weather to change. "You have to go when customers want to go across. You have to ride the weather and the river," he explains. "It's kind of like the lobster fishermen. You have to go. You can't say, 'I'll go home and take a nap and take you across later.'" Sheaffer did not consult the weather forecast a few years ago when he made an emergency run to reunite a woman and her mother. He crossed, at nearly full throttle, in twelve minutes

Millersburg ferry captains and crossing stories go back almost two centuries. In 1790, Daniel Miller, a farmer, teacher, minister, and Revolutionary War soldier, purchased nearly a thousand acres of land and rights to operate a ferry and to fish for shad at this place. In 1807 he plotted the town, sold its first lots, and gave it his name.

Miller did not actually operate the ferry. Successive owners of the ferry rights began transporting customers in the early decades of the nineteenth century. They rowed large boats in high water and poled canoes and flatboats when the river level fell. A ferryman launched a side-wheeled steamboat for the first time in 1873. This boat towed a flat loaded with cargo and required the building of the ferry wall to ensure a constant pool. The first stern paddle wheeler, a converted coal dredger, slipped into the water in 1905. All subsequent ferryboats have been stern-wheelers.

In the late 1980s, a Millersburg bank bought the boats and turned them over to the Ferry Boat Association, which operates them with the aid of substantial donations and grants. The association now runs and markets the operation as a tourist and historic attraction, promoting Millersburg's transportation heritage while recognizing that no one plans to ride this ferry as an exercise in efficiency.

Because of the ferry, Millersburg still recognizes the Susquehanna as an integral part of the community. The paddle-wheelers are launched each May in conjunction with the town's Cherry Blossom Festival and the Roaring Bull Canoe Race. On the Fourth of July, the community sponsors a concert at its riverfront park and sets off fireworks above the water. Labor Day is Stern-Wheeler Day: Decorated rafts cruise the water while a street carnival and live entertainment fill the park.

Tina Fetter is a past chairperson of the Ferry Boat Association and owner of Tina's Sandwich Shop, just across River Street from the ferry landing. "The ferry is what Millersburg is all about," she told *Apprise*, a regional magazine. "Without it, we'd be just another town on the river. If the ferries ever died, it would be just like a death in the family."

Scores of other Susquehanna ferries passed away long ago. Occasionally they left their names to places (Fishers Ferry, Clarks Ferry, Shenks Ferry, McCalls Ferry) or to roads (Ferry Street in Athens, Simpson Ferry Road on the West Shore across from Harrisburg) or to buildings (Wright's Ferry mansion in Columbia). Many, especially those on the lower river, started operating before the Millersburg Ferry. The first, the Susquehanna Lower Ferry, began crossing at the mouth of the river in 1695. By 1788, at least seventeen ferries crossed the final seventy-five miles of the river in Pennsylvania and Maryland.

Simple fords were more numerous and often predated ferries. Given the Susquehanna's shallowness, finding a fordable spot for foot or horse passage was not difficult. It was

The original Falcon *ferryboat docked at the Millersburg Landing sometime before 1910. The boat towed the car on the barge across the Susquehanna from Perry County. (Pennsylvania State Archives, Harrisburg.)*

difficult, especially in the rocky lower river, to find a spot even enough to cross with a wagon. Early settlers stabilized fords with flat rocks. Later residents laid out fords on dam breasts.

Fords and ferries (and later bridges) often coexisted. Timothy Dwight, president of Yale College, forded the North Branch near Unadilla, New York, in the autumn of 1804 because the ferryboat was unavailable and a bridge had not yet been completed. "There was nothing left us, therefore, but to cross a deep and rapid ford," he wrote. "Happily, the bottom was free from rocks and stones."

If Dwight had taken that ferry across the relatively narrow river, he would have been poled in a scow or other small boat. Earlier ferry owners had employed canoes or dugouts. In the nineteenth century, operators turned to rope ferries. Ferrymen grasped a rope cable stretched across the river and pulled themselves and boats ahead on the water or, less commonly, employed horses to haul boats by pulling heavy ropes wound on capstans.

Operators generally located ferries upstream of riffles, which slowed and deepened water. Where riffles were insufficient, as at Millersburg, they built seasonal ferry walls.

Communities often developed around ferrying points. John Wright's Ferry, established on the east bank of the river in 1730, became Columbia. John Harris's Ferry, started on the same side three years later, became Harrisburg. These ferries were equally popular. In the early years, scores of people awaited passage in dugouts that could carry a ton or more. Later, as many as 200 wagons lined up to await passage on the larger flatboats. Sometimes they waited several days.

Ferries made good businesses. Wright's Ferry, situated on a direct line from Lancaster to York and at one of the few gaps in the river hills, enriched John Wright and his son. John Wright Sr. built a ferry house and his own substantial home and became a community leader in Columbia. John Wright Jr. took charge of the western end of the ferry and built a ferry house and tavern at present-day Wrightsville.

No one could simply find a likely spot along the river, haul out his boat, begin a ferrying service, and make a fortune. Colonial governments regulated early ferries and granted patents for their operation. Various entrepreneurs vied for the trade. The Wrights had two primary competitors, one north and one south.

William Anderson's ferry ran between Marietta and Accomac, about three miles north of Wright's Ferry, where the river is considerably narrower. John Wright objected to the granting of a patent for this ferry but lost for two reasons. One was pragmatic: water often fell so low at Columbia that boats needed an alternative route. The other was geographic: while Wright's accommodated travelers from Philadelphia by way of Lancaster, Anderson's served traffic moving from New England and New York by way of Reading. Their trade rarely overlapped and most travelers eventually preferred Anderson's route.

In the same year Wright started his ferry, Thomas Cresap established a service about four miles south at Blue Rock, on the west bank of the river, opposite the present town of Washington Boro. A Marylander, Cresap settled in territory that Pennsylvania and Maryland disputed. The disagreement led to the survey of a line between the two colonies in 1763 by Charles Mason and Jeremiah Dixon. Pennsylvania did not recognize Cresap's ferry; Maryland did. John Wright and other Pennsylvanians had political as well as economic reasons to want Cresap and his ferry removed.

According to Cresap's account, he had just begun to pole two Pennsylvanians from the east bank toward his ferry landing one autumn afternoon in 1730 when the two raised guns and ordered him to return to shore. To avoid capture, Cresap struck at the two with his pole, but they overpowered him and tossed him into the river. Cresap could not swim and would have drowned had he not found footing on a rock.

Violence escalated as armed Pennsylvanians repeatedly crossed the river and Cresap retaliated. After Cresap and his associates killed a man, Pennsylvanians burned his cabin and imprisoned him. In the summer of 1737, King George II freed Cresap and calmed hostilities between the warring colonies. Unable to abide the peace, Cresap abandoned his ferry and moved west.

Wright's Ferry survived all competition and continued operating, under a succession of owners, until 1924. At that time, the ferryboat captain was George Leitheiser, a Civil War veteran who had served as a boatman on the Susquehanna and Tidewater Canal. Blown into a rock by a storm shortly before the ferry service ended, Leitheiser coped with a hole in his hull and, according to a newspaper account, "lots of excitement, especially among the women passengers, a few of whom became hysterical."

Limited in capacity and constantly challenged by low water and bad weather, ferries had been superseded by bridges in many places on the Susquehanna's branches a century before Leitheiser wrecked his boat. The Pennsylvania legislature authorized eight long bridges on the lower Susquehanna in 1809. High water or ice destroyed most of them within a few years but new bridges quickly replaced them.

At Columbia, for example, Theodore Burr's 1814 covered bridge lasted only until 1832, when floodwaters drove huge chunks of ice through it.[6] Union soldiers burned its replacement, also a covered bridge, to stop advancing Confederate troops before the battle of Gettysburg.[7] The third bridge lasted until 1896, and both automobiles and trains used a fourth bridge. Motorists demanded a new concrete bridge, solely for motorcars, so a fifth bridge at the approximate location of Wright's Ferry carried the Lincoln Highway (Route 462) across the river in 1930. A companion bridge began carrying Route 30 traffic in 1972.

Many of the Susquehanna's major crossing points have similar histories—of multiple bridges built throughout the nineteenth and twentieth centuries at or near the locations of ferries or fords. Because of the width of the lower river, many of these bridges set records for length. The first and second spans at Columbia were the longest covered bridges (5,690 feet) in the world. At just over 360 feet, the covered bridge at the lower river's narrowest point at McCalls Ferry was the longest single-span timber-arch bridge ever built in the United States. The 7,500-foot-long 1930 bridge at Columbia, with twenty-eight spans, is one of the longest concrete-arch bridges in the world. With forty-eight arches stretching 3,830 feet across the river above Harrisburg, the 1902 Rockville Bridge is the world's longest stone-arch railroad bridge.[8]

Where length is not an issue, some of the river's most picturesque bridges span its beginnings. The little concrete bridge that carries Main Street across the river's outlet from Lake Otsego at Cooperstown stands at the approximate location of the first bridge—a tall pine tree felled across the stream in 1786. At McGees Mills in Clearfield County, the only remaining covered bridge on the West Branch has carried one lane of traffic since 1873.

But no bridge crossing conveys anything like the nostalgic kick of cruising the Susquehanna on the anachronistic Millersburg Ferry. Agitation for a bridge at Millersburg during World War I and again in the 1930s and early '50s nearly brought results that almost certainly would have stopped the last of the old-time ferryboats. But, as the state decided then and there and at other times at various locations, this long and winding, broad and shallow river cannot be bridged, as it cannot be diked, all along the way.

Juniata River

I wish you could see on a summer evening, the bright silver

surface of the noble Susquehanna . . . or spend a tranquil

evening, as I did, in the groves of Duncan's Island, within

the gates of the Blue Ridge, near the mouth of the Juniata,

listening to the murmur of the rivers, or the song of the

mocking-bird.

—Charles Joseph Latrobe,
The Rambler in North America, 1836

THE TRIBUTARY JUNIATA RIPPLES over riffles to meet the Susquehanna at the southern end of Duncan's Island. Drivers crossing the Clarks Ferry Bridge over the Susquehanna may not notice the Juniata's half-mile-wide mouth. The extensive road and bridge works in the Amity Hall–Clarks Ferry area tend to overwhelm the natural scenery, which itself is complex.

Two large and very different islands dominate the area. One is Duncan's, which has been developed with a variety of Route 11/15 "strip" businesses, including Island Auto Sales and Island Concrete. Duncan's actually belongs to both rivers. The two-mile-long island is bordered on the west by the Juniata and on the east by the Susquehanna.

The mouth of the Juniata defines the island's southern end. A secondary mouth once skirted Duncan's on the north. Old rivermen called this second mouth "the gut." Current islanders refer to it as "the crick." While working on the Juniata Division of the Pennsylvania Canal in the early 1830s, workers filled this gut with earth excavated from the canal. For the better part of two centuries, Duncan's has not been a real island, except during big floods when the Juniata overflows into the Susquehanna along the old gut.

Haldeman's Island, also about two miles long, lies just east of Duncan's. The narrowest sliver of Susquehanna water separates the two. Haldeman's remains largely in its natural state as State Game Lands no. 290. The wider swath of the mile-wide Susquehanna washes past Haldeman's eastern shore.

Many generations of Native Americans camped on these islands. Their favorite place seems to have been the southern tip of Duncan's, where they could take advantage of good fishing in both rivers. Workers digging the canal channel through this area cut into a large burial mound. They hauled away hundreds of cartloads of human bones. Mixed with tons of dirt, these bones helped to fill in the Juniata gut and dam the entire Susquehanna, providing a pool deep enough to tow canal boats from east to west.

This expansive upriver view (ca. 1930s) shows, from left to right, the town of Duncannon on the west shore, the Juniata River entering the Susquehanna, Duncan's Island (relatively undeveloped), Haldeman's Island, and the main course of the Susquehanna sweeping around the islands on the right. Clarks Ferry Bridge crosses the Susquehanna. (Pennsylvania State Archives, Harrisburg.)

"The original canal would have gone through the gun shop. It would have gone through the Outfitters. There's an itty-bitty portion of the canal left right over there." Eric Reeser is talking about Reeser's Gunshop and Gunsmithing, which he owns; Greg Smith's Surplus and Outfitters shop; and a canal remnant nearby. The two stores flank Route 849 at Duncan's tip, just across the Juniata River bridge from Duncannon and just before that road joins 11/15. Reeser's family has owned this land at the rivers' confluence for decades.

An amiable young dealer in firearms, Reeser looks out across the Susquehanna from the point. "You can walk almost clean across the river here," he says. "There's one area, just on the other side of that grass section in the middle, that gets a little deep, then it goes back to shallow again."

The Susquehanna ordinarily is so shallow here that you can see heavy timbers on the bottom, crossing the river like railroad ties. These timbers supported the covered bridge that permitted both land traffic and mules towing canal barges to cross from Clarks Ferry on the eastern shore to Duncan's. The canal then split, with the main branch running up the Susquehanna's western shore to Northumberland and the Juniata Division running along Duncan's Island to Amity Hall, then crossing to the west side of the Juniata and following it. "It's a good fishing spot—especially where these two rivers meet," says Reeser. "There's a big hole right in there, less than fifty yards off the point. The fish kind of congregate in that hole. They come in there and they swirl right there where the two rivers meet."

A pronounced diagonal line, similar to the division of waters at Northumberland, extends from Duncan's point, separating the Susquehanna and Juniata. The larger Susquehanna pushes back its contributor. John Cunningham, whose family owns Riverfront Campground, along the Susquehanna just south of the confluence, says the line provides the best place to fish: "When you have two rivers come together, the one will stop the other. Fish are lazy. All they do is lay there and let the food come to them. It's the best buffet around."

Anglers launch boats from the campground or walk across the end of Duncan's, where concrete and stone remains of the old bridge and canal works form a buffer against erosion when the Juniata goes on a rampage. They may wade far out into both rocky rivers to catch muskies and walleyes, channel catfish and bass.

Native American residents also appreciated plentiful fishing opportunities, as well as easy water access to distant points in three directions. Several ancient trails follow the Juniata for the same reason the state began building the canal along that valley before extending it up the West Branch: the Juniata provides the most direct path from the Philadelphia market to Pittsburgh.

When completed in 1834, the entire Juniata system included a state-owned railroad from Philadelphia to Columbia, the canal up the Susquehanna and along the Juniata to Hollidaysburg, the Allegheny Portage Railroad across formidable mountain ridges between Hollidaysburg and Johnstown, and another canal from Johnstown along the Conemaugh and Kiskiminetas to Freeport and then down the Allegheny to Pittsburgh. Pennsylvania's less efficient response to the Erie Canal was sometimes called "the Great Canal."

The Juniata Division began in the canal basin at Amity Hall, on the northern end of Duncan's, and ran 127 miles to Hollidaysburg, crossing the Juniata several times and, on occasion, running in the river itself. The canal provided the first major east–west transportation route in America and immediately opened the Juniata Valley to settlement.

Philip Houlbrouke Nicklin followed this route in the 1830s before he wrote his travel book with the alliteration-littered title *A Pleasant Peregrination through the Prettiest Parts of Pennsylvania, Performed by Peregrine Prolix.* Approaching Clarks Ferry, Nicklin observed the canal skirting Peters Mountain;

and separated from the Susquehanna by an enormous wall of stone and earth, it debouches through a wide opening of solid masonry into the mighty river, here converted into a lake by an immense dam. As the boat entered the river, the horses ascended to a gallery high in the air, attached to the side of a great bridge of timber, which here extends its numerous and expanded arches across the river, and thus drew us across the wide expanse of water. Having passed the river, the boat entered the canal on the south-western side of Duncan's Island, through a superb lock of solid masonry; the romantic river Juniata discharging its limpid waters into the Susquehanna close on the left.

Charles Dickens traveled this way on a trip from Baltimore to Pittsburgh in 1842. "Sometimes, at night," Dickens reported of the canal segment along the Juniata in *American Notes,* "the way wound through some lonely gorge, like a mountain pass in Scotland, shining and coldly glittering in the light of the moon, and so closed in by high steep hills all round, that there seemed to be no egress save through the narrower path by which we had come, until one rugged hillside seemed to open, and, shutting out the moonlight as we passed into its gloomy throat, wrapped our new course in shade and darkness."[9]

Much of the Juniata flows through a narrow, meandering valley, with occasional tall cliffs hovering over river travelers. The most dramatic gorge runs for about three miles between Jacks Mountain and Clear Ridge near Mount Union. Outside the towns along its banks, the Juniata riverscape remains largely green, with mountain forests yielding to substantial farmland near the mouth. Like the Susquehanna, it is a pleasant, rural, unnavigable river.

And, like the Susquehanna, the Juniata is formed of substantial branches. The Frankstown Branch begins west of Altoona and runs about fifty-six miles before joining the river. The shorter Little Juniata starts east of Altoona and curves south to join the Frankstown Branch above Huntington, where the Juniata officially begins. Several miles below the Frankstown–Little Juniata confluence, the Juniata's longest tributary enters. The Raystown Branch flows a hundred miles from Bedford. Thirty of those miles are widened by Raystown Lake, the 1970s flood-control project that created the largest unnatural body of water in Pennsylvania.

The Juniata itself is only 100 miles long but, thanks to its extensive tributaries, drains some 3,400 square miles. That makes it the Susquehanna's second largest tributary (if the West Branch is considered the first) and Pennsylvania's sixth largest river overall. An observer may find that hard to believe while overlooking the shallow, rocky, becalmed mouth gently commingling with the Susquehanna. Until it floods, the Juniata (also known by anglers as "the Juice") is a sleeper.

Harrisburg: Water Gaps

The river was cut by the world's great flood and runs over

rocks from the basement of time.

—Norman Maclean, *A River Runs through It*

Amid this mob of mountains glides the Susquehanna to the sea.

—N. P. Willis, *Letters from Under a Bridge*

A visitor to Reservoir Park, a singular 600-foot hill accessible from Harrisburg's Walnut Street, might not expect to enjoy one of the most spectacular views of the Susquehanna's valley. But here it is: from the peak of the park, about a mile from the Susquehanna, one looks north to three flat-topped ridges, incised by the river up to a depth of 850 feet. The mountains range into the distance, with the river running through them like a path plowed through drifted snow.

Blue (also known as First), Second, and Peters mountains all impressively stop dead at the water's edge on both sides—dramatic evidence that water conquers rock. These are three of the Susquehanna's five water gaps. From this vantage point, the taller Second Mountain obscures Third Mountain and its gap. Mahantango Mountain, the northernmost of the series, stands well upstream and out of sight near Montgomery Ferry. This spectacular section of river and hills—from Mahantango to Blue Mountain—is a national natural landmark and a geologic puzzler of the first order.[10]

These sandstone Appalachian ridges are as hard as rock anywhere in the Susquehanna Valley. They are so hard that at Blue, Second, and Peters mountains they squeeze the river to its narrowest measurements between Sunbury and Chickies Rock, near Marietta. They are so hard that their streambed remnants, running as riffles across the water between mountain ridges, remain as substantial impediments to navigation.

For two centuries, geologists have debated why the river cut through these mountains. Practically everywhere else along its route, the Susquehanna swerved when possible to avoid heavy rock cutting. At the water gaps, the river barreled straight through the tough stuff. Theories abound, some of them half-baked. The earliest: an enormous inland ocean burst through the mountains in its quest for the Atlantic, catastrophically carving huge gaps in solid rock. Later geologists believed the river took advantage of fractures or worn ridges in the rock when it chose the precise location of each cut. Once settled in the fracture, running water eroded rock over millions of years—slowly for the most part, more quickly when melted glacier water coursed down the valley.

In 1889 William Morris Davis, in a paper titled "The Rivers and Valleys of Pennsylvania," proposed a plausible theory that remained popular for decades but is no longer supported by many geologists. He said, simply, that the river is older than the mountains. The river ran through the area—on a relatively flat surface called the Schooley peneplain—before geological forces uplifted the region. As the mountains rose, the river, already embedded in the landscape, continued to cut through rock, but not nearly as much rock as earlier theories suggested. This is an easy idea to like. All you have to accept is that the water was always in that place, a moving but immovable object. This irrepressible horizontal force continued to cut away as the earth heaved rock upward.

William Sevon, of the Pennsylvania Geological Survey in Harrisburg, takes issue with this theory. A longtime river watcher who loves to think deeply about the Susquehanna's changes over eons, Sevon proposes a complex variation. Millions of years before the Susquehanna began coursing south from what is now New York across Pennsylvania and into the Chesapeake, Sevon believes, the water in this entire region ran the other way. It drained northwest, toward Ohio.

To understand this radical older drainage pattern requires a leap into the distant past, hundreds of millions of years ago, when an inland body of water called the Appalachian Sea extended from Newfoundland to Alabama. To the southeast of this sea lay tall mountains whose front may have lodged in the vicinity of Philadelphia. Mud, sand, and

Three of the Susquehanna's five water gaps are visible from a downriver vantage point near the National Civil War Museum in Harrisburg's Reservoir Park. (Photo by Christine Brubaker.)

gravel eroded from these mountains. Streams flowing northwest deposited this sediment in the Appalachian Sea and along the sea's margins. Eventually the pile of accumulated sediment stood many miles thick, all cemented together to form various kinds of rock.

About 260 million years ago and over a period of 10 to 20 million years, the continent of Africa collided with North America in a cataclysmic event called the Alleghanian Orogeny. This spectacular collision created another huge mountain range. Computer modeling by Penn State

University researchers indicates that this range, the Alleghanian Mountains, measured between 2.2 and 2.8 miles high and between 155 and 220 miles wide.

As these mountains formed, enormous pressure from the impact of the collision of continents squeezed rocks in the Appalachian Sea area into many folds, called anticlines and synclines. Then the Alleghanian Mountains began to erode. Streams flowing from them, still toward the northwest, carried sediment that had been deposited on top of the new anticlines and synclines. For a few million years, water continued to drain as if nothing had changed, except for the formation of the new mountain range.

About 230 million years ago, Africa split from North America and the Atlantic Ocean washed between. At the same time, a narrow inland basin formed between the present locations of Gettysburg, Pennsylvania, and Newark, New Jersey. Sediment from the highlands still existing in the Philadelphia area began filling this basin from the southeast. A smaller amount of sediment ran in from the north, indicating that some streams were beginning to flow from northwest to southeast. Deposition in this basin may have stopped 200 million years ago. Maybe.

Sevon pauses to run his hand through his white hair and ponder the next 100 million years of geologic history. "Nothing is really known about what happened in Pennsylvania between the end of deposition in the Gettysburg-Newark Basin and about 100 million years ago," he says, "but the scenario was probably something like this." Over the next 100 million years, the mountains in southeastern Pennsylvania gradually eroded away to low hills. Streams developed on the southeast side of these mountains and flowed into the new ocean. Then these streams began to erode headward—extending their length by cutting into material at their headwaters—from the southeast toward the northwest. Sevon believes that a stream that would become the Susquehanna River formed in this way. It gradually cut inland from the Atlantic, across the remains of the former mountain range in southeastern Pennsylvania, across the Gettysburg-Newark Basin, and finally through the rocks formed in the area where the Appalachian Sea had been.

"Why did it choose a path through the five water gaps north of Harrisburg?" Sevon asks. He looks hard at the multicolored Pennsylvania geology map on the wall of his Harrisburg office. "Probably because it was headed in that direction and deviated only slightly from its course because of now long-disappeared variations in the rocks."

As it eroded headward, the lengthening Susquehanna cut across northwestward-flowing streams that were still draining hills remaining in what is now the anthracite coal region. The growing river pirated these streams, pulling their flow south with it. The Juniata is a prime example of a river the Susquehanna captured by stream piracy. The West Branch may be another example. Maybe.

The reason for the uncertainty about much of this scenario relates to research done by C. Wylie Poag, a geologist with the U.S. Geological Survey at Woods Hole, Massachusetts. Poag studied data from extensive seismic profiling and from numerous drill holes in the Baltimore Trough—a deep ocean area off the mid-Atlantic coast. While interpreting patterns, types, and thicknesses of sediment in that trough, Poag discovered several things. Among them: sediment from the Susquehanna did not appear until about 120 million years ago, and the amount of deposition varied considerably over time.

Poag found enormous amounts of sediment, indicating that considerable rock has been eroded by the Susquehanna since it began contributing to the Baltimore Trough. During the past 16 million years alone, the Susquehanna and its tributaries have eroded more than half a mile of rock from the surface of Pennsylvania. This means that the landscape and the position of the river may have been considerably different 16 million years ago, let alone 260 million years ago.

"Keep in mind that we're talking about a situation that is not only occurring in the distant past but it's occurring probably several miles in the air above us," Sevon explains. "That's the hard thing to conceive. A lot has gone on since then. An immense amount of material has been eroded. When you start pushing what happened back that far, you're making many guesses."

Translation: the theory of water gap formation may change again.

Harrisburg: Renewal

Twenty years ago, this was a sewer. Today it's been cleaned

up—the cities, the people are coming back to the river.

—Secretary of the Interior Bruce Babbitt, speaking of the Susquehanna and defending the Clean Water Act at Harrisburg, 1996

Standing on Harrisburg's Front Street in the winter of 1807, the English adventurer Fortescue Cuming surveyed the Susquehanna: "The view from every part of this street is very beautiful, both up and down the river, about five miles each way—terminated upwards by the long ridge of the Blue mountains, through a gap in which . . . the river rolls its rapid current. . . . Several islands add to the beauty of the view, particularly one, on which is a fine farm of nearly one hundred acres just opposite the town."

Cuming examined Harrisburg, then crossed to the West Shore on a ferry flatboat. Workers had cut a channel through the Susquehanna's ice, probably downstream from the farmed island (now called City Island) that so impressed Cuming. Some men on the ferry used iron-pointed wood poles to break a thinner layer of new ice in the channel. Others stuck their poles into the river bottom to hold the boat against the current. Still others poled the boat ahead. Cuming timed the passage at twenty-two minutes before continuing his journey on foot.

The observant traveler followed a popular route. John Harris Sr. began operating his ferry sometime after 1705. Because of the ferry, Harrisburg became a significant stop on the trail leading across the river to Carlisle and on into the wilderness. Harrisburg's first entrepreneur is buried along the river near his ferry landing and not far from an impressive limestone-and-dolomite house built by his son, who founded the city and gave it the family name.

The Harrises controlled the riverfront throughout the nineteenth century, so the railroad and canal had to go around the back side of town. Unlike the river's other sizable cities—Binghamton, Wilkes-Barre, Williamsport—Harrisburg is not separated from its waterway by major highways or industrial buildings along rails. Nor do levees block the view. Situated on an elevated plain some twenty-five feet above the river, Harrisburg has suffered severe flooding but not the catastrophic inundations that have ruined other Susquehanna towns.

The wide swath of green Harris land (now part of Riverfront Park) separates the river from the elegant mansions along Front Street. These homes, many now converted for commerce or social service, face the broad water, as does the capitol building, three blocks back. Stephen Sills designed the imposing structure so that it would look out over the Susquehanna—the primary water route to the commonwealth's interior.

Harrisburgers relate directly to their river. They wade into it to fish. They boat on it and swim in it. They hold their major celebrations on and alongside it. "It's a really friendly river," says Cindy Adams Dunn, director of the Pennsylvania Audubon Society and a longtime river user. "Anyone with old sneakers can walk out into it."

Harrisburg has not always been friendly to the Susquehanna. Two major renewals restored the integrity of the city's relationship with its river.

Residents began drinking the Susquehanna in 1841. Previously they had drawn water from wells and from Paxton Creek, which cuts through the city from north to south before joining the river. Efforts to tap into area springs for a more general supply failed, as did early attempts to channel Susquehanna water into town. After two disastrous fires swept several blocks in 1837, citizens got more serious about providing a steady supply of water.

They built an elaborate municipal water works on Front Street, pumped river water to a large reservoir in what would become Reservoir Park, and distributed it throughout the growing city. The waterworks, with an imposing 230-foot standpipe, attracted early tourists.

By 1900, that facility could not ensure a constant supply of quality drinking water. At least two dozen towns poured raw sewage into the river upstream, just as Harrisburg poisoned water for users downstream. Intensive dredging of coal and sand constantly stirred the soup, causing a murky and sometimes foul-smelling liquid to spill from water taps. Moreover, tin cans, ashes, and other debris discarded by residents who had lost touch with their environment littered the riverbank.

Near the close of 1900, the formidable civic improver Mira Lloyd Dock decried the disaster that the city's water and waterfront had become in a catalytic speech to the Harrisburg Board of Trade. She showed a hundred stereoptican slides comparing Harrisburg's "hideous conditions" to the environment in cleaner American and European cities. Wisely, she also emphasized the "cash value of cleanliness and beauty"—a message she knew her audience of community pillars would not ignore.

The *Harrisburg Telegraph* began agitating for pure water, parks, paved streets, and other city improvements and printed a song, to be sung to the tune of "Marching through Georgia":

When we stroll at the riverfront upon a summer's day,
The perfume that we must inhale is not like new-mown hay.

Progressive residents, organized as the Harrisburg League for Municipal Improvement, promoted a bond issue to finance major public works. In 1902, Harrisburgers passed that measure and elected Vance McCormick mayor to implement the improvements.

Enter J. Horace McFarland, a local business leader who printed 200 garden catalogs and cared deeply about the appearance of his city and country. McFarland took photographs of trash, billboards, and other eyesores in Harrisburg and especially along the Susquehanna and Paxton Creek. He photographed raw sewage floating in river and creek. Then he showed his pictures to civic and church groups. "The streets where you live are more ugly than the fields where beasts live," he told them. Beyond ugliness, he claimed, the polluted water they drank provoked an unusual number of typhoid cases.

As McFarland's crusade (he called it "the awakening") began to succeed, the newly formed American Civic Association elected him president and sent him across the United States to ring similar alarms in other cities. McFarland and the association also lobbied for the national park system. These efforts were part of the City Beautiful Movement, which spread across the nation during the early years of the twentieth century, transforming urban life by improving sanitation, transportation, and recreation. Some efforts did not succeed, the 1911 Better Binghamton campaign among them.

The movement in Harrisburg sparked the city's first renaissance. Between 1902 and 1915, the city increased its park acreage from 46 to 958 and its miles of paved roads from

1851

DINTAMAN'S MOTOR BOAT, ROW BOAT AND CANOE LIVERY.
No. 1122 N. Front Between Herr and Cumberland Street Harrisburg, Pa.
SALE AND STORAGE PAVILION, TWO HUNDRED BOAT CAPACITY
Agents for Morris canvas canoes, W. H. Mullins Pressed Steel Boats and Ferro Gasoline Engines.

Dintaman's Boat Livery handled scores of motorboats, rowboats, and canoes on Harrisburg's Front Street. William W. Stoey, who operated a taxidermy shop two doors from the livery, took this photo "with tourists" in September 1909. (Pennsylvania State Archives, Harrisburg.)

four to seventy-four. City engineers installed a sewer system to intercept the waste that had been feeding directly into the river. They built a concrete channel to keep Paxton Creek within bounds and a huge conduit to drain its floodwaters into the Susquehanna before they passed through the city. "You'd think it was a canal," wrote the local historian Marian Inglewood about Paxton Creek in 1925, "so quiet and docile it has become."

⮊ *Dozens of men work on Harrisburg's concrete steps as a steam dredge helps from the river in September 1914. The project runs nearly three miles along the Susquehanna, stabilizing the riverbank and providing a barrier against minor flooding. (Pennsylvania State Archives, Harrisburg.)*

The largest improvements—those that gave Harrisburg a national reputation—transformed the riverfront. The city built a dam at the end of Dock Street in 1913. The dam deepened the Susquehanna significantly for miles upstream. Although it became one of the most dangerous low-head structures on the river, the Dock Street Dam improved the water supply, reduced opportunities for mosquitoes to breed in low water, and provided some control during flooding.

Engineers constructed an impressive series of concrete steps from the city's plain down to the water. The steps ran nearly three miles along the riverfront, from the dam to the site of the current governor's mansion. They stabilized the riverbank and invited citizens enjoying Riverfront Park to extend their attention to the water.

Perhaps most important, the city developed Fortescue Cuming's favorite island. Harrisburg purchased City Island and constructed a water filtration plant there to remove sewage and coal from drinking water before piping it beneath the Susquehanna to the old pumping station on Front Street.[11] The city also built athletic fields and a grandstand, an amusement park and picnic grounds, and formalized a municipal bathing beach at Sandy Point, on the island's northern tip.

Harrisburg paved this guarded beach with concrete in 1925 and it remains popular. "I don't know of any other city of this size anywhere in the northeastern United States that has a bathing beach out here in the middle of the river in a large metropolitan area," says Ted Clista, a retired state water quality director. "In that sense, it speaks to a pretty good quality of water in the Susquehanna."

Boating increased on the water deepened by the Dock Street Dam. In the years leading up to World War II, the Harrisburg entrepreneur George Reist rented out hundreds of canoes and sailboats from floating boathouses. His *Reist Kipona* dance boat, an enormous platform covered with thousands of colored electric lights, glided along the Susquehanna each summer evening with an orchestra on board.

But even as the band played, inner-city Harrisburg decayed. Harrisburg's population fell from 89,500 in 1950 to 53,000 in 1980. Dozens of businesses left town. City services declined with a declining tax base. The U.S. Department of Housing and Urban Development ranked Harrisburg second worst among America's "distressed cities." The city lost its credit rating. Falling apart, Harrisburg again neglected its waterfront.

Stephen Reed, Harrisburg's big-idea mayor for the past two decades, sparked the city's second revitalization. He encouraged massive downtown investment in retail businesses, hotels, and museums. He spruced up the city's parks, notably Riverfront Park, which now hosts gardens and historical memorials all along the river. (These include a monument erected in 1915 to celebrate the accomplishments of the City Beautiful Movement; the city rededicated it to honor the "Second Renaissance" in 1991.) Most significant, Reed decided to redevelop City Island and make it and the Susquehanna once again the city's focal point.

The mayor commissioned a City Island study. When the report recommended that the island be maintained as a natural park with benches and trails, Reed ignored the advice and did what he wanted to do. He compressed the "nature walk" into a sliver of trees on the island's West Shore side and jazzed up the rest of the island. He built Riverside Stadium to house the Harrisburg Senators, an unusually successful professional baseball franchise. He improved the concrete beach for the swimmers who returned to enjoy improved water quality. He encouraged entrepreneurs to add food concessions, an arcade, and a miniature golf course. The city constructed two island-based marinas, which quickly filled with pontoon boats. City Island's multiple amusements began to draw tens of thousands of visitors

⤳ The Pride of the Susquehanna *docks at one of two marinas on City Island. Passengers enjoy regular dinner cruises along the Harrisburg waterfront. The view is upriver from the Walnut Street Bridge. (Photo by Christine Brubaker.)*

from a region far beyond Harrisburg.[12]

Now when Harrisburgers celebrate, they go to their river. The riverboat *Pride of the Susquehanna* schedules symphony and fireworks cruises during Fourth of July and Labor Day festivities. The Harrisburg Symphony plays on a barge. The century-old Kipona Festival on Labor Day weekend includes canoe races, concerts, arts and crafts displays, and fireworks over the Susquehanna. These celebrations continually remind residents that they live directly on a river.

"The most harmonious cities are those whose buildings can be reflected in a river that flows easily between them, going about its business as a vital artery in urban metabolism," writes Lyall Watson in *The Water Planet.* Harrisburg's buildings stand too far back from the river to be reflected in the water, but otherwise the sentiment suits a city that alternately has rejected and embraced the Susquehanna and finally has accepted it as an essential element of its nature.

Harrisburg: Ice

No river in the United States east of the Rocky Mountains

is subject to greater movement of ice than the Susquehanna.

—Edwin F. Smith, superintendent of the Susquehanna
and Tidewater Canal, 1903

The idea of all this ice is unreal. I've never seen anything

like this. I never thought it would be like this. Never.

—Barbara Sterne, Harrisburg resident, after Susquehanna
ice scoured the Shipoke section, 1996

Early on the afternoon of January 20, 1996, broken ice propelled by a river running ten feet above flood stage jammed behind Harrisburg's Walnut Street Bridge. Chocolate-milk-colored water coursing at high speed pressed this ice against the old iron bridge and tried to push it farther. The tension shook telephone polls on shore. A crowd of flood oglers felt the earth move.

The Walnut Street Bridge runs from Harrisburg to City Island and then on to the West Shore. Water and ice pressure buckled a middle section of the West Shore segment as five people began to walk out there. Tina Manoogian-King, Harrisburg's parks and recreation director, ran onto the bridge and screamed for these people to get off. Three returned rapidly to the West Shore; two ran over the breaking bridge toward Harrisburg. Within minutes, the section ripped free. Two more sections soon joined it in the roiling river. The liberated force of water and ice pushed these bridge parts downriver into the Market Street Bridge. The crowd stared in disbelief.

This bridge had been weakened by even higher floodwaters in 1972. Dubbed "Old Shaky," the oldest surviving Harrisburg bridge and the oldest metal span bridge in the United States had been preserved as an exclusively pedestrian path to the island. More people ordinarily would have been walking on the popular bridge on a Saturday afternoon. Fortunately, most Harrisburgers had anticipated the danger.

The collapse of the Walnut Street Bridge was the most dramatic event during the flood of 1996, but it represented a small part of Harrisburg's overall damage. Floodwater-driven chunks of ice practically clear-cut City Island, breaking up or pushing off much of what the city had built there. Ice packs as abrasive as granite boulders destroyed sections of the steps leading from Riverfront Park to the river. Eight feet of water and chunks of ice as large as automobiles, and sometimes encasing automobiles, covered parts of the city. When the ice and water receded, foul-smelling mud remained in hundreds of homes. Harrisburgers suffered through the cleanup well into spring.

This ice flood was unusual in the scope of its destruction, but not unique. The circumstances of the catastrophe's origin were unique. The wicked weather leading up to the January flood was just the beginning of what would become the wettest year ever recorded in the Susquehanna Basin. Severe early-winter storms generated snowfalls about forty inches above normal. Up to three feet of that snow fell in a blizzard on January 7. On January 19, a warm front with high winds and temperatures melted some of the snow but left a thirty-inch base throughout much of the basin. On that remaining snow pack fell two to five inches of rain. The rain shot directly into streams feeding the Susquehanna. No one had ever seen water rise so rapidly on the tributaries or on the Main Stem. And then, on January 20, the river's twelve-inch ice cover broke.

The ice flood swamped every waterway in Pennsylvania but hit the Susquehanna Basin particularly hard. Fourteen people drowned in the Susquehanna or its tributaries. Four died when an ice jam broke on Lycoming Creek, propelling a four-foot wall of water toward the West Branch at Williamsport. Ice jams damaged all hydroelectric dams on the Lower Susquhanna. Boxcar-sized blocks of ice thrust up on the shore at Creswell, near Safe Harbor Dam, derailed a 122-car Conrail train.

Because it narrows suddenly at several locations and is cluttered by islands and dams and other obstructions, the Lower Susquehanna is plagued by more ice jams and the flash floods they release when they break than any other river in the East. Of the more than fifty substantial floods recorded at Harrisburg since the 1780s, most have been

ꙮ *Floodwater and ice dislodge sections of the Walnut Street Bridge on January 20, 1996. This photo, taken from the West Shore, shows City Island covered by water and ice, with Harrisburg's skyline in the background. (Historical Society of Dauphin County—The John Harris/Simon Cameron Mansion Museum, Harrisburg, Pennsylvania.)*

caused by ice jams and sudden thaws. Floods carrying ice packs often do far more damage than high water by itself. Water may rearrange the landscape, but ice rearranges it and chews it up.

Before the unusually warm winters of the late 1990s, ice thick enough to walk on or even drive across formed between January and March of most years. If a cold spell lasts long enough, ice can stretch for a hundred miles, with lighter "new" ice snaking through older layers. If cold holds even longer, sheet ice can deepen and become grounded. Heavy, grounded ice is the most dangerous when it breaks loose.[13]

When more people depended on the river for their livelihood, the opening of the channel in spring was a major community event. Everyone who lived near big water knew when the ice was about to break. Riverside residents could hear it cracking and popping and rumbling from miles away. Those close enough could feel the rush of air that precedes great movements of ice.

Residents of river communities stopped what they were doing and gathered to celebrate. Jacob Gossler wrote about his experience at Columbia in 1888: "The 'break-up' in the spring, which, singularly enough, almost invariably occurs at night, is an event! The inhabitants on both sides of the river announce it by the blowing of horns and conch-shells and the exhibition of lights. They may indulge now in the extravagance of rockets! The roar of the cracking ice and the rush of the river, accompanied by the noise of the horns and shells, and the flashing lights, is weird and exciting!"

Communities no longer turn out en masse to watch ice crack in the spring, but veteran river watchers never miss it.

Donald Oyler lives in a home where the Conodoguinet Creek runs into the Susquehanna at West Fairview, directly across from Harrisburg. He boats and fishes on the river and he waits for the ice to break each spring the way other people watch for first flowers and migrating birds.

"Sometimes you can really hear it coming," he says. "Oh, boy, it cracks. Especially at night, when it's quiet, then it begins really roaring along—until it jams. Then you hear it grinding, you know, and sometimes it will slide under other ice." Oyler points out at the broad river sprinkled with small islands just north of City Island. "Out there one year a big piece of it started to go overtop of other ice. Then it jammed against an island. Then it went *under* the ice that was there and you could see it lift the whole sheet of ice up in the air."

The winter of 1994 was unusually cold and snowy. Thick ice formed early. Then temperatures fluctuated in late February and March, causing ice to thaw and refreeze for several weeks. The ice cracked hard for the first time one late February afternoon. "A buddy and I were standing in front of the house talking and I heard this just like thunder," Oyler recalls, "and I looked up the river and I seen it starting to crack and shove, and in only a matter of minutes it was out here and it hit these trees along the water and starts to jam against them. Then it ran up the creek 'cause the creek was open and it just took all them trees along the creek and laid them up against the bank like matchsticks."

Oyler warms to a cold subject: "Other winters ice hits the end of an island and in a matter of minutes there'll be fifty feet of ice sticking up out there. I went out and boated around one of those tall jams. I didn't get too close. It eventually let loose. Half of it came down at once and made waves. It was high—maybe thirty, forty, fifty feet. That was somethin' to see."

Oyler does not speak with similar awe about the flood of '96. The white rubble that jammed behind the Walnut Street Bridge held back a pond of water that infiltrated Oyler's home. "We had forty-eight inches inside the house," he says. "The lower rooms were just exactly half full." When the bridge broke and the ice jam let loose, the house rapidly drained. Oyler had to replace much of his first-floor furniture, but he knows the flooding could have been much worse. Catastrophic floods have shoved millions of tons of ice down the river during the past two centuries. Hundreds have drowned in Susquehanna ice floods; thousands have lost homes.

The first substantial records of an ice flood on the Susquehanna date to March 1784. "The Great Ice Flood" followed an unusually cold winter that featured a brief January thaw and sudden refreezing of large chunks of ice that had started moving downstream. "The ice, which had floated the day before, was suddenly obstructed," reported Dr. Benjamin Rush of Philadelphia, "and in the Susquehanna the obstructions were formed in those places where the water was most shallow, or where it had been accustomed to fall. . . . The ice in many places, especially where there were falls, formed a kind of dam, of a most stupendous height."

The spring thaw occurred on March 15. Refrozen mounds of ice at intervals held back melting water. The river behind the jams rose many feet in a few hours and then burst loose in a torrent of water and ice. "The ice broke up in the Susquehanna and the water rose 30 feet high and swept away houses and barns," someone wrote in an old book of tax records in Lancaster County. "Many people, also many cattle drowned."

Water and ice stripped the riverbanks above Harrisburg and crashed into what would become the city, depositing large quantities of ice between the river and Paxton Creek. An early Dauphin County historian noted that the 1784 flood convinced John Harris Jr. not to lay out his town on the lower grounds (now Riverfront Park) between his new stone house and the Susquehanna.

Ice floes ruined bridges and damaged canals on the Susquehanna and its tributaries throughout the nineteenth century, but the ice flood of 1904 outdid them all. After early March rains melted ice that had reached depths of two and three feet, the flood hurled house-sized hunks of ice downstream, grinding up islands and shorelines all the way to the Chesapeake. The "ice freshet" obliterated the dam at Shamokin Riffles; backed up the water of the Conestoga River, which ruined most of the buildings in the village of Safe Harbor; and destroyed scores of boats in a massive pile of ice at the end of the line in Havre de Grace.

The ice flood of March 1936 remains the "spring" flood of record for the Susquehanna. After an unusually cold winter, the river's three-foot ice cover began melting in late February. Continually warming temperatures and seven to nine inches of rain in early March contributed to a major breakup of ice about March 12. Severe flooding began with high water and ice the next day and continued well after the ice had passed, with water rising until March 21 at most locations. Because the greatest rise began on March 17 on upper reaches of the river, many people refer to this event as the St. Patrick's Day Flood. Exceptional devastation extended from the headwaters of both branches to the Chesapeake.

In Harrisburg, the flood closed the city's bridges and many highways for more than a week and the river did not completely return to its bed for a month. Ice destroyed gas mains and power lines. High water submerged and rendered useless the city's pumping station and City Island's water-filtering plant. The city rationed water for weeks. Many residents seemed dazed by the changes in the landscape and in their lives.

Despite the horrendous human suffering and property damages the flood caused along the riverfront, Harrisburg turned down a levee proposed by the Corps of Engineers and authorized by the National Flood Control Act. City officials made that decision after nearly a decade of debate on the merits of a levee, with flood-control advocates citing the economic advantages of protecting real estate and opponents criticizing Harrisburg's proposed share of construction costs. Trumping all arguments was the reluctance of most residents, especially owners of the mansions along Front Street, to lose their capital view of the Susquehanna. The city government indefinitely deferred local cooperation with the Corps of Engineers in 1945. Harrisburg remains the only large city on the Susquehanna without a protective levee.[14]

The 1996 flood forced many people to think about better ways to deal with future flooding. The National Weather Service and the Corps of Engineers reconsidered methods of forecasting ice jams. The Susquehanna River Basin Commission established the Interstate Committee on Emergencies, Jams, and Meteorological Systems (the acronymically memorable ICEJAMS) to examine ways to improve flood management from Harrisburg to the Chesapeake. Congressional representatives along the river persuaded their cost-cutting colleagues to abandon plans for a radical reduction in the Susquehanna's early flood-warning system. Everyone will be better prepared, flood experts said, the next time ice jams dam the flow.

Harrisburg: Drought

A river is more than an amenity, it is a treasure. It offers a necessity of life that must be rationed among those who have power over it.

—Supreme Court Justice Oliver Wendell Holmes, 1931

As Governor Tom Ridge declared a drought emergency in thirty-two Pennsylvania counties in late September 1995, he observed that the Susquehanna's exposed rock ridges formed bridges from bank to bank. The governor could have walked across the river on dry rocks at several points north and south of the artificially high water created by the Dock Street Dam. Some area residents did that. Others tossed picnic baskets in the backs of their pickups and drove out to islands.

After several months of below-average precipitation and the driest August on record, the river had fallen to its lowest level since the 1960s, running at a fifth of its normal flow and at the slowest velocity in seventy years. The Susquehanna fell so low that sections of the riverbed, uncovered since spring, had turned to meadowland.

Anglers stalked bass like trout in shallow, vodka-clear water undisturbed for weeks by falling rain or moving sediment. Boaters stood frustrated on docks, unable to use water ragged with rocks. Lacking sufficient water to power turbines, hydroelectric dams limited generation to three hours a day. Farmers drew record amounts of water from what was left of the Susquehanna to irrigate withering crops. Nearly everyone else in the Susquehanna Basin, according to the governor's order, faced mandatory water restrictions.

The basin suffered through one of the worst droughts of the century that year and then endured the record wettest year (and highest river flow to the Chesapeake) in 1996, only to return to drought in 1997. The first half of 1998 was unusually wet, the second half abnormally dry. Rainfall picked up during the first few months of 1999, then stopped abruptly in the spring. Governor Ridge declared another drought emergency that summer as groundwater and streams dropped to their lowest levels in more than a century and the power plants stopped generating entirely. It took record rainfall dumped by two hurricanes in September to mitigate that drought.

The feast-or-famine water pattern of the 1990s had been established with a drought in 1991–92 and substantial flooding in each of the next two years. This fluctuation is not unusual in a humid basin where average annual rainfall totals about nine inches more than in the country as a whole but a hard, fractured rock surface holds relatively little groundwater. Thanks to the basin's speedy runoff, Susquehanna droughts can turn severe within half a year.

The historical register of droughts is not so complete as the flood record because people tend to forget dry times. Floods are more dramatic events, with definite beginnings and endings and multiple tales of woe. By comparison, droughts are nonevents: they usually begin and end slowly and are all but impossible to forecast. Droughts eventually may empty wells and kill the corn, but the average resident of the river basin does not pay much attention because the river itself is doing no visible harm.

One of the earliest mentions of a Susquehanna Basin drought appears in the diary of Christopher Marshall at Lancaster in November 1780: "It's said that the Susquehanna and Conestoga rivers through the long drought [are] so low that people may walk over them by stepping from stone to stone." A Lancaster County newspaper reported that during the spring of 1832 cattle had been driven from bank to bank of the Susquehanna, a sight the oldest inhabitant had never seen before.[15]

While installing the first river gauge at Harrisburg in 1891, officials said the lowest-known water on the Susquehanna had been measured in 1803. That drought and others uncovered the lower river's many rocks, including a vast field of distinctive rocks with holes in them near Falmouth, several miles south of Harrisburg. Farmers frowned at their browning fields and called these potholed stones "hunger rocks."

Before the 1990s, the most significant extended Susquehanna droughts of the twentieth century occurred in the early 1930s, the early 1940s, and the mid-1960s. The Reverend Harry L. Lindsay Jr., whose family lived in a cottage on the Susquehanna north of Harrisburg, recalled that during the Dust Bowl days of the '30s the river nearly dried up, and so did duck hunting. The '60s drought hit bottom in September 1964, when monitors reported lowest levels all along the river. The all-time low-water record for Harrisburg is 1.83 feet, recorded on September 13, 1964.

The drought of the 1960s was the last major low-water event that did not require intervention to resupply the Susquehanna with water. The droughts of the 1990s spawned the first water-supply crises because the number of industries drawing water from the river had increased substantially.

Residents of the Susquehanna Basin use more than 5 billion gallons of water every day. More than 80 percent is surface water taken by thirteen thermal-power generating plants, usually from the Susquehanna itself. These plants return 97 percent of that water to the river, at a much higher temperature.

Municipalities—Binghamton, Danville, Muncy, Columbia, Havre de Grace, and several smaller towns directly along the Susquehanna—place a distant second to the power plants. Lancaster and Chester also pipe water

directly from the river. Chester, on the Delaware River, sells some of its river water to Wilmington, Delaware. Many residents of these cities have no idea they are drinking Susquehanna water. Cleansed by chlorine and other chemicals, processed river water would win no awards for distinctive flavor.[16]

In a class by itself, Baltimore may draw more water from the river than any other municipality. During drought emergencies, the city had been drawing up to 137 million gallons a day from the Conowingo Pool through a pipe 52 miles long and 9 feet in diameter, incongruusly called the Big Inch Line. In 1998 Baltimore announced plans to draw even more water during drought emergencies without consulting the Susquehanna River Basin Commission. The SRBC challenged this plan in federal court and the two parties eventually compromised. Baltimore is restricted to 64 million gallons a day during droughts, but at all other times may take up to 250 million gallons.

Large industrial and agricultural enterprises consume most of the rest of the water removed from the basin. The Procter & Gamble paper products company near Mehoopany uses about 10 million gallons of Susquehanna water daily. In reaction to the droughts of the '90s, more farmers are taking water from the Susquehanna and its tributaries. Lancaster County's irrigated acreage doubled between 1992 and 1997.

While domestic use of Susquehanna water actually has declined in recent years, thanks in part to water-conserving toilets and low-flow shower heads, consumptive use nearly doubled in the last three decades of the twentieth century.

Low water at Harrisburg about 1900 exposes rocks rarely seen and part of the river bottom. (Historical Society of Dauphin County—The John Harris/Simon Cameron Mansion Museum, Harrisburg, Pennsylvania.)

(Water is consumed when it is taken out of the river and not returned. It either evaporates during energy production; becomes part of a product, such as concrete; is absorbed by plants during irrigation; or is diverted to another river basin.) The SRBC worries that accelerating withdrawals, if they continue during droughts, could endanger not only the quality of river water and the fishery but the levels of fresh water in the Chesapeake Bay.

In 1971 the SRBC ordered major consumptive users within the basin (those that draw more than 20,000 gallons per day over a thirty-day period) to replace that water or shut down during droughts. The SRBC reserved replacement water in the Cowanesque and Curwensville reservoirs for this purpose, and is considering increasing storage capacity in other Susquehanna reservoirs.

After the 1991 drought, the SRBC also began to look more critically at diversion of water out of the basin. In 1997 the commission said that it would not approve any such transfer unless the applicant proved that it had made a strong effort to conserve water supplies within its own basin, a standard that has long been applied in the less water-rich West and that has guided the SRBC's response to Baltimore's request.

The SRBC has been less successful in convincing farmers to acknowledge that they owe something for consuming water. Pleading unique circumstances, agricultural interests have forestalled proposed regulations that would force them to pay for using more than the 20,000-gallon daily standard for irrigation during droughts. Agriculture remains the only major consumer of water in the Susquehanna Basin exempt from water-replacement regulations.

During public hearings on agricultural consumption of water in the mid-1990s, SRBC officials grew weary of listening to local farmers and friends of agriculture raise their voices in concern that their water use might be regulated. Paul Swartz, the commission's executive director, seemed pleased when Dr. Paul Hess, attending one of those public hearings in Harrisburg, countered that argument: "One must realize that the waters of the basin are not private waters, but are the waters of the people. Users may use the waters by riparian rights or permits. But the water still belongs to the people, and the people have a constitutional right to its protection."

Royalton

To those of us who know, a bass is a very special fish—a breed apart from other freshwater species. A catfish, walleye or pickerel may make a delicious meal but only a bass really "strikes" and fights to the end to stay alive in the stream.

—Dr. John D. Long, "Bass Fishing in Lancaster County," 1990

A newspaper reporter asked Charles Miller Howell which of his many lifetime activities he took the most pride in. The Lancaster gravestone manufacturer and community leader, eighty-one years old in the spring of 1895, backed into his answer: "Well, the church should come first, but there are many better churchmen than I am," he said. "I'm proud of the favors bestowed on me by my Masonic brethren, but there are more worthy Masons than I. I've been lucky in politics and feel great pride in having beaten the Whig and Know Nothing candidates for county treasurer, but perhaps some other man could have beaten them more easily." Howell paused. "I'm proud of my home and its surroundings," he said, "but, taking one consideration with another, I take more pride in black bass fishing than anything else."

Howell, who had taken thirty-one bass from the

Susquehanna at Safe Harbor on the Tuesday before the newspaper interview, considered himself "the luckiest fisherman on the river." Thousands of anglers have followed his inclination as the Susquehanna has become one of the most popular bass fisheries in the eastern United States.

The river's shallow water and rocky bed provide an ideal habitat for bass, both largemouths (also known as black bass) and smallmouths (also known as bronzebacks). They thrive all along the river—in Lake Otsego and the Bakerton Reservoir, at Tioga Point, and just below the riffles at McKees Half Falls, at the mouth of the Juniata, and in the Conowingo Pond.

Imported from the Ohio River just before Charles Howell's fishing days ended, smallmouths have superseded the bigger but less frisky largemouths as the Susquehanna's prime fish in recent decades. Thousands of anglers practice the precision casting and expert handling of line required to bring in a feisty specimen. Some prefer to wade into the shallow water and rock-hop the river (even though, as someone once said, negotiating the slippery, uneven bottom of the Susquehanna feels like walking on greased bowling balls). Some use boats, often with outboard motors so propeller blades won't break on rocks. Others fish from inflatable boats as they float down the river. Still others glide kayaks into hard-to-reach shallow and rocky places.

An increasing number of bass anglers seek direction from dozens of guides who know the Susquehanna and its tributaries. Dedicated anglers work the water on the coldest days of winter and on the hottest days of summer; they are out there on the midsummer night when Miller

mayflies hatch in a blizzard over the water, launching smallmouths on a feeding frenzy.

Bob Clouser, smallmouth guide and creator of Clouser's Deep Minnow fly, lives in Royalton, a small river community just below Harrisburg. He operates Clouser's Fly Shop out of his house, about half a mile from the Susquehanna. Charles Miller Howell would have liked Bob Clouser. Their lifetime priority is the same.

Clouser worked as a meat cutter for twenty-six years. When he was not cutting meat, he carved the guts out of smallmouth bass preparatory to frying the fish for his family. When the meat market closed two decades ago, Clouser opened his fly tackle shop and guide service. He quickly became known as the best guide in the fifty or so miles nearest his home fishing grounds—a range of river that also happens to provide the best habitat for bass anywhere on the Susquehanna. Half of his customers live somewhere in Pennsylvania. The rest drive or fly here from all over the world.

"Walleye draw people here when walleye season opens, and muskies put a few guys on the river," Clouser says. "But smallmouth bass is the main sport fish for this river. It's the strongest freshwater fish, ounce for ounce, I've ever caught. It's aggressive. It's a jumper."

Clouser has been tying his own flies since his father gave him a fly-tying kit for his fourteenth birthday. In the early 1980s, he made a successful bass fly that looked like a crayfish, one of the bronzeback's favorite snacks. He followed with the Clouser Swimming Nymph, which imitates an emerging Miller mayfly. Then came the incomparable

Bob Clouser of Royalton created Clouser's Deep Minnow fly and pioneered catch-and-release smallmouth bass fishing on the Susquehanna. (Photo by Christine Brubaker.)

Clouser Deep Minnow, often called simply a Clouser. Underwater, the Deep Minnow's lead bug eyes and silver tinsel imitate the behavior of minnows, sculpin, and baitfish. To smallmouths, trout, salmon, and other sport fish, this weird contraption looks like a gourmet lunch. With its hook pointing upward, the better to snag a fish as it bobs along the Susquehanna's rocky bottom, Clouser's Deep Minnow is the most popular underwater fly in the world.

Clouser transports eager anglers out into the river on his 16-foot flatboat stripped of seats and anything else that might interfere with fly casting. He knows every hole and riffle in this section of the Susquehanna. He knows where the fish congregate, and it is a rare day when Clouser's company does not catch multiple bass.

Smallmouths prefer to hang out in sheltered spaces, so Clouser looks for them on the front sides of rock ledges and the back sides of islands. His favorite hunting areas are fish weirs. The piles of heavy rocks, planted in V patterns all along the river bottom, are easy to spot in low water from a low-flying airplane. Much as the Native Americans formed weirs or eel racks, early settlers created these weirs a century and more ago to trap migrating shad and eels. Today bass follow their food into the weirs, which provide excellent habitat for crayfish and small minnows, mayfly nymphs, and other insects. When flooding or ice jams wreck the weirs, Clouser repairs them, shoving boulders into place with a winch and a slingshot-like holder. He likes the old fish traps because "the history's there, the mystery's there, and also the fish are there."

About the same time that he began guiding anglers on

the Susquehanna, and not coincidentally, Clouser stopped eating bass. If he and an increasing number of other bass fanciers kept everything they caught, he reasoned, the Susquehanna's smallmouth fishery could be depleted. So Clouser became a prophet of catch-and-release fishing. He made all the anglers he took out on the river toss back what they reeled in. "I don't care what size it is, any kind of harvest is going to hurt a fishery, and it also depletes from the enjoyment of somebody else being able to use that fish," Clouser says. "I've changed a lot of people's attitudes about catch-and-release fishing."

In the mid-1980s, Clouser and other serious fishermen noticed that large numbers of good-sized bass no longer populated the Susquehanna. Too many fishermen were competing for too few fish. Whereas 16-inch smallmouths had been caught commonly in previous years, hauling in a 12-incher made a respectable fish story by the end of the decade. Clouser, Bill Roberts, and other area anglers formed the Susquehanna Smallmouth Alliance to lobby the Pennsylvania Fish and Boat Commission for more stringent limits on smallmouth catches. After several years of discussion, the commission in 1991 raised the size limit for smallmouth keepers from 12 inches to 15 inches and reduced the creel limit from six to four per day south of the Dock Street Dam. Bigger bass began to thrive in that region, so in 1997 the commission extended the four-fish and 15-inch regulations from the inflatable dam at Sunbury to the Maryland border.

At the urging of the Smallmouth Alliance, which quickly became the largest smallmouth bass club in the country, the commission also tightened rules for a proliferating number of fishing tournaments that undermined the fishery. Too many tournaments allowed entrants to kill fish or remove them from the spot where they were hooked and return them to alien water, where they sometimes died. Since the commission began requiring all tourneys to include live wells in boats and otherwise clean up their programs, the smallmouth fishery has stabilized.[17]

A strong bass fishery is important not only so that weekend anglers can hook a fancy fish but because smallmouth bass are the "indicator species" for water quality in the Susquehanna. Larry Jackson, a fisheries biologist with the Fish and Boat Commission, has assessed water quality in the Susquehanna from Sunbury to York Haven Dam since the late 1970s. Working out of the Huntsville Hatchery, south of Carlisle, Jackson has spent many nights electrofishing on the Susquehanna and Juniata. He zaps fish, checks them for size and disease, and releases the groggy specimens to the river. Though the smallmouth population in places remains stressed by overfishing, Jackson knows the fishery's future is positive. He recorded the largest number of smallmouth fry in the Susquehanna in six years while electrofishing during the summer of 1999.

"The Susquehanna is a tremendous smallmouth bass fishery," Jackson says. "I don't think you could ask more of a river flowing in front of the state capital. You can go wet-wading for smallmouth bass and catch good numbers of them and look over your shoulder and see the capitol building in the background," he says, smiling as he realizes he is on a roll on his favorite subject. "That's water quality.

That's habitat. That's pretty impressive."

You don't have to catch fish to recognize how healthy they and the river they thrive in are, says Jan Jarrett, who loves to canoe the river when she is not lobbying for environmental issues in Harrisburg. "Most places you can see the bottom in six feet of water," she says. "It's full of fish, full of fish. Smallmouth bass out the wazoo. Huge catfish. Carp. Muskies. The river's full of protein. There's great insect communities. You turn over a rock and you see all kinds of mayflies. The river is clearer. It's cleaner. It's spectacular—one of the best rivers in the state."

Still, when Bob Clouser catches and releases fish, he does it not only to save the fishery but because he no longer trusts the contents of a Susquehanna fish fillet. "The water quality is better as far as visible pollution is concerned," he says. "What we don't see, I'm afraid, is still there—the chemicals being washed out of the farms, the mercuries. Because of the amount of that stuff that comes down the river, I would be more leery today of eating a smallmouth than twenty-five years ago."

The Pennsylvania Department of Environmental Protection and the Fish and Boat Commission began monitoring toxic chemical pollutants absorbed in fish tissue in 1976. When toxic levels approach or exceed FDA and EPA standards, the state advises the public to limit or stop fish consumption. The only section of the Susquehanna where anglers are perennially warned not to eat any fish extends from the mouth of the Lackawanna River at Pittston, several miles downstream. The primary problem is toxic PCBs.

EPA studies show that releases of toxins within the Chesapeake Bay's entire watershed, including the Susquehanna, have declined significantly since 1988; but some scientists believe federal and state tolerance levels and the amount of toxins still being released are too high. They would agree with Clouser that no fish is safe to eat.

A coalition of national and state environmental groups claimed in 1996 that the Susquehanna receives more toxic chemicals from industries than any other waterway in Pennsylvania. Nearly 2 million pounds of toxins were dumped legally into the river in Pennsylvania from 1990 to 1994. The groups claimed that the actual volume of toxins, with ammonia leading the list, may have been twenty times that amount.

State officials and other Susquehanna monitors countered that toxic chemicals, diluted in river water, pose no hazard to fish or humans. "We are a huge drainage basin—27,500 square miles," said Susan Obleski, spokeswoman for the Susquehanna River Basin Commission. "There are no signs of toxic impact. The allowable limits are designed on the ability of the river to dilute and handle these amounts."

A debate over what level of toxicity should be permitted in drinking and fishing water will continue as long as people have differing opinions about what amount of toxic chemicals triggers cancer, birth defects, or simple food poisoning. Lancaster continually monitors raw Susquehanna water captured at Columbia and piped to residents. The city never has reported a problem with excessive toxic chemicals in its water supply.

Three Mile Island

On March 28, 1979, and for several days thereafter—as a result of technical malfunction and human error—Three Mile Island's Unit 2 Nuclear Generating Station was the scene of the nation's worst commercial nuclear accident. Radiation was released, a part of the nuclear core was damaged, and thousands of residents evacuated the area. Events here would cause basic changes throughout the world's nuclear power industry.

—Text of Pennsylvania Historical and Museum Commission marker along Route 441 near Three Mile Island

On March 28, 1979, as a result of technical malfunctions, human error and corporate criminal acts, T.M.I. Unit 2 had a nuclear meltdown. In the nation's worst commercial nuclear accident, over 100,000 residents evacuated, radiation was released resulting in serious health effects to thousands, and eventual deaths. While Unit 2 is shut forever, the government allowed Unit 1 to reopen in 1985 against the overwhelming vote of area citizens. T.M.I Unit 1 continues to radiate the public.

—Text of mock historical marker erected temporarily at Three Mile Island by antinuclear activists in March 1999

MIDWAY THROUGH *The China Syndrome,* a melodramatic movie centered on a fictitious accident at a nuclear power plant in Southern California, a physics professor explains a meltdown to Jane Fonda and Michael Douglas. If the cooling water surrounding the reactor core were to disappear, he says, the nuclear fuel would melt through the bottom of its containment vessel and enter groundwater. The fuel would vaporize the water, blasting radioactive clouds into the atmosphere. This radioactivity, the professor adds, "would render an area the size of Pennsylvania permanently uninhabitable." After March 28, 1979, the reaction to that remark in central Pennsylvania movie theaters was personal and often audible.

Release of *The China Syndrome* coincided with the most serious commercial nuclear accident in the United States. A very real near-meltdown ruined an almost new reactor on Three Mile Island (TMI), in the Susquehanna River ten miles south of Harrisburg. Tens of thousands of people fled their homes, suppressing attendance in theaters within twenty miles of TMI during the week after the accident. They returned to a reactor filled with radioactive rubble that forever changed the way Americans think about nuclear power and the way TMI-area residents think about using river water to cool uranium.

Only the Mississippi River takes more heat from nuclear plants than the Susquehanna. One reactor continues to operate at TMI. Two reactors make power at Peach Bottom, on the York County shore thirty-five miles downstream. Two others generate electricity at Berwick, on the North Branch. Even before the accident at TMI, some people

ϝ   *Three Mile Island, viewed from upriver. The cooling towers of the nuclear reactor's Unit 1 continuously expel water vapor. The worst commercial nuclear accident in U.S. history ruined Unit 2 in 1979.* (Lancaster *[Pennsylvania]* New Era.)

called this section of the Susquehanna the "hot river valley."

The Susquehanna Steam Electric Station at Berwick, owned by PPL Utilities, has manufactured power relatively uneventfully since 1985. The same cannot be said for the operation at the Peach Bottom Atomic Power Station. The federal Nuclear Regulatory Commission (NRC) shut down Peach Bottom in March 1987, citing frightening failures to perform to minimal standards. Control-room operators had been napping and playing video games on the job. Other employees had been selling drugs in the plant's parking lot. A third of the plant had been contaminated by low-level radiation, and pipes and other parts of the system were falling apart. Nuclear industry experts called Peach Bottom "an embarrassment to the industry and to the nation." The NRC closed the plant for nearly two years while its operator, Philadelphia Electric Company, replaced personnel and cleaned up the mess.

Peach Bottom's reactors and Unit 1 at Three Mile Island all began manufacturing atomic power in 1974. At the time, the nuclear industry claimed its technology would transform the world of energy, producing electricity so cheaply that it would not be worth metering. Industry flacks worked hard to convince Americans that new plants were so well designed that they could not fail. They said a nuclear meltdown, the so-called China syndrome, was impossible.

If radioactivity never could escape from sturdy containment vessels, promoters said, what would be the danger of building nuclear reactors on the banks of rivers or even on islands in rivers? There they would have plenty of water to mitigate the intensely hot process of producing nuclear power.

To the nuclear engineers of General Public Utilities (GPU), TMI's New Jersey–based owners, Three Mile Island seemed a near-perfect place to build a power plant. Some 400 acres of sandy soil covers this bedrock island, largest in the Susquehanna. (The U.S. Department of the Interior figured TMI's length at three miles, but it actually extends about two and a half miles.) The island lies only 300 feet from the Susquehanna's eastern shore and so could be bridged easily.

GPU designed TMI Unit 1 to produce about 860 megawatts of electricity at full capacity. The company spent $410 million building the unit, then turned over management to Metropolitan Edison (Met Ed), its central Pennsylvania subsidiary. Unit 2, designed to produce 900 megawatts and built at a cost of $700 million, did not go on line until 1979—just three months before the accident.

The two units' four hourglass-shaped cooling towers loomed 355 feet above the river, low enough not to present a dangerous obstacle to planes taking off from Harrisburg International Airport, some two and a half miles north of the island's northern tip. Just in case, GPU reinforced the reactor containment buildings to absorb the collision of a Boeing 707.[18] Then GPU stepped back and let Met Ed, a company that had no experience operating a nuclear reactor, manage both units.

The primary coolant system of a pressurized water reactor is a closed loop of distilled water kept at an average temperature of about 575°F. This water circulates from the reactor core, where it is heated by the fission process in uranium, through pipes to a steam generator. There the water

of the primary coolant system transfers heat to water in a secondary, feed-water loop without ever coming into direct contact with it. This process transforms water in the secondary loop into steam and the steam blasts through turbine blades that drive a generator to make electricity. Water in a condenser, cooled by drafts in the cooling tower, returns the steam to liquid form so it can recirculate, just as the primary coolant is recirculating. The only part of this wet process ordinarily visible outside the plant is escaping water vapor in the form of a white plume billowing from a cooling tower.

Operating at 97 percent of full power at the time of the accident, TMI Unit 2 was drawing 15,000 gallons of water a minute from the Susquehanna. After heating the water, the plant cooled it to a temperature slightly warmer than the water it joined when it was discharged downstream.

On Wednesday, March 28, 1979, TMI Unit 1 had been shut down for several weeks for refueling and Unit 2 was operating under automatic control. No one anticipated that anything unusual would occur at the plant that morning. No one on duty had been trained to deal with a reactor emergency, largely because no one in the nuclear power industry or in the government regulatory agency believed such an emergency would ever occur.

Frederick Scheimann, foreman of the shift at Unit 2, described the noise the reactor made as it shuddered violently at 4 A.M. "All of a sudden, I started hearing loud, thunderous noises, like a couple of freight trains." Scheimann rushed from the basement to the control room, leaving behind two maintenance men who, attempting to clear a clogged pipe, had cut the flow of water into the feed-water loop. That error had forced Unit 2's turbine and reactor to shut down automatically with a booming jolt. It also had caused the reactor to belch the first of several releases of radioactive steam into the atmosphere.

By the time Scheimann got to the control room, routine emergency procedures had been activated mechanically. Three emergency feed-water pumps had begun flushing cooling water around the reactor core. That would have solved the problem if three valves had done what they were designed to do. Two valves mistakenly left closed by workers two days earlier prevented water from the emergency feed-water pumps from reaching the core. Worse, another valve jammed open, allowing 220 gallons of radioactive water a minute to drain in the other direction, out of the reactor. That water flooded the floor of the reactor's containment building and flowed on into an unsealed auxiliary building.

Operators in the control room misunderstood what was happening in the reactor for several hours and so turned a dangerous situation into a disaster. Misreading water and pressure level monitors, they believed too much water was flowing into the reactor. About 7:30 A.M. they turned off a set of three additional emergency feed-water pumps—the last potential source of coolant to the burning core. Then they opened a drain line to remove even more water from the reactor. From the moment they opened that drain, Unit 2's ruin was irreversible.

Not one instrument in a control room jammed with measuring devices told operators how much cooling water was inside the reactor at any time that morning. A combination of mechanical and operator errors and the simple lack of an effective gauge of water level propelled Unit 2 toward meltdown.

As the coolant drained away, temperatures in the partially uncovered core rose to more than 5,000°F, melting sixty-two tons of the core—about half the entire mass—and tons of other material. The top five feet of the core disintegrated and fuel rods containing uranium pellets shattered. Then a twenty-ton slug of uranium melted through the floor of the reactor chamber to the bottom of the containment vessel and other uranium melted through the chamber's wall. Only the reactor's steel bottom and sides stood between that uranium and the island's groundwater.

Finally realizing they had been trying to fight a fire by, in effect, shutting the hydrants and cutting the hoses, control-room operators began pumping water to cover the core just before noon. That water followed the uranium and cooled it, stopping the meltdown. Operators stabilized the core about nine hours after the accident began.

Experts later estimated that TMI came within a half hour to an hour of the type of total meltdown that ruined the Chernobyl reactor, which spewed radioactivity over a large area of Ukraine and well outside the Soviet Union in 1986.

The worst of the damage to Unit 2 occurred by the afternoon of March 28, but the worst of the public nightmare did not begin until Friday, March 30. Until then, Met Ed and NRC spokesmen repeatedly reassured people living near the plant that they were in no danger, that a meltdown could not happen, and that relatively little radioactivity had been released from the plant during the incident. They did so partially because they emphasized positive spin on nuclear power over public safety and partially because they really did not know the extent of the damage.

Impudence or ignorance guided almost all official comment until plant engineers realized the reactor's core had suffered extensive damage. Early Friday morning, radioactive steam blew out of Unit 2 without warning and everyone in central Pennsylvania soon understood that the problem was much worse than they had been led to believe. Plant officials proposed the possibility of more unplanned releases of radioactivity and some experts began to worry about a hydrogen bubble exploding in the top of the reactor. Governor Dick Thornburgh ordered pregnant women and young children to leave the area. Tens of thousands of other people also abandoned their homes that weekend. But the bubble dissipated by Sunday and many experts began to speculate that the incident was over. They were right, although the NRC did not determine that the reactor had been fully stabilized until a month after the accident.

Some scientists in the health radiation field claimed then and maintain now that radioactivity released from Unit 2 caused cancers in humans, deformations in livestock, and aberrations in plants, such as three-foot-tall dandelions. Hundreds of area residents believe their health problems originated with radiation released from TMI. In 1996 a federal judge dismissed more than 2,000 physical damage

claims filed against GPU, holding that the plaintiffs had not clearly linked their poor health to the accident. A federal appeals court reinstated most of those lawsuits in 1999, and the Supreme Court concurred the next year. Surviving plaintiffs are proceeding with claims under Court-imposed conditions limiting expert testimony on radiation and its consequences for health. Other cases have been settled out of court, with sealed resolutions.

More than a dozen studies, including the original review by the President's Commission on the Accident at Three Mile Island and a University of Pittsburgh report released in 2000, have reached a conclusion at odds with the plaintiffs' claims: all of these studies say only a tiny amount of radiation moved off site and could not have caused significant health problems. But no one knows definitely how much radiation the reactor released because monitors set to register up to 1,000 rems went off-scale for several hours during the accident; all estimates are at best educated guesses.

Whether the accident caused physical damage or not, it created widespread psychological turmoil. Psychologists and antinuclear activists examined trauma within the immediate population as carefully as the government studied radiation releases. More studies probably have been done of psychological responses to the accident at TMI than of any other event in history.

Met Ed began decontaminating the plant immediately. That process ultimately cost nearly $1 billion, involved thousands of workers and tons of robotic radioactivity scrubbers, and removed most of the 294,500 pounds of nuclear debris in the reactor and auxiliary building to a storage area in Idaho. Workers left tons of other solid nuclear material in the reactor. It will remain there until well into the current century, when its radioactivity will have decomposed slightly and will be less hazardous to cleanup crews.

Compared with the dangerous and time-consuming disposal of this solid nuclear junk, getting rid of more than 2 million gallons of radioactive water seemed relatively simple. Just dump the contaminated water into the river, the reactor's operators suggested. Let the Susquehanna dilute the radioactivity and wash it on into the Chesapeake and out to sea.

The City of Lancaster and a regional antinuclear group, the Susquehanna Valley Alliance, sued to prevent this discharge from contaminating the city's drinking water and the river in general. Residents of the area, even those who continued to support nuclear generation of power without reservation, found the water-dumping plan unacceptable. The City of Baltimore, hoping to draw more water from the Susquehanna in the future, also expressed alarm.

Under pressure from legal action and public opinion, the utility installed filtering equipment to remove most radioactive elements from this water, then slowly boiled it in an evaporator. GPU evaporated the last gallons of water in the summer of 1993—more than fourteen years after the accident.

Tons of solid nuclear waste—both from the accident and from previous and subsequent operations at Unit 1—will remain on the island until the nation adopts a permanent storage place. Three Mile Island has become, as one observer noted, "one of the most dangerous radioactive waste storage sites in the world," and Unit 1 is scheduled to continue manufacturing nuclear power and radioactive waste until 2014.

Periodically the nuclear industry and the NRC recognize TMI-1 for running an efficient operation. Periodically some glitch occurs at the plant that reminds everyone of 1979. In December 1997, for example, area residents received an unwelcome reminder of TMI's history when GPU and NRC officials admitted that the valve that had jammed open in 1979, allowing coolant to spill and helping to precipitate the partial meltdown, had malfunctioned again. Safety changes had been made since the accident, officials assured the public, so the valve, stuck open this time from 1995 to 1997, could not have caused another serious problem.

Susan Stranahan helped cover the accident at TMI for the *Philadelphia Inquirer* in 1979. Fourteen years later, she concluded this about the incident in *Susquehanna, River of Dreams:* "The Susquehanna has survived every assault human beings have inflicted to date, but they still hold in their hands the capacity to render a whole region uninhabitable. All that is required are a few careless mistakes, and humans have clearly demonstrated themselves quite capable of that. Perhaps in response to this brush with disaster, there has developed among many who live along the Susquehanna a heightened sense of protectiveness and concern for the river, as well as for the living things coexisting there."

Perhaps. After the NRC permitted TMI-1 to restart in 1985, concerned citizens pressured the state and the counties surrounding TMI—Dauphin, Lancaster, and York—to install radiation monitors. The area's media quickly report anything unusual that occurs on the island. Antinuclear activists remain engaged. Before the NRC approved the 1999 sale of TMI to PECO Energy (which has since merged with other utilities as Exelon Nuclear), local officials dissected every aspect of the deal.

But people want to get on with their lives. Central Pennsylvania's largely conservative residents are not prone to hold a grudge against any industry, especially one that employs hundreds of area workers. A few vehicles still sport a bumper slogan wildly popular with some drivers just after the accident: "No one died at TMI."

Most residents have relearned how to be comfortable with the clouds of steam billowing continuously from TMI's cooling tower. Weekend river rats ignore the white puffs while docking at the Tri-County Boat Club at TMI's northern tip. Jet pilots fly right over the reactor without giving it a thought.

Thousands of people live within a few miles of Three Mile Island and the population is increasing. In the spring of 1979, the *Harrisburg Patriot-News* called Goldsboro, the village across from TMI on the Susquehanna's York County shore, "the ghost town of the Atomic Age." Goldsboro has risen from the dead: the state's second-fastest-growing community nearly double its population in the 1990s. An entire generation has grown up without personal experience of an accident that, thanks to luck as much as anything, did not poison the Susquehanna and render central Pennsylvania uninhabitable.

Conewago Falls: Geology

The diabase is here pocked by uncounted numbers of large and small potholes. There are also many large blocks containing potholes, some large enough to allow adult persons to crawl from bottom to top. The river-sculpted shapes in the diabase include bowls and tubs in which to sit, as well as wave and ripple-like forms more commonly seen in seashore sand. Here they occur in very hard rock.

— Donald M. Hoskins, former Pennsylvania state geologist, describing potholed rocks at Conewago Falls

The wild falls at Conewago, ranging over ragged terrain for three-quarters of a mile below Three Mile Island, provide an unexpected bump in the broad, shallow river. Here thousands of water-carved black and gray rocks create one of the most expansive pothole fields in the United States.

Although cut into a hard diabase sill, the potholes seem incongruously soft and curvaceous. Some observers have called the rocks' graceful sculpting "sensuous." Others, reminded of a sterile lunar landscape, are unnerved by the sight. In *Pennsylvania's Susquehanna,* Elsie Singmaster reported that thousands of visitors ogled the potholes during abnormally low water in October 1947. They saw "the curious and fantastic forms into which the hard rock had been carved. No doubt many were glad when rain fell and the potholes were filled and the tortured rocks again covered from view."

In lowest water, you can walk across the river on these rocks, some as small as golf balls, others as large as tractor trailers. Some of the holes in the rocks are the size of marbles, others deep and wide enough to hide a bear. Some are filled with drought-dried fungi. Others, still holding water from the last flood or rain, shelter snails, or crayfish which have eaten the snails and left their shells. Here you may find mosquito larvae, there Asiatic clam shells or bits of coal. And over there an alder bush has taken root in dirt washed into a pothole the size of a paint bucket.[19]

What concentrated force cut these perfect holes and smoothed the sides of the rocks around them? Early geologists believed that small rocks drilled into larger rocks and, swirling around and around over thousands of years, gradually abraded holes. As the holes enlarged, bigger stones washed in to continue the work.

Henry David Thoreau explained this theory of pothole creation: "A stone which the current has washed down, meeting with obstacles, revolves as on a pivot where it lies, gradually sinking in the course of centuries deeper and deeper into the rock, and in new freshets receiving the aid of fresh stones which are drawn into this trap and doomed to revolve there for an indefinite period, doing Sisyphus-like penance for stony sins, until they either wear out, or else are released by some revolution of nature."

Bill Sevon, the Pennsylvania Geological Survey geologist in Harrisburg, and Glenn H. Thompson Jr., retired as a geologist from nearby Elizabethtown College, have a differ-

ent theory. They believe hydraulic vortices cut these holes. Vortices roil in the tail races of big dams. They are varsity versions of the smaller but equally deadly boils beneath Binghamton's Rockbottom and other low-head dams. Thompson calls them "underwater tornadoes." The geologists say these hydraulic vandals sought out weaknesses in rocks, particularly the points of intersection of two cracks, and employed sand and silt to abrade the surfaces, much as if they were sandpapering them. Abrasion enlarged the tiny potholes and then bigger and stronger vortices carrying more sand and silt widened and deepened the potholes at a more rapid rate.[20]

This process has been completed—for now. The present Susquehanna at average flow cannot expand potholes and floods don't last long enough to do the job. Mud, not sand, composes the sediment load these days, so the tools required to begin the work are no longer in the water. Sevon and Thompson believe only a glacial flood could have created conditions under which wild water and servile grit could begin to abrade so many holes in rocks.

Water flowing at average volume wears away rock over millions of years. Massive ice and floodwater can move and cut rock overnight. Sevon believes a glacial ice flood may have upended some of these rocks. Truck-sized boulders weighing nearly 100 tons obviously have been rolled along the riverbed because potholes in some of them are upside down. The geologist thinks one of the earliest glacial floods moved these rocks. The catastrophic release of water when Lake Lesley's ice dam burst south of Williamsport may have done the job.

☙ *Low water during a severe drought in 1963 drew these visitors to the potholed rocks at Conewago Falls. Geologists believe glacial floods employed abrasive sand and silt to smooth the sides of rocks and cut holes inside them, creating one of the largest pothole fields in the United States. (Lancaster [Pennsylvania] New Era.)*

When the outburst from upstream rolled into this area, Sevon writes in an article for *Pennsylvania Geology,* "at Conewago Falls, where the valley narrows within a few hundred feet to half its upstream width, discharge would have been maximized, and water depth may have exceeded 100 feet. The violence of extreme turbulence would have been concentrated in the two bank-marginal channels, and erosion of diabase would have been severe. . . . All in all, it would have been an extraordinary event."

The ice-overs in the Susquehanna's valley began about 2 million years ago and ended less than 15,000 years ago. During the period, ice sheets pressed south from Canada and melted back again at least four times. As glaciers advanced, they blocked northern drainage, forcing northward-flowing streams to become Susquehanna tributaries and augmenting the river's flow. During massive meltdowns, the river ran far wider and far deeper, rapidly eroding rock and washing broad terraces of sand and gravel downstream.

Glaciers advanced below Berwick, on the North Branch, and as far as Lewisburg, on the West Branch. Geologists know where the glaciers stopped because they deposited their moraines there. They also know what work glacial melt did below those dumping points. Clear evidence of landscape changes made by enormous amounts of floodwater punctuates the river's passage all the way to the bay.

Much of this evidence is clearly visible in valleys of the Susquehanna broadened and deepened to accommodate floods whose volume the New York geologist Herman Fairchild thought may have swelled several times larger than Niagara Falls. Some of the most intriguing manifestations

are hidden beneath sections of the Main Stem drowned by backwater from hydroelectric dams.

Constructing Holtwood Dam a century ago, workmen employed a cofferdam to divert the Susquehanna from its eastern shore. This structure exposed the river bottom in that area for the first time. Surprised engineers found a depression running more than a mile along the riverbank. The depression varied in width from 200 to 300 feet and in depth from 40 to 60 feet. It was by far the biggest hole anyone had ever seen in the riverbed.

Cary T. Hutchinson, chief engineer for the Holtwood project, surveyed the river bottom from Turkey Hill, south of Columbia, to Port Deposit. He discovered five more depressions, all running along the eastern shore, from one and three-fifths miles above Safe Harbor to just north of Conowingo. These spoon-head-shaped depressions ranged from nearly a mile to two miles long and up to 500 feet wide. Hutchinson measured the deepest point in the Bear Island depression south of Holtwood. The bottom of that hole was 130 feet deep—30 feet below sea level.[21]

Addressing the Geological Society of America in 1916, Edward B. Mathews called these depressions "deeps." He thought they must have been formed by the force of water passing through ancient narrows in the river just above each or by temporary increases in the volume of the entire river. Both scenarios could have increased erosive force, scooping out the holes.

Glenn Thompson has a variant theory. He believes that during glaciation a microclimate may have existed along the river gorge, creating special conditions to form these depressions. Tall cliffs shade the western water most of the day, so Thompson thinks that side of the river may have frozen over semipermanently during one or more of the glacial advances. The warmer east bank would have welcomed the river's only channel of open water. Turbulent water running along this narrowed course would have carried sand to erode the deeps, creating a deeper channel to accommodate the volume of floodwater.

Geologists' speculations compete with folklore regarding the ability of the deeps to suck animate and inanimate objects into their depths and beyond. The wildest stories involve Job's Hole, the southernmost of the deeps, just north of Conowingo Dam. Logs thrown into this hole supposedly whirled around before plunging down, never to be seen again. Some people said the hole had no bottom, others that it led to a subterranean cave running to the Chesapeake. The most flamboyant tale featured a fellow who pushed a malfunctioning car off the riverbank into the hole. Half a year later he spotted the vehicle in Baltimore. It was in good condition, still sporting its license plate. The new owner said he had discovered the car lying in shallow water near the mouth of the bay. He had pulled it out and started it running again.

John Walker, owner of Lancaster Scuba Center, had heard some of these tales and wondered what he might find at the bottom of a deep. He dived seventy feet into one of the huge holes. "It was dark. It was black. I couldn't see anything," he says. "I think there was coal swirling around down there." The diver never got to the bottom of that hole and says he will not venture into a deep again.

Conewago Falls: Navigation

There is a charm to me in an in-navigable river, which brought me to the Susquehannah. . . . I like the city sometimes, and I bless heaven for steam-boats; but I love haunts where I neither see a steam-boat nor expect the city.

—N. P. WILLIS, *Letters from Under a Bridge*

WHEN THE WATER RUNS LOW at Conewago Falls, no sizable boats can thread their way through the boulders. When the water runs high, rolling noisily through ranks of potholed rocks, creating whitecapped standing waves, boats of any size take a risk. In flood, with the water dropping twenty-three feet in less than a mile, Conewago can be more tumultuous than any other falls on this river.

"Susquehanna River is navigable with Canoes quite from the Lakes at the Head to the Falls at Conewaga," the mapmaker Lewis Evans wrote after his journey up the Susquehanna with John Bartram and Conrad Weiser in 1743. "Conewaga is the only Falls which tumbles headlong in this River. Below this are three or four others which are passable only in Freshes. By Reason of so many bad Falls this River has not yet Inland Navigation; nor is it indeed capable of any from Conewaga downwards."

Most early rivermen did not try to negotiate Conewago (a Native American word meaning "at the rapids") unless a spring freshet filled the river, submerging most rocks. Before the first Conewago Canal was constructed in 1797, almost all downriver traffic stopped at Middletown or adjacent Port Royal (Royalton). Crews unloaded cargoes and transported them overland to Philadelphia. The few boats that got past Conewago stopped at Marietta or Columbia, short of the rapids downriver. In 1809, Fortescue Cuming counted twenty-one falls, shallows, and rapids that impeded navigation on the Susquehanna—many of them downriver from Conewago.

Even less traffic passed upriver through Conewago. Instead, wagons transported goods overland from Philadelphia or Baltimore to Middletown. An early writer explained that it was not economical to attempt to move a boat of any weight up the falls because this effort "required 30 to 40 men a great part of the day, and an expense of five pounds or six pounds at least, to accomplish this work; for the men are obliged to perch and scatter themselves (as it has been humorously expressed) like *black-birds* on the rocks, and to drag their burden shifting from rock to rock through the whole length of the falls."

The Pennsylvania General Assembly appointed the first commission to examine ways to improve the Susquehanna's lower channel in 1771. That study found obstructions to navigation, especially at Conewago, too great to overcome. In addition to the practical concern, Philadelphians lobbied against improvements because they feared rival Baltimore business would benefit more from a navigable lower channel. The project died.

In 1783, Baltimore investors announced plans to build a nine-mile canal along the east side of the river from just above Port Deposit to Love Island, near the Pennsylvania line. The nine-lock Susquehanna Canal would bypass Smith's Falls and other obstructions and encourage trade between Maryland and the interior of Pennsylvania. When the canal finally opened in 1803, however, many boatmen avoided it because it was narrow and carried a strong current.

Although the Susquehanna Canal eventually failed, its potential spurred Pennsylvanians to counter with their own project on the west side of the river at Conewago. In 1792, representatives from Philadelphia and several communities on or near the river formed the Conewago Canal Company to dig this first canal in Pennsylvania. The mile-long, 40-foot-wide project employed two locks. At its grand opening in November 1797, workmen drilled holes in part of the diabase shelf that extends beyond the riverbed, filled the holes with sticks of dynamite, and fired them as an "amature cannon" for the pleasure of Governor Mifflin Thomas and 500 spectators.

In 1814 the company dug a second mile-long Conewago Canal to circumvent the falls on the east side of the river, from Dauphin County into Lancaster County. Two decades later, the Pennsylvania Canal incorporated the eastern Conewago Canal.

By facilitating travel downstream, the Conewago canals for the first time promoted lower ports over Middletown. Columbia soon became Philadelphia's primary port of entry on the river. However, the canals never were as popular as their promoters had hoped. Arks began running the river in the mid-1790s. With their shallow draft, they could pass through the falls relatively safely in high water. In greater numbers, rafts followed arks. Considerable traffic on the river after 1800 saved several hours of travel time and a 50-cent toll by avoiding the canals. Unlucky rafts paid dearly for taking the risk.[22]

River traffic remained largely seasonal. Thanks to the Susquehanna's shallowness and rockiness, most boats could count on moving long distances only during spring's high flows. For many would-be shippers, that was no way to run a river. The Susquehanna never achieved the transportation prominence of other rivers of its size and historic importance because it is naturally unsuited to the task. Politicians rarely appropriated adequate improvement funds, so efforts were sporadic and, for the most part, unsuccessful.

Earliest attempts to clear the river course employed fire and water. At low water, rivermen piled driftwood around large boulders at river's edge. They burned this wood, heating the rocks to a high temperature. Then they dumped cold water over the rocks to fracture them into smaller chunks that they could remove more easily. Occasionally workers shattered boulders with dynamite.

Breaking rock was backbreaking work. Commissioners appointed to examine and improve the Susquehanna between Columbia and the Maryland line in 1823 found signing contracts with local workers nearly impossible because labor in the river was fatiguing and debilitating, and the task had to be suspended in high water. The difficulty of this labor, coupled with the building of canals and the success of early railroads, eventually persuaded most politicians to abandon efforts to make the Susquehanna shipworthy. However, the possibilities of a navigable river remained

evergreen to some dreamers, especially steamboat fanciers.

In 1852 Eli Bowen wrote in *The Pictorial Sketchbook of Pennsylvania,* "There is really no serious impediment—the fall [of the river], upon the whole, is not too great to be overcome without dams or locks. Three or four millions of dollars, judiciously expended, would render it navigable, beyond doubt, for steamboats of the largest class."[23]

As various players fretted over making practical improvements to Susquehanna navigation, another set of characters strove politically to declare the river navigable (and sometimes unnavigable) on paper. The secretary of war issued the first official commentary on the subject in 1787. On removing military stores from Springfield, Massachusetts, to Carlisle, Pennsylvania, he said, "Were the Susquehanna River navigable for boats, and also the creek which runs through Carlisle [the Conodoguinet], the stores in Philadelphia might be transported to that place."

In 1789 and 1790, as representatives of the fledgling federal government engaged in lengthy debate over where to locate the national capital, the Susquehanna figured significantly and its navigability became a key issue. Representatives more or less seriously considered the river towns of Northumberland, Harrisburg, Columbia, Peach Bottom, and Havre de Grace for the nation's political center. U.S. Representative Thomas Hartley of York said Wright's Ferry (Columbia) would make a perfect capital because it is accessible by river from the Atlantic Ocean and "the distance is nothing more than to afford safety from any hostile attempt." Representative Fisher Ames of Massachusetts maintained that the Susquehanna "is navigable to the head of Lake Otsego." He documented that assertion by describing General Clinton's speedy trip on his manufactured flood during the Revolution.

Failing to convince their skeptical colleagues that the Susquehanna was navigable, Hartley and Ames reversed tactics, arguing that a usable waterway was not essential after all. What really mattered, they said, was to locate the capital near the center of the nation. Southern Pennsylvania, near the Susquehanna, fitted their bill.

Geographically, perhaps, but not politically: Southern representatives pulled the capital to the shores of the Potomac.

The boatability of the Susquehanna faded from the national agenda for a century. In 1890, Congress formally declared the Susquehanna navigable under the Rivers and Harbors Act, listing the river along with truly navigable waterways such as the Mississippi and the Hudson. The designation pleased Pennsylvania's delegation to Congress but did nothing to alter reality.

A dozen years later, U.S. Representative M. E. Olmsted directed the Army Corps of Engineers to examine the river's navigability. Olmsted's rival in the 1902 election had promised to make the Susquehanna navigable by oceangoing vessels all the way to Northumberland. Olmsted wanted to prove he could not do it.

The engineers reported that such a project would be possible but prohibitively expensive at $1 million per mile: "The problem presented for consideration is that of improving for purposes of navigation a nontidal river which drains an area of nearly 30,000 square miles, has worn a channel through hard primitive rocks, is generally shallow, has a steep gradient, and much of the way abrupt rocky banks, and is subject to destructive floods." The Susquehanna is not worth the effort, said the corps. Olmsted's opponent lost a major issue and Olmsted won reelection.

In 1904, Secretary of War William Howard Taft sealed the Susquehanna's future by designating it a nonnavigable stream above the Maryland border. This declaration opened the way for businesses to build dams and bridges without seeking congressional approval. If the river was not navigable, after all, why should Congress care if it was obstructed?

First in line, the Pennsylvania Railroad constructed a bridge across the river at Havre de Grace. York Haven and Holtwood dams soon followed, rendering the Susquehanna forever useless to vessels from downriver.

In 1914 U.S. Representative J. Hampton Moore of Philadelphia attempted to overturn Taft's decision. He told Congress that passageways could be built through the big dams and a series of small dams and locks could be added to provide "plenty of water for navigation and power also, all the way up to Harrisburg." He cataloged the various steamboats, gasoline-powered boats, canoes, ferryboats, and coal barges operating in limited sections and said they argued for the river's navigability. Moore claimed that "it is well established by the courts that if a stream can be used for commerce or trade in any form to any substantial extent, even for the floating of rafts of logs or lumber, it is a navigable stream."

Moore convinced his colleagues. They declared the Susquehanna navigable again. However, they never appropriated money to construct the grand navigational system that might have made Moore's dream work. Instead, the massive hydroelectric plant at Conowingo, approved the year before Moore made his pitch, cut off upriver travel for water craft of any size at ten miles above the Chesapeake.

And so the Susquehanna remains navigable by congressional decree from its mouth to the Pennsylvania–New York border. The West Branch officially is navigable as far as Lock Haven. Given this designation, the bulk of the Susquehanna is eligible for federal programs undertaken by the Corps of Engineers. These projects include flood control and limited channel dredging—but no improvements that would in any way disturb the dams, the major impediments to true navigability.

Ray Lybolt of Tunkhannock, who has lived along and used the river since the 1920s, knows the Susquehanna is special because it is not navigable. He is happy that nothing much larger than his canoe can traverse the river over long distances. "I'm glad there isn't more industry on our river," he says. "If our river was navigable, I'm sure that our town would have had more industry—just as it did during the time we had the canal—and as a result we would have more industrial pollution."

This "navigable" river is not navigable: that is its curse, and its salvation.

York Haven

Between York Haven and the mouth of the river there is a fall of about 270 feet. The mean annual discharge at York Haven from 1891 to 1904, inclusive, is about 40,000 second-feet. By applying the rule that 11 second-feet of water falling 1 foot equals a horsepower with 80 per cent efficiency it is seen that between York Haven and the outlet of the river there [are] about one million horsepower running to waste.

—John Hoyt and Robert Anderson, *Hydrography of the Susquehanna River Drainage Basin,* 1905

A close observer on the riverbank at Conewago Falls watches water flowing at a slight angle toward the Chesapeake, an unusual sight on the relatively level Susquehanna. Because the river drops more steeply at the falls than at any other short run along its course, this was the obvious place to construct the first major power dam. The York Haven Water and Power Company began operating a small hydroelectric plant at Conewago Falls in 1904. During the next three decades, other companies built larger dams downriver at Safe Harbor, Holtwood, and Conowingo. Today the Susquehanna's fifty-five miles between Conewago and the bay host one of the heaviest concentrations of electricity-generating units in the world.

Unlike most rivers, where hydroelectric projects are built nearer the source than the mouth because that's where the action is, the Susquehanna falls more rapidly at its end than at its beginnings. When a river acts this way, hydrologists say it has an inverted profile. From its risings in New York, the Susquehanna meanders nearly 400 miles with an average drop of about 2.5 feet per mile. Then from Conewago to the Chesapeake it picks up speed, falling nearly twice as fast, at

4.7 feet per mile.

The Susquehanna is the only river on the Atlantic coast with an inverted profile, largely because it is one of the oldest rivers and flows through a long-eroded landscape. The geologist Bill Sevon explains: "The Susquehanna's headwaters do not occur in mountains because there are none. The headwaters are nibbling ever so slowly because stream gradient is low. However, at the mouth of the river a large sediment load has been poured into the Baltimore Trough in the Atlantic. As a result, there has been offshore loading that depresses the trough. This depression is compensated by onshore uplift." This uplift along the lower river, combined with a lower sea level during the latest ice age, encouraged increased erosion. Thus the greater gradient downriver.

Early Americans acknowledged this striking attribute of the Lower Susquehanna. In a report on ford and ferry possibilities on the Susquehanna in 1778, Continental Army scouts noted that from Harris's Ferry to the river's mouth, "the fall of the land is very rapid, as one can judge by the rapidity of the current and the number of Falls that are found there."

At the beginning of the twentieth century, electricity entrepreneurs decided to tap all of this "horsepower running to waste" to light up a considerable portion of the East Coast. The power companies recognized that the river fall here would produce electricity profitably, especially when other factors blended with the quickened current to provide almost ideal conditions for development.

Not only does the river drop rapidly at the point where all of its major tributaries have increased its volume to near maximum, but the river hills from Harrisburg to the bay provide a natural reservoir for all this water. (This is particularly the case in the deep Susquehanna Gorge, extending from Turkey Hill to the Chesapeake. In fact, the river falls at its steepest pitch in the 43 miles below Columbia—5.39 feet per mile.) From Conewago to the bay, where water transport is difficult, power production is easy. At this point the river also provides power to the people with facility and therefore some thrift. The Harrisburg-Lancaster-York region is the most populous and economically vibrant along the Susquehanna's route, providing a thriving immediate market for power; nearby markets in Philadelphia and Baltimore draw the excess.[24]

York Haven, then the largest power plant in the United States, shared the nearby hamlet's name, provided by relieved raftmen who had washed through Conewago Falls. Workmen constructed a mile-long wing dam of rubble masonry at the northern end of the falls, actually submerging some of the rapids and potholed rocks in York Haven's three-and-a-half-mile pond called Lake Frederic. This dam runs from the powerhouse on the west bank at a sharp angle upriver, anchoring near the southern end of Three Mile Island. The relatively short dam at the foot of Red Hill contains the river's smaller channel on the other side of TMI. The angled dam channels the river toward the western shore and into a head race that passes into York Haven's U-shaped forebay. From there water plunges twenty-one feet through the power plant's small turbines. The turbine wheels in turn drive shafts connected to electric generators.

York Haven can generate up to 20,000 kilowatts of electricity under optimum conditions. That is now meager voltage by Susquehanna standards.

As Mayor J. Barry Mahool of Baltimore turned on the current at the Susquehanna's second hydroelectric plant in October 1910, he said, "The big Susquehanna River is now working for Baltimore, so here's to the Pennsylvania Water and Power Company; may it live long and prosper!"

With a maximum capacity of just over five times York Haven's and plenty of customers lined up behind the City of Baltimore, Holtwood Hydroelectric Station became at once the largest producer of electricity in the United States and the second largest dam in the world. Only the Nile's Aswan Dam was bigger. The fifty-five-foot-high concrete wall at the site of the old McCall's Ferry held back eight miles of water (Lake Aldred), which the plant spilled through ten enormous turbines.

This place was perfect for dam building. Not only does the river fall rapidly at McCall's Ferry, but the hills channel it narrowly, creating a compact current to drive the turbines.[25] The last dam built before the federal government began licensing such projects, Holtwood proved immensely profitable for Pennsylvania Water and Power and its successor, PPL Utilities.

Conowingo Hydroelectric Station displaced Holtwood as the Susquehanna's largest dam in 1928. Philadelphia Electric Company sited the huge concrete structure five miles south of the Pennsylvania border, about four and a half miles north of tidewater, at a crucial series of rapids. ("Conowingo" is a variation of "Conewago.") From 1926 to

York Haven hydroelectric station was the nation's largest power plant when it was constructed in 1904. This is its powerhouse, viewed from the west shore. (Photo by Christine Brubaker.)

1928, nearly 4,000 men labored to build a 105-foot-tall concrete wall and the powerhouse, relocate sixteen miles of Pennsylvania Railroad track, and reroute Route 1 over the breast of the dam.

Conowingo was Earth's largest water-power generator at the time, called by some "the eighth wonder of the world." Its seven original turbines could generate up to 252,000 kilowatts of power. Philadelphia Electric Company added four larger turbines in 1964, increasing capacity to 512,000 kilowatts. All of this electricity travels to the greater Philadelphia area, where at peak production it provides power for 3 million people.

The water backed up by the dam became Conowingo Pond, which stretches for just over fourteen miles, nearly to Holtwood. This pond inundated miles of shoreline. The little town of Conowingo, two miles upriver, disappeared beneath the water. Near the upriver end of this pond, at Muddy Run, Philadelphia Electric started up the nation's largest pumped-storage hydroelectric unit in 1968. On a bluff 400 feet above the Susquehanna, the company built a 4,400-foot earthen dam, longest in Pennsylvania, across Muddy Run ravine. The dam created an enormous reservoir.

During periods of low demand, usually at night, the company pumps water from the river up to the reservoir. During the day, when the demand for (and price of) electricity rises, the operation releases reservoir water to flow by gravity through eight giant turbines back into the river. Each of these turbines can produce up to 110,000 kilowatts. So Muddy Run's maximum capacity is substantially larger than Conowingo's.[26]

In the spring of 1930, some 4,000 Safe Harbor Water Power Corporation workers began building a series of cofferdams that would dry the river bottom and allow the building of a permanent dam at the confluence of the Susquehanna and Conestoga, about eight miles upriver from Holtwood. Safe Harbor Dam, which currently generates up to 417,000 kilowatts, would be the last hydro unit built directly on the lower river. Next to Conowingo, it is the largest dam. Its ten-mile pool (Lake Clarke) is the second longest.

The four dams have changed the Lower Susquehanna from a free-flowing, rock-encrusted wild river into a series of four placid ponds. In the forty-three miles from Columbia to tidewater, the Susquehanna's current runs unfettered for only eight: a mile in the tailrace below Safe Harbor Dam, two miles below Holtwood, and five miles below Conowingo. The dams block fish travel, trap mounds of ice in winter and enormous amounts of sediment in all seasons, and alter the habitat of their ponds in numerous, complex, and mostly negative ways. The tradeoff is a region wired to a degree that would amaze Thomas Edison, one of the earliest official visitors at the enormous river blockage at Holtwood and inventor of so many of the things that require so much of the electricity produced here.

Brunner Island

I have waded in the Susquehanna downstream of the Brunner Island power plant when the warm discharge area was over 100°F. This temperature is more like a hot tub than a river and is too warm for nearly all gamefish. . . . Come fall and winter however, these discharges are like fish magnets. Water temperatures in the discharge zone of fifty to sixty are common during this time and quite welcome for both fish and fishermen.

—Christopher Beatty, *Susquehanna River Guide*

THE DRIVER HAS JUST FINISHED LOADING 1,200 pounds of live hybrid striped bass into his big truck. He is making small talk now with the man who sold him the fish. Brent Blauch owns Susquehanna Aquacultures, a company that grows bass along the Susquehanna in York County. Blauch and the driver are joking around before the truck pulls out. The driver's English vocabulary is limited, so he is having some difficulty keeping up.

"You ever have pheasant?" asks Blauch. The driver does not understand, though he is smiling and nodding his head. "It's a bird," Blauch explains. "A kind of bird. Ring neck. Pheasant. Wild bird. It's like a chicken. Chinese chicken."

"Chinese chicken?"

"Yeah. Ring neck. Bird. You understand bird? Chinese bird? Pheasant?"

"O.K. I eat chicken," says the driver, laughing at this strange conversation. He understands chicken. He does not understand pheasant. Closer to the business at hand, he understands fish.

"We have chicken in Canada," he says. "We have none of these fish." He laughs again. "Best fish in the world."

The driver is taking away $4,000 worth of hybrid striped bass (a cross between striped and white bass) and a story about a funny kind of chicken. It is Tuesday. He will be back on Friday to buy a similar amount. He will transport all these live fish to Toronto's Chinatown and distribute them to wholesale fish markets. Chinese Canadians will buy the fish and take them home and eat them. Friday's truckload of central Pennsylvania fish will be steamed live in Toronto's Chinese restaurants on Saturday evening.

"They used to go to Mississippi to pick up striped bass," Blauch says after the driver has begun his long trip north. "We're better because we're closer and our fish last. They go in the tank in Toronto and they're a little more resilient to stress. We have some losses, but not like the indoor farms. Our fish become much more tolerant to changes in their environment, and so they adapt and survive better."

The driver from Toronto has taken his supply of fish on a raw day in early December. The air temperature is in the 30s. The river temperature is in the 40s. These hybrids would not be happy in such cold water, but they are not in cold water. Susquehanna Aquacultures grows its hybrid striped bass in Susquehanna water warmed to 60°F or more—warm enough to take winter business from southern fish farms.

If PPL Utilities were not making electricity by burning coal at Brunner Island Steam Electric Station, Susquehanna Aquacultures could not exist. The Brunner Island plant, squeezed onto the northern end of a long, narrow island just south of York Haven, uses river water as coolant and Susquehanna Aquacultures channels the discharge through its fish farm. Blauch buys his fingerlings from those southern farms where the Chinese used to buy grown specimens and raises them in Brunner Island's thermal stream. A highly polluting utility provides warmth for a highly prized fish. An environmental lemon produces a piscatorial lemonade.

Second only to Peach Bottom Atomic Power Station in amount of electricity produced along the Lower Susquehanna, Brunner Island employs three coal-fired units to turn river water to steam. The steam drives turbines that generate up to 1,495,000 kilowatts.

Brent Blauch holds a hybrid striped bass, one of thousands of fish that his business, Susquehanna Aquacultures, raises from fingerlings in Susquehanna water. The water is warmed to 60°F or more in all seasons by emissions from the adjacent Brunner Island Steam Electric Station. (Photo by Christine Brubaker.)

PPL has been spewing tons of coal pollutants into the air through Brunner Island's two chimneys since 1961. After passage of the Clean Air Act of 1990, the utility dramatically reduced the release of nitrogen oxide and sulfur dioxide. Federal and state guidelines require further reductions because Brunner Island remains among the nation's top emitters of pollutants that produce smog and degrade Susquehanna and Chesapeake water. It is also one of the

larger emitters of heated water into the Susquehanna—some 730 million gallons a day. Brunner Island and the nuclear stations at Three Mile Island and especially Peach Bottom all have localized thermal impacts on the river. Brunner Island has the largest effect.

The hot water discharged from Brunner Island hugs the river's west bank, elevating the water temperature significantly for seven or more miles downstream. In winter, when fish are sluggish elsewhere in the Susquehanna, smallmouth bass swim and feed as if it's springtime in the Brunner Island discharge. Year-round anglers take advantage. "Over the Christmas holidays, it's like the first day of trout season," says Brent Blauch. "People are lined up shoulder to shoulder to fish along the warm water."

Shortly after the units went on line at Brunner Island, PPL decided to use this thermal stream to demonstrate that warm water pouring out of a power plant could have a positive influence on the environment. (Negative impacts of overheated water include intrusion on fish spawning and egg hatching and encouragement of noxious aquatic growths.) PPL built dikes to channel a fraction of the warm water outflow through a twenty-acre fish farm directly below the power plant. The operation tried unsuccessfully to raise catfish and experimented briefly with shad and an exotic African fish.

In the late 1980s, PPL decided it had spent enough money on the project and offered to lease the farm. Blauch was working as a consulting engineer in upriver coal regions. He wanted a new challenge.

He has regretted that decision only once. The

Susquehanna topped the island's dike in January 1996. Floodwaters killed all his fish and wrecked most of his equipment. He had to start raising fish all over again and had nothing to sell until the spring of 1997. All his customers returned.

"I don't see our situation here as any different than any other kind of critter farm, like a little poultry operation," explains Blauch, who considers himself a fish farmer in every way. "We buy things and feed them and grow 'em up to big ones. It takes a twenty-four-hour attention span. There's a lot of husbandry and keeping them happy."

During most of the year, Susquehanna Aquacultures pumps water from Brunner Island's discharge canal into its own reservoir. This warm water flows by gravity through nineteen raceways filled with hybrid striped bass. During the summer, when the river itself is warm and the water discharged from the utility is too hot for bass, the operation pumps river water directly through the raceways. In either case, the operation uses water only once. Fish swim constantly in a fresh flow.

Blauch tries to keep the water at 70 to 75°F. In the summer, the temperature sometimes rises higher. In the winter, if some of Brunner Island's units are shut down for maintenance, the temperature may fall considerably lower. If the plant shuts down entirely, the fish farm is in trouble, although striped bass are more tolerant of cold water than some other fish and can survive a few days of frigid temperatures.

As the fish grow, Blauch moves them from raceway to raceway and eventually into a truck bound for Toronto or New York or central Pennsylvania markets. The fish live most of their lives—a year or more—swimming in this manufactured current and manipulated climate.

Blauch babies his fingerlings. He keeps them in large round tanks so he can control their growth before moving them to the raceways. He employs several people, but often feeds the fingerlings and culls the dead himself. He also keeps several dogs to bark off the birds that would love to swoop into the fingerling tanks and raceways and make a meal of some of his 250,000 fish.

PPL officials originally thought raising fish this way could become a popular idea. They were wrong. Blauch's operation is unique in Pennsylvania. There are only a handful of similar utility-based operations elsewhere in the country. Catfish farming is becoming a major industry in southern ponds and fish farming in general is growing in popularity worldwide, but not in used coolant.

Blauch looks wistfully from his bass raceways to the dike that separates his farm from the Susquehanna. "I got into this business because I like to fish," he says, "but I haven't had much time to fish. I can't get over, when I do get out there, how much life is in this river. You'd be amazed at the different types of life that you encounter—small organisms and larva and all kinds of fish."

Blauch knows that not everyone shares his high opinion of Susquehanna water: "Some people say they don't want to eat fish that come from the river. I tell them if you can drink the water, the fish are probably not going to like it. Do you drink water where a flounder lives? The Susquehanna is one of the best fisheries around; that tells all you need to know about the water quality."

Marietta

A seeming eccentricity in the design of the borough is the peculiar manner in which the town sprawls for a mile and a half along the river but is little more than a quarter or half a mile wide. The principal reason for this is that at the time of the laying out of the villages river trade had assumed large proportions and was for many years the main element of business in the town. River frontage, therefore, was vital to the survival of the town.

—*History of Marietta,* 1962

WHILE LOCK HAVEN AND WILLIAMSPORT were principal markets for West Branch logs, most rafts headed for distant Marietta. In the spring of 1827, six years before the Pennsylvania Canal opened, 1,631 rafts and 1,370 arks passed Harrisburg. Many of the lumber rafts stopped at Marietta, several miles downstream from the adventurous rapids at Conewago. Buyers moved lumber by good roads from Marietta to Lancaster and Philadelphia.

Raftmen separated the Susquehanna into three divisions. The first extended from Clearfield to Lock Haven, the second from Lock Haven to Marietta, and the third from Marietta to Port Deposit, at tidewater. The river is relatively sluggish at all three end points, so they became obvious places to stop.

Running from Lock Haven to Marietta, rivermen lashed most lumber rafts into fleets of two. Each fleet carried at least a four-man crew: a pilot, two steerers, and someone to help anyone else in a pinch. These fleets usually paused at White House (Highspire), about 6 miles downstream from Harrisburg. There Lock Haven pilots yielded to White House pilots, who specialized in maneuvering rafts through Conewago and on to Marietta.

From Marietta south, raftmen broke fleets into single rafts. Expanded crews of six to nine men guided these rafts through the hazardous waters from Columbia to tidewater. Few upriver men piloted rafts below Marietta; lower-river pilots who lived in Marietta, Columbia, and nearby areas carried on from there. They had to navigate dangerous spots, including the point at Turkey Hill, Cully's Falls just below McCall's Ferry, the Horse Gap at Peach Bottom, and the Hollow Rock in Bald Friar Falls. Below these rafting points, as below Conewago, local rivermen often maintained boats to help rescue raftmen if they stove on rocks and wound up in the drink.

Many rafts that did not stop at Marietta continued to Port Deposit, a port of deposit for lumber. There raftmen lashed their timbers into floats of about nine rafts, some of which "floated" on top of others. Big boats towed these floats through the Chesapeake Bay to Chesapeake City, on the Chesapeake and Delaware Canal. Workmen reshaped the floats into long rafts called lockings and towed them along the canal to Delaware City, on the Delaware River. There they transformed them into floats once more and towed them up the Delaware to northern markets.

Getting the rafts to Marietta or Port Deposit was the short part of the raftmen's round trip. Unless they paid to ride a canal boat, or a rail car in later years, raftmen walked home. From Clearfield to Marietta by water might take two or three days. The return journey—175 miles or so on paths along the river they had just descended—required five to six days of hard walking. The men had to keep moving, especially in early spring, in order to meet another raft coming downriver. In *Rafting Days on the Susquehanna,* James Herbert Walker says his father rode seventeen rafts into Marietta one spring and walked back to Clearfield County each time.

Returning raftmen ordinarily traveled in groups, and riverside hotels and taverns flourished, thanks to their patronage. A tavern stood every four miles or so along the "Big River," the raftmen's term for the wide Lower Susquehanna. Some raftmen made a point of stopping at each for a drink. Often they imbibed considerably more when they stopped at a hotel for the night. Raftmen with sore feet poured liquor into their shoes as a healing agent.

As the raftmen walked, they played musical instruments or sang, developing an impressive repertoire. Group singing, especially with well-lubricated vocal cords, could reach impressive volume on tunes such as "Captain Jinks of the Horse Marines" (who fed his horse on corn and beans) and "The Daring Young Man on the Flying Trapeze." Their rowdy drinking and singing, not to mention the reckless nature of rafting itself, prompted N. P. Willis to worry that rafters might become a "sympathetic *corps,* whose excitement and *esprit* might be roused to very dangerous uses."

Lumbermen returning by train also imbibed liberally. Dr. Robert Lowry had decidedly mixed feelings upon hearing his most famous hymn, "Beautiful River," sung by inebriated lumbermen in the early 1870s. The Baptist minister and University of Lewisburg (Bucknell) professor listened to the men "repeating the chorus in a wild, boisterous way. . . . I did think that perhaps the spirit of the hymn, the words so flippantly uttered, might somehow survive and be carried forward into the lives of those careless men, and ultimately lift them upward to the realization of the hope expressed in the hymn."

No matter how much fun getting drunk and singing loud might have been, going home was never the highlight of a raftman's tour. Rafting downstream was the big adventure. A contemporary of West Branch raftmen wrote: "This trip, when made for the first time was as much of an event—aye, more—in the history of the life of a young man, as is a trip to Europe today; nor was any one considered a true lumberman—a hero—until he could tell some wonderful story about 'what I saw at Marietta last spring.'"

What raftmen saw at Marietta was a town rivaling nearby Columbia as a center for river business. Marietta's Scots-Irish settlers had built their houses facing the river, some of them with lumber rafted down it. In addition to James Anderson's Ferry, river-related businesses included boat building, lumber milling, and, after 1833, the Pennsylvania Canal. In 1814 Marietta numbered among its residents nine lumber merchants, twenty-one carpenters, twenty-one joiners, four river pilots, three ferrymen, one pastor, and fourteen tavernkeepers.

For every Hiestand or Grosh or Duffy who made a small fortune from the river, many other Mariettans fell short. James Mitchell, a Clearfield County raftman, said upriver men were surprised that so many Marietta residents would beg for food and search for chips of wood on rafts to use as kindling the next winter. They encountered this type of wood-chip scavenging nowhere else on the river.[27]

Wood for fuel was relatively scarce because early settlers clear-cut trees to plant crops, build houses, or help manufacture charcoal for the early iron industry. When iron furnaces converted from charcoal to anthracite in the 1840s, the focus of many Mariettans turned from the river and the lumber trade to the canal and a trade in coal and iron.

Thanks to nearby ore mines, ubiquitous limestone (used as flux in the ironmaking process), and coal transported from the Wyoming Valley by way of the Pennsylvania Canal, Marietta became a miniature Pittsburgh after 1845. Through the end of the nineteenth century, eight furnaces operated along a mile-long band directly on the Susquehanna's floodplain between Marietta and picturesque Chickies Rock, which juts into the Susquehanna just downstream. They turned out tons of pig iron for shipment by canal and later by rail.

Hundreds of immigrants settled in Marietta and Columbia specifically to work in the mines and furnaces. German ironworkers joined the area's already substantial Pennsylvania German population. Irish and Welsh and later Central Europeans came in even greater numbers. These people altered the ethnic character of the Columbia-Marietta region as noticeably as immigrant coal miners transformed the Wyoming Valley and Cambria County.

The furnaces flourished for several decades and then slowly declined as the iron industry discovered huge supplies of ore in Minnesota and the superior coking qualities of bituminous coal in western Pennsylvania. Pittsburgh put "Little Pittsburgh" out of business.

June Evans, an assistant professor of sociology and anthropology at Millersville University, has been searching for artifacts at the site of the Henry Clay furnace, near Chickies Rock, for more than a decade. Dr. Evans and her students have had to dig through several inches of sand, fine coal, and dirt to get to the ruins. Regular floods have deposited this material throughout the floodplain, creating a beachlike effect in low places where summer archaeologists have not disturbed it. Here one sees what Marietta's Front Street might look like after a flood if a railroad embankment did not protect it from an onslaught of river sediment.

Front Street sits about a football field's length from the river. The rail line runs between river and street on a bed elevated several feet. The Pennsylvania Railroad raised the line to protect the rails, not the town, although the embankment has served as a semi-effective levee. Marietta is adding impervious material to the embankment's river side to transform it into a true dike.

In minor floods, the Susquehanna remains in the boat clubs and parkland on the river side of the embankment, but big water always finds a way to get into Marietta. In 1972 the town suffered as much damage as any community on the Lower Susquehanna. The river never overflowed the railroad embankment; water came straight up through satu-

    The Philadelphia artist Edmund Darch Lewis painted hundreds of landscapes in Pennsylvania, New York, and New England. The Susquehanna at Marietta, *completed in 1871, depicts Marietta and its iron furnaces, looking upstream from Chickies Rock. (Mr. and Mrs. James A. Miller, Marietta, Pennsylvania.)*

☙ *The painter-poet Lloyd Mifflin of Columbia took this photograph of his cousin Martha Mifflin standing on Chickies Rock, south of Marietta. The camera is pointed downstream. The Pennsylvania Railroad's Low Grade Line, completed in 1906, cuts off a slice of river, creating shallow Kerbaugh Lake at the left. River riffles lead to the Columbia bridge in the distance. (Lamar Libhart, Harrisburg, Pennsylvania.)*

rated ground between the rail line and Front Street.

Bob Shank ordered employees to pile everything on the bar of his popular Front Street tavern. "She'll never come over the bar," he said. The 1936 flood had not come over the bar; the river had crested about eight feet above flood stage. In 1972 it crested twelve feet above. Shank marked his wall where water from both floods stopped rising. The second mark is close to the first-floor ceiling.

More than a thousand people, nearly a third of Marietta's residents, evacuated the borough in 1972. They returned to flooded Front Street properties that seemed beyond repair. Some owners abandoned their homes and the borough condemned them. A few residents advocated bulldozing the entire floodplain inside the railroad embankment, but volunteers helped clean up the mud and new people moved in and saved most of the buildings.

Shank's Tavern began serving raftmen in 1814 and Bob Shank is not about to abandon the saloon now. He no longer trusts the bar to hold his valuables if the river rises. When a forecast calls for high water on Front Street, he moves everything to higher ground.

Columbia

There rushes the River,—both Surveyors understanding by now 'tis not only a River, being as well the Boundary to another Country.

—Thomas Pynchon, *Mason & Dixon*, describing Charles Mason and
Jeremiah Dixon viewing the Susquehanna from the east shore

On his way from Philadelphia to York in 1796, Isaac Weld Jr. crossed the Susquehanna at Columbia because he believed its ferry used better boats than ferries up- or downstream. "The Susquehannah is here somewhat more than a quarter of a mile wide," Weld reported, missing the Susquehanna's true width by a mile, "and for a considerable distance, both above and below the ferry, it abounds with islands and large rocks, over which last the water runs with prodigious velocity: the roaring noise that it makes is heard a great way off."

The first Englishman to travel extensively in the United States and write critically of his experiences, Weld clearly appreciated the Susquehanna setting. "The scenery in every point of view is wild and romantic," he wrote of the riverscape he could see from his ferryboat. "In crossing the river it is necessary to row up against the stream under the shore, and then to strike over to the opposite side, under the shelter of some of the largest islands. As these rapids continue for many miles, they totally impede the navigation, excepting when there are floods in the river, at which time large rafts may be conducted down the stream, carrying several hundred barrels of flour."

Much of that flour, as well as coal, whiskey, and lumber, stopped at Columbia, an important port on the Lower Susquehanna when Weld passed through and for many decades thereafter. Thanks to its direct highway connection with Lancaster and Philadelphia, Columbia also became a prime transportation center for passengers moving east to west. In later years, even more travelers arrived by canal and rail to cross the river here. At Columbia, a steady

~ *In 1812 Pavel Petrovitch Svinin, secretary to the Russian consul general in the United States, portrayed Wright's Ferry crossing from Columbia to Wrightsville in* A Ferry Scene on the Susquehanna River at Wright's Ferry, Just above Havre de Grace. *The flat-bottomed boat carries a lady and gentleman and their chaise, a coachman, three foot passengers, and two ferrymen rowing the boat. Chickies Rock stands in the background. (The Metropolitan Museum of Art, New York, Rogers Fund, 1942.)*

stream of humanity passed over the Susquehanna into "another country."

The town was eight years old when Weld described it. Samuel Wright, grandson of the first ferryboat operator, had laid out the place, renaming Wright's Ferry for Christopher Columbus in hopes that it might become the nation's capital. Settlers built the first homes on Front Street, in the floodplain. The land slopes only gradually from the water, so most well-to-do residents moved well up the hill. Some of them lost their river view when huge piles of lumber and warehouses occupied the riverfront. Shad fisheries and produce markets, sawmills and coal yards soon shared the busy floodplain.

Joshua Gilpin, traveling with his family from Philadelphia to Pittsburgh in 1809, stayed at the ferry house on Front Street preparatory to crossing the river. The mass of merchandise washing down the Susquehanna and the trade on shore impressed him. "Columbia is seated on the lowest point where the Susquehanna is safely navigable," he wrote in his journal. "Columbia is therefore the grand depot of all the produce of this vast river which waters a great part of Pennsylvania. . . . The produce now brought consists of abt. 100,000 bbls flour, 300,000 bus of wheat; an immense quantity of lumber—a great deal of coal, iron, whiskey, beef, pork, & in fact all the productions of the country."

The next morning a man rowed Gilpin and his family across the river in a small bateau. "The water not being high the stream was extremely tranquil & the current by no means rapid," Gilpin observed. "We could every where see the bottom the water being quite clear—the bottom is very uneven, appearing composed of numberless rocks—the deepest part was now not more than 5 or 6 feet but so shallow in many places that our boat which drew only 5 or 6 in[ches] of water almost touched."

Five years after Gilpin crossed, the first bridge eased traffic flow over the Susquehanna. Meanwhile, raft traffic increased each spring, jamming the waterfront. Columbians petitioned the state for permission to regulate access to the town's wharves and landings in 1817. The legislature complied after reviewing a Senate report that stated, "The owners of rafts who bring lumber down the river occupy so much space along shore, as to render it either impracticable or dangerous for boats loaded with grain to approach the warehouses for the purpose of unloading."

Boat pilots discharging human cargo at Columbia also faced potential danger. Isaac Shields, a free black English man, settled in Columbia early in the nineteenth century and helped spirit slaves out of Maryland. Shields and later his son, Isaac Shields Jr., secreted slaves in a false-bottomed wagon and carried them to Wrightsville, then polled them over to Columbia in a boat.

Several other black Columbians helped operate this major station on the underground railroad. Stephen Smith, a lumber dealer in Columbia and later Philadelphia and the wealthiest black man in mid-nineteenth-century America, was a leader in the movement. He and William Whipper employed escaped slaves in their riverfront lumber yards. Other escapees worked in coal yards and many remained in Columbia for the rest of their lives.[28]

As Columbia began to resolve its river transportation

problems in the 1820s and '30s, it benefited tremendously from alternative transport. Unlike most river towns, where trade benefited first from canals and later from railroads, Columbia received its canal and railroad at the same time. As a result, trade really boomed in the 1830s. In the early '30s, workers extended the Pennsylvania Canal by sections northward from Columbia. In 1840, the Susquehanna and Tidewater Canal, running from Wrightsville downriver to Havre de Grace, opened for traffic on the other side of the Susquehanna. To connect the canal sections, mules walked a towpath on the Columbia bridge, pulling canal boats between Columbia and Wrightsville.

Meanwhile, the Philadelphia & Columbia Railroad reached its Columbia terminus in the spring of 1834. A 1,924-foot inclined plane dropped cars ninety feet to river level, where a team of mules drew them across the river on rails laid on the new bridge. Alternatively, mules dragged cars for a short distance along Front Street track to the canal basin and outlet lock for shipment north. By 1836 the Philadelphia & Columbia was operating thirty-four steam locomotives—more than any other railroad in the United States.

Rail and canal traffic grew rapidly from the mid-1830s and Columbia's riverfront teemed with competing freight and passenger lines. Freight could be carried in practically any direction to and from Columbia and arriving passengers had their choice of crossing the Susquehanna on the bridge or transferring to the canal. Philip Houlbrouke Nicklin chose the canal when he came here in 1835.

Columbia, Nicklin wrote in a book published the next year, "is a thriving and pretty town, and is rapidly increasing in business, population and wealth. There is an immense bridge here, over the Susquehanna, the superstructure of which, composed of massy timber, rests upon stone piers. . . . Here is the western termination of the Rail Road, and goods from the seaboard intended for the great West are here transhipped into canal boats."

After spending several hours at Columbia, Nicklin boarded a Pioneer Line canal boat and continued his trip northward. "The pretty town of Marietta is two miles above Columbia, on the same side of the river," he wrote. "That part of the river lying between the two towns, in some points of view resembles closely the scenery of Harper's Ferry, and is quite equal to it in beauty and sublimity."

Most travelers chose railroad over canal. By 1839, more than 50,000 cars traveled the Philadelphia & Columbia each year. Long lines of cars waiting to use the inclined plane reminded older residents of wagons that had backed up at the ferry. A new rail line entering Columbia from the southeast at river level resolved the inclined plane problem in 1840, but other modernizations came slowly. The railroad used horses to draw some cars until 1844 and mules switched cars along Front Street until a switching engine arrived in 1882. All this activity ensured that the town's waterfront would remain industrial, more like Williamsport's floodplain than the grand residential section along the shore at Harrisburg.

In 1857 the state sold its vast canal and railroad system to the Pennsylvania Railroad. The Pennsy continued to run locomotives across the 1834 bridge and its successor, initi-

The Columbia Canal Basin before a hurricane destroyed the town's last covered bridge across the Susquehanna in 1896. The outlet lock joins the Susquehanna at right. Notice the extensive cargo docks and numerous boats and railroad cars. None of this activity occurs on the Columbia waterfront today. (Columbia [Pennsylvania] Historic and Preservation Society.)

ating its first through service, from Philadelphia to York by way of Columbia, in 1870. Nine years later, traveling on that line or possibly another upstream, Robert Louis Stevenson observed the Susquehanna before issuing the most famous remark anyone has ever made about it. "And when I had asked the name of a river from the brakesman, and heard that it was called Susquehanna, the beauty of the name seemed to be part and parcel of the beauty of the land," he wrote in *Across the Plains*. "As when Adam with divine fitness named the creatures, so this word

Susquehanna was at once accepted by the fancy. That was the name, as no other could be, for that shining river and desirable valley."

By the time the Susquehanna enchanted Stevenson, Columbia had passed its prime. River and canal traffic had declined dramatically and rail lines elsewhere were drawing more trade. Today all river-related businesses except one marina are gone. The gritty riverfront is filled with railroad tracks, abandoned brick warehouses, Columbia's and Lancaster's water-intake plants, Columbia's sewage outflow, and the town's landfill.

Residents of Columbia, Wrightsville, and Marietta periodically discuss ways to lure tourists with tales of their colorful river history. Columbians have proposed sprucing up the waterfront and building a transportation museum, but little changes in this tired river town. Most travelers these days, zipping across the Susquehanna on the Route 30 bridge, barely notice as they bypass the place.

Columbia Dam

Poor Shad! Where is thy redress? Who hears the fishes

when they cry?

> —Henry David Thoreau, *A Week on the*
> *Concord and Merrimack Rivers*

Wipe out a river's spawning run and you have diminished

the very springtime.

> —Tom Horton, *Bay Country*

As the silvery American shad swam in from the Atlantic and began to ascend the Susquehanna to spawn each spring, Columbians residing in a riverside neighborhood called Fishtown plucked the migrating specimens out of the water by the thousands. The whole village might have been called Shadtown two centuries ago, says the local historian Reeves Goehring, because so many shad filled the Susquehanna and so many Columbians fished for them.

Describing these shad runs, Jacob Gossler wrote in 1888: "Columbia was famous for its shad, which, when I was a boy, were caught there in immense quantities and of excellent quality. . . . The shad are not so numerous in the Susquehanna as they were in my time, when they were so plenty that five to ten dollars per hundred was esteemed a fair price; and the farmers came from far and near to secure a wagon load, to be salted down, like mackerel, for future use."

This fertile fishery changed abruptly in 1839 as workmen completed a six-and-a-half-foot-high dam of white pine cribs filled with stones a mile below town. Ponded water behind this dam created a basin in which canal boats could float in all seasons between Columbia and Wrightsville. Fish could not swim over this dam: it eliminated all shad fishing above Columbia.

The shad-fishing region had been truncated earlier in the decade by similar canal dams constructed first at Nanticoke, at the southern end of the Wyoming Valley; then just below the confluence of the Susquehanna's branches; then at Clarks Ferry, where the Juniata joins the Susquehanna. People who had come to rely on shad for income furiously denounced this first major damming of the river.

"Immediately after the erection of the river dams the shad became scarce, the seines rotted, the people murmured, their avocation was gone," Gilbert H. Fowler told the Pennsylvania Commission of Fisheries in 1894, when the Bloomsburg-area fisherman was eighty-six years old, "and many old fishermen cursed Nathan Beach for holding the plow and the driver of the six yokes of oxen that broke the ground at Berwick for the Pennsylvania Canal."

An anonymous poet, calling his lament "A Dam Nuisance," expressed a common opinion of the Columbia Dam:

[Spring] hears the fisherman's tale of woe
From Havre de Grace to Otsego . . .
For the savory shad is seen no more
Above Columbia's smoke-wrapt shore. . . .
Through the centuries we'll sing the psalm,—
"O dam Columbia! Columbia Dam!"

The dam not only blocked the annual shad migration but ended free passage of arks and rafts on the run of the river. The economic importance of the canal, however, outweighed all complaints to the legislature. For what turned out to be a few years of modest success for the Pennsylvania Canal system, the dams at Columbia and elsewhere segmented the Susquehanna, ruining the most fertile shad fishery in the eastern United States and one of the largest fisheries of any kind on any river.

"They came in such immense numbers and so compact," said Gilbert Fowler, "as to cause a wave or rising of the water in the middle of the river, extending from shore to shore." These shad were as large as they were numerous, as bones found in archaeological digs attest. They ranged from two pounds for those caught on the lower river to thirteen pounds if they swam past nets and hooks all the way to Towanda or Athens and matured. Many fish weighed twice as much as today's specimens.[29]

Born in freshwater, the anadromous shad swam downriver and spent most of the four or five years of their lives in the ocean, returning to freshwater only to spawn and die when they reached sexual maturity. Their birth waters included the sources of the North Branch near Cooperstown, the streams running into the river near Lock Haven and perhaps farther upriver on the West Branch, and "cricks" in the foothills of the Alleghenies near Hollidaysburg, on the Juniata.

Early river watchers knew precisely when each spring's run would begin. A long, thin, dark-brown insect called a shad fly preceded the fish on the river. The shad frog made its seasonal debut. Dogwoods and shadbush trees bloomed. Bloodroot (a.k.a. shad flower) unfurled its white petals. Spring sprang with the shad run.

Native Americans must have fished for shad through thousands of springs. Archaeological and early historical evidence suggests they used rock weirs to guide fish into a box or chest; spears, gigs, and bows and arrows to kill them; and sieves to extract them from the water. George Henry Loskiel, a Moravian missionary, described their way of fishing for shad in 1788. After driving the fish into a box with poles and by making "an hideous noise," he said, "Indians stationed on each side of the chest take them out, kill them and fill their canoes. By this contrivance they sometimes catch above a thousand shad and other fish in half a day."

Native Americans also fished from the shore. One of their favorite fishing places is now called Indian Steps, near Airville, in York County. Here they carved holes into rocks as footholds from which to spear shad or catch them in bow nets, large, hand-held wood-and-mesh devices dipped into the water. Settlers supplanted Native Americans on these "steps." "Here men stood in long lines and waited their turn to dip for shad," wrote one historian. "As soon as a man caught a shad he would step aside and go to the end of the line and wait his turn for another chance to dip his bow-net into the water. Old inhabitants will tell you that often a hundred or more men and boys would be lined up at this point."[30]

Early fishermen realized that the most efficient way to capture shad in large numbers was with a seine (also called a "haul seine") pulled along the river by two boats. Men poled the boats ahead, trapping fish within a half circle formed by the stretched net. The boats touched shore, closing the semicircle, and fishermen extracted the shad.

As shad was a staple in the Native Americans' diet, so it became one of the most common foods for the conquering Europeans. Numerous early Susquehanna settlements—from Cooperstown to Wyoming to the West Branch Valley—owed their continuing health to the spring shad run and salted fish stored for winter. Some people called shad "poor man's salmon" because a shad sold for a dime or less in the early years of the nineteenth century. Settlers bartered shad: one shad might be traded for a pound of sugar, 100 for a bushel of salt. Republican operatives traded shad for promised votes in a party primary at Columbia in 1880.

News of the abundance of Susquehanna shad helped persuade Connecticut settlers to move to the Wyoming Valley before the Revolution. During the Yankee-Pennamite Wars, they fought with Pennsylvanians in part over control of the best shad-fishing sites. The large number of widows created by the Yankee-Pennamite and Revolutionary wars prompted Wyoming Valley fishermen to set aside the shad run's first Sunday for "widows' hauls." All shad caught on that day went to widows and orphans. At one widows' haul midway between Wilkes-Barre and Plymouth, fishermen caught and donated an estimated 10,000 shad.

That was an unusually large but hardly a record haul for one fishery, on widows' day or any other. Fishermen in the Berwick area reported collecting 11,000 and 12,000 fish a day. Here's the record: In April 1827, Thomas Stump, operating what was then the largest shad fishery in the United States, laid a seine across the mouth of the river at Havre de Grace. No shad or any other fish could swim out of the Chesapeake past that seine. Because a fierce wind limited activity on the river, Stump had to leave the seine in the water for four days and nights. During that time, all fish that swam to the head of the bay encountered this big mesh trap. The fishermen spent more than three days pulling the seine to shore and several more days distributing its contents to Maryland and Pennsylvania residents, some of whom dumped the plentiful fish on their land as fertilizer.

After adding up the hundreds of wagons that left the river filled with shad and herring and striped bass, Stump estimated that he had caught 15 million fish.

More typically, fishermen caught several hundred shad a day during the early decades of the nineteenth century. Individual catches declined as more fisheries opened all along the river and its tributaries. At Columbia, the pillars of the community—John and James Wright and Robert Barber—managed three early shad fisheries along the shore. Subsequently, dozens of island fisheries forced shore operations to share the catch. Upriver, between Northumberland and Towanda, at least forty separate fisheries operated seasonally at the height of shad fishing.

These fisheries rarely had difficulty selling their product. Farmers drove wagons many miles to stock up on shad for the winter. After road builders extended the Lancaster-to-Philadelphia Turnpike to Columbia in the late 1790s, shad began feeding a much larger populace. These farmers sometimes stayed at the river for as much as a week, holding lively jamborees. Hotels and taverns built to accommodate them would, in later years, serve raftmen.

But this lucrative fishery, including shad canneries operating all along the river, had begun to decline even before construction of the canal dams. Early grist- and sawmill dams blocked off the narrow upper river and many lower tributaries. Levi Beardsley, an early Cooperstown settler, recalled that shad and herring continued to run the Susquehanna all the way to Lake Otsego until small dams downriver obstructed their ascent after 1800. Various laws required dam builders to use fishways or ladders, but these

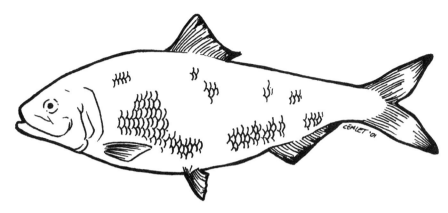

〜 *The American shad, once the Susquehanna's premier fish, lost its spawning run with the building of the Columbia Dam and other canal structures early in the nineteenth century. (Drawing by Chris Emlet.)*

devices, if installed at all, rarely worked.

Because more people lived along the Lower Susquehanna, these fisheries had the market clout to restrict fish passage to the north. Periodically resentment flared upriver. In 1814 representatives of northern Pennsylvania counties accused fishermen in Columbia and other Lancaster County river communities of "so constantly scouring" the lower river that most shad had no chance of swimming past them. The Pennsylvania legislature responded by dividing the river into sections and closing those sections on staggered days to allow fish to swim farther upstream. Unfortunately for upriver fisheries, no one enforced this rule.

Fisheries upriver also protested downstream fish weirs, which functioned like dams to stop shad and also hampered navigation. Pennsylvania prohibited construction of weirs on the Susquehanna in 1700 and again in 1761 and 1771. New

York did likewise in 1788. Fishermen virtually ignored these dictates.

Both Maryland and New York protested construction of the canal dams without success. Fishermen below the dams who suddenly found easier pickings joined canal lobbyists in support of each new obstruction. Then they fished as if there would never be another shad run. "After the erection of the Columbia Dam, the people who dwelt below seemed to think that the future of the shad fishing industry in the Susquehanna was about at an end," wrote William E. Meehan in his 1893 history of Pennsylvania fishing, "for they threw all discretion to the winds, and adopted all kinds of outrageous methods of taking fish."

Fighting for the best fishing places and trying to restrain downstream fishermen occasionally escalated into "shad wars." In the late 1850s, Columbia seine fishermen traveled downriver to Safe Harbor to destroy weirs, baskets, and other shad-fishing tools. Their intended victims met them with rocks, boat poles, and a cannon made at the Safe Harbor Iron Works. The Columbians abruptly retreated, ending the Great Safe Harbor Shad War. Another fish fight in 1860 claimed the life of a York County fisherman.

Deteriorating water quality began to depress the quantity of fish about the same time dams and overfishing below them took a toll. Tanneries and other industries pumped increasing amounts of fish-killing poisons into the water. Clear-cutting of timber promoted soil erosion. Coal added acid. River dwellers joked that a blend of coal dust and sewage contributed to the unique taste of Susquehanna shad.

The decline of the fishery prompted the Pennsylvania legislature to name a commissioner for the restoration of inland fisheries in 1866. Seven years later, the legislature expanded the post into a three-member commission, predecessor of the modern Pennsylvania Fish and Boat Commission. The first commissioner, Colonel James Worrall, had a singular mission, impossible for him to complete, as it turned out. The legislature told Worrall to concentrate on restoring shad and other migratory fish to the Susquehanna.

Worrall persuaded the state to ban the netting of shad within 200 yards of a dam sluice or passageway, where the fish tended to congregate; but when officers attempted to enforce the restriction at the Columbia Dam, fishermen destroyed their boat. The state also required owners of the canal dams to build fishways or open chutes so that shad could pass over or through the structures. The upstream dams refused to construct such passageways and the Pennsylvania Supreme Court eventually upheld their rebellion.

Owners of the Columbia Dam attempted a series of fish chutes between 1866 and 1886, with limited success. An illegal process called "shingling" reduced the effectiveness of these passages. Columbia fishermen connected wood or tin shingles by a cord to an anchor and sank the anchor in the fishway. The current kept the shingle in motion, frightening shad so they would remain below the dam.

In an effort to circumvent the lower fisheries, Worrall and the other commissioners began hatching shad directly in the Juniata River and at a hatchery in Marietta. They transported millions of young shad to the Susquehanna's tributaries. The U.S. Fish Commission expanded efforts to stock shad in the Susquehanna in the 1890s. Many of these fish did not live long in strange waters, however, and the authorities eventually abandoned their efforts.

What the fish commissioners could not accomplish, a hurricane did. The storm that swept Columbia's third bridge off its piers in 1896 also ruined most of the deteriorating canal dam. The canal had long since been abandoned, so there was no reason to repair its dam. Shad once again had free passage all the way to the Juniata. Within years, a thriving fishery, though a shadow of the predam enterprise, returned to the Susquehanna and Juniata.

Harry Hall of Columbia said he could net hundreds of shad with a single sweep of his seine after the dam came down. John Detweiler of Long Level, on the west bank of the river just below Columbia, told the *Columbia News* he was catching nearly a thousand shad each night at the height of the run in the spring of 1903.

The shad's reprieve was brief. Construction of the York Haven Dam shut down migration above Conewago Falls in 1904, and the Holtwood Dam six years later sealed off Columbia from shad once again. Most residents hailed the building of these hydroelectric dams and the power they would bring to central Pennsylvania without worrying about their effect on the Susquehanna's lower course or the migratory fish that could no longer swim upstream.[31]

The Columbia painter and sonneteer Lloyd Mifflin understood that Holtwood would alter the Lower Susquehanna and everything in it. In the last lines of "To Pennsylvanians on Damming of the Susquehanna," Mifflin called on the river itself to do what men too timid to condemn the construction would not do:

> Thou mighty Stream! alone vent thou thy wrath:
> Rise! till a thousand torrents thundering roar
> Headlong, and in thy wild, avenging path,
> Sweep this abomination to the sea!

While prosaic shad fishermen dreamed of dynamiting Holtwood into oblivion, the Fish Commission took positive action to overcome the obstacle. After shad refused to use fishways at Holtwood, commissioners began netting fish below the dam and transporting them above York Haven so they could continue running up the river. Many of these fish died and relatively few of their offspring survived the return trip through the turbine blades of the dams' generating units. When Conowingo blocked all but the first miles of the river to fish migration in the late 1920s, the commission abandoned its circumvention effort. The Susquehanna's "abomination" had won total control over river traffic.

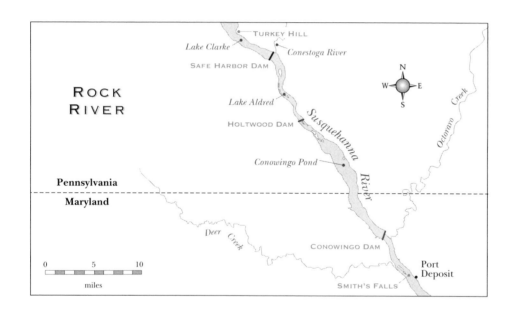

ROCK
RIVER

TURKEY HILL

Lake Clarke

Conestoga River

SAFE HARBOR DAM

Lake Aldred

HOLTWOOD DAM

Susquehanna River

Conowingo Pond

Octoraro Creek

Pennsylvania

- - - - - - - - - -

Maryland

Deer Creek

CONOWINGO DAM

Port Deposit

SMITH'S FALLS

N
W · E
S

0   5   10

miles

Rock River

Turkey Hill

It is not possible to step twice into the same river.

—Heraclitus

In time and with water, everything changes.

—Leonardo da Vinci

Just downriver from Columbia, the Susquehanna expands to its greatest breadth before Turkey Hill abruptly punches in from the east, pinching the waterway to half size and shifting the flow southeast. Between here and the Chesapeake, the river runs within the confines of the Susquehanna Gorge, the most impressive geologic feature of the Lower Susquehanna Valley.

Craggy metamorphic ridges (popularly known as the "river hills," poetically described as the "Susquehanna Highlands") rise precipitously from 200 feet to over 500 feet above the water along much of the course. They constrict the floodplain to a narrow swath on either side, just enough space to run railroad tracks along the east bank and the canal along the west, but allowing no room for a highway. Many of the river's final tributaries plummet down steep ravines, but otherwise these highlands are impenetrable for miles at a stretch.

Turkey Hill itself towers nearly 400 feet over the river, but will rise to at least 550 feet and become the area's tallest feature as Lancaster County steadily heaps its residents' solid waste on top. Here on the gorge's gateway ridge, an observer at the main lookout enjoys a panoramic view north toward the broad water and relative lowlands at Washington Boro and Columbia. Elsewhere along the ridge, hikers take in a less expansive view of downriver cliffs.

If not for the deepened water behind Safe Harbor Dam, a hilltop visitor also would see remains of a crystalline ridge spanning the Susquehanna from Turkey Hill to the York County riverbank. Before dam pools formed, these rocks and similar eroded ridges elsewhere in the gorge provided major impediments to navigation. Turkey Hill's ridge remnants presented an especially severe problem because the channel runs close by the hill. In a little booklet promoting Susquehanna navigation in 1796, Jonathan Condy identified the rock remaining in the water at the foot of Turkey Hill as the one major feature that should be blasted out of the lower river because the geography would not allow circumvention by canal.[1]

In the late summer and autumn of 1801, the Pennsylvania government and the Susquehanna Canal Company of Maryland employed Benjamin Henry Latrobe to clear the rock at Turkey Hill and other obstacles from the river's lower course and to complete a survey of the 40 miles of waterway from Columbia to Havre de Grace. Latrobe spent $10,000 blasting rock, hoping to open the channel along the east bank for adequate boating and rafting. He filled several notebooks and sketchbooks during this extensive work, drawing features along the river and remarking on specific improvements he made. "Although much remains to be done," he reported, "yet the work of this season has removed all the obstructions which were formerly so

formidable, as to render the attempt to descend the river hazardous to the lives of those who undertook it."

Latrobe's removal of rock and sediment, like all previous and subsequent efforts of the kind, was only partially successful. Sediment from upriver quickly drifted in to Turkey Hill, blocking the channel again. His lasting achievement is a seventeen-foot-long map of the survey area. More than an extraordinarily large surveyor's map, this is a practical artist's conception of the river and its geologic setting two centuries ago.

Latrobe later would become famous for designing the U.S. Capitol and other exceptional neoclassical buildings, and he surveyed the Susquehanna and drew his map with the same care he would give to his architectural drawings. The map shows the river's navigational courses, tributary streams, islands, falls, rapids, and ferry crossings, as well as the rock formations, forests, and farmlands running alongside. Latrobe used pencil, pen and ink, and watercolor, and carefully shaded tree and hill areas. In a letter to his wife from the field, the surveyor described the Susquehanna scenery as "savage" and "beautiful." His map conveys both attributes.

Christian Hauducoeur, who had mapped the Maryland portion of the river gorge in 1799, also worked on the Maryland section of the 1801 survey. He found that changes had occurred in navigation channels and in the forms and locations of islands in just two years. Latrobe incorporated this information on his map. Both Latrobe and Hauducoeur employed more sophisticated surveying tools than the average American land surveyor of the time. They may have made errors, but their work compares favorably with less detailed maps drawn in subsequent decades.

In his notebooks and in a letter to Governor Thomas McKean, Latrobe provided substantial supplemental information. He showed a special interest in Turkey Hill. "The most formidable obstruction in Pennsylvania below Columbia was perhaps Turkey hill fall," Latrobe explained to McKean. "The river after spreading to the width of nearly two miles, suddenly contracts itself on breaking through the mountains to the width of 60 chains or 3/4 of a mile. The whole bed is obstructed by high ridges of Rocks extending in regular lines directly across from shore to shore, while at the same time it is choked by rocky islands."

Anyone who expects to see that view near Turkey Hill today will be surprised. Practically everything has been altered. Stephen F. Lintner, writing in *The Papers of Benjamin Henry Latrobe,* explains:

The landscape so meticulously portrayed by Latrobe has changed drastically since he surveyed it. Tilled fields have returned to woodlands, alluvial islands have been continuously modified by flood and ice, and roaring gorges have given way to power dams. The sediment in the channel, formerly a golden sand, is now a mixture of sand, slag, and fine coal dust derived from upstream mining wastes. The channel itself is reduced in width, while the adjacent floodplain level has risen rapidly in elevation due to the massive influx of coal-laden sediment. Approximately 60 percent of the river channel mapped by Latrobe is submerged by the reservoirs of three twentieth-century dams.

The most obvious change in the past two centuries is the ponding of the river behind the dams. Latrobe described a wild river alien to today's measured flow. Dammed water covered multiple sets of falls mentioned repeatedly in Latrobe's notebooks. "From [the Susquehanna's] first entrance into the Turkey Hill, to the tide," he wrote several years later to Secretary of the Treasury Albert Gallatin, "there is no part that deserves the name of a sheet of smooth water."

Less obvious is a change in the river's width. Latrobe measured a two-mile width just above Turkey Hill. The river is now 1.6 miles wide at this place. Reduced by the better part of half a mile, despite the deepening of the water by Safe Harbor Dam, the river remains at its widest anywhere from Cooperstown to Havre de Grace.

The two-mile measurement might be a surveying error, but other observers corroborate it. R. Dudley Tonkin in *My Partner, the River* says the Susquehanna remained "over two miles wide" at this rafting point in the late nineteenth century. C. W. Bump also cited a two-mile width on his tour down the river in 1899. George Kraft, who lives several hundred yards from the Susquehanna at Washington Boro, believes the river was substantially wider because he has dug into hard river gravel in his basement. Steep slopes along the western shore suggest that most of a wider river must have spread beyond the present eastern shore. If so, Turkey Hill would have jutted even more dramatically into the wider flow.[2]

Latrobe climbed Turkey Hill. He found his view obstructed by trees, but he saw enough looking north to

≈ *As Benjamin Henry Latrobe surveyed the Susquehanna from Columbia to Havre de Grace in 1801, he recorded dozens of scenes with pencil and watercolor. He captured this view looking upriver from Turkey Hill, which juts into the river below Columbia. Round Top and the point of the Hellam Hills are visible on the York County shore (left) and Columbia sprawls on the Lancaster County side. (Maryland Historical Society, Baltimore.)*

☙ *This view upriver from Turkey Hill shows Susquehanna island configurations different from those Benjamin Latrobe sketched two centuries ago.* *(Photo by Christine Brubaker.)*

make a comprehensive sketch. Several years later, the British diplomat Sir Augustus J. Foster, also finding trees in the way, observed that "the channel is shallow . . . and there are several Islands covered with Trees in it, while the opposite Coast is high and shows some Cultivation."

Today's view upriver from Turkey Hill (reached by way of a trail leading off River Road south of Washington Boro) has been improved by a cut in the trees. The spectacular panorama features an expansive river with an island configuration radically different from the one Foster observed and Latrobe mapped and sketched.

"The landscape of the lower Susquehanna which Latrobe surveyed in 1801 has changed very little in terms of the general visual perception," explains Stephen Lintner in an analysis of the lower river. "Detailed field examination, however, indicates that the channel of the Susquehanna River has been transformed by changes in land use. . . . The details of the contemporary landscape in the study area, the engineering structures, the islands and the floodplains are man-made."

A physical geographer, Lintner began exploring the phenomenon of river change as a science editor of Latrobe's papers. In 1983 he completed his dissertation for Johns Hopkins University, "The Historical Physical Behavior of the Lower Susquehanna River, Pennsylvania, 1801–1976." Using Latrobe's survey as a base, Lintner examined changes that had taken place in a 7.8-mile section of river from Marietta to Turkey Hill.

Lintner combined his own physical observations and historical readings with analyses of Latrobe's survey and maps of the area made by Latrobe in 1801, T. H. Poppleton in 1824, the U.S. Geological Survey in 1902–10, the Safe Harbor Water Power Corporation in 1929, and the U.S. Geological Survey in 1969–72. He relied heavily on archives of the Safe Harbor Water Power Corporation, including surveys and photographs of this section of river before and after construction of the dam.

Lintner found that millions of tons of coal sediment washing down the river, along with accelerating erosion of millions of tons of soil, had made the most radical changes. Fine coal, when wet, formed a sticky slime that coated and blackened the original orange silt clay of the Lower Susquehanna's islands and banks and built up those features by several feet. Pushed around by high water and ice, these masses of coal and silt constantly altered the sizes and shapes of islands and steadily reduced the width and depth of the main channel.

As human manipulation of the river evolved, the Susquehanna changed again and again. From its earliest years, the coal reclamation program widened the channel. Then backwater from Safe Harbor Dam covered most of the islands and rocks and coal and silt and everything else. The dam became a huge trap for sediment, and coal and silt falling into the shallower areas of the impoundment rapidly reduced the width of the channel and regenerated and expanded old islands, many of them at locations that approximated their previous positions. New islands joined them.

Lintner estimated that the area covered by islands between Marietta and Turkey Hill increased 72 percent—

from 250 acres in 1801 to 431 acres just before completion of the dam in 1931. Island acreage expanded dramatically to 1,800 in the study area by 1973—a 317 percent increase from predam measurements. Much of this acreage lies in what is essentially a dead-water zone along the east shore between Washington Boro and Turkey Hill.[3]

As the "Pennsylvania Navy" expanded the coal reclamation program in the 1940s and '50s and the anthracite industry declined, coal sediment in the river dropped sharply. Simultaneously, improved land management practices reduced soil runoff. The Susquehanna in the Latrobe-Lintner study area stabilized by the 1970s.

Lintner predicted in 1983 that "the man induced depositional trend [since the 1840s] will continue to be reversed by an erosional trend which will remove major channel deposits, reduce island areas and undercut the sides of elevated floodplains in the study area." He cautioned, however, that "increased urbanization and highway construction could contribute significant amounts of sediment and reverse this trend at some locations."

In fact, they did. Floods periodically scour out thousands of tons of soil and transport them to the Chesapeake, but constant erosion from developed land replaces most of this loss. So far, the sizes of channel and islands have not noticeably changed since Lintner measured them. The river's elevated banks remain relatively stable. The larger changes that human intervention provoked over a century and a half may take that long to reverse themselves. With dams manipulating the flow, full reversal may never occur.

Lake Clarke

When the erection of the three power dams converted a turbulent river into a chain of placid lakes, residents along the shores began to adjust themselves rapidly to the new condition. They found that they had exchanged the rugged beauty of the river for the quieter beauty of lake country; and they found that by the exchange they had gained an expanse of inland water ideally suited to recreation and relaxation.

—P. Stewart Macaulay, *Baltimore Sun*, 1933

Gary Trautman might as well live on Lake Clarke. He spends most of his time on the ponded Susquehanna water behind Safe Harbor Dam. He toils during the week as a Safe Harbor mechanic, patrols the lake with the Lancaster Flotilla of the Coast Guard Auxiliary on weekends, skippers young Sea Scouts in reconditioned boats a couple of nights a week, and operates a Lightning gib in the Susquehanna Yacht Club's Wednesday-night races. In his spare time, he fishes for Lake Clarke smallmouths.

All these activities used to be more fun when the lake was less crowded. An explosion of boats—residents of Lancaster and York counties alone own more than 25,000 licensed vessels—has transformed this section of river into a speed course. Many of the new "boats" are personal water-

⪧   *Gary Trautman pilots one of several reconditioned boats he uses to help young Sea Scouts learn their way around Lake Clarke. Trautman also patrols this Susquehanna "lake" behind Safe Harbor Dam with the Lancaster Flotilla of the Coast Guard Auxiliary. (Photo by Christine Brubaker.)*

craft, popularly known by the brand name Jet Skis. Jet Skis have changed everything on Lake Clarke.

"They're like a dirt bike in the water," says Trautman, a forty-something river rat whose disdain for Jet Skis is shared by many boaters and anglers. "They'll jump your wake and they'll think nothing of crossing your bow. Jet Skis have created a whole new scenario on the river. The Fish and Boat Commission has beefed up the police. We have to patrol a lot more frequently with the Coast Guard Auxiliary and other boaters have got to be a lot more aware."

On a perfect summer weekend, Lake Clarke, like Lake

Frederic upriver and Lake Aldred and the Conowingo Pond downstream, is filled with pesky Jet Skis, high-horsepower motorboats with water skiers in tow, fuel-efficient pontoons, twenty- and thirty-foot sailboats, small fishing inboards, and a sprinkling of canoes and kayaks. Clarke is only ten miles long, with an effective navigation area two miles shorter from the upstream end. Pack hundreds of boats into eight miles of river on a Sunday afternoon and a stint on Fish and Boat Commission police duty or Coast Guard patrol can be challenging.

"It gets crowded out there, plus a lot of people use the river for party time," says Trautman. "They'll go out and they'll get drunk with their friends and race up and down the lake. They don't have any regard for the responsibilities they have on the water, and then we have trouble."

Trouble includes occasional crashes and creative boating behavior that Trautman finds hard to believe. He once watched a young man ride his personal watercraft in circles around his girlfriend. She was bouncing up and down in the water, gasping for breath as the unending wake washed over her. "I pulled alongside in the Coast Guard Auxiliary vessel and hailed the Jet Ski owner and questioned if he was operating his vessel in a safe manner," says Trautman. "He didn't answer, but he did stop. I don't have time for horseplay in the water because something can happen in an instant."

Before the dam, when the water was wild, this sort of situation could not have occurred. Even if powerful motorboats and Jet Skis had been available in the 1920s, they would have been useless in the rocky river. In fact, boating just for fun was not popular in the first years after the dam turned a whitewater river into a flat-water pond. Most boaters went out to cast for bass, pike, and perch stocked in place of the shad and herring that no longer swam up the river. This was then the largest "lake" in Pennsylvania; it drew anglers from all over the state. Purely recreational powerboats and sailboats came along much later, and with them multiple boat launches and marinas.

The Safe Harbor Water Power Corporation owns all of Lake Clarke's shoreline, stretching back to the bridges at Columbia. The utility leases the land to residents and river-front businesses. The Norfolk Southern rail line reduces commercial enterprise, restricts boating access, and ruins aesthetic appeal along the Lancaster County side. On the York County side, at Long Level below Wrightsville, marinas and sailboat clubs thrive. Here Gary Trautman launches his varied boats and the Franklin & Marshall College crew practices during racing season.

Lake Clarke even has its own tour boat, operated by Steve Trupe and Chip Debus of Columbia. They transport passengers up and down the water, pointing out the sights— Turkey Hill's intrusion, canal remnants, island summer cottages. Trupe and Debus's River Rats Tours and Grill pontoon often stops at "the sandbar" in the Conejohela Flats, off Washington Boro. Passengers swim in the Susquehanna's shallows and play volleyball on a beach composed largely of coal fragments, known as "Pennsylvania sand."

All these recreational enthusiasms overlap on Lake Clarke. Anglers get furious at motorboaters and Jet Skiers who drive close to fishing boats or shore, stirring up the water and scaring away anything with gills. Sailboaters become equally incensed if operators of stinkpots (an old, uncomplimentary term for powerboats) don't give them the right of way. And swimmers just take their chances in the churning pool that Lake Clarke becomes on sunny summer weekends.[4]

Friction among groups with different ideas of how to use the river erupts in unusual ways. Summertime river baptisms, conducted peacefully in this area for centuries, now may be interrupted by the roar of an outboard. A Columbia resident explained the problem in a letter to a Lancaster newspaper in 1997: "Boats coming in and out of the water made noise and really jeopardized the people both in the water and along the side. I know the boaters have a right to the waterway, too, but I'm sure they could arrange to have their boats in or out of the river before this ceremony starts, not wait until it begins. Where is their compassion for their fellow human beings?"

As the region's population and the popularity of deep-water recreation increase, so will conflicts, largely between motorized river recreationists and people with more traditional plans. Gary Trautman spends his summer weekends trying to keep peace between them.

"Jet Skis are the worst offenders," he maintains as he drapes the Coast Guard Auxiliary banner over the bow of his boat and prepares to monitor another day of frenetic recreation. "They agitate you if you're sailing or fishing— just like a doggone fly you can't get rid of. Fortunately, the interest in Jet Skis seems to be fading. I think they're on their way out."

Safe Harbor

Along the rivers great dams are being built and the pictographs, our sole surviving examples of very early American graphic art, are being buried beneath the waters. The natural erosion of stone in many places has been the means of destroying many records, and Indian "picture rocks" are but a memory in many localities.

—Donald Cadzow, *Petroglyphs in the Susquehanna River Near Safe Harbor, Pennsylvania,* 1934

In the summers of 1931 and 1932, Pennsylvania archaeologists made moving pictures of the Susquehanna River in the vicinity of Safe Harbor. The grainy black-and-white film, bouncing on the screen, shows a turbulent river ripping through the gorge below Turkey Hill. The water rushes around dozens of elephant-sized boulders and rolls over hundreds of smaller rocks that create impressive standing waves. This tempestuous channel might be the upper Youghiogheny or the Lehigh at Rockport. It is difficult to associate this boulder-strewn stretch of white water with today's docile river.

This rocky, raging river no longer exists, except in severely muted form immediately below each hydroelectric dam. The placid reservoirs between dams have submerged the rest of the natural river. Also beneath these dam pools lie the primary subjects of the archaeologists' film and the objects of their summer expedition: the "picture rocks" of the Susquehanna.

A general concern that Pennsylvania's native culture had not been adequately examined and a specific concern that many of the aboriginal petroglyphs in the Susquehanna would be inundated by backwaters from Safe Harbor Dam spurred the expedition. Several academic researchers and amateur archaeologists had examined these rocks and their captivating carvings of birds, animals, human beings, and more abstract figures. Donald Cadzow, archaeologist with the Pennsylvania Historical Commission and leader of the expedition, made the first systematic study of all rocks in the area.

Petroglyphs on two features that would disappear beneath Safe Harbor's backwaters captured Cadzow's primary attention. Medium-sized Walnut Island lies in the center of the river, about midway between the dam and Turkey Hill. Creswell Rock, a large boulder, sits close to the shore at Turkey Hill. Cadzow's workers used a pneumatic drill to cut sixty-eight sections from the hard mica schist of Walnut Island and Creswell Rock. They loaded these heavy rock cuttings into boats that carried them through the rapids to Safe Harbor. The State Museum in Harrisburg and the Conestoga Area Historical Society in Lancaster County display several of these rocks.

The expedition also examined Big Indian and Little Indian rocks, large boulders directly below Safe Harbor Dam. Because these rocks would be only partially covered by water, Cadzow decided to leave their petroglyphs in place. He made plaster casts of them.

Cadzow's notes describe the petroglyphs in detail and

much of his film illustrates the process of cutting and casting the rocks and boating the samples to shore. He lost interest in the petroglyphs during the latter stages of the expedition as he began to examine significant Shenks Ferry and Susquehannock sites at Safe Harbor and Washington Boro. Although massive looting of town sites, fire pits, and burial grounds had preceded the expedition, Cadzow found thousands of objects, which he hauled back to the State Museum.[5]

Cadzow believed petroglyphs on Walnut Island and Creswell Rock may have been created by an earlier group of Native Americans than the carvings on Big and Little Indian rocks, which are less complex and abstract. He speculated that the later carvings had been made by an Algonkian group from the settlement at Shenks Ferry. (Archaeologists no longer use the term "Algonkian" in this way. Cadzow apparently referred to the Woodland culture, and Shenks Ferry settlements date to the Late Woodland period.)

The archaeologist suggested possible meanings for many of these pictures, often relying on interpretations of petroglyphs elsewhere. He said a human head with horns may depict a chief and a snake may symbolize an evil spirit. However, Cadzow concluded in his 1934 report on the expedition that "there is no positive proof that the symbols had the same meaning to their makers hundreds of years ago as they have to surviving groups of the same stock, or to people who lived thousands of miles away."

Cadzow approached the petroglyphs more seriously than most of his colleagues, who considered the carvings' ori-

⤝ *David Herr Landis sits on Big Indian Rock in the river just below Safe Harbor with a fellow Lancastrian, Justin Roddy, in 1896. Landis was among the earliest amateur archaeologists to examine Big and Little Indian Rocks' petroglyphs. He photographed the carvings after filling them with lampblack. No one has seen this much of Big Indian Rock since Holtwood Hydroelectric Station raised the water behind its dam in 1910. (Hershey Museum, Hershey, Pennsylvania.)*

gins so obscure as to render their study worthless. He and later commission archaeologists who shared his interest succeeded in placing Big and Little Indian rocks on the National Register of Historic Places in 1978. And then an amateur rock sleuth discovered many more of what he likes to call "glyphs."

Paul Nevin, a carpenter who restores old houses, lives in

a converted sawmill on an unnamed Susquehanna tributary upriver at Accomac. The mysterious petroglyphs captured Nevin's attention in the early 1980s. On warm summer days, he paddled out to Big and Little Indian rocks. He compared what he saw on the rocks with what Cadzow had recorded. Then he examined nearby rocks. He found dozens of petroglyphs on five other rocks that Cadzow had not noticed, or at least had not mentioned in his report. Nevin cataloged more than 300 carvings on the seven rocks.

Through careful observation over several years, Nevin developed a much larger view of the Safe Harbor petroglyphs than Cadzow had imagined. He presented his ideas at a symposium on "rock art" at the State Museum in 1991 and has refined his thinking since. Nevin agrees with Cadzow that the petroglyphs may have been created by a Woodland culture, most likely from the Shenks Ferry settlement. He thinks the carvings may have conveyed information about a tribe's boundaries or hunting grounds, or they may have signified events or sacred places. The precise meaning of the petroglyphs may be obscured by time, but Nevin does not believe speculation about their meaning is therefore idle.

Big and Little Indian rocks and the five others Nevin has discovered (he calls them Turkey Track, Eagle, Circle, Conestoga, and Footprint because of distinctive pictographs on them) seem to spill out into the Susquehanna from the mouth of the Conestoga River. Nevin believes this is no coincidence. In addition to the Shenks Ferry settlement at Safe Harbor, a major Shenks Ferry site has been excavated along the Conestoga at Millersville. Nevin thinks the Native Americans may have carved those rocks to indicate the tributary's significance to them.

Along with dozens of specific carvings Cadzow had ignored or seemingly misrepresented, Nevin discovered series of "dots" and "bird tracks" carved all over these rocks. He believes the dots may represent constellations and the bird tracks may point to significant land features. "Each rock has its own character," he says. "They have certain figures in common, and there are some unique figures, too. They're also different from those at Bald Friars down the river. It's incredible to me that there's not some sort of interpretive center that recognizes this site. There aren't any more extensive sites than this in the Northeast."[6]

Nevin formed the Susquehanna Kalpulli to preserve Native American culture and the petroglyphs. The regional chapter of the Society for Pennsylvania Archaeology joined the campaign. The preservationists want to place plaques on the rocks explaining their historic value and they hope to purchase surveillance cameras so they can monitor the rocks. They have posted signs at boat ramps warning against vandalism.

The earliest chiseled date is 1880 and the most flamboyant faux petroglyph is a large dovelike bird with a flower dangling from its mouth. Nevin says chiselers have been busy in recent years, augmenting pictographs with their own initials. While petroglyphs elsewhere are protected in state and national parks, the Safe Harbor carvings are exposed to anyone with a hammer and chisel and a boat to float to the rocks. Meanwhile, acid rain gradually erodes and ice floes seasonally scar the petroglyphs. If they are not protected, Nevin fears, they may follow their submerged kin into oblivion.

Although many archaeologists continue to find better things to do than consider the enigmatic petroglyphs, the Eastern State Rock Art Research Association, formed in 1996, has recognized the importance of studying and preserving the Safe Harbor petroglyphs. "It's just been in the last few years that some archaeologists are willing to stick their necks out and say, well, maybe there's something more to the petroglyphs," notes Nevin.

He knows there is something more when he stands on Footprint Rock. Footprint Rock remains underwater except when Holtwood draws down Lake Aldred each autumn for dam maintenance. Then the rock and its two footprints emerge. Cadzow did not record them, although they appear on earlier researchers' charts. The prints are of bare feet, with toes splayed, the way toes operate when they have never been confined by shoes. Nevin has stood several times in the pictoprints on that rock, which lies near all of the other carved Susquehanna rocks stretching out from the Conestoga River. "Those footprints fit your feet just like a pair of shoes. You can stand right in them," he says. "When you stand in those footprints, you look directly at the mouth of the Conestoga."

Conestoga River

Cows crossing a ford make a picture that, like that of geese on a green common, has long been close to the affections of men. In *American Scenery* (1872) . . . there are more pictures in which creeks and cows are associated than there are pictures on any other subject. . . . The conjunction is natural.

Water is the life of a landscape and cows the most picturesque of farm beasts. . . . A picture of stream and cows, of mill and streamside road, is sure to be in the experience of us all and to awaken loved memories.

—CORNELIUS WEYGANDT, *The Blue Hills*, 1936

On the front page of the *New Era*, I was surprised to see a photo of a cow in a stream portrayed in a positive light. Overgrazing and streambank destruction by cows are serious problems on a par with soil erosion and nutrient overloading across the farmlands. If all streams had vegetative buffer strips at least 20 feet wide, there would be less flooding, improved fish habitat, better tasting municipal water and clearer conditions for swimming and canoeing.

—REUBEN WEAVER III, Ephrata farmer and farm preservationist, in a letter to the *Lancaster New Era*, 1991

STANDING ON FOOTPRINT ROCK in the Susquehanna, looking toward the mouth of the Conestoga, a visitor surveys the eastern end of Safe Harbor Dam and the western end of the Conestoga River's verdant valley—a rigid industrial construct imposed on an ancient natural landscape. If William Penn had done what he planned to do at "The Point," where the Conestoga runs into the Susquehanna, this place would look very different today. Perhaps the Susquehanna

The Susquehanna viewed from the west shore three months before workers began build-*
ing Safe Harbor Dam. River volume was average on the day of the photo, January 4, 1930.
Notice the multiple rocks and extensive island acreage, much of which is underwater today.
On the east side, the Conestoga River enters the Susquehanna beneath a bridge on the
Pennsylvania Railroad Low Grade Line. (Safe Harbor Water Power Corporation, Lancaster
County, Pennsylvania.)

would be a very different river.

Penn set aside 100,000 acres, with twelve miles fronting on the Susquehanna, as one of his Pennsylvania manors. He called his project the Second Settlement. Some historians believe Penn planned to develop the commonwealth's original capital here rather than at Philadelphia, on the banks of the Delaware. In an advertisement inviting prospective settlers in 1690, Penn praised the area: "That which particularly recommends this settlement is the known goodness of the soyll and the scituation of the Land, which is high and not mountainous; also the Pleasantness, and the Largeness of the River being clear and not rapid, and broader than the Thames at London Bridge."

Safe Harbor may have received its name from Penn's settlement plan. Pennsylvania's founder proposed to open a shipping channel from the Chesapeake through the Susquehanna and far enough up the Conestoga to create a "safe harbor" just above its mouth. Although neither the grandiose transportation plan nor any part of the manor ever materialized, enterprising settlers built their own village on both sides of the Conestoga. They responded first to trade on the Susquehanna, then to a slack-water canal on the Conestoga connecting the "Port of Lancaster" with the Chesapeake.

Later, in the middle of the nineteenth century, the Safe Harbor Iron Works built a town of its own, including a large manufacturing plant and homes for its workers. The company extracted ore from nearby hills and boiled river water to make steam, which powered an engine that hauled coal from canal boats up an inclined plane to the plant. As the Iron Works faded at the end of the century and Susquehanna floods repeatedly backed water up the Conestoga to inundate Safe Harbor, residents abandoned and demolished many of the town's structures.

And then Safe Harbor changed again. The building of the dam and a new village for key personnel of the Safe Harbor Water Power Corporation resurrected the place in the 1930s. The utility created a park along the Conestoga, with Little League ballfields and the preserved last lock of the old

Conestoga Canal in the floodplain. Now the dam and the park are all that many people know about activity at this historic confluence.

Unlike the water washing past the boom-or-bust settlement at its mouth, much of the rest of the sixty-mile-long Conestoga flows through a tranquil, settled landscape of centuries-old Lancaster County farms. Particularly in the river's upper reaches, these farms are owned by Old Order Amish and Mennonites. Until recent years these Plain farmers, and many of their "English" neighbors as well, have worried little about the effect their picturesque dairy cows and beef cattle have on the river.

As acid mine drainage is the primary pollutant of water in the West Branch and some sections of the North Branch, manure is the worst contaminant in the Lower Susquehanna Basin. Whether cows defecate or urinate directly into a stream or let loose in the milking barn, they contribute much of their waste to groundwater and waterways feeding the Susquehanna and the Chesapeake. Filled with nutrients, that manure eventually poisons the bay and its fishery by feeding algae, which deplete oxygen in the water as they die and decompose. In this way do cows kill fish.

Agriculture is one of Pennsylvania's primary industries and Lancaster is Pennsylvania's premier agricultural county. Nearly 100,000 cows are Lancaster's sentimental and financial favorite among farm animals. More dairy cows per acre crowd Lancaster than any other county in the United States. Local farmers cannot grow enough cows of their own. Amish families travel to Vermont each winter to import more.

Lancaster has more laying hens than any other county in the country and plenty of other animals, hundreds of thousands of which are crowded into the county's 300 "factory farms." Some 17 million cows, chickens, hogs, and other animals create nearly 5 million tons of manure a year—about 20 percent of Pennsylvania's total. That is far more than the land can absorb. The nitrogen in manure on overfertilized fields dissolves in rainwater and moves rapidly into creeks and rivers.

Hercules cleansed the Augean stables, where cattle manure had accumulated for several years, by diverting the courses of two rivers and flooding away the filth. The Conestoga River and its tributaries do much the same every day for Lancaster County's outdoor stables, and in flood do the job even faster. The Conestoga is the Susquehanna's foremost manure conveyor, with the highest concentrations of nitrogen and phosphorus.

The Conestoga is also one of the most active conveyors of sediments, transporting an average of ten tons of dirt from each acre of its watershed each year—nearly double the state average. On many days the Conestoga is chocolate brown and viscous—"too thick to drink," as someone has said of the Mississippi, "too thin to plow." Erosion is heavy because landowners have almost entirely deforested the upper Conestoga watershed. Some farmers plow right up to the edge of the river and its tributaries and plant acres of row crops that cannot hold topsoil.

The tons of manure and soil that wash daily into the Susquehanna through the Conestoga's mouth contribute substantially to the high levels of nutrients and low quality of water in the Chesapeake. Environmentalists and government regulators have recognized this for many years and have struggled to promote change. The process has been difficult because many farmers in the Conestoga Valley are determined to preserve traditional agricultural practices and most Amish shun government funds allocated for manure management or anything else. The ability of these farmers to work the land matches the superior quality of the soil. Their capacity to deal with conservation issues varies from farm to farm.

In 1993 the American Rivers organization listed the Susquehanna among the thirty most endangered and threatened rivers in the country because of what its nutrient load does to the Chesapeake. Many Pennsylvania farmers questioned whether their part in the process was as significant as that of Maryland farmers, closer to the bay. When Pennsylvania in 1996 listed the Conestoga and nine other Lancaster County waterways among the state's most polluted streams, farmers paid closer attention; but some still considered the problem unrelated to their particular cows mucking about in the water.

If some farmers do not get the connection between what they do on their property and excess loads of nutrients and sediments in the Chesapeake, however, they do understand the effect manure has on their immediate environment. When cows stand in the river but will not drink from it—in fact, must be fenced away from sewage trenches because they prefer lapping that liquid to taking water from the Conestoga or its tributaries—the problem is hard to miss. When residents cannot drink from their own polluted wells,

the message is delivered even more directly.[7]

The message is actually two decades old. In 1981 the federal Rural Clean Water Program chose the Conestoga and nineteen other rivers across the nation for study and corrective action. The program recommended a number of best-management practices to help clean up the river, including less generous use of fertilizer to reduce nutrient overloading and improved tilling and planting techniques to conserve soil.

In 1983 the governors of Pennsylvania, Maryland, and Virginia signed the first joint agreement to address the Chesapeake's problems. Four years later the governors detailed what they believed their states should do by the end of the century. Among other commitments, the 1987 agreement called for a 40 percent reduction in the flow of nutrients to the Chesapeake by 2000. Better manure management, improved equipment in some sewer systems to remove nitrogen, and a ban on phosphate detergents have substantially reduced nutrients carried by the Conestoga and other Susquehanna tributaries, but the 40 percent goal has not been reached.[8]

Pennsylvania discussed instituting manure regulations for years before the legislature passed the first such bill in the nation. When the Nutrient Management Act took effect in 1997, most farmers found it acceptable, if overly intrusive.

In 1998 the Environmental Protection Agency began writing the first federal manure regulations. These and other federal guidelines helped drive the Chesapeake 2000 Agreement, a continuation and expansion of the 1987 pact. The newer document proposes to continue improving the bay's quality through 2010 by reducing development as well as water and air pollution in the watershed lying within Pennsylvania, Maryland, Virginia, and the District of Columbia. (New York, Delaware, and West Virginia have pledged in a separate document to curb the flow of nutrients to the bay.)

The agreement extends the 40 percent target for reduction of nutrients. If this voluntary effort does not sufficiently improve water quality, the EPA threatens to impose mandatory federal regulations in 2011. These regulations would include a calculation (called total maximum daily load) of how much pollution the Chesapeake could receive and still meet water quality standards.

Inspired by their own sense of land stewardship as much as or more than by government prodding, groups of concerned farmers and conservationists often focus on the feeder streams first. Farmers are fencing their stream banks to keep cows on the far side of picturesque. Others are replanting stream banks, creating forest buffers and adopting no-till farming techniques to prevent erosion.

Most farmers now are aware that they tend to overfertilize their fields and have cut back on commercial fertilizer. An increasing number are turning to produce farming, which of course creates no manure but requires its use. Others have used wetlands to trap nutrients and reduce rapid runoff and erosion after rains

Scientists are working on ways to cut the amount of nutrients that enter an animal so that less will come out. The less protein in feed, for example, the less nitrogen in manure. Experimenters are feeding cows and chickens an altered diet and adding enzymes that increase digestion of phosphorus and therefore reduce the amount excreted.

Some initiatives to transform manure have been financially as well as environmentally successful. One Conestoga Valley hog farmer extracts methane gas from his liquid manure, uses the gas to power his operation, and sells the odorless residue to produce farmers. Another mixes manure with garden wastes and newspaper to create a stable fertilizer that can be sold and stored for later use.[9]

The other option is to take land out of farming altogether. Commercial and residential development does so regularly in fast-growing Lancaster, although one of the most successful farm preservation programs in the country partially offsets that effect. The state-federal Conservation Reserve Enhancement Program has begun to remove 100,000 acres of prime farmland from production in twenty counties in the Lower Susquehanna Valley. This program pays farmers not to grow crops while encouraging them to cultivate stream buffers.

Nutrient pollution, as any agricultural agent readily acknowledges, is not exclusively a farm problem. Leaking septic tanks and runoff from overfertilized lawns in Lancaster's sprawling suburbia also contribute to the problem. The Lititz Run Watershed Alliance is reducing pollution to one of the Conestoga's tributaries outside the primary agricultural district. The association has improved Lititz Run's eroded channel through Lititz Borough, removed a dam so that fish can move freely up- and downstream, and diverted a Lititz Run tributary into wetlands that trap sediment. The EPA calls the Lititz Run project one of the twelve best stream-restoration efforts in the country.

Along the more highly developed lower Conestoga, the Lancaster Inter-Municipal Committee has developed a Conestoga Greenway running from Lancaster to Safe Harbor. Plantings along the greenway will help reduce runoff and a recreational path will lure residents back to the river.[10]

This effort to reduce pollution and increase environmental awareness in and along the Conestoga and its tributaries is replicated throughout much of the Susquehanna Basin, which hosts half of Pennsylvania's cropland and two-thirds of its livestock. The Susquehanna transports 66 percent of the Chesapeake Bay's nitrogen, 40 percent of its phosphorus, and 25 percent of its sediment load, so there is much work to be done. Some Susquehanna regions have been slower to accept direct responsibility for polluting the Chesapeake than the Conestoga Valley. The farther a farm lies from the Chesapeake, the less the quality of bay water may concern a farmer who wants to make a decent living raising cattle or hogs or fowl.

"I remember when Chesapeake Bay problems arose and they started this study and everyone was being condemned. Lancaster County took all the punishment because they're the closest to the bay," recalls Ted Keir of Athens. Serving as vice chairman of the Bradford County Conservation District in 1983, Keir attended the signing of the original Chesapeake Bay agreement. "But I said, 'Isn't this a joke! We've got over four hundred miles of river and they're blaming the farmers in Lancaster County for polluting Chesapeake Bay.'"

With the help of the Chesapeake Bay Financial Assistance Funding Program and other sources of aid, more farmers are cleaning up their operations. Until informed by federal officials, Jeff Bechtel, a Susquehanna County dairy farmer, did not know that his cow manure, which flowed into Wyalusing Creek and the Susquehanna, washed all the way to the Chesapeake. In the mid-'90s Bechtel installed a manure containment area next to his barn, a gravel barnyard to replace the mud his cows had slopped around in for years, and other progressive fertilizer and sediment stoppers. "From a health standpoint alone," Bechtel said at the time, "getting the cows out of that muddy barnyard was worth it."

He also took his cows out of the stream. They still look picture pretty in the field, and they stay a lot drier beneath the knees.

Conowingo Pond

The most complete and permanent destruction of a river is by a dam. The rapids, streamside plants, and valley landscape are flooded. The current stops and the chemistry and temperature of the water change. Deep water blocks sunlight and stops the growth of bacteria and other building blocks in the food chain. Creatures needing the current to deliver food have nothing to eat.

—Tim Palmer, *Endangered Rivers and the Conservation Movement*

Motoring through the lightly inhabited Lower Susquehanna Gorge, a driver encounters a blazing incongruity: an orange neon sign startles the night sky. This flashy marker stands on the breast of Conowingo Dam, which carries U.S. Route 1 across the mile-wide water. Rising 20 feet above the 105-foot dam, the sign says simply: "Conowingo Hydro Electric Plant." The message might well be: "This is the beginning of the end of the Susquehanna." Conowingo is the river's last and largest and most impregnable barrier.

When workers began building Conowingo in 1926, in preparation for the start of hydroelectric operations two years later, they blocked all upriver traffic from the Chesapeake, ten miles away. They also plugged the downriver flow. As far as bay/river ecology is concerned, the most significant things the dam stalled from the north were flowing water and the sediment and pollutants drifting in it. From the south, the dam kept shad and all other fish from ascending. As the twentieth century progressed, these effects would concern environmentalists more and more.

Conowingo's federal operating license mentioned nothing about the quantity of water operators might keep flowing downstream. So Philadelphia Electric (PECO) maximized power production and profits by following a water-flow policy that periodically cut off all water moving through Conowingo's turbines. This procedure caused no problem during periods of high water; but PECO also stopped the river during low flows. On weekends especially the utility ponded water to run through its turbines on Monday mornings.

The occasional result was a relatively dry riverbed, with a few deep spots and a lot of shallow puddles. The broken stream extended for over three miles, until Octoraro and Deer creeks contributed fresh water to redevelop the river. Over the years, millions of fish died in pools of stagnant and oxygen-starved water, often creating a summer stench that drove away weekend anglers and angered riverside residents.

When Conowingo's fifty-year license came up for renewal in 1976, the Federal Energy Regulatory Commission said it would issue only one-year extensions until PECO convinced the commission it was not harming the river with its low-flow policy. The Maryland Department of Natural Resources, which believed Conowingo was doing harm, proposed new procedures. These included a guaranteed minimum year-round release to ensure sufficient water and oxygen and a substantial increase in the daily release during spring spawning months.

PECO initially objected to any change in its operations, claiming a guaranteed constant release would cost at least $1 million a year in lost hydroelectric power, a cost that consumers would have to bear. A few fish kills now and then, the utility suggested, did not justify the expense.

As the kills continued, U.S., Maryland, and Pennsylvania officials began to question PECO's operations more closely. In a 1979 report, the Susquehanna River Basin Commission found that Conowingo significantly altered river flow, particularly during low-flow season. The agency concluded: "The existing storage [in Conowingo Pond] cannot simultaneously meet the needs for hydropower peaking generation, year-round minimum release, water supply withdrawals and pool elevation for recreation and fishing purposes." Therefore, the SRBC said, choices would have to be made to

The Conowingo Hydroelectric Plant, pictured from Cecil County, Maryland, on the Susquehanna's east shore, blocks the river's flow four miles above its fall line. The orange neon sign on the powerhouse and lamps over U.S. Route 1 illuminate the Conowingo Pond and the night sky. (Photo by Richard Hertzler.)

provide the maximum hydroelectric benefit without severely undermining competing interests.

Those interests included anglers and environmentalists concerned about life in the river immediately below the dam; the cities of Baltimore and Chester, which wanted to be able to draw out water when necessary; and powerboaters, who demanded sufficient water in the pond on weekends so they could motor anywhere without knocking into rocks.

Under continual assault from many aggrieved parties and local politicians who had to listen to their complaints, PECO reluctantly altered its procedures. In the 1980s it began to maintain a minimum flow of 5,000 cubic feet per second through the dam and to use aerators to inject oxygen into the water. PECO never stopped dumping large amounts of water at any time. So the low-flow kills have ended, but water surges that accompany peak power production continue to provide adventures for fish and fishermen directly below Conowingo.

In addition to regulating natural water flow, Conowingo Dam blocks millions of tons of sediment from passing naturally on to the Chesapeake. About 3 million tons of eroded sediment wash down the Susquehanna each year and lodge behind the big dams. Much of the sediment is dirt. The dirt mixes with sand, coal, and chemicals to create a dark, mayonnaise-like paste. Without the hydroelectric plants, most of this conglomerate would wash directly into the Chesapeake. As it is, about two-thirds of it stops behind the dams.

Actually, it stops only behind Conowingo because the holding ponds behind Safe Harbor and Holtwood reached their capacity many years ago. Anything new floating down the river passes over those reserves and sticks in the Conowingo Pond. About 43 million tons of sediment are trapped in Safe Harbor's Lake Clarke, 14 million in Holtwood's Lake Aldred, and 185 million behind Conowingo. With up to 2 million tons washing in each year, Conowingo may reach its capacity—about 225 million tons—in a little over two decades.[11]

Once sediment fills Conowingo Pond, the U.S. Geological Survey warns, a "time bomb" will hit the bay. All sediment entering the Susquehanna—the equivalent of 100 railroad cars a day—will begin passing over the dam and washing into the Chesapeake. The bay will suffer a 250 percent increase in the load of suspended sediments, a 2 percent increase in nitrogen, and a 70 percent increase in phosphorus. The sediment will reduce the amount of light in the bay's water and smother aquatic life. Additional nitrogen, phosphorus, and other toxic chemicals embedded in the sediment could poison the bay's crabs and oysters and the commercial and recreational fishing industries that depend on them. "It will be gradual, but eventually it will affect the entire bay, all the way down to Virginia. The sediment will kill everything," said Mike Langland, the Geological Survey hydrologist who directed the seven-year study leading to the 1998 report. "There's no doubt [an ecological disaster] will happen; it is just a question of how fast."

How fast depends on several factors, one of which is the effectiveness of efforts to reduce the amount of sediment flowing into the Susquehanna. If farmers and developers control erosion, homeowners restrict the amount of fertilizers they use on lawns and gardens, municipal sewage-treatment systems clean their waste more thoroughly, and the state seals more debris in abandoned coal mines, this disaster can be delayed.

But slowing the flow of sediment does nothing to reduce the amount already behind the dam. "A river like the Susquehanna is so big, it's got a tremendous memory," says Dr. Robert Summers, director of technical and regulatory services for the Maryland Department of the Environment. Summers has long been involved with Susquehanna water quality and early in his career specifically monitored the Conowingo discharge. "What we see coming out of the mouth of the Susquehanna today is probably more of an indication of what people were doing on the land a decade ago than what they're doing now."

To dredge one year's contribution of sediment would cost an estimated $28 million. Dredging previously accumulated material would cost tens of millions more. Worse, dredging would stir up heavy metals and coal in the water, and some of that material would wash over the dam. Additionally, no one knows what to do with the matter removed from the water. Piling toxic mud throughout the Lower Susquehanna Valley does not appeal to anyone.

Dam owners are not taking any initiative to resolve the problem.[12] They say they do not produce the sediment and should not be held responsible for removing it. In 1999 the EPA's Chesapeake Bay Program and other involved agencies created a task force to recommend options for dealing with the issue. Meanwhile, nature is doing something to reduce sediment behind the dam, but in a potentially catastrophic way.

The flood of 1996 scoured nearly 12 million tons of sediment from behind the three dams—most of it from behind Conowingo—along with the other dirt the swollen river carried through from upstream. All told, the flood pumped 15 million tons of nutrient-saturated sediment into the Chesapeake. That is approximately sixteen times the average annual sediment load contributed by the Susquehanna. Langland's USGS study estimated that this unscheduled cleansing of Conowingo's reservoir set back the "time bomb" by five or six years.

Scientists say this flood caused little harm because it hit the bay when winter had repressed biological activity. Had the river flooded in spring or summer, the outcome would have been different. Another Agnes-sized flood in season would cause big trouble. That flood washed an estimated 34 million tons of sediment into the bay over ten days. About 22 million tons came from behind the three dams, most of it from Conowingo Pond. The sediment smothered huge areas of Chesapeake grass beds and killed crabs, clams, and shad. Turbit H. Slaughter, a geologist with the Maryland Geological Survey, said at the time, "What has happened in the Susquehanna has never happened like this before in the recorded history of man. There is no precedent that can even compare with it. Compressed overnight we saw a geological process that should take hundreds of thousands of years."

Unless someone develops a magic method to dispose of mountains of underwater muck, the Chesapeake faces either an expanded annual flow of poisoned dirt from the Susquehanna that could kill the bay slowly or a potentially catastrophic flood that could kill it fast.

Conowingo Dam

The dam hurt the river. It had been swift moving and the fishing was great. There's nothing up there but catfish now. I remember the day I took up fishing. A man stopped in a Chevy sedan. He opens the back door and there, from one door to the other, is a rockfish with his tail bent up against the door. I went out and bought my first rod and reel. I caught a rockfish. I quit fishing though when the fish quit. It's just not a fair trade, especially considering what they charge for electricity.

—Pierce Bates of Maryland, recalling in 1977 how he fished below
Conowingo Dam in the early twentieth century

Conowingo Dam is the largest hydroelectric plant ever constructed all at one time and it was built to last forever. The 4,648-foot-long dam is grounded on gabbro, a hard granite that extends across the river and up both banks. Between August 1926 and January 1928, workers poured 435,000 cubic yards of solid concrete on top of this granite base. No one has ever poured more concrete at one place.

Conowingo is the largest gravity-rooted hydro structure on Earth: only its own enormous mass holds it steady in the Susquehanna's course. The record flood of 1972 pushed the dam's center two inches downstream. It has not budged since.

The multistory, cathedral-like windows spanning Conowingo's powerhouse reflect the scope of a world-class engineering achievement, but they do not reflect the river. Most of the panes are translucent and do not reflect anything. Translucence was the original plan, now checkered by transparent panes. Don Taskey, the last PECO Energy guide fired before the cost-conscious utility ended plant tours in 1999, explains: "Typically, in the spring, the plant begins to lose some panes. The fishermen snap their lines back toward the building and hit the glass with their sinkers. The original glass is replaced with clear panes."

On practically any day of the year in good weather and all through summer nights, scores of anglers line a narrow catwalk running the length of the Conowingo powerhouse to fish in the dam's churning tailrace. Scores more take their stand with rod and reel in Fisherman's Park, which extends from the dam along the river's western shore. The more adventurous jump into the river in chest waders or edge motorboats up toward the dam when it is not spilling big water.

An increasing number of these anglers, especially on the catwalk, are of Eastern European or Southeast Asian ancestry, people who prefer catfish and carp to bass or perch. Using balls of dough to attract carp and "stinkbaits" of shrimp to draw catfish, Ukrainian and Romanian and Vietnamese anglers from Philadelphia and Baltimore and Washington haul in fish enough to fill wheelbarrows.

Other fishers also gather here, but they are not clunking their sinkers into Conowingo's windows preparatory to landing a fat carp. Under optimum conditions, scores of birds hover over the tailrace or stalk in the shallows, waiting to zoom in for baitfish washing out of the turbines. Ospreys and great blue herons and common merganser ducks and a dozen types of gulls congregate below Conowingo to feed on the small stuff. Bald eagles swoop straight down into the churning white water to scoop up larger prizes.

The choice is extensive. Just as the first few miles of the Susquehanna below Cooperstown are filled with fish that thrive in both the river and Lake Otsego, so fish below Conowingo include specimens from both river and bay. Of the 103 species recorded throughout the Susquehanna River drainage, 78 have been collected below the dam. They include smallmouth and largemouth bass, walleyes, tiger muskies, northern pike, white perch, striped bass (more commonly called rockfish), and American and gizzard shad.

Except for the gizzard shad (also known as mud shad, thanks to their gag-a-gourmet flavor), the numbers of all these fish are depressed. Except for the singular triumph of creating the best angling spot on the lower river at the place where all fish must stop swimming upstream, the magnificent Conowingo Dam has done nothing to improve Susquehanna River fishing.

After 1926, most species continued to thrive on both sides of the dam, but the customarily huge spring migrations of anadromous fish—silvery American shad and herring, alewives, rockfish, white perch—stopped dead at Conowingo. Here, in Ralph Gray's memorable line from a 1950 *National Geographic* article, the fish "circle dumbly before the mystery of concrete."

In the two decades after 1926, as commercial shad netting continued and sport fishing began, the fishery below the dam seemed as strong as ever; but then it began to fall apart. Richard Gerstell, who reeled in his first shad a few miles below Conowingo in the late 1930s, recalls that decline in his comprehensive history of American shad in the Susquehanna:

> Between 1950 and 1965, fishing pressure on the river was clearly on the increase, while fishing pleasure decreased markedly. Delays and hassles in getting boats in and out of the water at marinas were frequent. On still days, the exhaust from countless boat motors formed a blue haze over the water. To avoid irritating tangles with the lines of other anglers in always-near boats, it was necessary to keep a close and constant watch, and that was not always enough. And to top it off, the day's catch was almost invariably much smaller than in prewar seasons. That is why 1965 was my last year of shad-fishing on the Susquehanna.

Bob Jobes of Havre de Grace remembers a commercial shad fishery still going strong below Conowingo in the 1960s and early '70s. Generally, commercial rigs fished at night and sport fishermen during the day. That way the sportsmen kept their boats out of the commercial fishermen's gill nets. "What you would do was go up as far as you could to the rocks at Port Deposit," Jobes recalls. "You'd let mesh net drift down with the current, with boats stretching it out and lanterns in the boats. And then there'd be someone waiting above you to let *their* net drift down with the current. You'd get all the way down, pick the net up, run back up, start all over again. And you'd keep on doing that all night long, till the shad stopped running. Sometimes there'd be a dozen commercial boats up there fishing like that. You'd see lanterns everywhere on the river."

Concentrated overfishing and water pollution in the limited stretch of river defined by Conowingo Dam steadily reduced the shad population. In 1960, sport fishermen caught an estimated 13,000 shad, nearly 2,000 of them in the dam's tailrace. By the time the state of Maryland banned all shad fishing twenty years later, biologists estimated that 4,000 shad remained in the upper Chesapeake and the Susquehanna.

Well before Maryland's ban, Pennsylvania renewed its efforts—begun with the appointment of the Commissioner for the Restoration of Inland Fisheries in 1866—to revitalize the shad population. In 1947 the state began studying the feasibility of constructing fishways to move shad above Conowingo and the other hydroelectric dams. Maryland and New York joined in later studies, and in 1969 the three states and the U.S. Fish and Wildlife Service formed what would later be called the Susquehanna River Anadromous Fish Restoration Committee. The committee added representatives from the Susquehanna River Basin Commission and the utilities operating the hydroelectric plants.

The dam owners, especially Philadelphia Electric (PECO), never wanted to build fishways. Just as PECO balked at dealing with issues of water release below and sediment and trash buildup above Conowingo, it also kept saying no to a fish passageway. PECO told the restorationists they had to prove that a shad fishery could be renewed on the Susquehanna before the utility would commit to building an expensive fishway.

And so the restoration effort began to assemble proof. Earliest efforts included capturing shad in the upper Chesapeake, marking them with small plastic identification tags, and transporting them by truck above the dams, hoping they would swim back down through the turbines and out to sea. Anglers below the dams earned 50 cents if they turned in tags they snagged with live fish attached. Nobody got rich, but numerous tagged shad survived the dam turbines and wound up on downriver fishhooks.

PECO finally agreed to open an experimental and relatively primitive fish lift at the western end of the powerhouse in the spring of 1972. The lift's operators increased water flow in the vicinity to fool migrating fish into thinking a passage existed through the dam. The shad followed the faux flow into an open-topped, elevator-like cage. Workers hauled this cage out of the river, separated shad from other fish, lifted them into a tank with circulating water, and trucked them above the dam.

Earliest operations collected a hundred or so fish a year, a number PECO said did not justify spending $300,000 annually to operate the lift. Recognizing that a few buckets of fish transported upriver each spring would not restore the Susquehanna's fishery in a hundred years, the restoration program began stripping millions of eggs from shad in the Delaware, Columbia, and other shad-rich rivers, fertilizing them with shad milt, and releasing the eggs directly into the

Upper Susquehanna. Many of these eggs failed to hatch. Many that did hatch made tasty meals for predators. Of more than 200 million fertilized eggs deposited in the river and its tributaries between 1971 and 1976, relatively few survived.

So the Fish and Boat Commission created the Van Dyke Hatchery to raise shad to survival size along the Juniata River near Thompsontown. Since 1976, hatchery workers have imported hundreds of millions of shad eggs from six other rivers and raised them to fry and fingerlings. They release them into the Juniata or Susquehanna, the waters of which biologically imprint the fish so they know where to return to spawn.

In addition, the shad restoration project transferred tens of thousands of mature shad from the Connecticut and Hudson rivers to the Susquehanna near Tunkhannock. Biologists inserted tiny radio transmitters in the stomachs of these shad and picked up their signals from receivers on shore. Many passed through the dams and out to sea. Turbines chewed up others.[13]

The Susquehanna's shad population began to increase rapidly in the 1980s. More and more fish swam to sea and returned to the river to reproduce. This success seriously undermined PECO's argument against installing a larger fishway. In 1986 Congress required the Federal Energy Regulatory Commission (FERC) to consider the effect of dams on fish and wildlife when it decided whether to license new and existing dams. At the same time, a FERC administrative law judge ordered PECO to build a second temporary lift and to allow enough water to flow through the dam at all times to support the shad fishery. "Fish pas-

sage measures," wrote the judge, "are a cost of doing business on a river containing anadromous fish populations."

PECO management planned to fight the ruling, but the drugs-and-video-games fiasco at PECO's Peach Bottom nuclear reactor undermined that decision. When the company brought in new management to clean up Peach Bottom, it announced a major shift in its Conowingo shad policy as well. PECO decided to build a permanent $12.5 million lift at the east end of the powerhouse and agreed to keep a constant stream of water flowing downriver for the spring shad run. "If we're going to use the Susquehanna for our purposes," conceded the new, improved PECO management, "we have to put something back into the river."

In the spring of 1991 the utility opened the largest fish lift in North America. As opposed to the older elevator on the dam's extreme west end, which transported fish to land until it closed in 1999, this is a true lift to higher water. Attracted by an artificially strengthened current, shad swim into a partially submerged concrete structure. They are directed mechanically into a large metal hopper and lifted through a 100-foot steel tower. At the top, released into a trough, they swim by a counting window and escape into Conowingo Pond.

The number of shad using the Conowingo lift has varied from year to year with changing weather and river conditions, but the trend has been toward larger numbers. More than 193,000 shad crossed the dam in the spring of 2001, eclipsing the previous record of 153,000 in 2000. The numbers of shad are rising in the entire upper Chesapeake Bay, according to annual surveys by the Maryland Department of

Natural Resources. Many of these fish are moving into the Susquehanna.

After Conowingo agreed to build a permanent lift, the other dam operators fell in line. Safe Harbor and Holtwood completed lifts in 1997 and York Haven finished the final passageway—a fish ladder, not a lift, over the little Red Hill Dam—in time for the spring run in 2000. Engineers demolished part of that dam and constructed a set of rising pools in weirs leading up and over the structure.

Until the spring of 2001, most of the shad that passed over Conowingo stopped in the Conowingo Pond, disappointing shad shepherds for two reasons: the fish were not migrating as far as they had hoped and poor spawning habitat in the pond reduces reproduction. But 54 percent of Conowingo's elevator riders in 2001 continued swimming over Holtwood and most of them negotiated Safe Harbor as well.

Those fish that keep swimming above the Red Hill Dam meet only one obstacle before they reach the confluence of the Susquehanna's branches at Northumberland. The state inflates the dam at Shamokin Riffles in late May to early June, when the shad are still swimming upstream. Only five shad swam that far in the spring of 2000, but thousands eventually will. The Department of Conservation and Natural Resources plans to provide a fish passage through the dam by the spring of 2004. Once the Fish and Boat Commission removes many small dams on tributaries throughout the watershed, fish experts hope that in time 2 to 3 million shad a year will disperse into every creek and river feeding the Susquehanna.

Anglers on the Lower Susquehanna are beginning to see

❧ *Conowingo's fish elevator, viewed from Harford County, Maryland, on the Susquehanna's west shore, stands at the end of the structure's impressive powerhouse, from which the dam continues running to the east shore. This largest fish lift in North America transports tens of thousands of shad over the dam each spring. Notice the turbulent water attracting shad to the lift.* (Lancaster *[Pennsylvania]* New Era.)

the fruit of the shad restoration program. Maryland has allowed catch and release of American and hickory shad during the spring spawning run for several years. Pennsylvania does not yet encourage catch and release, but that may change as shad increase in number.

Shad are a particularly attractive fish to catch and release because they play hard to get. "They're a tremendous fighter. They will run with your line and pull it out," says Rich Wood, a shad restoration promoter with the Fish and Boat Commission. "Not only are they valuable for commercial fishing, they're a great recreational fish."

Catch-and-keep fishing may not be many years off either,

says Richard St. Pierre, a U.S. Fish and Wildlife Service officer and coordinator of the restoration committee's technical operations. If the number of shad passing upriver each spring continues to triple every four years, the few fish that anglers take out of the swim will not substantially affect the larger numbers. "The whole purpose of the program is to create a high-quality fishery," says St. Pierre, a soft-spoken fifty-five-year-old biologist who has spent most of his working life on this project. "The average angler on the Delaware only keeps one out of two shad he catches. Shad don't keep too well, and how many kids are going to eat a bony shad?" If the number of shad continues rising at current rates, St. Pierre says, the target of at least 2 million fish on the upper river will be achieved in about twenty years—"and that's a wild guess, given all kinds of variables, from El Niño to fish response to multiple dams."[14]

These fish will run into New York, St. Pierre predicts, although he doubts they will swim all the way to Cooperstown. "The river is different than it was two hundred years ago," he says. "Back then, the fish were coming in considerably earlier in the season." Today's later shad runs are not likely to reach the beginnings of the river before the water hits the prime spawning temperature of 70°F. When shad stop to spawn, they are done migrating. "Geography and climate," says St. Pierre, "run against us in New York."

On Packer Island, some 118 river miles upstream from Conowingo and 172 miles short of the New York border, Stan Rohrbach looks forward to the day when the first major shad run arrives at the confluence of branches. There the fish will have to decide which path to take, and the retired Shikellamy State Park director believes hundreds of anglers will offer them another choice—on the end of a fishing line. The Northumberland-Sunbury area will become a "boom town," he says, with "wall-to-wall" fishing on the island and at the park on Northumberland's Point.

"The fishery here," he maintains, "would be out of sight."

Smith's Falls

[At the head of the Chesapeake Bay] dwell the Sasquehannocks, upon a River that is not navigable for our Boates, by reason of Sholes and Rockes; but they passe it in Canoos.

—*A Relation of Maryland* (London, 1635)

THOUSANDS OF ROCKS AND BEDROCK islands protruded from the floor of the Lower Susquehanna before the dams pooled the water. The Susquehannocks learned to circumnavigate these obstacles in their light dugouts, no doubt using the Chesapeake's high tide when practical to help drive them up the watercourse as far as present-day Port Deposit and then threading their way through the rocks beyond.

The most substantial impediment in this section is Smith's Falls, which stopped Captain John Smith's progress in the summer of 1608. A river-wide ridge of sizable boulders just upstream from Port Deposit composes the "falls." Provided with a reasonable flow, these rocks produce considerable white water. They mark the river's fall line, or the approximate head of the Chesapeake's moon-driven tidal flow.

Once they made it over Smith's Falls and two more sets of riffles spaced at half-mile intervals upriver, Susquehannock canoeists ordinarily could paddle easily to their villages on Octoraro Creek and at Washington Boro. But in low water, at low tide, they may have spent time paddling in zigzags or even walking their canoes over and around rocks stretching well up the course.

Rocks still regulate the river below Conowingo. Edward Gertler is impressed by the "incredibly ledgy and jagged bottom" of the Susquehanna over the first four miles downriver from the dam. He writes: "At low water this creates a rocky maze, without parallel, that not only demands good water reading ability, but also requires the boater to have an intuitive sense to decipher where, in a 3,000-foot-wide panorama of pure rock, enough water gathers to float a boat." At least one boat map describes points between Port Deposit and Conowingo as "foul" with rocks.

Some people call Smith's Falls and similar upstream configurations "rock bridges" because in low water it is almost possible to walk all the way across the river on them without getting wet. The Susquehanna is the only Chesapeake tributary that has exposed rocks in its lower course, and these riffles surprise motorboaters roaring upstream from the open bay. Innumerable pilots have grounded their boats before acknowledging the rigid geology of the Susquehanna Gorge.

Early in the summer of 1588, just weeks before the English navy and bad weather wrecked the Spanish Armada half a world away, the first European explorers ventured up the Susquehanna and foundered on the rocks. Their leader was not John Smith, the English adventurer cited in modern texts as the first European to "discover" the Susquehanna, but Vicente González, a Spanish captain. Determined to explore the Atlantic coast and locate and destroy the English outpost at Roanoke Island, North Carolina, the Spaniards launched González from St. Augustine, Florida. The captain knew the territory: he had transported a doomed group of Jesuit missionaries to the Chesapeake in 1570.

González commanded a group of thirty sailors and soldiers, including Juan Menéndez Marques, who made a brief account of the six-week voyage. They rode in a small bark that had sailed from Spain to Cuba the previous year. Pedro Menéndez Marques, Florida's governor and uncle of Juan, described this boat as "a vessel very fast of sail and oar." González failed to discover the English on the Carolina Outer Banks before sailing on to the Chesapeake Bay. He investigated the mouths of several of the bay's rivers and coves. One of these rivers clearly was the Susquehanna: it was full of rocks.

The expedition entered the Susquehanna at high tide. The current at the mouth impressed González because it ran more than three fathoms (eighteen feet) deep with the tide. Rather than travel up the river at night, the captain sailed less than a mile into the Susquehanna, dropped anchor, and rested.

With a low tide at dawn, according to the summary of the trip, "it was almost a miracle that the bark avoided the great rocks by which the river was enclosed from one side to the other." Shouting out orders to dodge rocks revealed on all sides, González barely escaped the rugged trap. As they passed into the bay, the relieved sailors spotted a dead shad floating in the water.

The Spanish had arrived on June 23, the eve of the feast of St. John the Baptist, and everywhere there had been rocks; so they named this river San Juan de las Peñas (St. John of the Rocks). San Juan de las Peñas is the only continental European name the Susquehanna has ever had.

González made a speedier trip back to St. Augustine, on the way finding evidence of the Roanoke colony's location. On the basis of his report, the Spanish planned to send a major expedition to eradicate the colony and build a fortress of their own, but the destruction of the Armada and other distractions intruded. When the English finally arrived at Roanoke Island with supplies, what has come to be called the Lost Colony had vanished without Spanish intervention.

In 1607—twenty years after the start of the colony at Roanoke—John Smith and a hundred English settlers established another colony, which would become the first permanent settlement, at Jamestown, Virginia. In 1608—twenty years after Vicente González rode the high tide just inside the mouth of the Susquehanna—John Smith passed the same way.

As he sailed the Chesapeake and the Susquehanna, Smith figuratively washed out the record of Spanish exploration. In the First Book of *The generall historie of Virginia New England and the Summer Isles,* which recounted New World explorations preceding his, Smith mentioned Columbus briefly but referred to no Spanish explorers. Many subsequent authors have done the same and González's memory has all but vanished. To the victors go the spoils of history.

In early June 1608, John Smith and twelve crew members set out in a clumsy two-ton barge with a short mast to explore the Chesapeake. Smith's crew depressed him. Only two men had any knowledge of sailing. The others probably spent a great deal of time rowing the bulky boat.

At twenty-eight, Smith was a stocky, full-bearded European war hero and survivor of several recent attempts on his life by Powhatans and his fellow Jamestown settlers. He sailed methodically and made careful notes. After a brief trip back to Jamestown, the explorers traveled to the head of the bay in early August.

"At the end of the Bay," Smith wrote in the Second Book of his history, "where it is 6 or 7 myles in breadth, it divides it selfe into 4. branches, the best commeth Northwest from among the mountaines, but though Canows may goe a dayes journey or two up it, we could not get two myles up it with our boat for rockes. Upon it is seated the Sasquesahanocks, neare it North and by West runneth a creeke a myle and a halfe: at the head whereof the Ebbe left us on shore, where we found many trees cut with hatchets."

Although Smith thought his barge passed only two miles up the Susquehanna, his "Map of Virginia" indicates that he rode the high tide all the way to the first falls—a distance of about eight miles. Smith labeled these boat-stopping riffles "Smyths Fales." He dropped anchor there. The anchor got so securely snagged in the rocks that the crew could not pull it up in the morning and had to cut it free.

The "small river like a creeke" that Smith ascended with the second tide probably was Deer Creek, which runs into the Susquehanna from the northwest just below Smith's Falls. When he went ashore at that creek, Smith encountered his first Susquehannocks. That meeting prompted a handsome illustration on his map and his famous description of the Susquehannocks as "Giants." On his way out of the bay, Smith encountered other groups of Native Americans, who killed one of his men. Gratefully leaving the Chesapeake and the Susquehanna behind, Smith returned to Jamestown with a melancholy mind.

The exploratory voyages of Vicente González and John Smith proved four centuries ago what generations of boaters following their path have failed repeatedly to disprove: from barely inside its mouth and all the way up, except where it is ponded by dams, the Susquehanna is not hospitable to boats. The longest nonnavigable waterway in the world remains a river of rocks.

⇌ *Smith's Falls, viewed through trees along the river's east shore, prevented Captain John Smith's sailing barge from continuing up the Susquehanna in 1608. Just upriver from Port Deposit, the falls mark the head of the Chesapeake Bay's tidal flow. (Photo by Christine Brubaker.)*

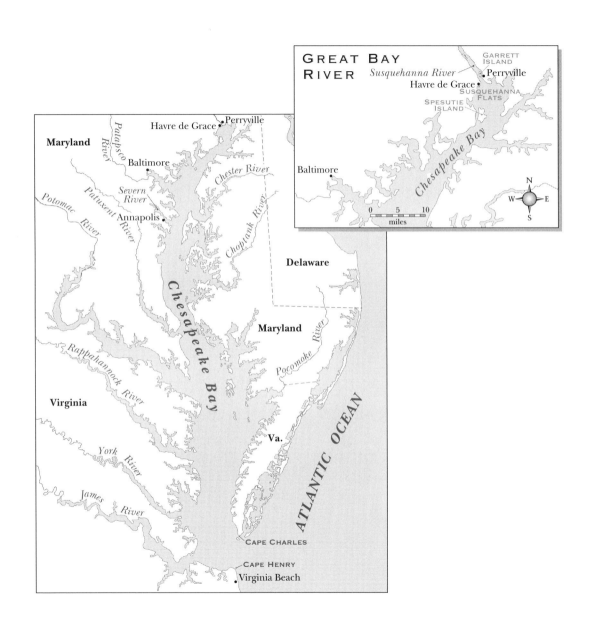

GREAT BAY
RIVER

Susquehanna River

GARRETT
ISLAND

• Perryville

Havre de Grace •

SUSQUEHANNA
FLATS

SPESUTIE
ISLAND

Baltimore •

Chesapeake Bay

N
W • E
S

0   5   10
miles

Maryland

Havre de Grace • Perryville

Patapsco River

Baltimore

Severn River

Chester River

Annapolis

Patuxent River

Choptank River

Potomac River

Delaware

Maryland

Pocomoke River

Chesapeake Bay

Rappahannock River

Virginia

Va.

ATLANTIC OCEAN

York River

James River

CAPE CHARLES

CAPE HENRY
• Virginia Beach

Great Bay River

Havre de Grace

People think there are lots of fish in the Susquehanna

River. If only they could have seen what it was like during

the first two-and-a-half decades of this century. I can

remember walking in fish up to my knees and participating

in a type of fishing no longer known on the upper

Chesapeake Bay.

—ARTHUR WILSON of Havre de Grace in a
Baltimore Sun interview, 1977

BECAUSE TRAVELING THE MAJOR overland route between Baltimore and Philadelphia requires crossing the Susquehanna at its mouth, probably more people have passed over here than at any other place. This was as true in the late eighteenth century, when George Washington crossed the river's end at least a dozen times, as it is today, when Interstate 95 carries one of the East Coast's heaviest streams of traffic from Havre de Grace in Harford County over to Perryville in Cecil.

The features that most contemporary travelers associate with the mouth of the Susquehanna River are its four bridges. After canoeing beneath them, Tim Palmer said these bridges "punctuated the difference" between river and bay. Every day these sturdy crossings—as impressive as the multiple spans at Harrisburg—convey thousands of people and hundreds of tons of freight. Vehicular traffic is constant on I-95 and Route 40. Amtrak passenger trains cross on the Pennsylvania Railroad bridge and CSX freights on the Baltimore & Ohio bridge. Because their progress from land across water to land is seamless, few travelers think much about the river below, let alone the effort their predecessors expended in crossing before the bridges were built.

From its start in 1695, Susquehanna Lower Ferry was one of the best-used and best-known shuttles on this or any river. Most travelers from the south passed over the Susquehanna by this ferry, crossing near where the Amtrak bridge stands now. The first six presidents crossed here. The Marquis de Lafayette crossed several times on the Lower Ferry. According to tradition, on the first of these journeys he compared the town on the Susquehanna's western bank to the little harbor of Havre de Grâce on the Breton coast. The name stuck.

Horses powered the Lower Ferry in the early years. Passengers and freight rode on one barge. Blindfolded horses occupied another barge lashed to the first. The horses walked on a treadmill to turn a paddlewheel that propelled both barges across the river. If bad weather, high tide, or ice made crossing dangerous, oarsmen rowed smaller ferries from bank to bank.

Rail lines arrived at the river in 1837, nearly three decades before the Philadelphia, Wilmington & Baltimore built the first bridge. In the interim, steam side-wheelers ferried PW&B cars, which were considerably lighter than contemporary cars. The second of these railroad ferries, the *Maryland,* a massive iron boat 238 feet long, could transport entire trains, including twenty cars and the locomotive. The crossing took eight minutes.

In January 1857 the *Maryland* chugged daily across the Susquehanna through thick ice, keeping a channel open. One night the ice upstream of the channel moved and caught the side-wheeler in a pack. Railroad workers laid a plank walkway on the ice from Perryville to the boat and passengers and their baggage passed over it to shore. The next morning they extended planks all the way to Havre de Grace. Passengers and baggage passed back and forth across the river in this way for four days before workers managed to free the steamer and reopen the channel.[1]

Getting across the river was easier than moving lumber and coal boats down the shallow, rugged course and out into a shallow bay. The Baltimore District of the Army Corps of Engineers began dredging the western banks of the bay near Havre de Grace just before the Civil War. In 1882 the engineers removed a shoal opposite a Susquehanna island just above Havre de Grace and opened a channel 200 feet wide and 15 feet deep from out in the bay to the river's mouth. The corps periodically dredges this channel to keep it open.[2]

Given sparse traffic on the river and upper bay, except for Sunday sailors, all the dredging was hardly worth the effort. Commerce from the river to the bay, consisting primarily of loads of lumber, cement, fish, and granite, declined dramatically, from 135,293 tons in 1905 to 37,936 tons in 1908, largely in response to completion of the dam at York Haven in late 1904. Hydroelectric dams even lower on the river eventually cut off all traffic from upriver.

The only substantial freight the river carries today runs out from a huge quarry on the west shore just above Havre de Grace. The Arundel Sand and Gravel Company ships barges loaded with thousands of tons of granite to locations throughout the Chesapeake and up and down the East Coast. Every day of the week, tugboats push these huge barges from the quarry, which now extends half a mile from the Susquehanna's shore into the river hills.

In the nineteenth century, Susquehanna-area granite came from quarries in hills near Port Deposit. Port Deposit granite often moved south by canal rather than river. Much of the other river traffic, especially large amounts of coal, also transferred to the Susquehanna and Tidewater Canal after it opened in the spring of 1840. For a brief period the canal spurred prosperity at Havre de Grace, its southern terminus. Businessmen anticipating a boom in canal trade arriving from Columbia-Wrightsville built many of the town's large brick homes.

But the river and bay remained the town's focus during most of the nineteenth century and the first half of the twentieth. Generations of residents relied heavily on the water for their livelihoods. Fishing was the main thing. Havre de Grace watermen fished in spring and summer. In fall and winter they gunned down ducks on the Susquehanna Flats, the shallow area at the head of the bay where the river dumps much of the silt it does not deposit behind Conowingo Dam. In winter, too, many men cut ice from the river and sold it for refrigeration.[3]

"This was the place to fish," says Bob Jobes, the forty-something waterman and duck decoy carver who lives on Havre de Grace's Otsego Street, named for the Susquehanna's mother lake. "This is sort of a lost part of the Chesapeake and the Susquehanna right here. It's always you hear about Tangier Sound, Rock Hall, Tilghman Island; but hey, this used to be—Havre de Grace, Perryville, Port Deposit—this used to be *the* place to fish."

When he investigated the head of the bay and the river in 1608, John Smith said he found an "abundance of fish, lying so thick with their heads above the water, as for want of nets, our barge driving amongst them, we attempted to catch them with a frying pan, but we found it a bad instrument to catch fish with." The Susquehannocks formally recognized the excellence of the fishery at the mouth of their river half a century later when they pointedly maintained rights to these fishing grounds in a treaty with the English.

The Susquehanna's major shad and herring markets developed at Havre de Grace, Port Deposit, Lapidum, and other villages near the river's mouth. One traveler counted fifteen seine fisheries here in 1796. About that time, fish-processing operations also sprinkled Havre de Grace, Garrett's Island, and other sites running upriver to Port Deposit. Rivermen cured and processed hundreds of tons of fish and packed them off to cities on the eastern seaboard.

Asahel Bailey of Havre de Grace revolutionized the area's shad and herring fishing in 1820 by inventing the "shad float," a fish factory on a raft. Fishermen towed these floats to sites on the lower river and in the Flats. They anchored them in midstream, where the current carried most of the fish trying to swim upriver to spawn. This positioning improved on casting seines from shore.

These floats—logs covered with flat wood floors—ran to as much as 300 square feet. Each contained several shanties that housed sleeping and dining quarters; a kitchen; an office; rooms for beheading, gutting, and washing fish; and a room with fish storage bins. A fifty-foot-wide "apron" made of oak slats sloped from one side of the float into the water and rested on the bottom of the river. Watermen used a small boat to stretch a huge seine out from the float. Then they hauled in the seine, impounding the fish and driving them up the apron onto the float. On a good day, one float could collect half a million fish.

The floats operated for just over a century, primarily gathering shad and herring, but also rockfish and carp, pike, salmon, and perch. "Whatever was in the river, we caught," the late A. Hughes Spencer told the editors of *Havre de Grace: An Informal History.* Spencer worked on the floats of his father's Silver, Spencer and Company just after World War I. "The herring was the most plentiful. I've heard my father say they'd give you all the herring you wanted if you'd buy shad for 10 cents apiece."

The late Arthur Wilson also worked on Silver, Spencer floats. "My job was to wade through the catch and throw back the white perch, pike, rock and other types not wanted," he recalled in a newspaper interview. "Slipping and sliding on the deck with rubber waders on I would then shovel the herring and shad into baskets. . . . The baskets were then taken to the cutting room where 20 men or more stood at a cutting table. After a basket of fish was dumped

before a worker, he would grab a fish and with two swift motions of the knife cut off the head and remove the entrails. These parts fell through a hole into the river."

Up to a hundred men worked on one of these floats. During the rigs' final seasons, in the mid-1920s, the workers received 90 cents a day plus room, board, and a daily jigger of whiskey. After the few weeks of the spawning run, itinerant workers moved on to other towns and Havre de Grace residents found other jobs. Arthur Wilson's father, for example, worked in the Arundel quarry.

The floats disappeared when shad declined in numbers and herring in popularity, but watermen continued to haul seines along the shore and an increasing number of sportsmen began using rod and reel in the current. Gary Pensell remembers an active river fishery in 1959, the year he and his father opened Tidewater Marina, one of Havre de Grace's five marinas. "When we first opened," he says, looking out at the mouth of the Susquehanna from his glass-walled marina office, "we could stand on the end of this dock almost any evening—it didn't matter what day of the week it was—and just count 'em, hundreds of boats. It looked like you could walk across the river on them."

The fishery soon declined and has never come back. Sometimes Pensell gets so disenchanted with the fishery in the bay and at the mouth of the river that he boats all the way up to Conowingo and fishes in the dam's tailrace, catching what the anglers casting from the dam's catwalk miss.

More than the fishery was worn out in Havre de Grace by mid-century. "When I came here [in 1953]," recalls Ellsworth Shank, affable curator of a museum in the former

⟿ *Harvesting fish in the Lower Susquehanna above Havre de Grace about 1920. From the 1820s through the 1920s, fishermen towed "shad floats" out into the river and the Susquehanna Flats and captured shad, herring, and other fish with huge seines. (Kenneth Kay, Havre de Grace, Maryland.)*

lockhouse of the Susquehanna and Tidewater, "it was mostly a bunch of sunken boats along the river. You didn't want to live on the water, it was so trashy looking."

Prosperous marinas and restaurants, several public parks, and too many condominiums have replaced the broken boats and the old town dump as Havre de Grace's Susquehanna riverfront has undergone a renaissance in recent years. So has the bayside—home to the popular Decoy Museum, the new Maritime Museum, and an elaborate boardwalk extending along the bay. Regular skipjack

◦ *The Havre de Grace historian Ellsworth Shank stands on a pivot bridge that allowed traffic to pass over the Susquehanna and Tidewater Canal at the lockhouse in Havre de Grace. Behind him the Susquehanna stretches to condominiums in Perryville. (Photo by Christine Brubaker.)*

cruises leave from the Tydings Park yacht basin.

"The river dominated in the town's early years," says Shank, "but it's always been a river *and* bay town. Compared to most towns, we have tremendous public water access. People really use the water here—the Susquehanna and the Chesapeake."

The Mouth

I drain a thousand streams, yet still I seek

To lose myself within the Chesapeake.

—Lloyd Mifflin

ANTICIPATING AN ATTACK BY WAY of the Chesapeake, Lieutenant John O'Neill set up three small artillery pieces behind a breastwork along the Susquehanna in Havre de Grace. The Irish-born soldier and his gunners called this meager assemblage the Potato Battery. They aimed their cannons southeast and waited. If British troops massing on nearby Spesutie Island tried to boat ashore in barges, the tiny gun crew aimed to blow them out of the water. The patriots hoped to deter the British from landing and doing to Havre de Grace what they had just done to Frenchtown on nearby Elk River: burn it to the ground.

There is no record of the Potato Battery's shot striking anything but water when 400 Royal Navy tars and Royal Marines washed into Havre de Grace at sunrise on May 3, 1813. The British killed a militiaman named Webster with a rocket, and all the defenders except O'Neill retreated. On recoil, a cannon bruised O'Neill's thigh and he limped to a nearby nail factory. He continued to put up a spirited defense with several other men before a contingent of Royal Marines captured them all. Then the British did torch

Havre de Grace, extending their penchant for firing American towns by damaging two-thirds of its sixty buildings. Fifteen months later they burned every public building in Washington but the post office.

Citing dangerous shoals and currents, the Maryland General Assembly eventually authorized construction of the Chesapeake's second lighthouse at Concord Point, just downriver from where O'Neill's battery had been located. In 1827 the legislators honored O'Neill's steadfast defense by naming him lighthouse keeper.

This lighthouse, deactivated and restored, and one of O'Neill's original cannons stand in the little park on Concord Point. The point anchors one end of an invisible line running across the Susquehanna. Here the river meets the Chesapeake Bay's tidal flow. In a way, John O'Neill recognized this division of waters by erecting his defensive battery near this point. The Maryland legislature clearly recognized it by building the lighthouse here.

"I tell people I don't know where God says, 'This is where the river meets the bay,' but then I show them the layout," says Ellsworth Shank, who began studying the lay of the land long before he became curator of the Lockhouse Museum in the 1980s. "I say the width of the river at the mouth is three thousand feet, approximately, but you go right beyond the end of Havre de Grace, where the lighthouse is, and all of a sudden"—and here Shank spreads his arms expansively—"shooo—it's five, six miles. At that point, the land necks back—and you have a corresponding point across the river."

Concord Point's counterpart on the Susquehanna's east

Workers built the Concord Point Lighthouse of Port Deposit granite at Havre de Grace in 1827. The oldest lighthouse in continuous operation in the United States was designed "to protect vessels from dangerous shoals and currents at the mouth of the Susquehanna River." (Photo by Christine Brubaker.)

shore is Perry Point in Perryville. To divide river from bay, draw a line between these points. This line is not a biological division of waters. Those who claim it is impossible to determine where river water ends and bay water begins are correct. The waters slosh between river and bay with the tides. In flood, the Susquehanna's channel propels freshwater miles out into the bay. In drought, the bay slops up into the Susquehanna, salting the drinking water Havre de Grace draws through pipes from the channel.

Nor is this a visible division of waters such as the diagonal line that separates the different-colored North and West branches at Northumberland. This split is more clearly defined by associated terrain. Here the coastal plain that surrounds all the rest of the Chesapeake begins changing to the Piedmont plateau, which produces the hills on either side of the river and the rocks in the river. From a boat well out in the bay, the waterway with the largest volume of flow on the East Coast of the United States looks rather puny as, clearly confined by ridges, it runs out into expansive coastal flatlands.

The Susquehanna River Basin Commission Compact confused the location of the river's mouth by defining it otherwise. The 1970 compact says the river's basin is "the area of drainage of the Susquehanna River and its tributaries into Chesapeake Bay to the southern edge of the Pennsylvania Railroad bridge between Havre de Grace and Perryville, Maryland." That bridge, the southernmost of the four spans, crosses a little less than a mile upriver from Concord Point. A handful of area residents will cite this legal definition if asked for the dividing point between river and bay, but even the SRBC confirmed Concord Point as the true geographical divide by erecting a mouth-of-the-river plaque near the lighthouse in 1995.

Tom Horton suggests yet another possible definition of the Susquehanna's mouth in *Bay Country*. He says the mouth might more correctly be located along a rough line across the Chesapeake between Solomons Island on the Patuxent River and Hooper Island on Maryland's Eastern Shore. This is some 90 miles south of Havre de Grace, nearly halfway to the bay's Atlantic outlet. Up to that point, before the Potomac pumps its substantial flow into the Chesapeake, Horton says, "at least ninety percent of the

freshwater comes from a single river, the Susquehanna, and this is more nearly its rightful mouth."

Of the Chesapeake Bay's nearly fifty major tributaries, the Susquehanna is the only requisite river. Without the Susquehanna's average daily flow of 25 billion gallons of freshwater—no matter how polluted by coal acid or cow manure—the 19 trillion gallons in its estuary would turn saltier and begin drying up.

When all that water flows through the river's mouth at Havre de Grace, it has traveled for up to six days since washing out of the Russian Orthodox Monastery's cedar swamp and Faber Farabaugh's fouled spring and the highlands of the Juniata. By the time they reach Concord Point, the waters of the Chenango and Chemung have mixed thoroughly with the waters of the Lycoming and Loyalsock, and they are about to be mixed again in the great blender of the Chesapeake.

The Flats

The ducks were so abundant on the Susquehanna Flats and surrounding areas up until about 1950 that it was actually not necessary to hunt them. It was only essential that the hunter or gunner select a location which the ducks frequented for food or rest and then be able to kill them, to guarantee a successful day.

—J. Evans McKinney, *Decoys of the Susquehanna Flats and Their Makers*

H. L. Mencken likened William Jennings Bryant to the Platte River: "a mile wide and a foot deep at the mouth." The Sage of Baltimore might have coined a simile closer to home. The end of the Susquehanna approaches that width and runs only a foot or two deep over the sediment load it has pushed into the Chesapeake.

Some of the finest topsoil from three states forms the Susquehanna Flats, a thirty-six-square-mile delta at the head of the bay. These expansive Flats range south from Concord Point and Carpenter Point to Spesutie Island and Turkey Point. All of that vast plain wants to poke its sandy soil above water. Here, given a low river flow and low tide, you could wade much of the way across the bay.

The Susquehanna has been carrying silt to the Chesapeake region since the drainage turned south. European settlement and deforestation speeded the process. The Department of Agriculture says as many as seven tons of soil erode into the Susquehanna from an acre of basin cropland in a year. Much of that sediment eventually winds up in the Flats.

This huge silt bar—what C. P. Hauducoeur labeled the "large shoal" on his 1799 map—helps make the Chesapeake one of the shallowest estuaries in the world. The average depth of the bay is twenty feet, but 10 percent of it, including the Flats, is less than three feet. This shallow delta reaching into a shallow bay may seem an appropriate extension of the shallow Susquehanna, but it is also a warning. Like the ponds behind the Susquehanna's hydroelectric dams, the Chesapeake Bay is filling with sediment. Unlike those ponds, the bay cannot pass sediment downstream. As the Chesapeake fills, it dies.

The Susquehanna Flats once provided perfect conditions for the cultivation of wild celery, eelgrass, and other submerged aquatic vegetation that filter polluted river water, attract migratory ducks, and shelter anadromous fish. Grass and wild celery grew so thick that the Flats might as well have been one huge island: boats could not pass through it. "It was difficult to take a boat out there," recalls Gary Pensell at Tidewater Marina in Havre de Grace. "At low tide it looked like a pasture. The entire Flats were covered with vegetation."

This exceptional fish and wildfowl habitat became one of the most popular sporting attractions on the East Coast in the nineteenth and early twentieth centuries. Residents of Havre de Grace and Perryville depended on the Flats as much as on the river for their livelihood, and hundreds of sportsmen came here to shoot into the sky or drop a line in water.

Each autumn, enormous numbers of ducks and geese—especially canvasback ducks, which dined almost exclusively on wild celery—flew in from Canada to spend the winter in warmer water. A seventeenth-century observer reported a flock of ducks a mile wide and seven miles long headed for the Flats. So many feathers in the sky encouraged slaughter. John Smith's adventurers killed 148 ducks with three shots in 1608. By the 1870s and '80s, when the Flats had become famous for canvasback hunting, hundreds of gunners were killing 5,000 ducks a day. William Dobson, a Havre de Grace hunter, is said to have shot 509 ducks himself one day in 1879. After one of his overused double-barreled

10-gauge shotguns exploded, he cooled the other in the water after each firing.

Most duck hunters used sinkboxes from the 1880s until Maryland banned them in the mid-1930s. These boatlike blinds floated almost submerged in the shallow water. Duck hunters lay on their backs in them—one observer likened them to a "tin coffin"—and fired into the sky. Other shooters used specially designed rowboats known as bushwhack rigs.

Successful duck hunting required a large number of decoys. J. E. McKinney of Havre de Grace estimates that hunters a century ago used about 40,000 decoys during a season on the Flats. Each sinkbox rig set out between 300 and 700. Bushwhackers used 75 to 125. Most of these fake ducks looked like canvasbacks, although a few simulated other waterfowl: redheads, blackheads, bluebills. Local residents carved these decoys, often from light and durable white pine rafted down the West Branch and Main Stem to Port Deposit.

The Flats' reputation for duck hunting spread far. John James Audubon came here to paint ducks and other birds. Wealthy men from New York and Philadelphia hired guides, bought decoys, and blasted away at Audubon's models. These well-heeled shooters, known as "sports," included J. Pierpont Morgan's son. "Jack" Morgan and friends from Long Island bought Spesutie Island in the 1930s.

A good time was had by all, except the ducks, which steadily declined in number throughout the twentieth century, especially after market gunners began shipping waterfowl out of Havre de Grace by the barrel. These commercial hunters stood by the dozen, firing 12-gauge shotguns from boats, sometimes at night with lights. Some employed small-bore "cannons" that could fire up to a pound of shot.

Joel Barber, an early twentieth-century poet, artist, and decoy collector, wrote about the commotion these hunters caused. A quatrain of "Off Havre de Grace" describes the killing Flats:

> For then it comes, across the Chesapeake—
> The roar of guns, like traffic on a bridge,
> And valiant canvasback come hurtling down
> Like ripe plums falling in a gale of wind.

Recognizing that hunters could not go on shooting hundreds of ducks a day without wiping out the canvasback population, the federal government ordered bag limits—twenty-five a day, then twelve, then two. Given bag limits and a ban on sinkboxes, duck hunters about 1960 began body-booting—standing in the Flats in rubber suits, surrounded by decoys, taking single shots.

Gunners alone did not do in the ducks. In order to grow more wheat, Canadian farmers drained wetlands where migratory Chesapeake ducks hatched, cutting the supply at the source. And then, in the 1970s, eelgrass and wild celery began to disappear from the bay. Many ducks simply stopped flying into the Flats for food. Those that continued to come here began dining on hard-shelled clams instead of celery. The new diet did not agree with them. The number of canvasbacks wintering on the bay dwindled from hundreds of thousands to hundreds.[4]

What killed the grass? Theories abound. The ecologically correct one: Nutrients and sediment washing down the Susquehanna overwhelmed most submerged aquatic vegetation. Biologists say excess nutrients, the very element grasses had been filtering from the water, stimulated the growth of algae, preventing the sun from ever reaching bottom grasses.

A complementary excess sediment theory claims that Tropical Storm Agnes delivered the coup de grâce at Havre de Grace as the Susquehanna pushed 50 million tons of storm-washed sediment onto the delta. That sediment created some 500 acres of real but temporary islands while covering thousands of acres of grass. Buried, or deprived of light by turbid water, the grass died.

Charles Jobes, Bob Jobes's brother, believes chlorine used to cleanse sewage released to the Susquehanna played a role in killing grass: "The Havre de Grace Wastewater Treatment Plant had a pipe running out into the channel just below town. You could see the chlorine boiling from the waste that they treated. It just came right up in the channel, and it smelled of chlorine like you wouldn't believe. It burned your nose. That chlorine kept the grass from growing."[5]

And some people say the wild celery and eelgrass failed in the Flats because one summer, several years before Agnes, the state of Maryland deliberately poisoned them. Harry Jobes, father of Bob and Charles, observed the poisoning, the decline of grass beds, and the collapse of duck and rockfish populations that thrived on that grass. The elder Jobes ("what's left of me," as he puts it) has retired to Aberdeen, on the bay just south of Havre de Grace. A gruff, chain-smoking old salt who has spent most of his life fishing and

⟨ *Bob Jobes, at the wheel, and Charles Jobes stand in their haul-seining boat at Tydings Park yacht basin in Havre de Grace. The modest boat holds two tons of rockfish, sufficient to accommodate the 1,250 pounds of fish per person that haul-seiners are permitted to take in a year. (Photo by Christine Brubaker.)*

boating on the river and bay, Jobes does not like to hear anyone suggest that overshooting or overfishing undermined the bay's wildfowl and fish populations. He says the state did that by poisoning their grassy feeding grounds so that an increasing number of "blow boats" from Havre de Grace marinas could sail in clear water closer to home.

"The state come up here and killed all this grass, killed all the larvae, killed all the fingerlings, killed all the bass, the yellow perch, the white perch, all over these flats," he says. "They poisoned everything from one shore to the other. By the acres they did it. Five feet deep they did it. There used to be a hundred thousand canvasbacks in the air and there were big globs of rockfish and yellow perch eggs hanging on the grass and they killed everything. It'll never come back."

Not everyone is so pessimistic. Grasses are multiplying slowly in some sections of the bay, thanks to a reduction in the Susquehanna's nutrient load and planting and transplanting of grasses. Submerged aquatic vegetation throughout the bay now covers an estimated 69,000 acres—about 12 percent of the original grassy area—although vegetation remains sparse in the Flats.

The restoration of grass must compete with human use of the bay. In the spring of 1995 the Maryland Saltwater Fishermen's Association accused watermen of contributing to the degradation of grasses by ripping out fragile vegetation as they haul-seined for rockfish. Throughout the bay, about twenty haul-seining operations employ boats to drag large nets around rockfish from June to November. The Jobeses are some of the last haul-seiners working in the Susquehanna Flats and occasionally up into the river.

Dr. L. William Schotta, a retired Millersville University professor and longtime Flats rockfish angler, protested haul-seining in a letter to Maryland officials: "In drifting my boat near a haul seine operation, I saw uprooted aquatic grasses entangled in the net and piles of uprooted grass floating nearby. It is not difficult to picture that a weighted net dragged through the fragile bay grasses in three to eight feet of water will tear much of the grass out by the roots." Schotta said the early destruction of the grasses, by poisoning and Agnes, should not be extended by haul-seining.

The Maryland Department of Natural Resources launched a major study of haul-seining's effect on grasses.

Biologists accompanied the Jobeses on their excursions into the Flats. After examining the nets' interaction with grasses in detail, the state determined that haul-seining was not damaging them.

Still, Maryland severely restricts haul-seiners' catches. The Jobeses believe the commercial limit—1,250 pounds per person—is designed to save rockfish for an increasing number of recreational anglers. "I just get the feeling the state don't want you to catch them," says Bob Jobes. "Everything's going recreational. They want to make it a total sports fishery and drive out the commercial fishermen."

The Jobeses resent this intrusion. They say the watermen were here first—before the sport fishermen or the sailboaters or any other competing water users—and contribute little, if anything, to environmental problems. But they also acknowledge reality: their future is not on the water, regardless of its quality. Along with dozens of other watermen in the Havre de Grace area, the Jobeses now spend most of their days carving realistic decoys of canvasbacks and redheads and other ducks rarely seen on the Chesapeake anymore. Harry has been memorialized in wax, holding a wax decoy, in Havre de Grace's Decoy Museum.

"Now we just carve decoys for people that collect them," Bob Jobes says, knitting his bay-beaten brow in resignation. "We still use wood decoys when we go out body-booting and a few people actually hunt with them on the Susquehanna up in Pennsylvania, but probably ninety-seven or ninety-eight percent of what we make are collectibles. It's a big folk art."

The craftsman looks over a roomful of realistic decoys he has carved and painted for buyers to display on den shelves in Bel Air or Baltimore. "Everything has changed," he says, patting the head of a half-carved canvasback. "So much activity used to go on in the Flats—fishing in springtime and hunting in the fall—and now it's nonexistent, none, zero. It's almost like you get up in early morning, May or November, and look out across those Flats and you wonder if you're in a different world because of what used to happen. It doesn't happen anymore."

The Bay

There is but one entrance by Sea into this Country, and that is at the mouth of a very goodly Bay. . . . Within is a country that may have the prerogative over the most pleasant places knowne, for large and pleasant navigable Rivers, heaven and earth never agreed better to frame a place for mans habitation.

—CAPTAIN JOHN SMITH speaking of the Chesapeake, 1623

DAVE GELENTER UNCURLS A CHANNEL MAP on the deck of the *Stanley Norman.* A couple of dozen central Pennsylvania landlubbers gather around as the Chesapeake Bay Foundation (CBF) skipjack glides through the mouth of the Severn River at Annapolis. Captain Gelenter has turned over his wheel to a mate so that he can explain this map of the Chesapeake. The deep blue on the map is deep water, he tells his Saturday sailors; lighter blue is shallower.

"Now does anyone know why there's a deep trench run-

ning down the Chesapeake Bay?" Gelenter asks as he points to the long dark-blue channel that splits the map.

Gelenter's listeners endure a brief, slightly uncomfortable pause. Then someone suggests tentatively, "It's the old channel of the Susquehanna?"

"That's right!" Gelenter practically shouts. In his years of guiding CBF educational tours on this old oyster boat, only occasionally has he received an answer to this question. He enthusiastically commends the speaker and directs everyone's attention to the beginning of the dark-blue channel at the head of the bay.

"Back before the last ice age, there was no Chesapeake Bay," he explains. "The Susquehanna River, which you see the mouth of—right here—used to run right down through here all the way to the Atlantic Ocean. Then the planet cooled down. The water got taken up into ice. Then the ice age ended, the earth warmed up, the ice was released, and the river valley was flooded. So the Chesapeake Bay is the flooded river valley of the Susquehanna."

The primary goal of CBF cruises on restored oyster boats is to heighten public awareness of the bay's fragile, endangered ecology. Later in the day the crew will illustrate dramatically how oysters filter turbid and polluted bay water by letting a dozen of them clear the water in one aquarium while the liquid in another, oyster-free tank remains opaque. The message is also clear: the more oysters, the better. But right now, Captain Gelenter is content to let this remarkable information about the Susquehanna make an impact.

"In a nutshell," he concludes his lesson in geomorphology, "that's how the bay came to be. These days ship channels still use the deep water from the riverbed, although there are places where it is dredged to maintain that depth."

As it sails farther into the Chesapeake, the *Stanley Norman* will cross the old Susquehanna trench where it runs sixty feet deep. Elsewhere the ancient course cuts up to twice that far into the bay's bed. All ship captains use this course to move seagoing vessels to and from Baltimore. They know that if they deviated from the old channel, they could ground their boats on its steep shoulders. Some of the bay's best-known residents—blue crabs and rockfish among them—also prefer to navigate in this trench, where they can feed on deeper reservoirs of plankton.

This channel is the latest of at least three ancestral courses that held Susquehanna water. As sea level has fluctuated over hundreds of thousands of years, the river has run to the sea three geologically evident times. At those times, the Susquehanna accepted water from all of the tributaries that currently feed the Chesapeake. The Patapsco and the Potomac, the Patuxent and the Pocomoke, the James and the York and the Choptank and dozens of other rivers contributed directly to the Susquehanna. All the water that now enters the Chesapeake from New York, Pennsylvania, Maryland, Delaware, West Virginia, and Virginia flowed into the Susquehanna. Then the rising bay flooded the river at least three times and the Susquehanna's dominance of the region's drainage suffered at least three times.

Geologists have traced these distinct abandoned river beds through the Chesapeake region. They all start at the head of the bay, near the current mouth of the river. The beginnings of all are covered by the deposition in the Susquehanna Flats. Each progresses toward the Atlantic,

ending in the vicinity of the current mouth of the Chesapeake, just north of Virginia Beach.[6]

The Atlantic overwhelmed the oldest channel 200,000 to 400,000 or more years ago when the Earth's warming environment melted glaciers, lifted seas, and flooded the Chesapeake region. When sea level fell again, draining the bay about 150,000 years ago, the middle-aged course formed. It eventually succumbed to the same forces as the first. The current Chesapeake Bay began drowning the youngest course some 15,000 years ago.

In the late 1980s, Steven M. Colman of the U.S. Geological Survey at Wood's Hole, Massachusetts, and other geologists found that the three channels originally ranged from about 150 to 200 feet deep and from 1 1/4 to 2 1/2 miles wide. With the aid of seismic-reflection profiles and a series of holes bored into the old streambeds, they also found that the channels rarely coincide.

The courses are named for the towns nearest them on Maryland's Eastern Shore. The youngest, Cape Charles, follows the deep blue on Dave Gelenter's map. The intermediate channel, Eastville, runs along the eastern margin of the bay. The oldest, Exmore, breaks even farther east; for the most part it is buried beneath the Delmarva Peninsula, outside the current Chesapeake.[7]

In separate studies, Colman and others discovered that both ends of the youngest abandoned course are fully filled with sediment (except where dredged), whereas the middle of that course remains partially open to create the shipping channel. Where has all the sediment come from? The answer should provide comfort for Pennsylvania's farmers, who have been ripped up one cornrow and down the next for allowing so much soil to wash down the Susquehanna: the Atlantic Ocean's continental shelf, eroding back into the bay, seems to be contributing more sediment than the river.

Extrapolating from this information, geologists estimate that the Chesapeake is half full and could fill entirely in 5,000 to 10,000 years. The actual time that process takes will depend on several variables, the most significant being fluctuation in sea level. A rising sea, propelled by global warming and other climatic factors, will extend the bay's life, but not forever.

After the bay fills in and becomes a marsh, and when sea level falls again, the Susquehanna will establish a new course to the Atlantic. Once again it will drain the entire region—a task it has performed, sporadically, for a quarter of a million years or more.

On a perfect summer Saturday, with tourists from the Lower Susquehanna Valley in tow, Dave Gelenter is not so concerned about when the river may reassert its primacy as he is about improving the quality of the water now in the river's estuary. Retaking the *Stanley Norman's* wheel, he instructs his mate to launch the oysters on their water-filtering binge. "We're out here to create awareness about the bay's ecology," he remarks, "and we want our Susquehanna friends in Pennsylvania to help us restore the bay." Captain Gelenter looks to his sails and heads for the Cape Charles trench.

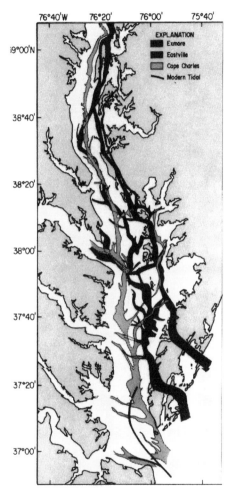

〜 *Three ancient abandoned beds of the Susquehanna, all beginning at the present mouth of the river, run through the Chesapeake region to the Atlantic Ocean. The oldest, designated Exmore, breaks east of the present bay. Eastville runs along the bay's eastern margin. The most recent course, Cape Charles, provides the Chesapeake's current shipping channel. (U.S. Geological Survey, Woods Hole, Massachusetts.)*

Epilogue: The Sea

Long before I set foot on a Chesapeake skipjack, my wife and our two children and I traveled to Virginia Beach on a long summer weekend. I no more anticipated encountering the Susquehanna River at a Virginia museum than I expected the ocean to dry up before we could jump into it.

A large plastic relief map lies horizontally in a box in the center of the geology room at the Virginia Science Museum on General Booth Boulevard, a short walk from the Atlantic. The map depicts the Chesapeake and its immediate drainage basin. The land areas are raised and water areas depressed. The map's most prominent feature: a deep, narrow cut running down the center of an only slightly depressed bay.

Press the exhibit's green button and the deep cut fills with water. Then water dribbles over the edges and floods the entire bay section of the map, until liquid fills all the depressed areas. The nation's largest estuary visibly submerges the deep cut, here labeled "Ancient bed of Susquehanna."

I pressed the green button several times, watching the water fill the depression and drain out and fill again and drain. I pressed on, well after the kids had lost interest. I considered what an extraordinary geologic event this had been and then—not a good vacation thought—realized how extensive this writing project was going to be. For the first time that spring, I had visited the Susquehanna's sources in upstate New York. Now I was playing with a Susquehanna exhibit at this beach resort a short drive from where the Chesapeake meets the Atlantic between the Virginia capes. I left the museum with a new and apprehensive appreciation for the size of the river and its bay and my task.

Since that summer when I first encountered the phenomenon of the Susquehanna in the Chesapeake, I have traveled along and on the river more times than I can count to collect stories for this book. Whenever I got too involved in local details upriver and lost sight of the Chesapeake, I pushed that green button in my mind and it all came together.

Ecologists love to emphasize the Susquehanna-Chesapeake connection—not its geological underpinnings so much as its biological consequences. Dave Gelenter cares deeply about the Susquehanna's impact on his bay's ability to rejuvenate itself. An aquarium full of horseshoe crabs and starfish reminds visitors to the Biological Field Station in Cooperstown of Lake Otsego's relationship with the Chesapeake. The Alliance for the Chesapeake Bay, concerned about the integrity of the bay's entire watershed,

describes the Chesapeake's ecosystem as ranging "from its origins at Cooperstown, New York, to its mouth in southern Virginia."

But geology runs deeper than biology. Eventually I would discover that the ancient Susquehanna did not stop at the present sea margin but washed even farther out to a constricted Atlantic. Geologists believe that when sea level fell radically, the river swept through the drained Chesapeake and kept right on rolling over dry land on the shallow continental shelf. Studies have traced a subtle topographic valley across the shelf from the present mouth of the Chesapeake to Norfolk Canyon, some 48 miles out to sea.

Forming a mental picture of this older, longer Susquehanna takes some effort. The Chesapeake's mouth is nearly 14 nautical miles across. From Cape Henry or Cape Charles, an observer cannot see the other side. Imagining a river a fraction of this size running across dry land out into dry land extending nearly 50 miles to the brine is no easier than visualizing the ancestral Susquehanna flowing out of the Adirondacks and slowly eroding, over millions of years, scenery that stood miles higher than the current landscape.

But whatever the Susquehanna looked like eons ago, and wherever it started and stopped, this river always has been larger than it appears. In the cosmic sense, as all water moves and mingles, the Susquehanna has no beginning or end, neither in space nor in time—and all of the water in it has come from everywhere.

AN AFTERWORD OF *Gratitude*

MORE THAN A HUNDRED PEOPLE who know and love the Susquehanna have contributed their substantial understanding of the river to this book. Most are quoted or credited in the text. Several contributors deserve special recognition.

Customarily, authors acknowledge spouses last. Chris Brubaker comes first, not only because she abided while I struggled to turn water into words but because her interest in natural history and the outdoors (she created the trail to the Susquehanna's scenic overlook at Turkey Hill) inspired this work. She also took many of the photos that enliven the type and paddled with me from York Haven to the Chesapeake.

Dave Schuyler, who teaches American studies at Franklin & Marshall College, read the manuscript first. He suggested important improvements and recommended the work to The Pennsylvania State University Press, for which I am especially grateful.

Joe Richardson, retired Franklin & Marshall biologist who has led field trips along the Susquehanna for many years and knows the river well, carefully read chapters on the North and West branches and suggested changes that significantly improved those sections.

Others who read parts of the manuscript include Ad Crable, Joe Homberger, Ted Keir, Paul Nevin, Bill Sevon, Ellsworth Shank, and Bill Sheaffer. All contributed to the value of this project. None is accountable for my mistakes.

The staffs of dozens of libraries, museums, archives, historical societies, newspaper offices, and government agencies along the Susquehanna and in Philadelphia, Baltimore, and Lancaster graciously assisted in assembling information and illustrations. Martha Tyzenhouse supplied the maps.

I thank Peter Potter, editor of The Pennsylvania State University Press, for quickly recognizing the importance of the Susquehanna as a subject and patiently helping me find my way from manuscript to published book.

Finally, I am grateful beyond measure to my parents, Mr. and Mrs. John H. Brubaker Jr., for encouraging me to do anything I wanted to do in life. This is it.

A NOTE ON *Sources*

HUNDREDS OF SOURCES, published and unpublished, have contributed to this writing. These were most influential.

The earliest lengthy books on the river were published between 1949 and 1955. Richmond E. Myers wrote the first and best, *The Long Crooked River.* A geologist and geographer, Myers probably understood the river better than anyone else. His Penn State University doctoral thesis, "The Development of Transportation in the Susquehanna Valley: A Geographical Study, 1700–1900" (1951), explores that aspect of the river's story in depth.

Elsie Singmaster, central Pennsylvania author of regional history and historical fiction, traced the river's course through Pennsylvania in an illustrated book, *Pennsylvania's Susquehanna,* in 1950.

Carl Carmer completed the best known of the Susquehanna books in 1955. *The Susquehanna,* a volume in the Rivers of America series, which Carmer edited, examines the history and folklore of the Susquehanna Valley.

Four decades passed before the next river book appeared. In 1993, Susan Stranahan, then a *Philadelphia Inquirer* reporter, published *Susquehanna, River of Dreams,* the first environmental history of the river. The book concentrates on the disastrous effects of human enterprise on the Susquehanna from the Wyoming Valley south.

Previous to these studies, three shorter works dealt exclusively with the Susquehanna. In 1796 Jonathan W.

Condy wrote *A Description of the River Susquehanna, with Observations on the Present State of Its Trade and Navigation* to promote the Susquehanna as a major transportation route. In 1893 Zenas J. Gray published *Prose and Poetry of the Susquehanna and Juniata Rivers,* an uneven collection with some charm. Charles Weathers Bump traveled the length of the Susquehanna in 1899 on assignment from the *Baltimore Sun.* The *Sun* published his entertaining columns in book form as *Down the Historic Susquehanna: A Summer's Jaunt from Otsego to the Chesapeake.*

In a class by itself, Stephen F. Lintner's impressive doctoral thesis for Johns Hopkins University, "The Historical Physical Behavior of the Lower Susquehanna River" (1980), compares a section of the Lower Susquehanna surveyed by Benjamin Latrobe in 1801 with the same stretch of river in 1976. Also of interest are Latrobe's original survey notebooks and the huge map he made of the Lower Susquehanna, both housed at the Maryland Historical Society in Baltimore.

Roger B. Stein's catalog for a 1981 exhibition, *Susquehanna: Images of the Settled Landscape,* at the Roberson Center for the Arts and Sciences in Binghamton, New York, reflects at length on what the Susquehanna has represented to artists, as well as the waterway's substantial impact on American history and culture.

Several works cover specific aspects of the Susquehanna's story in exceptional detail. These include Richard Gerstell's *American Shad in the Susquehanna River Basin: A Three-Hundred-Year History* (1998); Charles F. Petrillo's *Steamboats on the Susquehanna: The Wyoming Valley Experience* (1993); Barry Kent's *Susquehanna's Indians* (1984); William Voight's description of the creation of the Susquehanna River Basin Commission, *The Susquehanna Compact: Guardian of the River's Future* (1972); and R. Dudley Tonkin's colorful account of the West Branch lumber industry, *My Partner, the River: The White Pine Story on the Susquehanna* (1958).

Walter F. Burmeister's *Susquehanna River and Its Tributaries,* vol. 3 in the Appalachian Waters series (1975), is the most complete canoeing guide to the river. Tim Palmer's *Rivers of Pennsylvania* (1980) includes the Susquehanna and several of its tributaries, also largely from a canoeist's perspective.

Noteworthy local and regional histories include Alan Taylor's masterful *William Cooper's Town* (1995); Peter C. Mancall's *Valley of Opportunity: Economic Culture along the Upper Susquehanna, 1700–1800* (1991); Oscar J. Harvey and Ernest G. Smith's six-volume *History of Wilkes-Barre, Luzerne County, Pennsylvania* (1909–30); John F. Meginness's *Otzinachson: A History of the West Branch Valley of the Susquehanna* (1889); Michael Barton's *Life by the Moving Road: An Illustrated History of Greater Harrisburg* (1983, 1998); and Peter A. Jay's *Havre de Grace: An Informal History* (1986).

Numerous articles in historical journals provide information available nowhere else, especially Arthur H. Wilson's two pieces titled "Literature Regarding the Susquehanna Valley" in 1943 and 1946 *Proceedings* of the Northumberland County Historical Society.

Relevant technical reports include the Pennsylvania Department of Environmental Protection's biennial "Water Quality Assessment"; publications of the Susquehanna River Basin Commission; and reports by the Chesapeake Bay Foundation, the State University of New York College at Oneonta's Biological Field Station at Cooperstown, and companies operating hydroelectric dams on the Lower Susquehanna.

The Alliance for the Chesapeake Bay publishes *Bay Journal,* a comprehensive monthly newspaper covering environmental issues related to the Chesapeake and its watershed.

Dozens of community newspapers report regularly on Susquehanna-related issues. They include the *Freeman's Journal* in Cooperstown; the *Binghamton Press & Sun-Bulletin* (especially "Returning to the River," a 1996 series by Dick Marsi); the *Times Leader* of Wilkes-Barre (especially "Susquehanna Sojourn," a 1988 series by Mary Ellen Alu); Williamsport's *Sun-Gazette;* the *Patriot-News* of Harrisburg; the *Lancaster New Era* (especially Ad Crable's "Outdoors" articles) and the *Intelligencer Journal,* both of Lancaster; and the *Sun* of Baltimore.

Detailed Susquehanna maps include U.S. Geological Survey maps, especially of headwaters areas; Howard Wm. Higbee's 1965 *Stream Map of Pennsylvania,* published by Vivid Publishing Inc. of Williamsport; the *Official General Clinton Canoe Regatta Map,* produced by the Bainbridge, New York, Chamber of Commerce in 1991; the Susquehanna River Tri-State Association's canoe map series for the Susquehanna in Pennsylvania north of Wilkes-Barre; and aerial photo fishing guides to the Susquehanna from Lake Frederic above York Haven Dam to the Chesapeake, published by Bass Chumps Publishing of Towson, Maryland, in 1994.

Notes

Spring-Water River

1. Identifying a primary source of the Susquehanna would not have made sense to colonial Americans. They also thought the river was much larger. When William Penn's agents purchased the Susquehanna territory north of Wyalusing from the Native Americans in 1683, terms of the deal clearly indicated that the Susquehanna River included all streams flowing into it above that point, among them the Unadilla, Charlotte, Chenango, and Chemung.

2. While Lake Canadarago and its feeder streams lie slightly farther north and farther from the Chesapeake than Lake Otsego and its sources, Otsego is generally considered *the* headwaters lake of the Susquehanna. Otsego is twice as large (4,200 acres vs. 2,000) and historically more important than its sister lake, so the stream that flows out of it is called Susquehanna. That said, writers and mapmakers often have promoted the lakes equally. The earliest relatively accurate map with any detail of the region, drawn by Lewis Evans in 1749, shows Canadarago and Otsego of similar sizes and does not designate a single source "from the Lakes at the Head of this Branch." Writing two centuries later, Richmond Myers in *The Long Crooked River* states simply, "The North Branch rises from the waters of Otsego and Canadarago Lakes." The Biological Field Station on Otsego refers to the Upper Susquehanna *Lakes* Region.

3. Otsego Lake has been described as the "overdeepened Susquehanna," just as the Chesapeake Bay has been called the "drowned Susquehanna." The river is longer, on both ends, than it appears.

4. Mark Twain mercilessly ridicules *The Deerslayer*'s description of the Susquehanna's outlet in his essay "Fenimore Cooper's Literary Offenses." Cooper says the stream is 50 feet wide at the outlet, Twain notes, but "it presently narrows to twenty as it meanders along for no

given reason, and yet when a stream acts like that it ought to be required to explain itself. Fourteen pages later the width of the brook's outlet from the lake has suddenly shrunk thirty feet, and become 'the narrowest part of the stream.' This shrinkage is not accounted for."

5. Debris filled the first few miles of the river in 1769 as well, according to the diary Richard Smith kept of his river exploration with the Mohawk scout Joseph Brant: "This River from the Lake Otsego is full of Logs and trees and short crooked Turns and the Navigation for Canoes and Batteaux requires Dexterity. Ed. Crogan is about to employ the Indians in the useful service of removing the logs next summer."

Long Crooked River

1. The sources of the Chenango, as well as of the Unadilla, actually lie farther north than the sources of the North Branch itself; but the North Branch's ultimate sources lie much farther east and so at a greater distance from the Susquehanna's mouth.

2. Many of Pennsylvania's 2,000 low-head dams afflict streams in the Susquehanna watershed. Settlers constructed them to provide water power for grist- and sawmills or to permit canals or steamboats or ferries to function. Many of them are no longer needed and the Pennsylvania Fish and Boat Commission is gradually removing them. State law requires elimination of all low-head dams south of the Juniata River's confluence with the Susquehanna. If a dam cannot be removed, it must be fitted with fish ladders to permit the Susquehanna's renewed shad population to run up tributaries to spawn.

3. Early canoeists approached a journey as a social experience. They expected to meet and greet many travelers. On their return from an assembly with the Six Nations in New York in the summer of 1750, Moravian missionaries named Cammerhoff and Zeisberger shot steep rapids above Tunkhannock. Then: "The Otcongo sorcerer, who was going down the Susquehanna, came towards us, and we paddled along for some distance, side by side. He inquired for news from the

Nations, and handed over his kettle into our canoe, bidding us eat and drink."

4. Some of these artifacts came from Carantouan, also known as Spanish Hill, an unusual flat-topped hill along the Chemung just northwest of Athens. An impressive parade of nineteenth- and early twentieth-century historians has identified this hill as the site of a large seventeenth-century Native American village. All of these historians—from nationally recognized scholars to chroniclers of the Susquehanna region—also have said that in 1615 the French explorer Samuel de Champlain sent a young assistant, Etienne Brulé, to Carantouan to enlist the Susquehannocks in an attack on the Iroquois. They say that at this time Brulé descended the Susquehanna to the Chesapeake. All of this is now accepted knowledge: On its travel Web site, Pennsylvania promotes Brulé as the first white man to descend the river and "set eyes on the picturesque hills and valleys of inland Pennsylvania."

But none of the story is true, according to the Pennsylvania archaeologist Donald H. Kent. Spanish Hill has yielded no evidence of seventeenth-century Native American occupation; all artifacts date to the sixteenth century. Moreover, Brulé left no account of his supposed Susquehanna trip. The only reference is in Champlain's writing, and he provides no details, does not even name the river; historians have simply assumed it to be the Susquehanna. "In all probability [Brulé's] story of descending a river was a fabrication," concludes Kent. Other archaeologists and enlightened historians agree.

5. Numerous historians have reported falling water levels throughout the Susquehanna Basin. O. J. Harvey and E. G. Smith provided the most detailed account of that change in the 1909 volume of their six-volume history of Wilkes-Barre. "The North Branch is of no great width," they wrote, "although forty and more years ago it was of much greater width and depth." The river at the foot of Northhampton Street in Wilkes-Barre had been measured as at least 800 feet wide in 1809. The U.S. Geological Survey in 1902 measured the width of the stream at the same place as 710 feet. Harvey and Smith said the Susquehanna's tributaries in the vicinity of Wilkes-Barre were not so sizable as they had been even fifteen or twenty

years before 1909. They speculated that the combined waters of any two of these tributaries, with the exception of the Lackawanna River, would have been insufficient to operate a single sawmill, whereas all had been capable power sources 100 years earlier.

6. Just upriver from Azilum, the massive Standing Stone projects some twenty feet above the water just off the river's western shore. This rock looks as if it toppled off a cliff and sank upright in the riverbed. It may have come from the top of a hill, but not from around here: a glacier swept this unusually large erratic down the valley. The Native Americans called Standing Stone Ossinepachte and carved petroglyphs on its surface. During General John Sullivan's march up the Susquehanna, a trigger-happy artillerist fired a shot at Standing Stone. The ball blew away a corner and with it some of the old carvings. Acid rain has worn away the rest.

7. The Department of the Interior has designated sections of the Delaware and the Allegheny as national wild and scenic rivers, but has not so designated this part of the North Branch or any other section of the Susquehanna itself. In 1998 President Bill Clinton named the Upper Susquehanna (Pittston to Sunbury) and Lackawanna rivers an American heritage river area. The designation allows an appointed federal "river navigator" to coordinate local, state, and federal environmental and economic initiatives in the region. Supporters hope the project will produce amazing results, perhaps including cleanup of one of the Susquehanna's most polluted stretches, but its aims differ substantially from creating a wild and scenic designation for the water itself.

8. Imaginative or hard-of-hearing white settlers somehow corrupted Wassawomeke, or a variation thereof, into Wiwaumic, then Wyomink, then Wyoming. The original Lenni Lenape word meant something like "great plains," which is how the grassy floodplain must have appeared before development. A Pennsylvanian who apparently knew the Lenni Lenape meaning of the word transferred it to the vast plains of the territory that would become the state of Wyoming.

9. Because of its composition, the buried valley of the Susquehanna today provides an excellent source of drinking water for Wilkes-Barre and nearby communities. Dr. Brian Redmond, a Wilkes University

geologist who has drilled several wells into the valley, says it runs some 100 feet deep beneath Wilkes-Barre and deeper elsewhere. Redmond expects that increasing numbers of residents will use the buried valley as a large and convenient reservoir of relatively pure drinking water.

10. A monument lists the names of the dead at St. Joseph's Roman Catholic Church in Port Griffith. Survivors and members of victims' families participate in a special mass there each year. The tragedy called the Knox Mine Disaster, one victim's daughter has said, ought to be called the Knox Mine Murders. State prosecutors charged officers of the Knox and Pennsylvania coal companies with involuntary manslaughter, violations of mining and labor laws, and income tax evasion. Six men served prison terms.

11. Such studies of acid mine drainage did not disturb some Wyoming Valley residents a century ago. They believed that mine water was good to drink because diseases, along with everything else, could not live in it.

12. Lime does not fully offset acid mine drainage until well below Harrisburg on the main stem. In a 1963 survey, P. W. Anderson found that water flowing along the east bank of the river at Harrisburg remained high in sulfate concentration, while the river along the west bank, channeling water from the Juniata and other less acidic west bank tributaries, carried considerably less pollution.

13. Wilkes-Barre has been hit hard by floods not only because of the river's narrow, winding course but also because of the Wyoming Valley's steep hills and slim floodplain—a situation common elsewhere in Pennsylvania. The U.S. Geological Survey says only 186 of Pennsylvania's 2,571 communities are safe from high water. The Susquehanna is particularly susceptible to flooding because of its huge drainage area. Also, many of its tributaries flow in the same direction as the prevailing storm centers. Many of its little streams drop precipitously, dumping floodwaters rapidly into the relatively shallow river and its tributaries. The Susquehanna River Basin Commission calls the basin "one of the most flood-prone" in the country and, for its size, "virtually without peer" in amount of flood damages sustained.

14. Most of these new structures occupy a floodplain that was covered by a dozen or more feet of water in 1972. Local officials encouraged renewed development to stabilize the tax base, and state and federal agencies did nothing to discourage them. Federal disaster aid helps most homeowners whether they are insured against flood or not, so there is little incentive to move out of the floodplain or purchase costly insurance. In 1972, only two residents of Wilkes-Barre had flood insurance. Many are still not covered.

LONG REACH RIVER

1. Henry Wilson Storey's 1907 *History of Cambria County*, an authoritative local study, is at first certain, then ambiguous about the source of the West Branch: "A spring on the farm of Andrew Strittmatter . . . is the accredited source of the west branch of the Susquehanna. Flowing in a northwesterly direction for half a mile, thence for an equal distance nearly west, the stream above mentioned is enlarged by another run, rippling down from Carrolltown, about a mile and a half to the northeast. This is the longer run of the two and is by some considered the source of the river."

2. The West Branch's early miles have been described in other ways. Nineteenth-century lumbermen called the first useful section of the river the Little Ditch. In the summer of 1683, when William Penn began negotiating with the Iroquois chiefs of New York for control of the river and lands on both sides of it, he declared his intention to secure the West Branch all the way to its source, or at least as far as "a place so out of the way that a small thing could not carry some people to it."

3. Underwater remnants of boom cribs are visible upstream of Williamsport and Lock Haven. Over the years, ice jams and floods removed many logs from the cribs and city work crews took out others to protect water skiers. In 1966 the Army Corps of Engineers examined some of the cribs remaining from the Williamsport Boom. The cribs had filled with sediment and were impeding navigation. The corps removed fifty-foot-long logs that had been wet for more than a century and had not begun to rot.

4. This practice of orienting the backs of nineteenth-century buildings to the river is not universal. In Binghamton, as in Lock Haven, many of the Victorian homes built closest to the river look away from it; but in Harrisburg, Sunbury, Wilkes-Barre, Williamsport, and many small towns such as Marietta, most riverfront homeowners look toward the Susquehanna. In some towns, most notably Williamsport and Columbia, nineteenth-century industrial growth along the riverfront pushed the river-facing residential area several blocks away from the water. When constructed directly on the river, commercial buildings usually face the street, for obvious reasons.

5. The Susquehanna creates challenges for canoeists who often must choose from among two, three, or more courses divided by islands. This has ever been the case. In the spring of 1750, Moravians traveling in the vicinity of Wyalusing reported that the river was "frequently so blocked up by islands that we could with difficulty find an opening through which to pass."

6. The Last Raft was not *the* last raft. In June 1976, O. Lynn Frank, author of the Clearfield Boy Scout canoeing guide, piloted a crew of twenty-five in a successful three-day, 63-mile raft trip from Miller's Landing in Clearfield County to Lock Haven. Lynn's raft matched the 1938 version in size, but the builders used chainsaws instead of broadaxes. Designed as a Clinton County bicentennial event, the trip ran smoothly because the organizers waited for highest water and limited their brief voyage to the most remote and least obstructed section of river.

BROAD, SHALLOW RIVER ⁓

1. Much of the water from the branches remains separated for more than 50 miles—to below Harrisburg. Throughout that distance, water flowing along the east shore is darker than water flowing along the west. (Coincidentally, water along the east shore also is deeper throughout most of that course.)

2. Both branches were naturally clear from their sources to the Chesapeake until European settlers polluted them. Before John Bartram and his party began their journey north from Shamokin in 1743, they borrowed a canoe and paddled a short distance up the West Branch. "We diverted ourselves with swimming," he reported. "The water was chin deep most of the breadth, and so clear one might have seen a pin at the bottom." Even in the coal-rich Wyoming Valley, the historian Charles Miner wrote to a Wilkes-Barre newspaper in 1860: "Is [the Susquehanna] not so limpid, so clear, that floating down in a skiff or canoe you may see everywhere, however deep, the sands at the bottom and mark the fish as they glide by and play around your boat?" As late as 1890, John Boyle O'Reilly, canoeing past Athens, said he had never seen river water "so clear and wholesome as the Susquehanna. . . . The water was about four feet deep all the way down, and the bottom was of small pebbles, every one as clearly seen as if laid on a mirror."

3. Cooper and the younger Priestley did not just stumble upon Northumberland. They and other British investors purchased nearly 700,000 acres running from Northumberland northward, between the river's branches, to the beginnings of Loyalsock Creek. They planned to sell lots to British immigrants, but the speculation failed as prospective purchasers investigated the wilderness and changed their minds. The most famous would-be settlers were the British poets Samuel Taylor Coleridge and Robert Southey. In 1794, when they were in their early twenties, Coleridge and Southey determined to create a "Pantisocracy" on the banks of the Susquehanna. Twelve couples would join this communal society. Each would work a few hours a day for the good of all and devote the rest of their time to creative and contemplative pursuits. Coleridge later said he and Southey chose the site for a reason befitting their idealistic plan: because of the "pretty and metrical sound" of the word "Susquehanna." The poets never came to America, so their utopia lived only in their minds as a potential "experiment of human perfectibility on the banks of the Susquehanna."

4. Where coal stops, so do Asiatic clams. Keller's beach is littered with their sun- and water-whitened shells among glittering specks of coal. The empty shells, up to one and a half inches across, are slightly lighter than coal and, by the time they reach shore, have split at the hinge. Fish biologists trapping shad at the base of Conowingo Dam

found the Susquehanna's first Asiatic clams in 1979. Multiplying furiously, they have clogged intake pipes at hydroelectric and nuclear power plants. By the early 1990s they had advanced into the North Branch and are expected to cover most of the river eventually. On the positive side, Asiatic clams are a sign of good water quality: Like black flies, they do not flourish in polluted waters.

5. The dredgers brought more than coal to the surface. Occasionally they dislodged ice cakes, which created a novel attraction when they floated to the river's surface in midsummer. More often, dredgers dug into pockets of methane gas created by decaying plant material. This gas bubbled to the surface in an odoriferous explosion that dredgers called "river flatulence."

6. The greatest of the early Susquehanna bridge builders, Burr also designed spans at the Upper Susquehanna Ferry in Maryland and at McCall's Ferry, Harrisburg, Northumberland, and Berwick in Pennsylvania. He used wood for all these bridges, including their coverings. Burr built a sawmill in New York to prepare timber and hired raftmen to float that timber to the bridge sites.

7. In June 1863, Union defenders established a defense line along the Susquehanna to keep Confederate troops from crossing on Harrisburg's Camelback Bridge or the Columbia Bridge and capturing Harrisburg. After an inconclusive skirmish on the West Shore, Confederate troops withdrew from the Harrisburg area. Other Confederates massed at Wrightsville, preparing to cross to Columbia. Outnumbered federal forces set fire to the pine and oak span, which burned and collapsed into the water. The Confederates turned around and marched to Gettysburg.

8. The Rockville Bridge replaced the nearby Northern Central Railroad Bridge in the Dauphin Narrows, just north of Harrisburg. Six of the older bridge's sixteen piers remain rooted in the river. On the central pier stands one of the Susquehanna's best-known landmarks: a miniature version of the Statue of Liberty. The four-ton statue, with Lady Liberty facing downstream, rises twenty-five feet above the thirty-two-foot pier. Eugene Stilp of Harrisburg sculpted the statue from fiberglass, wood, metal, and glass. "Some environmentalists want to take it down because it ruins the natural view of the river," says Stilp,

"but a lot of people, especially older people, say it gives them a lift when they drive by and see it out there on the water."

9. Canal boats had company in the canal. Nearly half a century after Dickens passed up the Juniata Valley by way of canal and river, the Landis brothers used both river and canal to canoe down the Juniata to the Susquehanna and on to Harrisburg. Henry K. Landis, who, with his brother, George, created the collection of rural Pennsylvaniana at Landis Valley Museum in Lancaster County, kept a diary of their sixteen-day trip during the summer of 1888. The Juniata was typically shallow that August and the brothers, in decked canoes, used the canal to circumvent the river's rare rapids and extensive low-water stretches. "Where the water was swift & rocky," Landis wrote, "we came by the canal which is pretty swift all along here." Over the last ten miles, from Newport to the Susquehanna, the brothers found the river uncanoeable and so stuck to the canal. They never did dip their paddles in the rocky Susquehanna, but canoed its canal all the way to Harrisburg.

10. Jack Kerouac was not positively impressed by the mountains just north of Harrisburg. The narrator in *On the Road* is walking along the river with "the Ghost of the Susquehanna," an old man bound for Canada: "We walked seven miles along the mournful Susquehanna. It is a terrifying river. It has bushy cliffs on both sides that lean like hairy ghosts over the unknown waters. Inky night covers all. Sometimes from the railyards across the river rises a great red locomotive flare that illuminates the horrid cliffs. . . . I thought all the wilderness of America was in the West till the Ghost of the Susquehanna showed me different."

11. The flood of 1936 disabled the filtration plant and the city began looking elsewhere for water. The City Island plant remained as a secondary source of treated water until Agnes fully destroyed it in 1972. Since then, Harrisburg has relied primarily on a 6-billion-gallon reservoir north of town. During drought emergencies, the city draws on the Susquehanna.

12. Only one of Reed's river development ideas failed. He had hoped to transform the treacherous low-head Dock Street Dam into a seventeen-foot-tall hydroelectric facility. He first proposed the project

in 1983. Citing multiple environmental concerns, DEP, the Fish and Boat Commission, and several conservation groups opposed the plan for more than a decade. In 2001, the city abandoned the hydroelectric project in favor of replacing the low-head dam with a slightly higher seasonal inflatable dam similar to Sunbury's, with a fish ladder to allow the passage of shad. Many environmentalists continue to oppose any increase in the dam's height.

13. The lower reaches of the river used to freeze more solidly. A century ago, John Mason reportedly skated from the confluence of the Susquehanna's branches to Harrisburg in half a day on a solid ice pack. Flanders Keller, the coal dredger of Port Treverton, drove a truck across the river just before the ice flood of 1936.

14. The Corps of Engineers examined Harrisburg again after the 1972 flood and recommended a levee to protect South Harrisburg, where most flood damage occurs. The Shipoke section, a quaint and trendy older area of homes near the Dock Street Dam, opted out of that plan. "People went to Sunbury and saw what they had done up there with that huge wall," recalls Joe Nell, who views Harrisburg across the river from his West Shore home at Wormleysburg. "They said, 'We don't want anything to destroy our view down here.'" When the engineers excluded Shipoke from the levee area, the cost of the project exceeded the potential benefit and they scrapped the plan.

15. Besides finding that they could cross the river practically anywhere on foot during a drought, early settlers and travelers discovered that low water could be a major source of disease. Shallows bred mosquitoes, which transported illness throughout the river valley. John Melish found "fever and ague" rife just south of Harrisburg in the first decade of the nineteenth century. Disease hampered commissioners appointed by Pennsylvania to examine and then make navigational improvements on the lower river in the 1820s. Commissioner Charles Trcziyulny reported that stagnant water produced "bilious fevers, agues, and all their concomitant evils," and that "the stench arising from these [carrion] and the stagnant pools, was such, as at times, almost to overcome us."

16. Ebenezer Cook did not worry about flavor when he drank Susquehanna water to cure a hangover three centuries ago. An early Maryland tobacco buyer, or "sot-weed factor," Cook often bought the weed near the mouth of the Susquehanna. He wrote humorous couplets describing his colorful experiences, published as *The Sot-Weed Factor,* when he returned to his native England (and embellished in a contemporary novel under the same title by John Barth). Cook employed this remedy after overimbibing:

> Waking next day with aking Head
> And Thirst that made me quit my Bed;
> I rigg'd myself, and soon got up
> To cool my Liver with a Cup
> of Succahana fresh and clear.

17. Fishing tournaments range from laid-back amateur contests sponsored by local clubs to competitive professional tourneys in which anglers vie for hundreds of thousands of dollars in prizes. Some of these contests go on for weeks or months. In 1991, professional and top-rated amateur anglers competed for $200,000 in the national Bass Masters Classic on the Chesapeake Bay and Lower Susquehanna.

18. Central Pennsylvanians discovered in September 2001 that the damage an errant Boeing 707 might do was no longer the appropriate standard for assessing the security of a nuclear plant. The Boeing 757 and 767 jumbo jets that terrorists commandeered and flew into the World Trade Center in New York City and the Pentagon in Washington, D.C., packed considerably more wallop than a 707. The NRC admitted that no nuclear plant had been designed to withstand the impact of a jumbo jet. Concern about such a scenario was more than theoretical. U.S. security officials said TMI was directly in the flight path of the hijacked jet that crashed in western Pennsylvania on September 11 and may have been its target.

19. To reach the potholes, exit Route 441 at the Falmouth Fish and Boat Commission access. From the parking lot, walk into the potholes and continue about half a mile upriver to the third power line. Turn toward shore and find a well-worn trail just downriver from the mouth of Conewago Creek. The path leads to the two-century-old canal towpath, which runs back to the parking lot.

20. E-an Zen, a University of Maryland scientist and expert on Potomac River geology, has identified another type of potholed rocks. They were eroded laterally as water pushed sediment against rock sides. Unlike vertical potholes, they are not circular; many have overhanging "roofs." Hydraulic vortices swirling sediment against rock began both types, Zen theorizes. On the Susquehanna, multiple lateral potholes are located on the Conowingo Islands, below Holtwood Dam.

21. In the autumn of 1801, the surveyor Benjamin Henry Latrobe dropped a 180-foot line with a lead weight on the end of it into the Susquehanna at a place known as The Neck, on the river's eastern shore in Lancaster County. The weight did not hit bottom there, or when Latrobe dropped the line into the water a little farther south along the eastern shore at McCall's Ferry. If Latrobe's measurements are correct, these holes had filled in considerably before the 1910 survey. Geologists say they do not fill in entirely because rushing floodwater periodically scours them.

22. The ride through Conewago Falls was always wild. In 1852, Eli Bowen described a raft trip:

We made the descent, several years ago, and can never forget the peculiar agitation of our nervous system, as our 'long, low' craft made the first plunge into the troubled waters! Gracefully sank down the front platform, and furiously swept the eager water over our thirsty boards! That plunge over, another and another followed in quick succession. Looking round, we were quite bewildered with the real wildness and magnitude of the scene—the white-capped waves sweeping by with tremendous force, and dashing their empty furies against the sturdy rocks, which the men at the oars, with the most *desperate efforts,* were trying to avoid.

23. Big plans for big boats always came to bad ends on the Susquehanna. John Arndt of Wilkes-Barre built a 12-ton schooner in 1803 and successfully sailed it down the river and the bay to the ocean. Encouraged by this singular success, Arndt planned to turn his hometown into an inland shipping port. In 1812 he completed a sixty-ton full-masted oceangoing vessel and sailed it down the river on a spring flood. Before the *Luzerne of Wilkes-Barre* could fight the British Navy, the ship had to defeat Conewago Falls. By the time the vessel reached Conewago, the river level had fallen and the ship ran onto the rocks. It remained stuck there through the next winter. An early thaw propelled ice through the boat, ruining it and John Arndt's dream of creating a port in the Wyoming Valley.

24. Westward expansion from Philadelphia guaranteed that this area would be settled first. Its population and economic prosperity have continued to expand, even as some other sections of Pennsylvania have declined. Lancaster and York have been among the fastest-growing counties in Pennsylvania for several decades. In contrast, population in much of the Susquehanna Valley has remained static, and Cambria County, on the West Branch, and Luzerne County, on the North Branch, have been among the state's largest population losers in recent years.

25. McCall's, the narrowest point on the river between Sunbury and the Chesapeake, was even narrower before construction of Holtwood Dam. In his 1801 survey of the Lower Susquehanna, Benjamin Henry Latrobe measured the width of the river at this point at an incredibly narrow 16 perches, or 264 feet. The covered bridge that Theodore Burr built across the river here in 1815 measured 360 feet. Widened by water backed up from Holtwood, the river at McCall's today remains less than a quarter of a mile wide.

26. In 1990 a group of investors, working under the title of Mid-Atlantic Energy Engineers, announced plans to build a second pumped-storage operation on the Susquehanna, this one at Cuffs Run on the York County side above Safe Harbor. The project would have generated far more power than Muddy Run and potentially as much as the nuclear plant at Three Mile Island. Local officials and residents universally opposed this plan. Lancaster's Manor Township objected strenuously, noting: "This area of the Susquehanna has been subjected to enough electrical generation projects! Three [actually four] hydro plants. Two [only one remains] steam plants. Two atomic plants. One pumped storage facility. The river can only support so much." Citing uncertainty in the deregulated power business, investors abandoned

the plan in 2000; but the president of Mid-Atlantic, William McMahon, said he thought the project eventually would be revived. "It's an ideal site," he explained. "You can only put these plants in a very few regions of the country. This is one of a very few. It's as environmentally friendly as you're going to get."

27. Less pecunious scavengers of larger pieces of wood lived all along the Susquehanna and tributaries. They were called Algerines, presumably for their North African counterparts who had plagued American ships along the Barbary Coast. These people often are romanticized as free spirits who made a meager living by fishing and pulling in stray driftwood to build homes and fires. In reality, many Algerines took advantage of the breakup of rafts or booms to guide as many logs as possible to shore and then resell them. The more aggressive Algerines stole unattended rafts and spar logs all along the river. They sawed off ends stamped with an owner's brand and sold the logs as their own. These "river parasites" took two of John Patchin's West Branch logs and cut off the stamps. Patchin relocated these logs while the Algerines were away from their camp and marked them again with his stamping hammer. When the Algerines returned, Patchin pointed to his stamps and lectured the surprised thieves: "Don't you know that when I put my stamp on the end of a stick it goes right through!"

28. Columbia has been cited as a place of origin for the term "underground railroad." Slaveholders tracking escapees to Columbia often lost all trace of them here, presumably because of the variety of transportation outlets. The mystified owners are said to have declared, "There must be an underground railroad somewhere." A similar origin claim is made for Ripley, Ohio, on the Ohio River.

29. Other big fish filled the river in those days, in numbers that are difficult to imagine now. The nineteenth-century river was "so crowded with fish that the nets would be broken," the state fish commissioner reported in 1869. These fish included perch, pike, mullet, suckers, catfish, and sturgeon. Lancaster's North Museum displays a 6-foot, 3-inch sturgeon caught in the Susquehanna near Bainbridge in 1846.

30. A York attorney, John E. Vandersloot, purchased this property

in 1907 and created Indian Steps Museum to showcase Native American culture. He extracted some of the "steps" before the water behind Holtwood Dam covered the site three years later. They are displayed in the museum.

31. Many anglers found better fishing in the ponds behind the dams than they had in the free-flowing river. In the years immediately after construction of Conowingo, the Federal Bureau of Fisheries, the Pennsylvania Fish Commission, and the Maryland Conservation Commission dumped 90 million perch and 10 million fish of other species into these ponds, which quickly became major recreational attractions.

ROCK RIVER

1. One of the earliest Susquehanna promoters, Condy believed the river could do more for American commerce than the Ohio and Mississippi combined. Assuming that removal of impediments or their circumvention by canal would open the entire river, Condy expected the Susquehanna to link the Atlantic Ocean with the Great Lakes. He described in detail how to bring this plan to fruition by connecting the river's tributaries, via short portages, with tributaries of the Allegheny and Genesee. Two centuries ago, Condy's ideas seemed sensible on paper. They had no validity on water.

2. Archaeologists take a contrary view. They believe the river was constricted to less than 1.6 miles before the building of Safe Harbor Dam, which widened it slightly. They base this theory on the location of major Susquehannock village sites at Washington Boro and Long Level on the opposite shore. "Before construction of the Safe Harbor Dam, the distance to the river's edge here at Long Level may have been several hundred feet greater," writes Barry Kent in *Susquehanna's Indians.* "That additional area of once-fertile alluvial soils, now inundated by the Safe Harbor backwater, was probably the location of some of the land farmed by the Susquehannocks." Whether one accepts the surveyor's measurements or the archaeologists' point of view, clearly the Susquehannocks' Susquehanna was not ours.

3. Island acreage in this portion of Lintner's study area now

changes seasonally. The Safe Harbor Water Power Corporation raised the level of its pond (Lake Clarke) by 10 inches for the first time in the summer of 1997. The extra water, used to create additional electricity, covered about sixty-four acres of grassy islands and mud flats off Washington Boro in an area known as the Conejohela Flats. The flats are fragile structures created by upriver silt, sand, and coal that poured into shallows on the east side of the river after installation of the dam. These flats have become a primary stopping point for thousands of migratory birds. Local conservationists, and especially birders, worried that higher water would damage the flats. Safe Harbor agreed to lower Lake Clarke to its former level during spring and autumn migration periods so that birds can use the flats. The compromise has worked: migrations have not been disrupted.

4. Bad boating behavior is a problem all along the river. Since 1984, nearly forty people have died in boating accidents on the Susquehanna's waters in Pennsylvania. Many did not know the territory. Most were not wearing life jackets. The Susquehanna misleads novice boaters because of its relatively placid appearance. Appearances are deceiving, according to K. Derek Pritts, waterways conservation officer for the Fish and Boat Commission: "Gallon for gallon, the Susquehanna is the most dangerous river in the state. It has treacherous currents, rocks, shallow areas, deep areas, all sorts of obstacles."

5. Archaeological sites pervade the Lower Susquehanna Valley. The Pennsylvania Historical and Museum Commission has registered nearly 200 sites in Lancaster County alone; many are located on or near the river. Two impressive Archaic sites (8000 to 1000 B.C.) are located *in* the Susquehanna, on Bare and Piney islands, well below Safe Harbor. From about A.D. 1300 to 1500 Shenks Ferry people occupied many sites along the river, including a town Donald Cadzow examined on a ridge just south of the Conestoga-Susquehanna confluence. The Susquehannocks supplanted the Shenks Ferry culture at Washington Boro. The archaeologist Barry Kent says Washington Boro "might well be considered the Indian capital of Pennsylvania from Paleo-Indian times to the beginning of the eighteenth century." Registered archaeological sites pepper the little village.

6. The only other petroglyphs in the bed of the Susquehanna stood at Bald Friars, Maryland, just below the Pennsylvania border. They were named for white quartz rocks (apparently resembling tonsured friars) that stuck up in the river before Conowingo Dam's backwaters flooded them. Historians removed many of these rocks. Some sit inside the Harford County Historical Society at Belair. Others rest outside, eroding, at the Cecil County Historical Society in Elkton.

7. The most toxic parts of nitrogen are nitrates, which pollute hundreds of Lancaster County wells. The human body turns nitrates into nitrite. Nitrite blocks oxygen from reaching body tissues and can cause "blue baby syndrome" in infants. In 1993 the Environmental Protection Agency said ten Lancaster County schools and businesses had excessive nitrates in their water. Half of these places were in the Conestoga River Basin.

8. Improved sewage treatment all along the Susquehanna has accounted for much of the nutrient reduction and better water quality. Pennsylvania told river communities to begin cleaning sewage in the 1950s. Only Wilkes-Barre persistently defied the order, pumping raw sewage into the Susquehanna until the late 1960s and providing only primary treatment (simply screening solid materials) until the late '80s. Pennsylvania required all Susquehanna treatment plants below the Juniata River to begin removing phosphorus in the '80s. Nitrogen discharges to the river and its tributaries are not controlled. (An experimental project at Lancaster's sewage treatment plant on the Conestoga is reducing nitrogen outflow. Bacteria in the sewage converts nitrates into a nitrogen gas vented into outside air.)

9. Programs to reduce the volume of manure have been offset in part by use of another form of fertilizer: sludge. Sludge is the solid matter, including human waste, left over after bacteria in a sewer plant have consumed more digestible material. Sludge supporters say it is a superior and safe fertilizer. Environmentalists oppose the spreading of sludge not only because more nutrients are hardly needed on most farms in the Lower Susquehanna Valley but because anything dumped into a sewer, including toxic metals from factories, may wind up on fields and eventually in water.

10. Greenways are gaining respect along the Susquehanna and its tributaries, although the process of persuading landowners to allow

greenways on their properties can be painfully slow. Greenways are in place or planned along much of Lancaster County's Susquehanna frontage from the Dauphin County line to Columbia. Maryland planners want to include both banks of the river in a Lower Susquehanna Heritage Greenway. The Susquehanna Greenway Partnership hopes to coordinate greenway development along the entire river.

11. In the summer of 1993, surveyors searching for a Mason-Dixon Line marker submerged in the pooled Susquehanna discovered dramatically how much silt has filled in behind Conowingo. The boundary between Maryland and Pennsylvania runs through the Conowingo Pond about five miles above the dam. Expecting the rectangular stone to be submerged beneath at least fifteen feet of ponded water on the river's western shore, the surveyors brought in scuba divers. The divers rowed a boat out to the site and jumped overboard, oxygen tanks, flippers, and all. They landed on a gravel-and-silt bar that kept their shoulders above water. They never did find the marker under all that sediment.

12. Dam owners have sufficient difficulty removing debris floating on top of the water. Until the late 1980s, the dams gathered floating trees and other river-swept debris and then sent the mass down to the next dam in a rush. Eventually a load of tree trash and other junk would hit the bay, annoying boaters and marina owners. Although dam operators claimed they could not do anything to prevent this problem, the SRBC insisted they must. Today debris is still passed along by the overflow dams at York Haven and Holtwood, but Safe Harbor and Conowingo use trash-harvesting barges to remove debris from the water.

13. While a significant minority of mature fish lose their heads attempting to return through turbines, shad restorationists say more than 90 percent of juvenile shad that make the same trip come through with scales intact. Turbines are like revolving doors, not blenders, for juvenile shad.

14. To transport additional fish above the dams, each facility eventually will have to add more elevators. St. Pierre does not emphasize that aspect of the program because "that's way off in the future and we don't want to scare our utility friends too hard."

GREAT BAY RIVER

1. Five years earlier, during one of the coldest winters of that century, the railroad had improvised a more dramatic transportation plan when river ice seemed thick enough to hold anything. Workers laid track directly on the ice. Pulled by horse-drawn sleighs, railroad cars passed from Perryville to Havre de Grace and back from January 15 to February 24, 1852. The railroad transported hundreds of travelers and 10,000 tons of freight, baggage, and mail in 1,378 cars without incident.

2. An outburst of ice originally opened this channel. According to the engineer C. P. Hauducoeur's notes on his 1799 map of the Chesapeake Bay and the Lower Susquehanna, the channel on the Havre de Grace side did not exist until the mid-1790s, when a "violent irruption in the breaking up of the Ice" gouged it out.

3. Icehouses operated on both sides of the river until well into the twentieth century. Hundreds of seasonal workers used large saws to cut thousands of tons of ice. They stored it in massive icehouses, then sold it to refrigerate homes and railroad cars in summer. William G. Whitney operated an icehouse at the Havre de Grace canal basin from 1882 to 1902. His diary emphasizes the hard work and often bad luck involved in ice cutting. One day in January 1891, for example, he and four men cut tons of ice out of the Susquehanna and towed it down the river through troughs cut in the ice. Before the crew reached the icehouse, wind-driven rain had washed it all away.

4. In recent years, some but not all waterfowl species have returned to the bay in larger numbers. Some hunters have abandoned the Flats, however, because they can find more ducks in the river. Thanks to conservation efforts by the Susquehanna River Waterfowlers Association, the duck population is rebounding all along the Susquehanna.

5. The chlorine problem has been resolved. Effluent from Havre de Grace has not conveyed chlorine into the Chesapeake since 1987, when the treatment plant began dechlorinating the 1.5 million gallons of wastewater it releases each day. The plant recently completed another upgrade, this time to remove nitrogen. One of the Susquehanna's

more sophisticated sewage treatment processes operates here at the end of the line. Pennsylvania's response to chlorine has lagged behind Maryland's. The state delayed in setting chlorine limits until the mid-1990s. R. B. Patel, the Department of Environmental Protection's wastewater section chief, explains the present policy: "We don't require dechlorination of wastewater per se, except in discharges into high-quality watersheds." Outside headwater trout streams, the DEP regulates only the amount of chlorine that may be discharged.

6. Many scientists believe the sixth largest meteor ever to modify the Earth crashed at the present mouth of the Chesapeake about 35 million years ago. The Atlantic rushed into the fifty-five-mile-wide, mile-deep crater immediately after the meteor's impact and left behind its salt when eroding sediment eventually replaced seawater in the hole. Geologists believe this crater helped draw the region's water southward and through it. During those times when the bay retreated, the Susquehanna alone flowed over the low ground of this ancient salt bed and out to sea. C. Wylie Poag, of the U.S. Geological Survey at Woods Hole, Massachusetts, has mapped the meteor's crater. It is centered on Cape Charles, Virginia, and extends beneath the bay and well out to sea. Thousands of vehicles a day cross it on the Chesapeake Bay Bridge-Tunnel.

7. Archaeological evidence of human habitation along the Susquehanna's ancestral channels is meager. Watermen occasionally dredge early artifacts from the bay, which of course carry no indication of precisely where they originated. In the late 1980s, the archaeologist Darrin Lowery located 11,000-year-old artifacts at Paw Paw Cove, directly on the Chesapeake. This is the only reported Paleo-Indian site on the Eastern Shore. Lowery believes the site was located at the headwaters of two small tributaries that emptied directly into the Cape Charles course.

Index